Crude Democracy: Natural Resource Wealth and Political Regimes

This book challenges the conventional wisdom that natural resource wealth promotes autocracy. Oil and other forms of mineral wealth can promote both authoritarianism and democracy, the book argues, but they do so through different mechanisms; an understanding of these different mechanisms can help elucidate when either the authoritarian or democratic effects of resource wealth will be relatively strong. Exploiting game-theoretic tools and statistical modeling as well as detailed country case studies and drawing on fieldwork in Latin America and Africa, this book builds and tests a theory that explains political variation across resource-rich states. It will be read by scholars studying the political effects of natural resource wealth in many regions, as well as by those interested in the emergence and persistence of democratic regimes.

Thad Dunning is Assistant Professor of Political Science at Yale University and a research Fellow at Yale's Whitney and Betty MacMillan Center for International and Area Studies. Dunning's previous work has appeared in *International Organization*, the *Journal of Conflict Resolution*, *Political Analysis*, *Studies in Comparative International Development*, and other journals. The dissertation on which this book is based was given the Mancur Olson Award by the Political Economy Section of the American Political Science Association (2008), for the best dissertation in political economy completed in the previous two years. Dunning's research interests lie in comparative politics, political economy, and international relations.

Cambridge Studies in Comparative Politics

Other Books in the Series

David Austen-Smith, Jeffry A. Frieden, Miriam A. Golden, Karl Ove Moene, and Adam Przeworski, eds., *Selected Works of Michael Wallerstein: The Political Economy of Inequality, Unions, and Social Democracy*

Lisa Baldez, *Why Women Protest? Women's Movements in Chile*

Stefano Bartolini, *The Political Mobilization of the European Left, 1860–1980: The Class Cleavage*

Robert H. Bates, *When Things Fell Apart: State Failure in Late-Century Africa*

Mark Beissinger, *Nationalist Mobilization and the Collapse of the Soviet State*

Nancy Bermeo, ed., *Unemployment in the New Europe*

Carles Boix, *Democracy and Redistribution*

Carles Boix, *Political Parties, Growth, and Equality: Conservative and Social Democratic Economic Strategies in the World Economy*

Catherine Boone, *Merchant Capital and the Roots of State Power in Senegal, 1930–1985*

Continued after the index

Crude Democracy

NATURAL RESOURCE WEALTH AND POLITICAL REGIMES

THAD DUNNING

Yale University

CAMBRIDGE
UNIVERSITY PRESS

CAMBRIDGE UNIVERSITY PRESS
Cambridge, New York, Melbourne, Madrid, Cape Town, Singapore, São Paulo, Delhi

Cambridge University Press
32 Avenue of the Americas, New York, NY 10013-2473, USA

www.cambridge.org
Information on this title: www.cambridge.org/9780521730754

First published 2008

Printed in the United States of America

A catalog record for this publication is available from the British Library.

Library of Congress Cataloging in Publication data
Dunning, Thad, 1973–
Crude democracy : natural resource wealth and political regimes / Thad Dunning.
p. cm. – (Cambridge studies in comparative politics)
Includes bibliographical references and index.
ISBN 978-0-521-51500-9 (hbk.) – ISBN 978-0-521-73075-4 (pbk.)
1. Democracy – Economic aspects. 2. Petroleum – Political aspects.
3. Natural resources – Political aspects. I. Title. II. Series.
JC423.D824 2008
321.8–dc22 2008018121

ISBN 978-0-521-51500-9 hardback
ISBN 978-0-521-73075-4 paperback

The Yale Program on Democracy generously provided financial support.

For my parents, Hap, Joby, and Ted

Contents

List of Figures — *page* xi
List of Tables — xiii
Preface and Acknowledgments — xv

1 DOES OIL PROMOTE DEMOCRACY? — 1
1.1 The Authoritarian and Democratic Effects of Natural Resources — 5
1.2 Explaining Variation — 15
1.3 Method and Plan of the Book — 25

2 THE FOUNDATIONS OF RENTIER STATES — 37
2.1 Sources of Rents — 39
2.2 Fiscal Effects: Natural Resources and Taxation — 45
2.3 Toward the Political Effects of Rents — 52

3 RESOURCE RENTS AND THE POLITICAL REGIME — 61
3.1 A Model of Coups against Democracy — 64
3.2 A Model of Democratization — 88
3.3 Discussion and Interpretation — 100

4 STATISTICAL TESTS ON RENTS AND THE REGIME — 107
4.1 Concepts and Measures — 111
4.2 Rents and the Level of Democracy — 121
4.3 Democratic Transitions and Breakdowns — 136
4.4 Assessing the Large-N Evidence — 140

5 THE DEMOCRATIC EFFECT OF RENTS 148
5.1 Case Selection: Probing the Mechanisms 149
5.2 Venezuela: The Rise and Demise of Rentier Democracy 152

6 RENTIER DEMOCRACY IN COMPARATIVE PERSPECTIVE 210
6.1 Chile: Class Conflict in a Rentier Democracy 213
6.2 Bolivia: Rents, Revolution, and Democracy 231
6.3 Ecuador: Oil Booms and Democratization 253
6.4 Botswana: An African Anomaly 258

7 THEORETICAL EXTENSIONS 268
7.1 Revenue Volatility 269
7.2 The Dutch Disease 272
7.3 Resource Ownership 274

8 CONCLUSION: WHITHER THE RESOURCE CURSE? 278
8.1 Crude Democracies and Crude Autocracies 279
8.2 Resources and Democracy: A Normative Coda 289

Appendix: Construction of the Simulations 293

Bibliography 297

Index 317

List of Figures

1.1	Coups against democracy	*page* 8
1.2	Explaining variation: a conceptual overview	19
3.1	The impact of resource rents on the incidence of coups	84
3.2	A net authoritarian effect of rents: the low inequality case	85
3.3	A net democratic effect of rents: the high inequality case	86
3.4	Rents and coups: the role of resource dependence	87
4.1	The effect of oil on democracy as inequality varies	123
5.1	Venezuelan government revenues from oil, 1921–2002	157
5.2	Real education and health spending in Venezuela, 1951–1990	163
5.3	Total and social expenditures in Venezuela, 1990–2006	185
5.4	Education and health spending in Venezuela, 1990–2006	187

List of Tables

4.1 Resource Rents, Inequality, and the Level of Democracy *page* 122
4.2 Industrial Capital Shares by World Region 129
4.3 Rents and Democracy in Latin America 130
4.4 Rents, Inequality, and Democracy: Probit Model 133
4.5 Resource Dependence: fGLS Estimates 135
4.6 Democratic Transitions and Breakdowns: Dynamic Probit Model 138
4.7 Rents and Coups: Probit Model 141

Preface and Acknowledgments

As this book goes to press, we are living in the midst of a petroleum boom akin to the two oil shocks of the 1970s. The per-barrel price of crude surpassed $100 in the first days of 2008, nearing in real terms the price records set during previous booms. For consumers in oil-importing countries, the rising price of petroleum represents an unwelcome cost and a source of inflationary pressure at a time of slowing economic growth. As in the earlier oil shocks, however, the sharply rising petroleum price implies an economic bonanza of epic proportions for oil-exporting countries. How will the boom affect economic and political institutions in those countries?

To analysts of the 1970s, a sustained petroleum boom could only boost the fortunes of oil-rich countries. Social-scientific theories suggested that rising national income would be good for democracy too. Yet, by the 1990s, scholars had begun to question the economic and political benefits of the first two oil shocks. Jeffrey Sachs and Andrew Warner, among others, presented research showing that the resource-rich countries had grown less, not more, than similar resource-poor countries (Sachs and Warner 1995); in another influential early discussion, Terry Karl asked why, "after benefiting from the largest transfer of wealth ever to occur without war . . . have most oil-exporting developing countries suffered from economic deterioration and political decay?" (Karl 1997: xv).

The answer seemed to be that a massive flow of natural resource revenues into the fiscal coffers of the state engendered perverse political as well as economic effects. Not only did natural resource booms cripple non-resource export sectors and inhibit various forms of productive economic activity, they also fostered corruption, weakened accountability, and heightened incentives for rent-seeking. Most relevant for this book, scholars began to argue what has now become nearly a new conventional wisdom: natural resources promote authoritarianism.

This book challenges this conventional wisdom as applied to the development of political regimes. It does not take issue with the claim that natural resource booms may sometimes heighten corruption or weaken institutions in various ways; nor does it contradict the assertion that they may support authoritarian regimes. Yet, this book attempts to refine such arguments by pointing out the ways in which resource wealth may also bolster democracy. Oil and other forms of mineral wealth can promote both authoritarianism and democracy, I argue, but they do so through different mechanisms; an understanding of these different mechanisms can help us understand when either the authoritarian or democratic effects of resource wealth will be relatively strong. Exploiting game-theoretic tools and statistical modeling as well as detailed country case studies, and drawing on fieldwork in Venezuela as well as Bolivia, Botswana, and Chile, I build a theory that seeks to explain political variation across resource-rich states.

For resource-rich countries today, this book suggests that the current boom will have more subtle effects than the present image of an authoritarian resource curse would suggest. Only time will tell to what extent the predictions of the theory are borne out by events. Yet, in trying to explain why petroleum and related kinds of natural resources sometimes seem to provide a blessing for democracy and at other times engender an authoritarian curse, this book provides a framework for thinking systematically about the contrasting political effects of natural resource wealth during the current export bonanza.

A first book provides a valuable (if daunting) chance to acknowledge the many personal and intellectual debts incurred during its conception; it is a pleasure to have the opportunity. I was blessed to have wonderful dissertation and oral defense committees as a graduate student at the University of California, Berkeley. Peter Evans and Gérard Roland provided models of engaged scholarship and encouraged me at important moments in my graduate career. David Collier has been a superlative mentor and a source of professional and intellectual encouragement nonpareil, as so many who have worked with him can attest. I am grateful to Ruth Berins Collier for her unflagging support and her very valuable guidance as the co-chair of my dissertation committee; during my first year in graduate school, Ruth also took me on as an editorial assistant at the journal *Studies in Comparative International Development*, a socialization experience that proved not only fun but also instructive. Finally, as the other co-chair on my committee, Jim Robinson did so much to inspire not only this book but also my faith that social science can tackle the most difficult and important questions while continually seeking to improve the means by which it does so; this book owes a great deal to him.

I have been fortunate to benefit from the guidance of many other mentors as well. David Freedman, who has shared his time and insights more generously than I could have ever hoped, taught me much about statistics and even more about social science. Bob Powell, in addition to providing an inspiring example through his own scholarship, gave me much-needed advice at a crucial point in the development of my dissertation; he also bestowed financial assistance that allowed me the time needed to obtain an M.A. degree in economics while pursuing my doctoral degree in political science. I am grateful to others, including Henry Brady, Laura Stoker, and Steve Weber, for their help and advice during my graduate studies. Terry Karl, whose scholarship helped to motivate some of the questions that led to this book, urged me to study political science in graduate school; I am grateful for the intervention.

Many people read portions of the manuscript and/or helpfully discussed its development with me. I would like to thank Jennifer Bussell, Alex Debs, Jorge Domínguez, Jim Fearon, Justin Fox, Scott Gehlbach, Stephen Haber, Patrick Heller, Stathis Kalyvas, Steve Levitsky, Pauline Jones Luong, James Mahon, Nikolay Marinov, David Mayhew, Victor Menaldo, Francisco Monaldi, John Roemer, Michael Ross, Ken Scheve, Ian Shapiro, Alberto Simpser, Richard Snyder, Hillel Soifer, Susan Stokes, Mariano Tommasi, Erik Wibbels, and Libby Wood. Nikolay Marinov helped with the formatting of figures in LaTeX and shared his rich data set on coups, while Serguey Braguinsky pointed me to useful references, Bill Clarke gave helpful advice on presenting the results of interaction models in Chapter Three, and Michael Gilligan generously shared data. Eddie Camp, Xiaobo Lu, Kaj Thomsson, and Kyohei Yamada suffered through a presentation of the game-theoretic material in my graduate class on formal models of comparative politics at Yale and made useful comments, as did Valerie Frey and Mario Chacón; Eddie Camp served as an excellent discussant at the Yale Comparative Politics Workshop, while Mario Chacón provided valuable research assistance. Stephen Kaplan was an enriching person with whom to discuss Venezuela and other topics. I received helpful suggestions on Chapter Five from Libby Wood and participants in her qualitative methods field seminar at Yale. Stathis Kalyvas and Susan Stokes kindly gave me guidance on the book's publication as well as much-appreciated advice on many other topics; in addition to moral support, Sue Stokes generously provided financial assistance through the Yale Program on Democracy. Jim Fearon graciously commented on two chapters of the manuscript that were presented at a conference on oil and governance at Stanford. I am especially grateful to John Roemer, who generously made many suggestions on the formal analysis in the third chapter, and to Michael Ross and to Erik Wibbels, who provided detailed comments on large portions of the manuscript. Jennifer Bussell and Ashley Dunning deserve some (they say all) of the credit for helping me come up with a title for the book.

No book involving field research could get researched or written without the help of many colleagues, contacts, and informants. The following individuals took their time to share with me their knowledge of Venezuelan politics or helped further my field research in other ways: Asdrúbal Baptista, Froilán Barrios, Gerardo Blyde, Mercedes Briceño, Gustavo Tarre Briceño, Rafael Gonzalez Cardenas, Jonathan Coles, Michael Coppedge, Javier Corrales, Moises Dorey, Steve Ellner, Luis Pedro España, Ramón Espinasa, Lupe Fajardo, Sergio Galvis, Gustavo García, Dorothy Kronick, Luis Lander, Daniel Levine, Christopher Mann, Osmel Manzano, Patrícia Marquez, Margarita López Maya, Luis Miquilena, María Eugenia Miquilena, Bernard Mommer, Francisco Monaldi, Richard Obuchi, Daniel Ortega, Alfredo Padilla, Alesia Rodríguez Pardo, Dick Parker, Michael Penfold, Rodrigo Penso, Mercedes Pulido, Fred Rich, Giuseppe Rionero, Francisco Rodríguez, Gustavo Romero, Samantha Sánchez, Arturo Tremont, Alfredo Torres Uribe, Ramón J. Velásquez, Alejandro Vicentini, Janine Vici-Senior, Ricardo Villasmil, and Stefania Vitale. I was fortunate to have an affiliation with the Instituto de Estudios Superiores de Administración (IESA) in Caracas, which offered me office space, administrative support, and, especially, a chance to interact with leading Venezuelan academics in a congenial environment. I owe an especially large debt to Francisco Monaldi, who helped to facilitate my field research in countless ways, provided extensive comments on my work, and, through many hours of conversation, helped me to understand much more than I otherwise would have about Venezuelan politics. I would also like to acknowledge the following individuals, who helped me on field research trips to Bolivia, Botswana, and Chile: Jorge Arrate, Lorgio Balcazar Arroyo, Willy Conradi, Ribson Gabonowe, Kenneth Good, Carlos Humud, Raúl Kieffer, Joe Matume, René Mayorga, Martin Mendoza-Botelho, Louis Nchindo, Neil Parsons, Joseph Ramos, Chris Sharp, Nicholas Terlecky, Richard White, and especially my friend

Arnold Bauer, who generously shared a small portion (but a large quantity) of his immense knowledge of Chilean history.

I was fortunate to receive excellent comments after presenting early versions of this material at Brown University's Colloquium on Comparative Politics; Harvard University's David Rockefeller Center for Latin American Studies; Stanford University's Center on Democracy, Development and the Rule of Law; the Yale Comparative Politics Workshop; and the Wallis Institute for Political Economy at the University of Rochester, as well as in the political science departments at Columbia University, New York University, Northwestern University, Ohio State University, the University of Chicago, the University of Illinois at Urbana-Champaign, the University of Virginia, and the University of Wisconsin–Madison. Early versions of this material were also presented at the meetings of the Empirical Implications of Theoretical Models (EITM) training institute at the University of California, Berkeley in June–July 2004, as well as at the Institute on Qualitative Research Methods (IQRM) (now the Institute on Qualitative and Multi-Method Research, IQMR) at Arizona State University in January 2004. The Institute of International Studies at the University of California, Berkeley generously supported my field research.

The anonymous reviewers made many helpful suggestions that greatly enriched the manuscript. I am also especially grateful to my editors at Cambridge University Press, Eric Crahan and Lew Bateman, for skillfully steering the manuscript through the review and production process, and to Margaret Levi for accepting the manuscript for publication in the Cambridge Studies in Comparative Politics series.

Finally, I am grateful for the many friends and family members who have supported me along the way. Márcia Treidler, Jennifer Walsh, Katya Wesolowski, and many other capoeiristas taught me lessons that could not have been learned elsewhere. Friends who preserved my sanity (or tried) in graduate school include Naazneen Barma, Taylor Boas, Margaret Boittin, Mark Haven Britt, Rebecca Chen, Brent Durbin, Miguel de Figueiredo, Matt Grossman, Dave Hopkins, Rebecca Hamlin, Amy Lerman, Keena Lipsitz, Sebastián Mazzuca, Simeon Nichter, Grigo Pop-Eleches, Ely Ratner, Sarah Reckhow, Jessica Rich, Erin Rowley, Kyra Naumoff Shields, Regine Spector, Sarah Snip Stroup, and especially Jennifer Bussell. I would also like to thank Dagan Bayliss, Elvin Geng, Ahwat Schlosser, Nicholas Terlecky, and Terry Wade, who will know why, and my family: the Berwyn Dunnings, the Fredricksons, Carolyn Geiger, Nan Margadant and Gudrun Klostermann, the Vogts, Ken Sorey and Case and Jay Dunning-Sorey, and especially my wonderful big sister Ashley Dunning, who has been a constant in the midst of change and always a source of inspiration. My cherished parents, Harrison Dunning and Jo Burr and Ted Margadant, have loved and supported me but also challenged and shaped me intellectually. For the latter reason as much as the former, this book is dedicated to them.

Crude Democracy:
Natural Resource Wealth and Political Regimes

1

Does Oil Promote Democracy?

The concept of a "crude democracy"—that is, a democracy fostered, supported, or sustained by oil wealth—is counterintuitive. Political scientists, policymakers, and pundits often assert that where oil or certain other natural resources are bountiful, democracy is not. Rulers of many resource-rich countries, from the Arabian Peninsula to the former Zaire, appear to have had great success in consolidating stable authoritarian polities; elsewhere, conflict over the distribution of resource revenues has seemed to promote political instability or even civil war but certainly not democratic regimes. In the aftermath of the U.S.-led invasion of Iraq in March 2003, for example, though some observers hoped Iraq's petroleum could be harnessed to pay for reconstruction and then to finance a stable democracy, other analysts worried that conflict over the division of oil revenues would inflame sectarian and regional tensions and ultimately undermine the prospects for democracy. The experience of many other resource-rich countries contributes to a pessimistic evaluation of democracy's chances in countries rich in natural resources. Commenting on the apparently robust association between oil wealth and autocracy, *New York Times* columnist Thomas Friedman pronounced a "First Law of Petropolitics" in the pages of the journal *Foreign Policy*: "The price of oil and the pace of freedom always move in opposite directions in oil-rich petrolist states" (Friedman 2006).

Behind this claim stands a large and growing, if more nuanced, academic literature in political science and related disciplines. According to many social scientists, the key to understanding the link between natural resources like oil and authoritarianism is to analyze the political incentives and capabilities associated with natural resource "rents"—that is, the extraordinary profits often associated with natural resource extraction, which frequently flow directly into the fiscal coffers of the state but require neither an elaborate tax bureaucracy nor the projection of the state's power into the domestic affairs of its citizens. By controlling the reins of government, elites in resource-rich countries may accumulate enormous personal wealth and may benefit more from taking costly actions to seize or maintain political control, rather than investing in other forms of economic or social power. Rulers who can rely on resource rents may have less need to share political power more broadly with citizens in exchange for tax revenues or other forms of support. Resource rents also appear to give authoritarian elites powerful technologies with which to ward off challenges to their rule: for instance, elites may use resource rents to strengthen the repressive apparatus of the state or to coopt the political opposition with material inducements. Although petroleum provides the paradigmatic font of resource rents, motivating the title and a major focus of this book, some other natural resources can also produce rents and thus are alleged to foster similar political effects. A growing body of empirical research, from case studies of resource-rich regimes in Africa and the Middle East to cross-national quantitative analyses, seems to support what has nearly become a conventional wisdom among many political scientists, policymakers, and pundits alike: resource rents promote authoritarian rule.[1]

As the literature on resource politics has itself noted, however, there are important anomalies to this claim. Norway's discovery of massive amounts of petroleum in the North Sea in the late 1960s and 1970s has not apparently destabilized Norwegian democracy, while diamond-rich Botswana is often described as a democratic success story and a political and economic oasis among the countries of post-colonial, sub-Saharan Africa. Aside from these often-remarked cases—which are sometimes "explained" with reference to the "pre-existing strength" of democracy or institutions of governance in such countries—there are many other examples that seem to defy the widespread notion that natural resource wealth fosters authoritarianism. In the first place, there are many democracies that are resource-*rich* without being highly resource-*dependent*, a subtle but important conceptual distinction that is sometimes elided in the literature on the effects of resource wealth: Australia, Canada, South Africa (today), the United Kingdom, and the United States are just a few obvious but important examples.

[1] Ross (2001), Barro (1999), Jensen and Wantchekon (2004), and many other analysts have argued that natural resources promote authoritarianism; see the further discussion in this chapter and in Chapter Two.

Beyond these apparent exceptions, however, lies a more radical possibility: rather than hinder democracy, natural resource wealth might instead *promote* it. A well-known literature on the historical evolution of democracy in Venezuela, one of the world's oldest oil exporters, makes precisely this claim. The idea that oil rents promoted democratic stability has been an important part of the received wisdom about Venezuela—a country that was, until fairly recently, among the most stable democracies in Latin America. As democracy after democracy in South America fell to authoritarian coups in the 1960s and 1970s, oil-rich Venezuela seemed an important exception; by the early 1980s, Venezuela had become a model for democrats throughout the region. In contrast, when the Venezuelan government's revenues from oil plummeted in the 1980s, a process that deepened in the 1990s for reasons discussed in this book, Venezuela's democracy was increasingly destabilized. Contra Friedman, oil rents and democratic stability have tended to move in the same, not opposite, directions in twentieth-century Venezuela.[2]

The apparent contradiction between the claim that oil promotes authoritarianism and the assertion that it has promoted democracy in Venezuela might provoke our skepticism about either the country literature or the recent, more general cross-national literature. To those who have argued that oil promotes authoritarianism, Venezuela is just another exceptional case—an outlier, in statistical parlance. Indeed, many observers have seen a growing centralization of power and an incipient authoritarianism in contemporary Venezuela, which they have taken as additional evidence in favor of the causal link between resource rents and authoritarianism. On the other hand, the fact that a wide range of country specialists have argued that petroleum promoted democracy in Venezuela might raise our concern that missing variables mediate the relationship between resource rents and the political regime type, and that these variables can help explain variation in observed outcomes across resource-rich countries.

A central contribution of this book is to help reconcile these competing claims. The analysis does not contradict the assertion that resource wealth promotes authoritarianism because, as I argue, there are indeed mechanisms through which resource wealth can promote the emergence or persistence of authoritarian regimes. However, there are also mechanisms through which resource wealth can promote *democracy*. As I show

[2] The most well-known statement that oil promoted Venezuelan democracy is Karl's (1987, 1997). See also España (1989), Naím and Piñango (1984), Rey (1989), and Urbaneja (1992).

in this book, the claims that resources promote authoritarianism and that they promote democracy are not mutually inconsistent. Resource rents can promote authoritarianism or democracy, but they do so through different mechanisms. An understanding of these different mechanisms can give us the analytic leverage needed to develop and assess a conditional theory about when the authoritarian or, alternately, democratic effects of resource wealth will be relatively important.

This study therefore aims not only to elucidate a democratic effect of resource wealth but also to propose and test a theory about the structural *conditions* under which the effect of resource rents will tend to be authoritarian or, instead, democratic. The argument can, in turn, help us explain variation in regime outcomes across resource-rich countries. There is substantial empirical and theoretical value to doing so: as I show in this book, the empirical relationship between resource rents and democracy is substantially stronger than many previous scholars have suggested. In Latin America, for instance, oil and other resources are *positively*, not negatively, related to democracy in time-series cross-section data. In addition, the in-depth case studies of Bolivia, Chile, Ecuador, and Venezuela developed in this book not only provide evidence on the mechanisms through which rents may promote democracy; they also show a positive intertemporal relationship *within* countries between the extent of resource rents and the stability of democracy. On its own, and along with other evidence I present in this book, these observations might pose some challenge to the idea that resource rents always promote authoritarianism because the relevant literature does not propose a theoretical reason to expect the effect of rents in Latin America to be different from the effect in any other part of the world.[3]

I argue here, however, that such cases are not democracies despite oil but instead are democratic in part *because* of oil or other natural resources. I suggest that a set of structural characteristics common to Latin American resource-rich countries amplify the democratic effects of resource wealth.

[3] However, Latin American and Caribbean cases figure prominently in previous analyses of anomalous cases. Smith and Kraus (2005) study five countries that are or have been "democracies despite oil": Congo, Ecuador, Nigeria, Trinidad, and Venezuela. Herb (2005) argues informally that there may be countervailing effects of rents on the regime, working, however, through different mechanisms than those emphasized in this study; among Herb's examples, Latin American and Caribbean cases also figure prominently (see his Table 1). Haber and Menaldo (2007) find a largely positive relationship between fiscal reliance on oil and the level of democracy in Latin America but argue that the net effect of oil reliance is, on average, close to zero. These and other valuable contributions are discussed further in Chapters Two and Four.

Other resource-rich countries outside the region that share these structural characteristics, such as Botswana (a case also studied in this book), also tend to be more democratic than other resource-rich peers. Far from anomalies, I argue that these cases represent a set of countries in which we should expect resource rents to have a relatively democratic, not authoritarian, effect. The empirical evidence presented in this book will help to buttress a key theoretical contention: the effect of resource rents is a *conditional* one, and variation in political outcomes across resource-rich countries is both coherent and at least in part predictable on the basis of the theory developed in this study.

What is the source of the contrasting political effects of resource rents? In the rest of this introductory chapter, I provide an initial elaboration of the theory developed in this book. The discussion is stylized, yet it conveys the key intuitions that undergird the authoritarian and democratic effects of resource wealth for which I argue. It also introduces my approach to the game-theoretic modeling of politics in resource-rich countries, an approach developed at length in the third chapter. I also use this discussion of the competing effects of resource rents to present a theory to help explain variation in regime outcomes across resource-rich countries. Finally, I close the chapter by discussing the method and plan of the book.

1.1 *The Authoritarian and Democratic Effects of Natural Resources*

As scholars of comparative politics have emphasized, there appear to be many ways that countries arrive at democracy. In general, there may be many different mechanisms through which democracy can be created, sustained, eroded, or destroyed (Shapiro 2003: 80–2; Tilly 1995). Important contingencies and indeterminacies are obviously involved (A. Przeworski 1988), a fact that does not in itself obviate the usefulness of seeking to understand structural and contextual constraints. Along with other factors (see O'Donnell and Schmitter 1986), the influence of economic development, economic inequality, and economic *interests* on the political regime has spawned a vast literature in comparative politics (B. Moore 1966; O'Donnell 1973; Rueschemeyer, Stephens, and Stephens 1992; Tocqueville 1835). The analysis in this book privileges the economic sources of political regimes, not because these are always the most important, but rather because the political effects of natural resource wealth must almost certainly depend on such economic factors.[4]

[4] See, however, Coronil (1997), who ties the impact of petroleum on politics in Venezuela in part to oil's semiotic and imaginative dimensions.

How does resource wealth influence the economic foundations of political regimes? One key characteristic of the natural resources on which I focus in this study is that they produce *rents*: super-normal (oligopoly or monopoly) profits, or the excess over the return to capital, land, and labor when these factors of production are put to their next-best use (Monaldi 2002a). Another characteristic, as Hirschman (1977) noted, is that the extraction of such resources tends to be capital-intensive and often takes place within the context of a geographically concentrated industry without widespread "linkages" to other productive processes. In much of the developing world and at various historical moments, mineral resources like oil have been directly owned and extracted by the state. However, even when they are not state-owned, and even in developed economies with strong liberal traditions of private sub-soil ownership, such natural resource sectors are often ready sources of revenue for the state. Asset immobility, geographic concentration, and the heavy sunk costs involved in the extraction of many natural resources create a tax base that is relatively inelastic and that can provide the state with multiple opportunities for appropriating rent (Mommer 2002: 108–18; Moran 1974; Wells 1971). In the contemporary era, crude oil is the quintessential example of a natural resource that produces "rents" for states, motivating the title and a major focus of this study. Yet, copper deposits, kimberlite diamonds, and other natural resources may produce rents and readily provide state revenues as well—while some natural resources do not.[5]

Together, these features of such natural resource sectors—that they produce rents, that they are often economic "enclaves," and that the rents they produce tend to be appropriated by the state—imply that their main political-economic influence often stems from their effect on patterns of public spending and revenue-generation (Beblawi 1987; Mahdavy 1970). The influence on public spending is obvious: because rents tend to be appropriated to an important extent by the state, they tend to be allocated or

[5] As discussed in the following chapter, kimberlite diamonds, which are geographically concentrated in underground pipes and generally involve substantial capital intensities in production, provide high barriers to entry for private actors but ready revenue sources for states; see Le Billon (2001), Snyder (2001), Snyder and Bhavnani (2005), and Isham et al. (2003). By contrast, alluvial diamonds, which are scattered via above-ground or subterranean waterways and tend to be relatively easily mined by individual citizens or other private actors, tend not to produce "rents" for the state. In Chapter Two, I provide a fuller conceptual discussion of "rents" and discuss reasons why some natural resources but not others may provide a source of rents for the state.

distributed by political authorities (Luciani 1987). The impact on revenue generation is slightly more subtle but no less important. For reasons I discuss at greater length later, resource rents can at least partially obviate the extent to which the state engages in more costly revenue-generating activities, including—particularly crucially for this study—the extent of taxation of citizens. Resource rents tend to pour directly into the fiscal coffers of the state, providing the Fisc with something akin to an externally generated "windfall" and also displacing taxation as an important font of public revenue (Beblawi 1987; Mahdavy 1970).

This analysis of the way in which rents may shape the fiscal basis of the state accords with the previous literature on resource-rich rentier states. I differ from much of this literature, however, in assessing the political consequences of this mode of state finance. I now turn from the influence of natural resources on the economic foundations of regimes to a theory of the influence of these foundations on regime outcomes.

By way of introduction, it may be useful to consider the following scenario. Suppose that under an existing democracy, rich elites have an opportunity to stage or support a coup against a democratic regime. Elites may weigh the expected costs associated with the coup itself (which may include, for instance, the likelihood of success or the probability of exile or imprisonment following an unsuccessful coup) against the anticipated costs and benefits of continuing to live under a democratic regime. Many factors are likely to influence these latter costs and benefits, but elites' economic interests may often play a role.

How might resource rents shape the economic costs and benefits of democracy to these hypothetical coup plotters? To pose a candidate answer to this question, consider Figure 1.1. The figure, which relates to a more elaborate model developed in the third chapter, depicts a stylized game between a relatively poor democratic majority and a rich elite. In the first move of this game, a relatively poor democratic majority sets economic policy. In the second move of the game, a set of relatively rich elites decides whether to stage a coup. I assume that there is some exogenous cost (ϕ^H) to staging a coup that is independent of economic interests (such as the risk that a coup fails, as mentioned above). In deciding whether to stage a coup, elites weigh the payoff to authoritarianism and the utility (or disutility) of democracy against this coup cost.

In this stylized world, there will be some critical value of the exogenous cost at which elites will be indifferent between staging and not staging a coup, given other costs and benefits associated with authoritarianism and

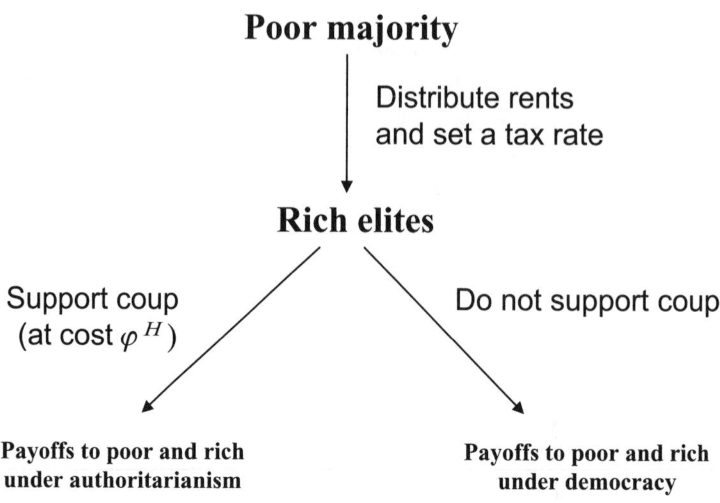

Figure 1.1 Coups against democracy.

democracy; for values of the cost that fall below this critical threshold, elites would prefer to support a coup than to live under a democratic regime. Factors that tend to increase the payoff to staging a coup and installing an authoritarian regime (left branch of Figure 1.1) will increase the incidence of coups, whereas factors that tend to increase the payoff (or decrease the disutility) to living under democracy (right branch of Figure 1.1) will decrease the incidence of coups.

Notice that economic policy in this simple game has two components: the distribution of the rents and the setting of a tax rate. First, because the resource sector supplies rents directly to the state, rents are distributed at the beginning of the game by the actors that control political power, here the democratic majority. If elites stage a coup, they are assumed to come to power and (at least until another change in political regime) to control the distribution of the rent. If elites do not stage a coup, the political regime remains democratic, and the democratic majority retains its ability to influence the setting of policy.

Second, the democratic majority also sets a tax rate on wealth or income. Suppose that rich elites and the poor masses receive profits or wages from economic production in manufacturing, agriculture, services, and other non-resource sectors of the economy. As a simplification—and to emphasize the distinction between these economic sectors and resource wealth—I refer to these non-resource sectors collectively as the private sector, to profits

to the exclusion of elites. Any number of factors, from political competition in multi-dimensional policy spaces (Roemer 1998) to lobbying (Grossman and Helpman 2001) and investments in "de facto" power by the rich (Acemoglu and Robinson 2006b) may limit the extent to which democracies actually redistribute (see Shapiro 2003, Chapter Five). The simplifying assumption that the poor set policy under democracy is meant to facilitate a comparison between democratic and authoritarian regimes; to be valid as a starting point, it should be the case that democracies tend to redistribute more than authoritarian regimes, on average.[10] These points are discussed further in the next two chapters.

It may also be important to point out at the start that the book builds an argument about the conflicting impacts of natural resource wealth on a certain kind of elite authoritarianism; that is, the book seeks to explain the contrasting effects of natural resource wealth on the strength of elite incentives to oppose Schumpetarian democracy. Though a large literature gives a privileged role to elite incentives, and though the kind of elite authoritarianism I discuss has historically been a prevalent form of non-democracy, it is surely important to recognize that elite incentives are just one factor affecting the emergence and persistence of democracy. Keeping this in mind throughout the development of the argument, as I discuss later in the book, may be helpful for placing scope conditions on the theory.

Finally, it is important to note that the analysis of the *authoritarian* effect of resource wealth in this book concurs in many ways with previous analyses. Indeed, because the focus here is on elucidating the relatively understudied *democratic* effect of resource wealth and on developing a theory to explain variation in regime outcomes across resource-rich states, the authoritarian effects of resource rents are explored in a somewhat "reduced form" fashion. Previous research has explicated a wide range of mechanisms through which resource rents might promote authoritarianism. Ross (2001: 332–7) discusses and tests three broad ways in which resources might hinder democracy: the "rentier effect," through which oil revenues "relieve social pressures that might otherwise lead to demands for greater accountability"; the "repression effect," through which "resource wealth may allow . . . governments to spend more on internal security and so block the

[10] Evaluating this point empirically, however, is complicated when viewed through the prism of a theory like Acemoglu and Robinson's (2006a): because the most unequal societies will not become democracies in the first place, comparisons of redistribution in democracies and autocracies may be subject to important sample-selection problems.

population's democratic aspirations"; and the [lack of] "modernization effect," in which "resource-led growth does not lead to higher education levels and greater occupational specialization . . . [and thus] should fail to bring about democracy." Other arguments linking resources to authoritarian rule elaborate in one way or another on one (or several) of these classes of mechanisms. For instance, the distribution of rents may be used strategically by elites to moderate demands for political reform or to "buy out" elements of the political opposition (Acemoglu et al. 2004; see also Robinson et al. 2006). In existing democracies, rents may engender a strong "incumbency advantage" that can inhibit political competition and promote creeping authoritarianism (Wantchekon 1999b, 2002); in authoritarian regimes, when elites can transfer resource rents directly to themselves and their supporters, they may exclude other groups from the direct benefits of the rents and thereby inhibit the development of autonomous challenges to their rule (Bueno de Mesquita et al. 2003: 94–5).[11]

For current purposes, the main point is that in much of the previous work on the authoritarian effect of rents, the distribution of rents is involved in one way or another in the argument—either because rents give political elites greater incentives to hold onto power through anti-democratic means or because they lend elites the capacity to resist pressure to share political power more broadly. This is a starting point for the models developed in the third chapter and elsewhere in the book. The core theoretical contribution of this study, however, is not to illuminate the authoritarian effects of rents, which have been better elucidated by previous analysts. Rather, the goal here is to elucidate the relatively understudied democratic effects of rents and to compare these effects to the authoritarian effects of rents posited by previous analysts. The theoretical models developed in this book allow us to study these two effects in the context of a single analytic framework and therefore allow us to generate hypotheses to explain variation in the political effects of rents.

In contrast to many existing claims about the political effects of resource rents, I argue in this book that resource rents can have both authoritarian and democratic effects: "crude democracy" is not an oxymoron. This book does not lay a special claim to advancing our understanding of the nexus between oil and authoritarianism, as the authoritarian effect for which it argues privileges mechanisms emphasized by other scholars. The principal

[11] See also Boix (2003), Jensen and Wantchekon (2004), Lam and Wantchekon (2004), Robinson (1997), and Wantchekon (2002).

contribution of this study instead is to elucidate an important and quite general mechanism that links resource rents to democracy and, especially, to *compare* this link to the mechanisms through which resources promote authoritarianism, in order to elaborate a theory that can help explain variation in political outcomes across resource-rich countries. The integration of the democratic and authoritarian effects of resources into a single analytic framework is important because it can allow us to generate hypotheses about the *conditions* under which one or the other effect may be relatively important. Indeed, the perhaps more interesting social-scientific question this study seeks to answer is what makes the authoritarian or, alternatively, the democratic effects of resource wealth more important. How can we explain variation in the political outcomes in resource-rich countries in comparative perspective?

1.2 Explaining Variation

Consider again the incentives of the stylized coup plotters in Figure 1.1. The discussion above emphasized that resource rents may have two opposed effects on the relative costs and benefits of staging a coup, net of the "normal" costs of coups.[12] On the one hand, control of political power implies control of the rents; thus, leaving political power in the hands of the democratic majority entails an opportunity cost for elites, particularly because it may be difficult for the majority to commit credibly to transfer some portion of the rents to the elite minority in the future. *Ceteris paribus*, it is therefore plausible that a boom in the resource sector should increase the benefits of taking power relative to the costs. On the other hand, one reason that rich elites might seek to take power in the first place may be to block redistribution under democracies, as many historical instances of coups in Latin America and elsewhere attest. Resource rents mitigate this threat of redistribution; because the redistributive costs to elites of democracy are lowered, incentives to undertake a risky coup may be reduced.[13]

In this schematic description (and in the richer formal models developed in the third chapter), there is a kind of horse race between the competing

[12] These "normal" costs may include the often significant risks of exile or imprisonment brought by failed coups, or the (at least temporary) economic as well as political disruption brought by successful as well as failed ones. See Chapter Three for further discussion.

[13] As I emphasized earlier and discuss later, these considerations may also be germane to understanding the incentives elites in an authoritarian regime who are considering democratization as a possible response to mobilization from below.

democratic and authoritarian effects of resource wealth. As a first step in explaining variation, it is useful to consider what variables might influence the relative importance of these opposed effects. When might the reduced redistributive costs of democracy be more important, relative to the resource-induced benefits of taking power through a coup?

This question is analyzed much more extensively in the formal analyses presented later in this book. To begin to answer this question here, it may help to introduce a stylized description of two different kinds of countries, which I will later connect to real cases. In each country, suppose that there are two economic sectors, a natural resource sector and a sector that includes manufacturing, services, or agriculture. Let us assume initially that revenues from resources accrue directly to the state, as implied by the idea that resource rents fall like "manna from heaven" into the fiscal coffers of the state; I justify this assumption further in Chapter Two (though later I also investigate the theoretical consequences and empirical value of relaxing it). In contrast to the state-controlled resource sector, private citizens are engaged in production in manufacturing, services, and agriculture, and in these sectors they reap rewards from profits or wages.[14] For lack of a better term, I refer to these non-resource sectors collectively as the "private" sector. Then, given that these two countries each have "resource" and "private" sectors, there may be substantial divergence along at least two basic dimensions, which will be important for our theory.

Imagine first country A, where the resource sector is a predominant force in the total economy: the ratio of resource rents to gross domestic product (GDP) is extremely high, so resource rents are very nearly the only economic "game in town." Moreover, to the extent there is any economic activity in the private sector, income and assets (such as access to capital, land, and so on) in this sector are distributed relatively *equally*. This country is "resource-dependent" as well as resource-abundant. (The distinction between resource abundance and resource dependence, introduced earlier, will be discussed further in a moment.) Moreover, inequality of private wealth or income provides little in the way of a potentially salient dimension of political conflict.

[14] I refer here to the "state-controlled" resource sector only for convenience; as I argue in Chapter Two, even resource sectors controlled by private companies may provide important volumes of rents for the state (Mommer 2002). However, the ownership structure may well matter, as I discuss later (see Jones Luong and Weinthal 2001a, 2001b, 2006 and Jones Luong 2004 on the role of the ownership structure in the resource sector).

By way of contrast, now consider country B. Here, the resource sector may be an important part of the total economy, but it is not preponderant: the ratio of resource rents to GDP is substantially lower than in country A, as there is important private economic activity outside of the resource sector. Furthermore, suppose that in this country there is also substantial inequality of assets or income in the private sector. In contrast to country A, private inequality provides at least a potential basis for political conflict.

In country A, because there is very little in the way of an important private sector, the mitigation of redistributive conflict may be of relatively little importance in shaping the incentives of our elite coup plotters. Moreover, to the extent such a sector exists, manufacturing or land assets may not be highly unequally distributed, so the economic basis for redistributive conflict may be relatively muted. Instead, we may expect conflict over the distribution of rents to be most prominent in shaping the incentives of elites. In other words, the mechanism through which I have argued that rents may promote authoritarianism may be relatively prominent.

In country B, on the other hand, the mitigation of redistributive conflict that is associated with resource rents may be a much more important source of political incentives for our elite coup plotters. Given the riskiness or other costs associated with a coup, elites may be more willing on the margin to play by the democratic rules of the game. Alternately, if the regime is instead authoritarian, incumbent elites who have significant private interests may be less prone to meet calls for democratic reform with repression, because resources mitigate the anticipated redistributive consequences of democracy—and this effect is relatively more important than in resource-dependent countries.

Of course, elites in country B may well desire to control the distribution of resource rents. Similarly, in country A rents may well limit redistributive taxation. Thus, both the "democratic" and the "authoritarian" effects of rents may be at work in both countries. It is simply argued here that the "democratic" effect will be more important in country B than in country A; this is because the indirect redistributive costs of continuing to live under democracy are substantially more important for shaping elite incentives in the former than the latter. In other words, when elites weigh the resource-induced benefits of a coup against the costs, they place relatively greater weight on the improvement to their payoff under democracy that stems from the mitigation of redistributive conflict. Elites in country B do not "like" democracy any more than do elites in country A, yet potential redistribution is more important in shaping elite incentives in country B than in country A, for reasons discussed further elsewhere in this study.

Having introduced this simple logic, it may be useful to develop more fully the conceptual and analytic framework that is implied in this discussion. Figure 1.2 depicts this framework. Our initial concern is with resource abundance, our most basic independent variable: is a country endowed with substantial natural resource wealth? Of greatest interest is the *conditional* impact of resource abundance, that is, how the political effects of resource wealth are conditioned by other variables. Nonetheless, the presence of resource wealth is obviously a sine qua non of the theory.

In the literature on the political effects of resource wealth, however, it is not resource abundance per se but instead the political effects of *rents* associated with natural resources like oil, copper, or kimberlite diamonds that are at issue. In particular, resource rents provide a particular kind of fiscal basis for the state, and it is this fiscal basis that is most important in determining the political effects of resource wealth. Given resource abundance, attention is restricted to "rentier states": those in which resource wealth provides a high proportion of government revenue (Herb 2005: 8; Luciani 1987: 72).[15]

What determines whether a resource-abundant state is also a rentier state? The main factor (though by no means the only, as discussed later) is the type of natural resource in question: not all natural resources readily produce rents for the public coffers. Natural resources such as crude oil or kimberlite diamonds are geographically concentrated, generally capital-intensive in production, and pose high barriers to entry for many private actors; they are, in turn, relatively easy for the state to tax, and taxing these sectors generally does not involve separating a wide swath of citizens from their private income. On the other hand, alluvial diamonds (which are scattered by riverbeds far away from underground pipes) and certain other minerals are geographically diffuse, demand little in the way of start-up costs, and may be relatively easily harvested by a wide range of private actors (Snyder and Bhavnani 2005). Taxing the latter kinds of resources may therefore be much like taxing other kinds of economic production by citizens; instead of falling easily into the coffers of the state, such forms of revenue generation may involve substantial distortionary and political costs. Just as obviously, primary commodities such as coffee or cocoa do not produce rents in the sense that term is used here. This distinction between resources

[15] The conceptualization of rentier states is discussed further in Chapter Two.

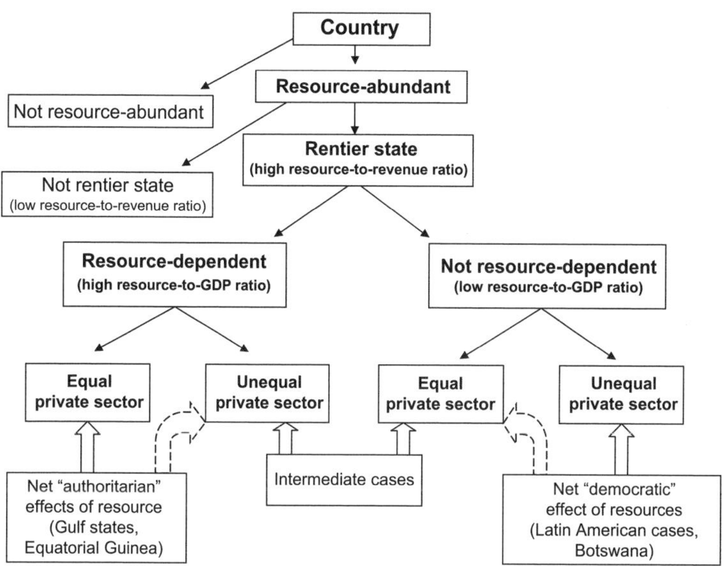

Figure 1.2 Explaining variation: a conceptual overview.

that produce rents and those that do not parallels a distinction in the literature on natural resources and conflict between concentrated, non-lootable or "point-source" resource and geographically "diffuse" resources that are "lootable" by private actors (Isham et al. 2003; Le Billon 2001; Snyder 2001; Snyder and Bhavnani 2005). In this book, attention is restricted to the former type of natural resources, for these are the resources that produce rents and thus are alleged to produce the political effects scrutinized in this book.

Moving down the branching diagram in Figure 1.2, the next useful distinction is between rentier states where the total economy is substantially dependent on natural resource wealth and those where it is not. As noted earlier, the definition of rentier states hinges on the extent to which resources provide the fiscal basis of the *state*. Yet this leaves substantial degrees of freedom with respect to the extent of development of private economic activity outside of the resource sector: resource rents may comprise an important proportion of government revenues without, however, making up as large a share of the overall economy. This is the source of the distinction between resource abundance and resource dependence.

To throw this distinction between resource-abundant rentier states and resource-dependent rentier states into sharper relief, it may be useful to compare typical Latin American resource-rich countries with many oil exporters in the Persian Gulf and West Africa. During Venezuela's oil boom of the 1970s, oil revenues provided more than 80 percent of the central government's budget, yet oil constituted only between 10 and 20 percent of gross domestic product.[16] Even during the boom, the private sector remained quite robust: Karl (1997: 42) reports that the participation of the private sector was 85.4 percent of GDP from 1970–1972 and 86.3 between 1973 and 1975, at the acme of the first oil boom.[17] In Chile, between the turn of the twentieth century and the First World War, the mining of nitrate supplied the majority of government revenues yet made up just 14 percent of GDP, on average (Blakemore 1974: 43–4; Mamalakis 1976: 38–9); the rest of the economy, and particularly the agricultural estates of the Central Valley, remained a crucial component of overall economic activity. Similarly, after the collapse of the nitrate sector and the rise of copper between the First and Second World Wars, revenues from copper came to finance up to 40 percent of annual government expenditures but constituted only between 7 and 20 percent of GDP (Moran 1974: 6). During Ecuador's oil boom of the 1970s, the national budget grew 21 percent in 1974, 32 percent in 1975, and 32 percent in 1976, much faster than the overall growth in economic product (Martz 1987: 51, 159, 404); in comparative perspective, Ecuador during the boom was a resource-*abundant* country but not a resource-*dependent* one.

Such cases present striking contrasts, however, with many resource-rich states in the Persian Gulf and in West Africa. In the midst of Saudi Arabia's oil boom of the 1970s, petroleum constituted upwards of 80 percent of government revenue, just as in Venezuela. However (though data are not as reliable), oil also appears to have reached nearly 80 percent of GDP during Saudi Arabia's boom, a pattern similar in other oil-rich Gulf states and in Africa but strikingly different from the pattern in many resource-rich countries in the Americas and in Europe. Perhaps the most extreme recent example of a resource-dependent state is Equatorial Guinea, a country of about 500,000 people that has become Africa's third biggest oil producer since large deposits of offshore oil were discovered in the mid-1990s. Due solely to the influence of these discoveries, Equatorial Guinea became the country with the second-highest per capita income in the *world*. The oil

[16] Author's calculations, *Ministerio de Energía y Minas*, various years; see also Baptista 2004: 73.

[17] This participation eroded subsequently, at least in percentage terms, as the public sector did grow during the boom, yet the private sector continued to contribute well over half of the total value of economic activity.

sector in Equatorial Guinea comprises more than 90 percent of GDP (International Monetary Fund 2005; McSherry 2006).

These examples suggest that there is a useful distinction to be drawn between rentier states in which the total economy (rather than simply the government) is relatively dependent on natural resources and those in which the degree of resource dependence is considerably lower. How is this distinction tied to the large-scale political outcomes this book seeks to explain? Casual inspection of the list of countries in the previous two paragraphs suggests that the resource-*dependent* countries tend to be more authoritarian than the merely resource-*abundant* countries. This book will argue that this is not coincidence; indeed, it will elaborate a theory in which greater resource dependence tends to privilege the authoritarian effects of rents.

Finally, to return to Figure 1.2, there are resource-abundant rentier states in which assets and income in the private sector are relatively *equally* distributed and those in which they are not.[18] In the models developed in Chapter Three, private inequality has a clear meaning: it is the share of *private* income that accrues to the rich. It is crucial to distinguish economic inequality in the private sector, however, from inequality that is due to the unequal distribution of rents themselves. The argument developed here concerns the impact of inequality in the distribution of non-resource wealth or income.[19]

According to the theory developed in this book, inequality of private income strengthens the democratic effect of resource rents. It is important to stress that this is not because inequality of private income is good for democracy. Just as in theoretical frameworks from Tocqueville (1835) to Acemoglu and Robinson (2006a), here high inequality itself is harmful to the chances for the emergence and consolidation of democracy. Inequality can engender more divergent preferences between elites and masses over

[18] For my purposes, equality is obviously more fruitfully conceptualized in continuous, not dichotomous, terms, as the model in Chapter Three makes clear. I simply describe "equal" and "unequal" private sectors here for heuristic purposes, as a way of mapping out basic contours of the argument.

[19] In the formulation of the models in Chapter Three, private income is assumed independent of the level of resource rents; I investigate the consequences of relaxing this assumption in Chapter Seven. In practice, as discussed both formally and informally elsewhere in this book, the unequal distribution of rents may be both an outcome and an important raison d'être of authoritarian regimes. Over the medium term or the long run, there may of course be important degrees of feedback between the distribution of rents and the extent of private asset or income inequality (see, e.g., Chaudhry 1997: 172–85). I discuss the consequences of this point for the argument elsewhere in the book.

redistribution, and because the preferences of poorer citizens for greater redistribution are assumed to be more influential under democracies (an assumption assessed elsewhere in the book), democracy is more costly to elites in more unequal societies. Yet where redistribution is a more salient concern for elites—precisely because there is greater inequality of non-resource income or wealth—the effect of resource rents in moderating redistributive conflict is more important. In other words, while inequality itself hurts democracy, resource rents mitigate the negative impact of inequality—and this effect of natural resources is more important (relative to the authoritarian effects of rents) in more unequal societies. This is, of course, a *ceteris paribus* claim that will be refined to some extent in the following chapters, yet this is what is meant by the theoretical proposition that inequality of private income can strengthen the democratic effect of rents.

Although I mainly leave empirical issues to subsequent chapters, it may be useful to note here that there is substantial cross-sectional variation in inequality in non-resource sectors, in resource-rich and resource-poor countries alike. One useful indicator comes from the industrial capital share, that is, payments to capital as a proportion of industrial value-added (i.e., payments to capital in non-resource manufacturing sectors, net of wages and salaries).[20] Using this measure, it is clear that resource-rich countries vary substantially with respect to the extent of inequality in non-resource sectors of the economy. For instance, compare the average capital shares in Latin America to those in the Persian Gulf: in the former region, industrial capital shares reach 80.2 on average, while in the latter, capital shares are 61.9 (see Table 4.2 in Chapter Four). There are important differences in the extent of non-resource, private inequality across resource-rich countries. The claim here is that these differences can also help us to explain variation in the net political effects of resource wealth.

Thus, at least two factors may help us to explain variation in political outcomes across resource-abundant countries: the extent of resource dependence and the level of private inequality. These are the two main variables that emerge as important in the comparative statics of the formal analyses in the third chapter. Of course, there is no claim that these are

20 Measuring the concept of private inequality raises important issues, as discussed in Chapter Four. The industrial capital share (in non-resource sectors) is the measure used in the cross-national empirical work in Chapter Four, where its utility as a proxy for private inequality in non-resource sectors of the economy is defended; the data come from industrial surveys conducted by the United Nations Industrial Development Organization (UNIDO) (see Ortega and Rodríguez 2006; Rodrik 1999).

the only structural factors that may condition the political impact of resource wealth; as discussed in Chapter Three and elsewhere, variables such as "state capacity," the historical moment at which resources are discovered or exploited, and other factors may also condition the political impact of resource wealth. However, it is argued that these variables help to explain variation in outcomes across resource-rich countries, and that they may do so because they shape the extent to which elites capable of mounting a coup against democracy (or preventing democratization) are concerned with redistributive pressures. By elucidating the conditions under which the authoritarian or democratic effects of rents tend to be relatively important, the theory can help to illuminate variation in comparative perspective, without appealing only to the (undeniably important) idiosyncratic aspects of particular cases.

As with my discussion of the dual democratic and authoritarian effects of rents above, it is useful to emphasize several points about this initial framework for explaining variation in outcomes across resource-abundant states. The framework is obviously highly stylized in a number of ways. As a heuristic device, the two economic sectors are imagined to be in splendid isolation from each other. This is appropriate as a conceptual starting point. As discussed above, the enclave-like character of rent-producing resource sectors (oil, copper, kimberlite diamonds, and so on) implies a low level of "linkages" between the resource sector and the rest of the economy, except through the channel of the political allocation of rents; indeed, this observation has motivated and informed a large literature on rentier states (see, among others, Hirschman 1977; Luciani 1987). Empirically, however, there may well be important feedbacks between the sectors. As many scholars have noted, a boom in the resource sector might inhibit the growth and even hasten the decline of other economic sectors, as in the famous "Dutch Disease," in which real exchange rate appreciations associated with resource booms damage other tradeable sectors, such as agricultural exports. Additionally, the approach distinguishes "private" inequality stemming from the unequal ownership of assets or claims on income in the agricultural, manufacturing, or service sectors from inequality that stems from the *distribution* of rents; the former might be thought of in terms of levels of "pre-existing" inequality, say, prior to a resource boom. In reality, at least in the medium to long term, resource rents may at least to some extent shape the extent of inequality everywhere in the economy (Chaudhry 1997: 175–7). These are important considerations, and they will be discussed elsewhere in this book. The wager, however, is that these are second-order concerns; it is useful to begin with a more stylized framework and then develop a more nuanced theory as the book proceeds.

Finally, I have suggested that whether natural resources can provide the fiscal basis for a rentier state depends primarily on the kind of resources concerned.[21] Readers may be justified in wondering, however, about the importance of other factors: for instance, are the fiscal regimes of certain kinds of states more prone to rentierism? It would be particularly problematic for the causal theory developed in this book if the political regime type itself determined rentier statism, yet it might also be the case that other institutional factors influence both the regime type and the fiscal take of the state; this could lead to misleading inferences about the impact of rents on the political regime. I take up this important issue in the next chapter, where I discuss the foundations of rentier states. I argue that neither theoretical reasoning nor empirical evidence supports the claim that the regime type conditions the fiscal take of the state: politicians in both democratic and authoritarian regimes can have strong incentives to maximize the rents the state receives from the resource sector, and the evidence suggests that both authoritarian and democratic regimes have sought to maximize rents. Nor, with one important exception, do factors such as the form of resource ownership or the overall economic orientation of the government significantly influence the propensity of the natural resource sector to supply rents to the state.[22] Rentier states may share diverse foundations, yet the presence of rent-producing natural resources tends to create a set of common forces that shape the fiscal basis of the state in similar ways. For purposes of developing this book's theory, it is useful to take these forces as a given, and to ask how the (exogenously determined) presence or absence of rents may shape the political regime, given various structural features of different societies. These points are argued further in the following chapter.

[21] This also does depend on the state of the world technological frontier: the mining of copper in nineteenth-century Chile was far less capital-intensive than the mining of the same resource in the twentieth century, when technological advances had made the mining of lower-grade ores increasingly possible.

[22] The exception to this point, and one explored in the following chapter, is that the form of ownership can matter where a concentrated domestic elite that is independent of the state owns and controls the natural resource in question. Then, unlike the theoretical framework described earlier, a resource boom unambiguously increases the incentives of elites to oppose democracy. This is a point that emerges from historical analysis of the Bolivian case (in the sixth chapter) and that is explored theoretically in the seventh chapter; it stands in tension with some recent work that has emphasized the advantages of private ownership of natural resources (especially Jones Luong and Weinthal 2006; see also Jones Luong 2004 and Jones Luong and Weinthal 2001b).

It is therefore useful to close this section by reiterating the key points. This study proposes a theory that illuminates the *conditional* political impact of natural resource wealth. Resource rents may have both democratic and authoritarian effects; the claims of previous analysts that resources promote autocracy or, alternately, democracy are not mutually inconsistent. The key task for comparative analysis is thus to illuminate variables or structural factors that tend to privilege the democratic or authoritarian effects of rents. I develop in this book a unified theoretical approach to confronting this analytic challenge; the framework developed here highlights several variables that may influence the relative salience of these two effects. In the discussion in this section, I highlighted the two most important factors, the extent of private inequality and the degree of resource dependence. The models developed in this book will show why these factors may matter and how they can help us explain political variation across resource-rich countries.

1.3 Method and Plan of the Book

This book uses a multi-method approach to investigate the impact of resource wealth on political regimes. The chapters that follow draw on several months of field research in Venezuela as well as secondary field research in Bolivia, Botswana, and Chile; the development of a series of game-theoretic models that probe the effects of natural resource wealth; conceptual elaboration of the core idea of the "rentier state"; and statistical analysis of cross-section time-series data on nearly all countries of the world. It is useful to say something at the outset about the contribution of each of these elements of the book to the development and testing of the overall argument.

In Chapter Two, I discuss the sources of rentier states, arguing that despite diverse foundations, countries rich in certain kinds of natural resources tend to converge on a set of fiscal arrangements that play an important role in my theory about the regime impacts of resource wealth. In this chapter, I further elaborate the concept of resource "rents," develop an approach to thinking about which natural resources provide rents, and review many of the insights of earlier literature on the fiscal basis of "rentier states." I also review some of the empirical evidence for the negative relationship between resource rents and taxation, which arises endogenously in the theoretical models of the following chapter and plays an important role in my argument about the democratic effects of rents. Finally, I discuss at greater length my basic approach to analyzing the economic determinants of democracy. These conceptual and empirical materials motivate and validate core assumptions as well as results of the theoretical models developed in the subsequent chapter.

I therefore use these conceptual elements as the basis for developing two related game-theoretic models in Chapter Three. In one model, a relatively rich elite in an existing democracy considers whether to support a coup against democracy, as in Figure 1.1 above, and the goal is to analyze how resource rents may shape the incentives of elites to intervene to overthrow the democratic order. In the other, incumbent elites in an existing authoritarian regime choose between possible responses to a "revolutionary" threat to their rule; these possible responses include repression, targeted transfers of resource rents and tax revenue to citizens when under threat ("buying out" the opposition), and democratization. Both of these models involve explicitly dynamic, infinite-horizon games, in which actors base decisions not just on their current economic returns but also on the anticipated future costs and benefits arising from their decisions today. In this sense, the two models are closely linked, despite obvious phenomenological differences between transitions from authoritarianism and breakdowns of democracy: the anticipated costs and benefits of democracy play a key role in shaping the choices of elites, whether the decision at hand involves foregoing a coup in an existing democracy or democratizing under an existing authoritarian regime.[23] In both models, resource rents shape elites' expectations about, inter alia, the future returns to democracy, but comparative statics analysis reveals the effects of resource rents to be mixed in these models. On the one hand, resource rents heighten the opportunity cost of democracy, because controlling the state in an authoritarian regime brings control of the distribution of the rents. On the other hand, the redistribution of private income through taxation, otherwise a disutility associated with democracy, is mitigated in a resource-rich society, lessening the relative attractiveness of taking costly actions (such as repression or coups) to maintain political power.

[23] In Dunning (2006), I analyze these two games jointly, in a fully intertemporal model in which there may be regime reversals in both directions, i.e., both coups against democracy and democratizations under authoritarianism. As I discuss in Chapter Three, however, this richer analysis comes at the cost of significant algebraic complexity and perhaps little in the way of added intuitions for the effects of resource wealth on the political equilibria. Because the comparative statics of that model are similar to those I derive in Chapter Three, I focus in this book on analyzing the relatively simple model of coups and the model of democratization separately.

Does Oil Promote Democracy?

One virtue of the formal models developed in Chapter Three is that they allow us to study these conflicting political effects of resource rents in a single framework. This helps us to generate hypotheses about the question of perhaps greatest social-scientific interest: under what conditions may the authoritarian or, alternately, democratic effect of resource wealth be more important? Because I emphasize that the *mechanisms* through which resource rents promote authoritarianism and democracy differ, the book's proposed answer to this question hinges on factors that will make one or another mechanism more important. In the models, there is a kind of "horse race" between the democratic and authoritarian effects of rents, and different variables will tend to strengthen one or the other effect, as discussed in the previous section. The predictions derived from the model are, to be sure, *ceteris paribus* propositions, and their empirical validity will depend on whether the theoretical model captures key economic sources of authoritarianism and democracy in resource-rich countries. On its face, however, the predictions of the model appear to help reconcile frequent claims that resource rents have had an authoritarian effect in many countries of the Persian Gulf and Africa—many of them highly resource-dependent countries in which high inequality may reflect the distribution of rent itself, rather than, say, "pre-existing" inequality of non-resource wealth or income—with the idea that rents may instead tend to promote democracy in the resource-rich countries of Latin America, where the ratio of resource rents to gross domestic product is substantially lower than in the countries of the Gulf, and a region in which inequality of non-resource income and wealth has been persistently high.

Chapters Four, Five, and Six are devoted to assessing the empirical evidence for these claims. The first important empirical task, which I take up in Chapter Four, is to revisit the cross-national statistical evidence on the authoritarian effects of resource wealth. From the perspective of the recent quantitative literature, for instance, the Venezuelan case appears to be simply an outlier (e.g., Barro 1999; Jensen and Wantchekon 2004; Ross 2001). Indeed, even if resource rents may have had a democratic effect in Venezuela, the generality of the democratic effect of resource rents would seem to be substantially limited by the apparently robust empirical association between resource wealth (actually, as I emphasize, resource *dependence*) and authoritarianism.

As I show in Chapter Four, however, the quantitative relationship between resource rents and democracy is substantially stronger than has been previously thought. Using cross-section time-series data on a global set of countries, and extending a data set from Hamilton and Clemens (1999) who provide a direct measure of resource rents, I find evidence that the empirical variation in regime outcomes across resource-rich countries is consistent with the propositions developed here. Inequality in non-resource sectors of the economy does appear to mediate the relationship between resource rents and the political regime, a finding that comes both from "direct" evidence—an interaction term model in which the estimated direct effect of resource rents on democracy is negative while the estimated effect of the interaction of rents and inequality is positive—and "indirect" evidence, in which I restrict the analysis to countries in Latin America, the most unequal region of the world (IDB 1998).[24] The relationship between resource wealth and authoritarianism also appears to reflect the relationship between resource *dependence* and authoritarianism, rather than resource rents per se. To be sure, there are important measurement and model specification issues involved in the statistical analysis, as I discuss further in Chapter Four. Yet given the prevailing belief among many students of the authoritarian "resource curse" that Venezuela may simply constitute an outlier, this new evidence suggests the usefulness of a focus on the democratic effect of resource rents.

Of course, other theories could plausibly explain this statistical evidence. In Chapters Five and Six, I turn to an extended analysis of several cases. Four of the five cases I analyze are located in Latin America, where—in part because of high inequality in non-resource sectors of the economy and a relatively low level of resource dependence, even among the most resource-rich countries of the region—the theory predicts a relatively democratic effect of resource rents; the other case, Botswana, shares similar characteristics. I discuss case selection issues further in Chapter Five. It is important to note here, however, that the main idea is not to assess the extent to which resource rents and the political regime covary in the ways predicted by the theoretical model; this task is undertaken in Chapter Four. Instead, the major goal of the case-study analysis is to assess the extent to which evidence on the mechanisms through which resource rents may have promoted or sustained democracy is consistent with the theory developed in this study. One way to put this is that the model developed in Chapter Three has observable implications, and an extended inquiry into the case-study evidence

[24] The positive and significant relationship between oil and democracy in a cross-section time series of eighteen Latin American countries between 1960 and 2001 persists to the exclusion of Venezuela from the analysis.

can assess the extent to which these implications are, in fact, observed. Another way to put this is that one wants to know whether "causal-process observations" (D. Collier et al. 2004) drawn from these cases are consistent with the mechanism through which resource rents are argued to promote democracy.

I begin in Chapter Five with a discussion of Venezuela in historical and contemporary perspective. In assessing the validity of the proposition that oil promoted democracy in Venezuela, I am able to take advantage of secular trends in the size of oil rents as well as new within-case (over-time) variation in political outcomes, not available to earlier scholars, to argue that previous analysts were justified in asserting a positive relationship between oil rents and democratic stability.[25] Indeed, unlike earlier analyses, the evidence presented here suggests that secular trends in the size of oil rents can help account not just for the past stabilization but also the more recent *destabilization* of Venezuelan democracy. Drawing on my fieldwork in Caracas and on the secondary literature, I argue that the growth of oil rents over the middle part of the twentieth century, by reducing the costliness of democracy in a highly unequal society, altered the incentives of elites to block or reverse Venezuela's transition to democracy in 1958. This was not, however, because elites received direct benefits from the *distribution* of oil rents themselves, as other analysts have suggested. Elites did benefit from the distribution of oil rents, yet political control of the state could conceivably have brought them even bigger direct benefits. Instead, the state's ability to extract ever-increasing oil rents from the oil sector nearly eliminated any *redistributive* demands that the democratic political system put on the Venezuelan economic elite. Whereas the breakdown of the brief democratic regime from 1945 to 1948—when oil rents were not nearly as important a source of government finance as they would later become—was precipitated by sharp class conflict and polarization, Venezuelan democracy after 1958 and particularly in the 1970s was characterized by a degree of class "compromise" and "consensus" that was highly unusual in Latin American countries during this period (e.g., Collier and Collier 2001; Levine 1978; Neuhouser 1992).

What is most striking about the Venezuelan case, given this earlier emphasis of country experts on class harmony, is the extent to which the class

[25] The methodological importance of observing within-case or intertemporal variation in the extent of resource rents and regime type across the relatively *longue durée* is discussed elsewhere.

divide reappeared as a salient basis for political conflict and mobilization beginning in the early 1990s. I argue here that the decline of oil rents as a source of public finance, which began in the 1980s and deepened in the 1990s for reasons I discuss in Chapter Five, was the most important factor contributing to this trend. Alternative explanations for class harmony after redemocratization in 1958, including explanations focused on the unique institutions enshrined in the "Pacto de Punto Fijo" and the Constitution of 1961, have a more difficult time explaining why class harmony was undermined in the wake of the decline in oil rents. To be sure, the institutions themselves were modified to some extent (for instance, with increasing political decentralization, the direct election of governors, and other factors), yet these institutional changes do not appear nearly major enough to account for substantial changes in the class basis of political identification, the wholesale collapse of support for the traditional Punto Fijo parties (AD and COPEI), and other transformations of the political arena. I argue here that the decline of oil rents contributed to the politicization of social class and the re-emergence of redistribution as a salient dimension of political conflict, in ways that are consistent with the theoretical framework developed in this study.

The renewal of redistributive politics in turn helps to explain the more recent destabilization of Venezuelan democracy over the past decade and a half. In the 1990s, with the rise of alternative parties such as Causa R, social class became a more explicit basis of political mobilization than perhaps at any time since the democratic interlude known as the *trienio* from 1945 to 1948. The election of Hugo Chávez to the presidency in 1998 heightened this trend. Initially popular also with some middle-class voters disaffected with the traditional parties but drawing his core support base from the nation's poor, Chávez initially moved cautiously on economic and particularly redistributive policy, maintaining a substantial degree of continuity with previous periods. By early 2001, however, in the face of low levels of oil rents and sharply declining popularity among his core support base, Chávez proposed an economic platform that was substantially more radical and substantially more redistributive than in earlier years of his presidency. I argue that this turn to redistribution, in the context of low oil prices, constituted a significant economic threat to the private elite and helped to mobilize substantial elite opposition to the regime—including, among a section of the business elite, support for a failed coup attempt against Chávez in 2002.

In the most recent years, the level of resource rents accruing to the Venezuelan state has risen impressively, beginning in 2003 in the wake of dramatic increases in world oil price levels. My discussion of the Venezuelan case therefore raises the important question of the influence of oil rents on the level of democracy in the most recent years. I take up this question at the close of Chapter Five. Many observers have correctly noted an increasing centralization of political power in Venezuela and indeed a decline in liberalism during the period of Chávez's presidency; some even classify the regime today as a "competitive authoritarian" regime, in which regular but marred elections are held. Although the idea that elections in contemporary Venezuela have been fraudulent is (thus far) without empirical merit, observers are correct to note a centralization of power and to raise the specter of greater future declines in Schumpeterian democracy. I discuss these issues at greater length in Chapter Five, but the question of relevance to this study is not the level of democracy in contemporary Venezuela. Instead, it is the impact of increases in *oil rents* on the political regime that is at issue. The evidence here appears mixed. On the one hand, there is evidence consistent with the idea of an "incumbency advantage" (Corrales 2006; Wantchekon 2002) associated with the recent rise in oil rents, one that may contribute to eroding electoral competition. On the other hand, analyzing data on elite attitudes toward economic policies of the incumbent administration and other variables, I argue that the mechanisms through which I argue that rents may promote democracy appear to be at work in contemporary Venezuela as well. It is difficult at the time of this writing to predict Venezuela's political future, though I propose some reflections in Chapter Five.

Taken as a whole, the Venezuelan case provides strong evidence not just that oil rents can promote democracy but that the mitigation of redistributive conflict is an important mechanism though which rents may have this effect. In fact, I find that a focus on the role of oil rents in mediating and moderating class and redistributive politics provides perhaps the most consistent explanation for cycles of authoritarianism and democracy in Venezuela in historical and contemporary perspective. Even so, knowledge of the Venezuelan case helped to motivate my approach to theorizing and modeling the politics of resource-rich countries. Because the Venezuelan case helped to generate the apparent contradiction that in part motivates this research, the positive relationship between oil rents and democracy might be of only limited relevance for assessing a general argument about the democratic effect of resource rents. And although the case study, perhaps most importantly, allows me to adjudicate between rival mechanisms through which oil rents could have had a democratic effect, skeptics might be justified in wondering whether there is not something idiosyncratic about the democratic effect of resource rents in Venezuela. That is, although the statistical evidence presented in Chapter Four suggests a more general relationship between rents and democracy, the mitigation of redistributive conflict may not in general provide the key mechanism through which resource rents can support the emergence and persistence of democracy in rentier states.

In Chapter Six, I therefore turn to briefer analyses of evidence from Chile, Bolivia, Ecuador, and Botswana. This evidence not only allows me to assess the generality of the democratic effect of resource rents in comparative perspective; it also, as it turns out, provides an opportunity to extend the theory in new and unexpected directions. In Chile, one of Latin America's longest-standing rentier states in the post-colonial period and also one of its oldest and most stable democracies prior to 1973, two resources (sodium nitrate and copper) provided an important fiscal basis for the state in different historical periods. Both resources also contributed to underwriting the mitigation of redistributive conflict, in ways discussed in Chapter Six, and very plausibly contributed to democratic stability in Chile. I discuss the evidence for this claim in Chapter Six and explore alternative explanations, while also discussing the relevance for the framework developed here of the coup of 1973. Although Chilean democracy fell victim in 1973 to perhaps the most famous anti-redistributive coup in twentieth-century Latin America, there is little evidence that copper itself either heightened redistributive conflict or promoted the turn to military rule. Instead, the most plausible interpretation of the evidence is that copper rents helped to mitigate redistributive conflict but nonetheless could not save democracy from its ultimate breakdown. I elaborate the argument further in Chapter Six.

Next, the Bolivian case partly confirms the intuitions underlying the general argument but partially suggests new theoretical directions as well. The tin barons who helped form the tiny oligarchy that ruled pre-revolutionary Bolivia (*la Rosca*, as this oligarchy was known) had substantial economic and political power, and they played an important role in resisting democratic reforms, appealing instead to the state to repress popular mobilization and strikes in the mines. The case of pre-revolutionary Bolivia therefore focuses attention squarely on the issue of resource ownership: because the tin sector was controlled by a domestic elite with substantial political power, tin rents plausibly *heightened* rather than reduced the economic disincentives associated with democratization for this small elite. After the Revolution of 1952, in which tin miners themselves played an especially critical role, the mines were nationalized, Bolivia redemocratized, and conditions for the establishment of a democratic rentier state seemed more propitious. Indeed, in the democratic period before the military coup of 1964, there is evidence that tin rents played a role in underwriting economic development, agrarian reform, and other measures while mitigating the economic threat to the elite. Yet, the capacity of the tin sector to provide rents to the state was limited by secular trends in the world tin market as well as by the aftermath of nationalization itself; by the end of the 1950s, it was aid from the United States—and not tin—which provided the major source of rent to the Bolivian state.[26] Finally, the gradual rise of the oil economy after the Revolution, and particularly the dramatic increase in natural gas reserves during the 1990s, promised a new source of rents for the central government. However, the location of oil and natural gas production in lowland departments such as Santa Cruz, rather than in the highland (*altiplano*) departments surrounding La Paz, also implied that the rise of natural gas rents plausibly shaped incentives for regional autonomy and secessionist movements as well. Thus, while the Bolivian case partially confirms the generality of the democratic effect of resource wealth, it also suggests the importance of patterns of resource ownership and of territorial control for the political effects of resource wealth. In Chapter Seven, I sketch an extension of the formal framework in Chapter Three to study the role of resource ownership, where I show that control of the resource sector by a small private elite, who must in turn be taxed by the state, may well heighten the authoritarian effects of resource wealth, as implied by some of the previous literature.

[26] As I note in Chapter Two, there is nothing in the definition of rent advanced in this study that precludes the study of rent from other sources, for instance, foreign aid. External assistance, however, is often disbursed strategically, sometimes carries conditions for various kinds of structural adjustment, and is sometimes conditioned on the regime type itself (Dunning 2004), thus complicating the assessment of causal influence of rents from this source. I therefore focus in this study on rents from natural resources, leaving the political effects of rents from other sources to future research.

I then turn to a brief analysis of oil and politics in Ecuador, where the rise of oil as a source of rents followed a military coup in 1972, initiated in part as a response to the imminent election of a left-wing mayor of the city of Guayaquil. Consistent with expectations from the literature on the authoritarian effects of oil, rents from oil production in the Amazon did finance the military budget during the 1970s and appeared to give the military government an important degree of state autonomy. Yet, inconsistent with the idea that democratic reforms and the price of oil always move in opposite directions (Friedman 2006), Ecuador redemocratized at the height of the second oil boom of 1979. The evidence suggests that the availability of oil rents as a source of public spending lessened the economic threat to elites that democracy posed: whereas the threat of redistribution had previously contributed to the breakdown of democracy in 1972, a vigorous policy of price and wage defense after redemocratization (e.g., a doubling of the minimum wage) came at a greatly reduced cost to private elites because of the new role for oil rents as the fiscal basis for the state. Consistent with the theory proposed in this book, oil rents appeared to limit redistributive conflict and contribute to democratic transition as well as consolidation in subsequent years.

Finally, I analyze the case of post-colonial Botswana, a diamond-rich rentier state and a nearly unique political and economic success story among the countries of post-colonial, sub-Saharan Africa (Acemoglu et al. 2003; Dunning 2005). At the time of independence from the British in 1966, Botswana was the second-poorest country in the world (Edge 1998: 343); between 1970 and 1997, Botswana achieved the highest average rate of economic growth in the world (Samatar 1999). Moreover, the identity of the highest office holder has changed three times since independence, the political opposition freely contests elections, social policies are routinely adjudged progressive, and there is a significant degree of media freedom, though the fact that the Botswana Democratic Party (BDP) has won every election since independence has engendered some debate about how democratic the country should be considered (see A. Przeworski et al. 2000: 23; also Good 1992 and Picard 1987).[27] Notwithstanding these debates, I argue that political competition is important and real in Botswana, and that the consolidation of the civilian regime took place even as diamond exports played an increasingly important role in the Botswanan economy; between

[27] The three presidents since independence have been Seretse Khama, Ketumile Masire, and Festus Mogae.

1976 and 1994, diamond exports increased by an average of 30.2 percent annually (Dunning 2005: 463). Botswana thus constitutes an important exception to the idea of a political or economic "resource curse," particularly when contrasted with the many resource-rich sub-Saharan African countries that are poorer today than they were at independence and/or that have long histories of authoritarianism in the post-colonial period. The theoretical model developed in this study is not consistent in all ways with the Botswanan case, yet I argue that it helps to explain important features of that case: in particular, why elections have not proved unduly threatening to the economic interests of the traditional cattle-owning Tswana elite.

As a whole, the evidence presented in this study suggests a revision to our understanding of the politics of resource-rich rentier states. The impression left by much recent work in this area is that the statistical evidence simply trumps any claim (by Venezuelanists or other scholars) that oil could have a democratic effect. Perhaps in consequence, an analytic focus on the conditions under which the authoritarian or, alternately, the democratic effects of resource wealth might become more important has been almost completely absent from the literature. I suggest here that the important and highly valuable literature on the authoritarian effects of resource wealth can be enriched by also considering the democratic effects of natural resource wealth. The evidence I present in this book suggests the empirical basis and, indeed, necessity of adopting a more qualified view.

This book will not, of course, explain all the variation in political outcomes across resource-rich countries; nor will it be argued here that the mechanism linking resource rents to democratic outcomes is salient for all resource-rich countries, even those that exhibit structural characteristics that should be propitious for the democratic effects of rents. The existence of apparent "anomalies" does not by itself invalidate the idea that resource wealth promotes authoritarianism. Nor, in the same spirit, does this book claim to explain all such anomalies. Rather, this book posits and explores a particular mechanism through which resource rents may promote democracy and compares it to mechanisms through which rents may promote authoritarianism. It does so theoretically, in the context of the game-theoretic analysis developed at length in Chapter Three; and it does so empirically, by testing the observable implications of the theoretical model with statistical analysis of cross-section time-series data and with largely qualitative "process tracing" of historical and contemporary evidence across a range of cases. Though the book will not explain all empirical anomalies, I argue that observable variation in political outcomes across resource-rich countries is consistent with the argument the book sets forth. Because resource rents have both authoritarian and democratic effects, explaining variation in political outcomes across resource-rich countries constitutes an important agenda for research on the effects of natural resource wealth.

2

The Foundations of Rentier States

This book proposes and tests a theory about the effects of natural resource wealth on the political regime. For purposes of developing this theory, I often take for granted that natural resource "rents" accrue to the state; this implies that extraordinary profits from natural resource production can provide a source of revenue for public spending. Much of the analysis then focuses on how the availability of rents in the fiscal coffers of the state shapes the development of political regimes; the third chapter, for instance, addresses the theoretical question of how the presence of rents may shape the chances for the emergence and persistence of democracy. The main theoretical contribution of that chapter, and of this book, is to argue that the flow of resource rents into the fiscal coffers of the state may have mixed effects on the propensity of countries to be democratic or authoritarian. In some settings, the democratic effect of rents will be relatively important, whereas in others the authoritarian effect will tend to triumph.

Yet this focus may seem to ignore an important prior question: how and why do states become "rentier states" in the first place? If, on the one hand, the reasons that rents tend to accrue to the state in some countries (and not in others) are related to countries' propensity to have democratic or authoritarian political regimes, then, at best, rents may serve as an intervening variable; at worst, empirical relationships between rents and the political regime may reflect the influence of unobserved confounding factors rather than causal relationships. On the other hand, if the propensity to become a rentier state in the first place is relatively independent of other factors that shape a country's propensity to have a democratic or authoritarian regime, then it makes sense to ask how the effect of natural resource rents on the political regime may be conditioned by the structural features of different countries, as I do in this book.

I argue in this chapter that with one important exception, the propensity to become a rentier state is independent of many other factors that might shape the propensity toward authoritarianism and democracy. I contend that the regime type itself does not strongly influence the state's absolute or relative "take" of the revenues produced by natural resource sectors. Nor does it matter greatly whether a central government appropriates rents from state-owned parastatals or instead from multi-national resource companies that provide tax and royalty payments to the state; both strategies can be relatively effective ways of generating rents, and rentier states exist where resources are privately owned as well as where they are state-owned. Even the overall economic orientation of a government—for example, whether economic policy tends in general to be "statist" or "liberal"—is relatively immaterial; as I show, otherwise liberal or market-oriented governments have adopted strikingly "rentierist" policies with respect to rent-producing natural resource sectors.

The exception, as I describe below, occurs when a concentrated and powerful domestic elite that is independent of the state owns and controls the natural resources.[1] In this case, domestic, non-state actors do mediate the supply of rents to the state; and capturing rents may carry a substantial cost in domestic political terms, making the factors that create rentier states in such settings of theoretical interest to the current study. Yet, as I argue, ownership of rent-producing natural resources by a concentrated domestic elite is the exception rather than the rule in resource-rich countries. And, where this form of ownership does exist, it is sometimes perturbed by disparate forms of encroachment on elites' resource wealth by the state; once the concentrated ownership of the elite is broken, I argue, the general theory developed in this book is relevant to understanding the political impact of resource rents. Even where a private elite's control of resources is unbroken, the theoretical framework developed here can be modified to analyze the political impact of resource rents (see Chapter Seven).

Thus, I maintain that the factors that shape the emergence of a rentier state do not generally have strong implications for the theory developed in this book. Rentier states may share diverse foundations, yet the presence of rent-producing natural resources tends to shape the fiscal basis of the state in similar ways across otherwise diverse countries. Having argued this, a key goal of this chapter is to describe how rents do shape the fiscal basis of the

[1] By "independent of the state," I mean that the elite is formally "private"; that is, the elite is not coterminous with the state itself, as in the case of the Saudi royal family.

state. I focus on the negative relationship between rents and (redistributive) taxation, a relationship that has been emphasized in a voluminous previous literature on rentier states; because this relationship plays a key role in the theory developed in the following chapter (where, however, it emerges as an endogenous result of the theoretical models), I review evidence for it in this chapter. I then close by discussing the broader literature on natural resource wealth and political regimes in greater detail than in the previous chapter.

2.1 *Sources of Rents*

In the contemporary era, oil is the quintessential example of a natural resource that produces "rents," motivating the title and a major focus of this study. Yet copper deposits, kimberlite diamonds, and other natural resources may produce rents and thereby provide the fiscal basis of a rentier state as well—while some natural resources do not.[2] This study is limited to the political effects of rent-producing natural resources because, in the important literature in political science on the authoritarian effects of resource wealth, rents are ultimately the alleged source of authoritarian rule.

Rent itself is defined by a super-normal level of (monopoly or oligopoly) profit; that is, resource rent is the economic return to natural resource extraction that exceeds labor and other production costs as well as transport costs and some "normal" return to capital. Alternatively but similarly, rent is the excess over the return to capital, land, and labor when these factors of production are put to their next-best use.[3] Yet, following the classic definition in Ricardian political economy, natural resource rent is also defined here as the payment to landlords in exchange for access to sub-soil resources. Thus, resource rent is the portion of the super-normal level of profit associated with some kinds of natural resource extraction that accrues to landlords. In the vast majority of important national producers of oil and other minerals in the contemporary world, this "landlord" is the national state (Mommer 2002: 108–18).

[2] Later in this chapter, I discuss some of the characteristics that might allow some natural resources but not others to provide the fiscal basis of a rentier state.

[3] Consistent with this definition, in some of the cross-national statistical analyses reported in Chapter Four, I extend a data set compiled by Hamilton and Clemens (1999), who measure the rent produced by various natural resources by subtracting estimated production costs and a normal return to capital from the market value of resource production—and thus provide a closer approximation to the idea of "rent" advanced here than in any other existing cross-national data set.

The characteristics associated with natural resource rents go well beyond this initial definition, as many analysts of resource-rich countries have noted. First, natural resource sectors tend to be relatively easily taxable, as the heavy sunk costs involved in the extraction of many natural resources create a revenue base that is relatively inelastic and that can provide the state with multiple opportunities for appropriating rent (Monaldi 2002a).[4] Second, because the extraction of these resources tends to be capital-intensive and often takes place within the context of a geographically concentrated, export-oriented industry without widespread "linkages" to other productive processes (Hirschman 1977), the resource sector tends to be endowed with the character of an "enclave" divorced from the rest of the domestic economy. Third, there is often a separation of labor between a landlord state, which merely collects rents, and a private producer (Mommer 2002), which in many developing countries and in many historical periods has been a foreign or multi-national resource company.[5] Although none of these characteristics is individually necessary, together these features of natural resource sectors imply that the main political-economic influence of natural resource rents stems from their effect on patterns of public revenue generation and spending (Beblawi 1987; Mahdavy 1970). That is, rent from natural resource sectors tends to exert an impact on the rest of the political economy primarily through its influence on the fiscal basis of the state.

An important point here, one already introduced in the first chapter, is that many natural resources do *not* readily provide rents to the state; this study is focused only on the political effects of rent-producing natural resources. What determines whether a given natural resource produces rents? In the recent literature on the relationship between natural resources

[4] As discussed later, of course, this is not true of *all* forms of natural resource wealth.

[5] In the vast majority of resource-producing countries around the world, sub-soil resources like oil and other minerals are taken to be a public utility in which the state reserves a sovereign interest based on the principle of eminent domain (even if it leases sub-soil exploitation rights to private concessionaires). Even in advanced liberal market economies such as the United States and the United Kingdom, private resource producers commonly pay royalties to the state; Mommer (2002), for example, presents evidence on the importance of resource rents in the United States, where, e.g., oil extraction on federal lands and waters requires royalty payments, as well as the United Kingdom and other countries. When production is undertaken by private producers, the payment of royalties evokes a Ricardian conception of rent, in which producers pay rents to landlords—here, the national state—in exchange for sub-soil access rights (Mommer 2002: 108–18). However, even when production is undertaken by a state-owned enterprise, there are still multiple opportunities for the state to capture inframarginal rents, for example, by taking advantage of differences in extraction costs across resource-producing countries (Mommer 2002).

and internal conflict, as well as in the literature on resources and economic growth, analysts have drawn a useful distinction between resources that are "diffuse," or geographically dispersed, and those that are "point-source," or geographically concentrated (Le Billon 2001; also Isham et al. 2003). A similar distinction has been drawn between "lootable" resources—that is, those that because of their geographical dispersion and low economic barriers to entry are more easily subject to predation by non-state actors—and "nonlootable" resources—those that, because of geographical concentration or capital intensities in production, instead tend to produce rents that accrue to the state rather than citizens (see Ross 2006; Snyder 2001; Snyder and Bhavnani 2005: 568–9). According to these distinctions, resources differ in the extent to which the revenues they produce are readily appropriable by the state or, alternately, non-state actors. For instance, the literature on resources and conflict has focused on the ability of potential rebels to fund insurgencies by appropriating natural resources (Collier and Hoeffler 1998a, 1998b; Ross 2006), yet has noted that not all natural resources provide equal opportunity to rebels: diffuse or lootable resources are easier for private actors, including rebel groups, to commandeer, while point-source resources instead tend to supply rents to the state.

As an example, already mentioned in the first chapter, consider the distinction between kimberlite and alluvial diamonds.[6] Kimberlite diamonds, found in subterranean lamproite rock formations, are geographically concentrated and tend to involve substantial capital intensities in production (Lujala et al. 2005: 543). They are often produced by large (multi-national) corporations or by state companies themselves, as in Botswana, where diamond production is undertaken by a joint venture company formed by De Beers and the government of Bostwana (which combination gives the name Debswana to the joint venture; Dunning 2005). Alluvial diamonds, on the other hand, are often scattered away from diamond pipes via systems of waterways and are, in consequence, relatively easily appropriable by small, private groups of citizens. While the mining of alluvial diamonds is rarely a source of substantial rents for the state, the mining of kimberlite diamonds often is. As Snyder and Bhavnani (2005: 568) note, for instance:

> Nonlootable resources provide favorable revenue opportunities for rulers. The large amount of capital and technology required to mine nonlootable resources profitably forms a natural barrier that excludes small-scale artisanal miners. This makes it easier

[6] Lujala, Gleditsch, and Gilmore (2005) refer to alluvial diamonds as "secondary diamonds" and kimberlite diamonds as "primary diamonds."

for the state to establish monopoly control over the resource because it eliminates the need to invest in coercive capacity to deter wildcat miners. Moreover, the low value-to-weight ratio that characterizes nonlootable resources attenuates 'agency problems' inside state-owned companies (e.g., theft of the resource by rogue employees).

Beyond mining technology, of course, is the question of market power: the markets for oil, diamonds, and copper (at least at some historical moments) have involved substantial monopoly or oligopoly elements, and this, of course, creates more substantial opportunities for the appropriation of rent. Yet what Snyder and Bhavnani (2005) call the "resource profile" (e.g., whether the resource is lootable or non-lootable) itself helps to determine whether the resource can provide the fiscal basis of a rentier state, given world markets that produce such monopoly or oligopoly sources of rents in the first place.

Yet, beyond the presence of particular kinds of natural resource endowments that, because of the characteristics outlined earlier, tend to produce rents, there appear to be few systematic predictors of which states become "rentier states"—that is, those in which natural resource rents provide a significant share of the government's revenues. For instance, it does not matter greatly whether a central government appropriates rents from state-owned parastatals or from multi-national resource companies that provide tax and royalty payments to the state. In both cases, a government may have strong incentives as well as the ability to extract a portion of rents from the resource-producing sector; and, crucially for the theory, in either case rents will flow to the state without substantial intermediation of domestic, non-state actors. To be sure, the taxation of parastatals or multi-national firms by governments may have effects on investment and exploration activities in the resource sector, thereby shaping the size of the resource "pie" over time; yet these effects are independent of both the regime type of the government in question and the identity of the resource producer. They are independent of the regime type because politicians in both democracies and autocracies can have strong incentives as well as the ability to maximize the state's take of resource rents.[7] And, they are independent of the form of resource

[7] One piece of evidence for this claim comes from the observation that both democracies and autocracies have expropriated multi-national oil companies; the founding members of the Organization of Petroleum Exporting Countries (OPEC), an organization originally designed to bolster the share of oil revenues captured by member states, included four autocracies (Iran, Iraq, Saudi Arabia, and Kuwait) and one democratic regime (Venezuela); the latter country, under the guidance of hydrocarbons minister Juan Pablo Pérez Alfonso,

ownership because governments can have many tools for extracting rents, whether resources are produced by parastatals or multi-nationals.[8]

Even if the state take is relatively independent of the form of resource ownership (with the exception noted below), and even if the political regime does not drive the fiscal treatment of the oil sector, it might be that other institutional factors influence both the regime type and the fiscal take of the state. Perhaps the mode of non-resource economic production or the general economic orientation of a government influences both regime type and fiscal take; or perhaps the state's claim on rents is related to the form of resource ownership, which might in turn be related to deep determinants of the political regime. It turns out, however, that the general economic orientation of a government (say, liberal versus statist) makes substantially less difference for the degree of rentierism in the resource sector than one might suppose. For instance, even in advanced industrial countries with the most liberal treatments of the resource sector (e.g., those that make allowances for private rather than state ownership or control of sub-soil resources), rent-producing natural resources tend to become important sources of fiscal revenue and can also displace other sources of revenues such as taxation. In the United States, for example, royalty payments on mineral resources in federal lands, including off-shore oil, have provided an important source of revenue for the federal budget; at the subnational level, the apogee of rentierism is perhaps the state of Alaska, where by 1980 the fiscal take (including federal taxes) reached 50 percent of gross income in the sector; in 2002, the value of the constitutionally mandated annual check that is received by eligible Alaskans and that is financed by oil reached $2,000, resulting in a *negative* state income tax (i.e., a net subsidy) (Mommer 2002: 158–60).[9] In sum, neither the regime type, nor the form

was the acknowledged leader of the organization at the time of its finding. The analysis of over-time evidence from various cases elsewhere in this book also supports this idea; in Venezuela, for instance, both democratic and authoritarian regimes have pressed for greater shares of oil revenues. See Chapters Five and Six for further discussion.

[8] In general, many factors make rents from natural resources more readily appropriable by the state than revenues from taxation of citizens, regardless of the form of ownership; see below and Chapter One for further discussion.

[9] Royalty rates in Alaska were increased from one-eighth of the value of produced oil in North Slope bidding in 1969 to one-sixth in 1973 to one-fifth in 1979, and there are also state production and corporate income taxes on the oil sector. The *Permanent Fund*, through which rents are distributed to citizens, was enshrined in the state constitution in 1976. Alaska has the lowest individual tax burden in the United States and is only one of seven states that do not levy an individual income tax; although the support of the U.S. federal government is key, so is the presence of substantial oil rents.

of resource ownership, nor the general economic orientation of a given society strongly influence the propensity of states to extract rents from the resource sector.[10]

The exception, as I described briefly earlier, occurs when a concentrated and powerful domestic elite that is independent of the state—that is, a formally "private" elite that is not coterminous with the state itself—owns and controls the natural resources. In this case, domestic, non-state actors do mediate the supply of rents to the state. Moreover, as explored elsewhere in this book, the form of ownership may then not be independent of a country's underlying propensity to have a democratic or authoritarian regime. For instance, as I argue in Chapters Six and Seven, when a concentrated private elite owns the natural resources, a resource boom unambiguously increases elites' incentives to resist or subvert democracy—a claim that differs from recent assertions in the literature that when petroleum industries are privately owned, oil may exert a positive impact on democracy (see Jones Luong and Weinthal 2006; also Jones Luong 2004 and Jones Luong and Weinthal 2001b). This is an important extension to the theory developed in this book and is discussed at greater length elsewhere.

Yet, as emphasized above, ownership of rent-producing natural resources by a concentrated domestic elite is the exception rather than the rule in resource-rich countries. Where this form of ownership does exist, it is sometimes broken by a social revolution or disparate encroachments on elites' resource wealth by the state; and once the concentrated ownership of the elite is broken, the theory discussed in this study is entirely pertinent. The Bolivian Revolution, discussed at greater length in Chapter Six, provides a leading example. Prior to the Revolution of 1952, the great tin mines in Bolivia were largely owned by three large families, the largest share being held by the baron Simón Patiño. This tin oligarchy—*la Rosca* as it was known—wielded an enormous influence over economic and political life in Bolivia, and it vigorously resisted popular mobilization aimed at obtaining a greater share of tin rents; movements toward democracy were vehemently opposed by the oligarchy, which instead invested a portion of tin profits in bolstering the repressive apparatus of the state. The Bolivian Revolution, however, resulted in the nationalization of *la Rosca*'s mines, and tin rents

10 The United Kingdom also established new royalties and other levies on the oil sector in the wake of the North Sea oil boom of the 1970s. However, the tax treatment remained highly favorable for the oil sector, and the overall fiscal take declined in percentage terms in the 1980s (Mommer 2002).

then filled (for a relatively short time, as it turned out) the fiscal coffers of the state. In fact, Bolivia democratized after its Revolution, as tin began to provide the basis for a classic rentier state.

For purposes of the questions probed in this book, it is therefore useful to think of rents as flowing more or less like "manna from heaven" into the fiscal coffers of the state, even though this is a radical simplification of the actual process by which the state captures rents. That is, we may usually take the factors that influence the supply of resource rents to the state as a given and ask how variation in the level of rents interacts with structural features of different countries to shape the political regime. The point here is not that the sources of rentier states are unimportant; the form of ownership, as just described, can sometimes matter in ways relevant to the questions probed in this book. The point is that in the great majority of resource-rich countries, natural resources come to provide a relatively ready source of revenue for the state, one that is less costly to extract than other potential sources of revenue. The level of rents may certainly then vary due to exogenous factors like world price movements. Taking for granted that resource rents accrue to the state is therefore a good starting point for exploring the political effects of rents across a great variety of states; in particular, it is a useful point of theoretical departure for scrutinizing the conventional idea that rents only promote authoritarianism.

2.2 *Fiscal Effects: Natural Resources and Taxation*

How do resource rents shape the fiscal basis of the state? As many analysts have emphasized, resource rents tend to displace other sources of revenue as the basis of public finance. Because the landlord state can often restrict access to the mineral-rich sub-soil, and because the resource tax base is relatively inelastic, a portion of revenues from the sale of mineral resources tends to pour directly into the fiscal coffers of the state; resource rents thereby provide the state with a source of public revenue that is akin to an externally generated "windfall" (Beblawi 1987; Mahdavy 1970). Moreover, generating revenue from the resource sector is generally less costly for the state than extracting revenue from other sources, in particular, from the taxation of citizens. Thus, resource rents can at least partially obviate the extent to which the state engages in costly revenue-generating activities in non-resource sectors of the economy—and, particularly crucially for this study, can obviate the extent of taxation of non-resource wealth. The negative relationship between resource rents and taxation plays an important role in the theoretical argument developed in this book. In this subsection, I therefore review the empirical evidence that this effect does occur before turning to some discussion of why it may occur.

There is abundant empirical evidence, both across and within countries, that resource rents do tend to displace other, more-difficult-to-collect forms of revenue such as income taxation. Indeed, analysis of the negative relationship between resource rents and taxation is a hallmark of the literature on the "rentier state" (inter alia, Anderson 1991; Beblawi 1987; Mahdavy 1970; Skocpol 1982). As Chaudhry (1997: 188) puts it, "There can be little argument that fiscal and bureaucratic developments are substantially altered during oil booms, with profound implications for a host of domestic relationships. The most important change is the decline in domestic taxation in general, and direct taxation in particular." Across a wide range of empirical, cultural, and historical contexts, one sees the same empirical patterns: resource booms lead to a decline in taxation and a decimation of extractive efforts on the part of the state.

Because the negative relationship between resource rents and taxation is so crucial for the argument developed in this study, it is worth detailing at some length various sources of empirical evidence for this relationship. In Saudi Arabia, according to Chaudhry (1997: 144):

> The oil boom created resource flows that made taxation unnecessary: the decline of the extractive apparatus followed. The rapidity with which the tax relationship and the tax bureaucracy changed belies an incrementalist interpretation; the dismantling of the extractive bureaucracy began almost immediately after the 1973 oil embargo. Most of the taxes on Saudis and fees on resident foreigners were withdrawn; foreign companies were given five year tax holidays (and extensions were granted thereafter); and personal income taxes on foreign workers were eliminated. The government canceled private-sector social security payments and began funding the General Organization for Social Insurance (GOSI) directly from the current budget. Unable to abolish the religious tithe outright, the government simply stopped collecting *zakat* in 1976.... Virtually all indirect taxes were eliminated as well. The mainstays of the old treasury, pilgrim fees and taxes on services in the holy cities of Mecca and Medina, were rescinded. Special fees on imported tobacco, overland tickets, the head tax, fishing taxes, and a variety of others were canceled in 1974, and the road tax—King Feisal's hard-won direct tax on salaried workers—abolished the same year. The carefully calibrated indirect taxes that had been the backbone of the import substitution regime met a similar fate.... The end of taxation, in turn, precipitated the rapid dismantling of the extractive bureaucracy.

As many analysts have noticed, this pattern is reproduced across countries and, within countries, across time. Soifer (2006) presents striking empirical evidence on the negative historical relationship between resource booms and taxation in nineteenth- and twentieth-century Peru and Chile. (I explore the latter case further in Chapter Six of this book.) In the mid-1840s, two decades after its legal independence from Spain, Peru experienced a dramatic fiscal boom driven by the export of guano, which was used as fertilizer in Europe. At the start of the guano boom, the per capita tax burden (average taxes paid by individuals) reached nearly ten Peruvian soles per capita; both head taxes and customs duties provided important sources of government revenue. By 1857, however, per capita internal taxes had fallen to under one sol per capita, even as government spending peaked. Soifer calculates that in no year between 1857 and 1873 did per capita taxes rise above 1.3 soles, while at the height of the boom government spending may have reached approximately ten soles per capita.[11] Whereas at the start of the guano boom, internal taxes constituted between 25 and 30 percent of total revenue in Peru, by the end of the boom internal taxes constituted a *near-zero* percentage of total revenue. In 1854, the head tax was eliminated, followed by the *contribución indígena*, and, in 1859, the tithe, which had been an important source of church revenue (Soifer 2006: 248, 251). As Soifer (2006: 248) puts it, "The guano boom coincided with the elimination of nearly all other forms of taxation as revenues from guano began to crowd out other sources of revenue." After the collapse of the guano sector in the 1870s, a fiscal problem compounded by the loss of mineral-rich (nitrate) provinces to Chile in the War of the Pacific, renewed state efforts to impose taxes in the territory met with limited success; for example, attempts to impose a poll or head tax led to a major peasant uprising in the mid-1880s (Soifer 2006: 256). By the first decades of the twentieth century, however, the per capita tax burden had increased tenfold, as export and particularly consumption taxes increased markedly. Peru's guano boom thus provides striking intertemporal (within-case) evidence for the negative relationship between resource booms and internal taxation.

A similar pattern obtained with respect to Chile's nitrate boom.[12] Internal taxation represented nearly 20 percent of total government revenue by 1850 (Soifer 2006: 263). The introduction of the *catastro* land tax in 1834 was followed by a prominent tax on the value of landholdings in 1853, which

[11] Soifer (2006: 251–2); for the government spending figure, Soifer cites Contreras and Cueto (1999: 118). These appear to be nominal rather than real values.

[12] Here I present summary statistics from Soifer (2006); other data on Chile gathered independently are analyzed further in Chapter Six.

soon constituted the most important share of internal taxes; an inheritance tax was also initiated, and direct taxes provided an increasing proportion of overall internal taxes (Soifer 2006: 267–70). These were taxes that fell on important economic interests in Chilean society; as Soifer (2006: 267) puts it, "By the end of the 1870's, the Chilean state generated significant revenue... reflecting the development of real extractive capacity on the part of the state." However, the seizure of nitrate-rich territory from Peru and Bolivia in the War of the Pacific and a subsequent boom in the value of nitrate production contributed to the near-dismantling of this sizeable tax apparatus. As Soifer (2006: 275–6) says:

> Internal taxes declined to a tenth of their 1885 level by 1895, and in that year and in 1900, essentially the only internal taxes collected by the national government were fees for stamps and official papers... during the nitrate boom, the central state's extractive capacity declined as taxes were eliminated in favor of other revenue sources that were easier to extract and imposed no direct costs on the population.

At moments of temporary depressions in the nitrate revenue, officials considered the imposition of customs duties and the resurrection of internal taxes; however, it was not until the end of the nitrate period after World War I that internal taxes were truly revived in Chile. Internal taxation tripled between 1913 and 1920 (Soifer 2006: 281), and the state generated more than 25 percent of revenues from taxation by 1920, as the result of the introduction of a property tax and other levies. As the discussion in Chapter Seven will show further, over-time data from the Chilean case strongly support the negative relationship between resource booms and internal taxation, a relationship for which the later copper boom in twentieth-century Chile will also provide evidence.

In Venezuela, a case studied at much greater length in Chapter Five, the rise of the oil economy also substituted for taxation as a source of fiscal revenue. To be sure, the tax base developed prior to the rise of oil, during the decades of the nineteenth and early twentieth century, was miniscule. Nonetheless, the steadily increasing relative importance of oil in the government's budget—from 6 percent in 1924 to 30 percent at the end of the 1930s, nearly 60 percent by 1958, and well over 80 percent during the 1970s (Ministry of Energy and Mines, various years; Urbaneja 1992: 88, 95)—also clearly inhibited the absolute growth of non-oil tax revenue. Attempts to raise personal taxes even incrementally in 1966, 1971, 1975, 1986, and 1989 all utterly failed, for reasons discussed in Chapter Five, not until the full effects of the decline in oil rents at the end of the 1980s had materialized that a significant tax (a non-progressive value-added tax) was successfully instituted, in 1993. Karl (1997: 121) shows that from 1977–1979, individual taxes in Venezuela were just 4 percent of total taxes, compared to more than 10 percent in a sample of eighty-six primarily developing countries with per capita incomes ranging from $100 to approximately $6,000, and mean income of $1,330 (in 1981 U.S. dollars). Compared even to neighboring Colombia, a country not often noted for its high tax rates, individual taxes in Venezuela during the oil boom were substantially lower (Karl 1997: 89). Even as late as 1989, non-petroleum personal and corporate income taxes were just 2 percent of non-petroleum gross domestic product (Rodríguez Balsa 1993). As Coronil (1997: 102) puts it, by the time of the boom of the 1970s, "the idea that [the] state's programs could be financed at least in part by citizens' taxes was simply absent."

Lest the cases discussed above suggest an opposite impression, the negative relationship between resources and taxation is not limited to developing countries. Indeed, Mommer (2002) presents striking evidence on the tendency of the resource sector to become an important fiscal basis of the state, even among states that are both developed and treat the resource sector in the most "liberal" ways (i.e., countries that give legal pride of place to private sub-soil ownership and private exploitation of rent-producing natural resources). In the United Kingdom, the petroleum boom of the 1970s led to the imposition of a special Petroleum Tax on the oil sector. In the United States, as mentioned in Chapter One, royalty payments on off-shore oil provide an important source of revenue for the federal budget; in Alaska, the fiscal take of the state government (including federal taxes) reached 50 percent of gross income in the sector. Each Alaska resident receives an annual check from the *Permanent Fund* (worth US$2,000 in 2002), as enshrined in the state constitution in 1976 (Mommer 2002: 158–60). Net tax payments by Alaskan residents are *negative*. Alaskans are subsidized, not taxed.

This extensive intertemporal evidence from within specific cases is matched by a robust cross-national pattern: taxes are lower in resource-rich countries. Karl (1997: 62) presents data on comparative tax rates of oil and non-oil producers. Among five oil-rich rentier states—Indonesia, Iran, Nigeria, Venezuela, and Algeria—non-oil tax revenue as a percentage of non-oil GDP reached an average of 11.32 percent between 1971 and 1973.[13]

[13] The idea of "non-oil GDP" has a rich history of conceptual development and empirical elaboration, particularly among a number of distinguished Venezuelan scholars; see Baptista (1997, 2004). The concept is discussed in more detail elsewhere in this study.

The average is pulled up by the Algerian outlier, where much of the means of production was socialized during this period; dropping Algeria, the average is 8.56 percent. In all other countries,[14] total tax revenue as a percentage of GDP in 1980 was 17.8 percent; even more strikingly, the percentage is higher in every category of income per capita, for 0–349 U.S. dollars per capita (where taxes averaged 12.9 percent of GDP) all the way to countries with more than US$1,700 in per capita GNP (where taxes averaged 22.7 percent of GDP). This impressive piece of comparative evidence provides substantial additional empirical demonstration of the negative cross-national correlation between resource rents and non-resource taxation.

Other cases in this book present evidence for a similar negative relationship between resource booms and other sources of government revenue such as internal taxation. Note, however, that although a decline in internal taxation on wealth or income is one important consequence of a resource boom, other kinds of redistributive policies may be affected as well. As the book's case studies suggest, for instance, resource booms may limit the extent of redistributive policies such as land reforms. In developing the formal analysis in Chapter Three, I therefore refer for convenience to a "tax" on income or assets. In fact, however, the impact of resource rents on other forms of (redistributive) revenue generation is countenanced by the theory developed here as well.

The book has not yet discussed *why* there is a negative empirical relationship between resource rents and (redistributive) taxation. There are undoubtedly several mechanisms that can account for this relationship. One straightforward explanation, which is important in the approach developed in the theoretical model of Chapter Three, is as follows. Taxation, whether proportional, progressive, or regressive, implies a constant marginal cost to private income within income brackets; for an individual or corporation that pays 34 percent on the margin, the marginal cost of raising taxes by 1 percent is a fixed proportion of private income or profits. Suppose, on the other hand, that individuals have (at least some measure of) declining marginal utility over public spending. Then a resource boom that pours revenue into the fiscal coffers of the state may affect the marginal benefit of public spending without, however, affecting the marginal cost of taxation in terms of foregone private income. If the behavioral rule implies equating the marginal cost of taxation with its marginal benefit, then, as Chapter Three

[14] Karl (1997: 62) does not say how many countries are actually comprised in "all countries," but it is presumably a global sample.

will show, a negative relationship between resource rents and preferred tax rates is induced. In particular, a resource boom may shape the preferred tax rate of policymakers, whether the policymaker in question is an "elite" or a "citizen" and whether the regime type is authoritarian or democratic.

Another reason a resource boom may lead to a decline in tax extraction could be put as follows. Resource rents are relatively costless for the state to collect, at least relative to other potential sources of public revenue; in contrast, taxation and other forms of extracting revenue from citizens may induce a greater aggregate cost (e.g., by encouraging the diversion of production to non-taxable activity or by promoting capital flight). In the absence of resource rents, states may be more willing, on the margin, to pay this aggregate cost. Yet, as I argue theoretically, resource rents alter the extent to which governments—including, centrally for the theory developed here, *democratic* governments—are willing to pay this aggregate cost in order to satisfy demands for public spending. As I explain further in Chapter Three, if there is a Laffer curve that maps tax rates to tax revenues, resource rents can shift the tax rate at which the marginal benefits and marginal costs of taxation are balanced. Whether this is the right or only mechanism through which rents reduce taxation, it is consistent with the empirical regularity widely noted by previous scholars: resource rents reduce taxation. At the very least, non-resource taxation often involves the creation of a capable state bureaucracy and requires costly monitoring efforts; it may also generate diversion of economic production into non-taxable activities. The incentives to engage in costly taxation may thus be substantially higher in the absence of resource rents than after a resource boom. One way to put this point is that although states may be relatively more willing to pay the aggregate distortionary costs of taxation in the absence of resource rents, a resource boom may contribute to a shift of the peak of the well-known Laffer curve, in which total tax revenues are said to initially increase with the tax rate but eventually decline.[15]

Ultimately, the mechanism through which resource booms lead to diminished taxation is not the most important part of the argument developed in this book, however. Though the negative relationship between resources and taxation is an (endogenous) result of the model in Chapter Three, the argument can also appeal to the empirical evidence from my cases and the

[15] Those on the Right and the Left generally accept the existence of a Laffer curve, even if they dispute the location of its peak: if taxes are 100 percent of total taxable product, one might reasonably expect taxable product to decline.

body of scholarship on resources and taxation in rentier states. What matters most for my argument is not the source of the negative relationship between rents and taxation, but rather its political consequences.

Before turning to these political effects of rents, it is useful to note that there is nothing in the definition of rents, or of the rentier state, advanced above that a priori limits the argument I develop in this study to natural resource wealth. Indeed, other sources of state rents—such as foreign aid—could well be considered. However, foreign aid is often disbursed strategically by donors; in particular, it may be disbursed conditional on the regime type of the recipient, a possibility that was empirically enhanced after the end of the Cold War (Dunning 2004). Thus, foreign aid not only adds additional strategic considerations into a theory of the relationship between rents and the regime type, but it also introduces problems in the empirical assessment of causal relationships, as the size of foreign aid (i.e., rents) may well be caused by the regime type rather than the other way around. Because the influence of natural resource wealth on political institutions has itself been a subject of major interest in political science, I focus in this study only on resource rents, leaving the possibility of generalizing the argument to other kinds of rentier states to future work.

2.3 Toward the Political Effects of Rents

Like previous analyses of the rentier state, the argument developed in this study thus hinges, in part, on the relationship of resource rents to the fiscal basis of government. However as described in Chapter One, I depart from much of the existing literature in assessing the institutional consequences of this mode of state finance. The purpose of this subsection is to discuss further the relationship of the theory outlined in Chapter One to the previous literature, to describe further core elements of the approach to democracy and authoritarianism I take in this book, and to pave the way for the formal theoretical analysis in Chapter Three. Readers who prefer to move more quickly to the development of the theory may wish to skip directly to Chapter Three.

According to a classic view on the origins of democracy, the need of rulers to commandeer revenue from citizens can play a crucial role in the emergence of representative institutions (e.g., Tilly 1985, 1990, 2004; also Bates and Lien 1985; Levi 1988; North and Weingast 1989). As the rallying cry of the American Revolution, "no taxation without representation," would imply, citizens may demand representation in exchange for giving up income as taxes; rulers may then be forced to extend political representation to citizens in exchange for tax revenue. Alternatively, in order to obtain debt finance from citizens, rulers may be forced to adopt institutions that credibly limit their own power to renege on repayment commitments (North and Weingast 1989). According to this general view, one source of the "representative bargain" between rulers and the ruled lies in the need of the former to raise tax or other forms of revenue from the latter. Moreover, the specific nature of the tax base can play an important role in shaping the degree to which representative institutions emerge. For instance, the greater the elasticity of the tax base—for example, the more mobility citizens enjoy in allocating productive activities between taxable and non-taxable sectors—the more likely it may be that rulers find themselves forced to extend representation in exchange for taxes from citizens (Bates and Lien 1985).

Drawing on this extensive literature on state formation and the origins of representative institutions, many political scientists have viewed the negative relationship between resource wealth and taxation as a source of authoritarianism in resource-rich countries. By providing rulers with a source of public finance that is independent of citizens' contributions to the Fisc, resource rents allegedly obviate the need for rulers to strike such a "representative bargain" with citizens and thereby hinder the emergence of democracy (Ross 2001: 332–3, 348–9). Beblawi (1987: 53–4), for example, writes: "With virtually no taxes, citizens are far less demanding in terms of political participation. The history of democracy owes its beginnings, it is well known, to some fiscal association (no taxation without representation)." Of course, this perspective subtly turns the slogan "no taxation without representation" on its head: although the phrase suggests that representation is a necessary condition for taxation, analysts of the authoritarian rentier state appear to suggest instead that taxation is a necessary condition for the emergence of representation. Yet, the core focus on the relationship between the fiscal basis of the state and the emergence (or non-emergence) of democracy echoes the long literature on the representative bargain involved in the state's taxation of citizens: the collection of resource rents requires little in the way of a bargain or contract between the king and his subjects (or the modern state and its citizens), and leaders in resource-rich countries are thus not forced to diffuse political power through representative and democratic institutions. As Bueno de Mesquita et al. (2003: 94–5) put it in a different but related argument, in resource-rich countries in which small "winning coalitions" support elites' hold on power, "leaders do not have to rely on the economic activity of residents to provide the resources they need to reward their supporters as much as when resources are absent. Without the need to hold in check their desire to appropriate income, leaders dependent on small winning coalitions can attempt to seize all of the pie."[16] According to much previous work, not only does resource wealth promote authoritarianism, but one of the mechanisms through which it has this effect is by diminishing the need of rulers to tax their citizens.

2.3.1 The Democratic Effect of Resource Rents

In contrast, I argue in this book that the negative relationship between resource rents and taxation can be an important mechanism through which resource wealth can contribute to the stability of democracy. Why might this be so? At least since Tocqueville (1835: 49–55, 128–36), political analysts have emphasized the importance of economic equality for explaining the introduction and persistence of democratic institutions. As abundant historical examples suggest, the enfranchisement of a relatively poor majority may contribute to the development of political cleavages based on divisions of wealth and income and, especially, to important political pressures for economic redistribution from the rich to the poor; and these pressures may clearly be greater in more unequal countries. The specter of redistribution through the ballot box, as the suffrage is expanded and disadvantaged groups are incorporated into the political arena, can make democracy more costly for elites and have clearly led to attempts to block or reverse processes of democratization. Latin American cases provide some of the paradigmatic examples of coups launched by the Right in order to block redistribution under democracy, as in Chile in 1973, Guatemala in 1954, or Argentina in 1976 (O'Donnell 1973; Stepan 1985). However, recent contributions in political economy have argued that the actual or anticipated redistributive consequences of democratization can more generally help to explain why democracy emerges and persists, or instead fails to do so, as well as the form that democracy takes (Acemoglu and Robinson 2001, 2006a).

The tendency of resource rents to displace other forms of revenue generation, including taxation, however, can make redistributive pressures less

[16] Bueno de Mesquita et al. (2003: 94) also note that in *large* winning coalition systems—i.e., where leaders must compete for the support of a relatively broad cross-section of society, as in a democracy—"the addition of rents from natural resources enables leaders to provide . . . public goods and cut taxes," which is the closest statement I have found in the existing formal literature to the democratic mechanism I emphasize here.

important in resource-rich countries. As suggested by the long literature on rentier states, and as the case-study evidence presented in Chapters Five and Six also attests, there is a negative relationship between resource rents and other forms of revenue generation, *including* various forms of redistribution such as proportional or progressive income taxation or land or other asset taxes.[17] Note that although the formal analysis in the next chapter assumes that redistribution takes place through taxes, the argument should not be understood to be limited to taxation; redistribution of land through agrarian reforms or other measures is certainly countenanced in the argument, as the case studies developed later in this study make clear. By providing a source of public spending that displaces redistribution from the rich to the poor, resource rents can reduce the economic cost of democracy to elites and thereby reduce their incentives to block or reverse processes of democratization. In a phrase, resource rents can underwrite democratic stability by reducing polarization over economic policy and particularly over redistributive tax policy.

To elaborate this argument further requires a further elucidation of the basic approach to the sources of democracy and authoritarianism, which motivates the formal analysis developed in the next chapter. Scholars of comparative politics have developed many different approaches to understanding processes of democratization as well as democratic breakdown, from the extensive literature on the role of intra-elite schisms in prompting transitions to democracy (O'Donnell and Schmitter 1986) to the literature emphasizing the international dimensions of democratization (Huntington 1991: 45–6). Although these traditions have generated many important insights and could be viewed as largely complementary to, rather than competitive with, the approach developed here, I build instead on recent research that emphasizes the role of mass mobilization and the politics of redistribution in explaining the emergence and persistence of democratic and authoritarian regimes (Acemoglu and Robinson 2000, 2001, 2006a; R. Collier 1999; Rueschemeyer et al. 1992). According to this tradition, the nature of the economic relationship between elites and masses can influence the emergence of democracy as well as the occurrence of democratic breakdown: as economic divisions between masses and elites widen, elites

[17] A proportional income tax may be redistributive in the sense that the value of payments from the rich exceeds the value of payments from the poor, while spending—if on public services or goods such as infrastructure that provide a benefit to all—tends to provide benefits on an equal per capita basis.

may also have stronger incentives to resist the introduction of democracy or, once democracy is established, to stage coups against the democratic order or to undermine the effectiveness of a broad franchise through institutional design or other mechanisms (Beard 1913; R. Collier 1999). Recent formal literature in political economy has helped to clarify the way in which inequality may influence the degree of economic conflict between elites and masses and thereby shape the incidence of democracy and authoritarianism (Acemoglu and Robinson 2001, 2006a). Departing from this theoretical approach and building on the previous literature on the fiscal basis of the rentier state, a central contribution of the model I develop in the following chapter is to clarify how resource rents may shape economic conflict and thereby influence the development of political institutions.

Given this framework, and as introduced in Chapter One, there are two main effects of resource rents on the development of the political regime. On the one hand, there is an "authoritarian" effect of resource rents, which echoes some of the prior literature on resource wealth and political institutions. Previous analyses have argued that resource wealth may provide incentives for the construction of "predatory" states (Robinson 1997).[18] A cursory review of fiscal politics in resource-rich authoritarian states suggests ample evidence for this claim. African leaders from Gabon's Omar Bongo to the former Zaire's Mobutu Sese Seko amassed large personal fortunes through control of their countries' resource sectors; in the Gulf states, Herb (1999: 31) reports estimates of the ruling families' share of total government expenditure that reach as high as 32 percent in the case of Qatar, 29.3 percent in Bahrain, 25.7 percent in Abu Dhabi, and 12 percent in more populous Saudi Arabia.

In the model developed in the next chapter, too, the desire of elites to control the *distribution* of resource rents can increase their incentives to hold permanent control of the state, which is the most certain way to

[18] Other scholars have noted a range of mechanisms through which resource rents may promote authoritarianism, from the promotion of an "incumbency advantage" that causes democratic institutions gradually to erode (Lam and Wantchekon 2004) to the formation of predatory authoritarian states (Acemoglu and Robinson 2006; Robinson 1997) to the long literature, discussed earlier, on the reduced need for rulers to strike "representative bargains" with citizens in resource-rich countries, and the model captures only some of the richness of these mechanisms. Other recent contributions to the literature on resource wealth and authoritarianism include Wantchekon (2002) and the relevant discussion in Boix (2003). See Ross (2001) for references to the extensive case-study literature.

guarantee continued access to these rents. Conflict over the distribution of resource rents can heighten the incentives of elites to maintain authoritarian institutions not just because political institutions allocate current power but also because they allocate *future* political power. For instance, elites may well be forced to transfer resource rents to coopt opposing groups that pose threats to their power; yet such threats may be temporary, and once strikes fail or popular mobilizations recede, elites can guarantee themselves a greater slice of the resource pie under authoritarian regimes. Thus, elites in resource-rich authoritarian regimes may be willing to pay a higher cost to repress threats to their power and therefore retain future control of resource rents. This image of authoritarian politics seems predatory, to be sure; yet, while there are authoritarian regimes that are not predatory, one is harder pressed to supply examples in resource-rich authoritarian countries.[19]

However, resource wealth affects economic conflict over the *redistribution* of non-resource income or wealth in an opposite fashion, and this is the source of the democratic effect of resource wealth in the model. Because resource rents displace taxation and other forms of revenue generation, they can also reduce the political salience of redistribution in democratic rentier states. Absent resource rent, democratic majorities may want to redistribute income away from elites to pay for public spending; other things equal, such redistribution increases the cost of democracy to elites. Yet, by displacing taxation as a source of revenue, resource wealth transforms the nature of this redistributive conflict. Just as with the authoritarian effect of resource rents, the democratic effect depends on the idea that political institutions allocate not just current but also future political power. Suppose, for instance, that elites are considering launching a coup d'état against an existing democratic regime. Even if redistributive policies are relatively moderate today, from the point of view of the elite, opportunities for coups may be fleeting; and tomorrow, when the coup threat has passed, democratic majorities may enact more radical policies. Yet, because resource rents endogenously reduce future redistribution as well as current redistribution, they allow democracies to credibly commit to limiting redistribution. Resource wealth therefore lessens the redistributive cost of democracy in the future as well as in the present.

Thus, rather than provide a mechanism through which resources promote authoritarianism, the reduction of the tax burden in the non-resource

[19] A partial exception may be Suharto's Indonesia (see Dunning 2005). On the distinction between "developmental" and "predatory" states, see Evans (1989).

economy is posited to promote the emergence and persistence of democracy. Of course, the image of political conflict on which the democratic effect of resource rents is based is clearly quite different from theories in which revenue-seeking rulers bargain with subjects over taxes (see, e.g., Bates and Lien 1985; Levi 1988; or North and Weingast 1989). On the one hand, compared to these relatively state-centric theories, the image of politics presented here might be considered relatively society-centric; as in various pluralist or Marxist traditions, the state is largely the arena for conflict between competing societal interests, rather than autonomous in its own right. However, this feature of the theoretical model developed in Chapter Three is largely an analytic simplification, and it provides a way to focus our attention on a understudied mechanism through which resource rents may promote democracy. On the other hand, the view that the negative relationship between resource rents and taxation undergirds a democratic effect of resource wealth *is* clearly in tension with the view of the recent literature that resource rents promote authoritarianism in part because they obviate the need for revenue-seeking rulers to strike a "representative bargain" with citizens. Sorting out the usefulness of these respective approaches to understanding politics in resource-rich countries is ultimately an empirical question, yet I will argue here that my approach does provide substantial insight into many (but of course not all) of the political effects of resource wealth. It also helps explain apparent anomalies to the claim that rents promote authoritarianism and—unlike many other theories—explicitly helps to explain variation in regime outcomes across resource-rich states.

The argument developed in this book is not the first to suggest that resource rents may not always promote authoritarianism, nor does it even claim priority in the argument that rents may instead promote democracy. As discussed in the first chapter, the idea that oil rents promoted democratic stability in Venezuela has been made by many experts on that country (España 1989; Karl 1987, 1997; Naím and Piñango 1984; Rey 1989; Urbaneja 1992). These analysts have emphasized different mechanisms through which oil rents promoted democracy. Rey (1989) and many others, for example, suggest that oil rents made Venezuelan politics a "positive-sum" game in which there were no losers (see also España 1989; Karl 1997; and recently, Buxton 2004: 115). Other analysts allude to the idea that oil eased social and economic tensions between different groups, including different social classes (Naím and Piñango 1984; Urbaneja 1992). Finally, the most well-known argument among scholars of comparative politics is perhaps the sophisticated analysis of Karl (1987; also 1997), who emphasizes structural changes induced by the rise of an oil-based economy, including rising rates of urbanization and the creation of a bourgeoisie with an economic interest in democracy (1987: 74). Though the argument developed in this book about the democratic effect of rents bears some similarity to each of these arguments, it also differs in important respects; in Chapter Five, I discuss why I believe the account developed here provides the most consistent explanation for the impact of oil on the secular development of the Venezuelan political regime.

The more important point, however, is that such accounts provide no way to explain variation in comparative perspective. For instance, these arguments do not explain why oil might promote democracy in a Venezuelan or other Latin American setting but instead appear to foster authoritarianism elsewhere. Viewed against the backdrop of the compelling, recently published statistical evidence on the apparently robust relationship between natural resource wealth and authoritarianism (Jensen and Wantchekon 2004; Ross 2001), the Venezuelan case appears idiosyncratic. The explanations of country experts thus appear less compelling because scope conditions or variables that could explain the varied impacts of resource wealth are not discussed.

Other scholars working with comparative evidence have also recently suggested a less-than-robust relationship between resource wealth and authoritarianism. Smith (2004) suggests that resource rents may promote regime durability but not affect the political regime type. Herb (2005) argues informally that resource rents promote authoritarianism by relieving governments of the need to tax but may also promote democracy by inducing at least some measure of economic development; analyzing cross-section time-series data, he finds a less robust relationship between oil rents and authoritarianism than previous scholars. Smith and Kraus (2005) examine five apparent exceptions to the claim that oil dependence promotes authoritarianism (Congo, Ecuador, Nigeria, Trinidad, and Venezuela), without, however, proposing a theory that explains why the effects of oil might be different in these countries than in authoritarian resource-dependent states. Among other valuable contributions to the literature, these important papers echo the effort of the current project to explain variation in the political effects of resource wealth yet examine quite different mechanisms and do not generate predictions about the conditions under which the net effect of resources would tend to be more democratic or more authoritarian.

The theoretical model presented in this book, and developed in the next chapter, is the first to attempt a systematic explanation of the varying effects of resource wealth on the political regime. It is certain, however, not to be the last word; as I suggest elsewhere in the book, this project suggests new directions for future research and also raises new questions even as it helps to answer other long-standing ones. Yet, this study takes important steps toward theorizing the varied political impacts of resource wealth, and it uses several kinds of empirical approaches to illuminate the usefulness of the theory. It therefore joins other recent work in calling for *conditional* theories of the effects of resource wealth and represents a theoretical and empirical advance in this direction.

3

Resource Rents and the Political Regime

This chapter turns to a formal analysis of the political impact of natural resource wealth. The analysis helps to reconcile the conflicting claims in the previous literature on this topic. On the one hand, in the two related models developed in this chapter, a natural resource boom makes holding political power more valuable because political power entails control over the distribution of resource rents. Consistent with a large literature on the authoritarian effects of resources, rents increase elites' incentives to stage a coup against an existing democracy; under an existing authoritarian regime, rents elevate elites' incentives to counter mobilization from below with repression or targeted transfers of revenue, rather than by democratizing.[1]

On the other hand, the analysis suggests that resource rents can also promote democracy, but through a different mechanism. By driving down the rate at which the poor want to redistribute private income away from elites under democracy, rents decrease the economic cost of democracy to elites. Rents can thus also reduce the incentives of elites to stage coups under existing democracies or to repress popular mobilization rather than democratize under authoritarian regimes. Consistent with recent cross-national empirical work as well as the case-study literature on the evolution of democracy in Venezuela, the models suggest that there may also be a democratic effect of resource rents.[2]

A virtue of the formal models developed in this chapter is that they permit the study of these conflicting political effects of resource rents in a single framework. This helps generate hypotheses about the question of

[1] The literature on the authoritarian effects of natural resource wealth is discussed in Chapters One and Two.

[2] For recent cross-national empirical work, see Haber and Menaldo (2007), Smith (2004), Herb (2005), and Chapter Four of this book. Venezuelan case studies include Karl (1987, 1997), Naím and Piñango (1984), and Rey (1989), discussed in Chapter Five.

perhaps greatest social-scientific interest: under what conditions may the authoritarian or, alternately, democratic effect of resource wealth be more important? In other words, the analysis aids in the task of developing conditional hypotheses that may help us explain variation in political outcomes across resource-rich countries.

The models suggest that the democratic effect of resources will be relatively important when the redistribution of non-resource income or wealth is a particularly salient concern for elites. In practice, two variables may play a key role. First, the comparative statics of the model suggest that the democratic effect of rents is stronger in societies with high degrees of inequality in non-resource sectors of the economy. Inequality can impede democratization, but resource rents mitigate the redistributive tensions that high inequality implies; as inequality grows and potential redistribution increases, the mitigation of inequality is a more important concern for elites, relative to their desire to control the distribution of resource rents. Then, in the horse race between the democratic and authoritarian effects of rents, the former tends to be stronger. Second, the authoritarian effect of rents is heightened by resource dependence, rather than by resource wealth per se. The intuition is similar: when resources are the only economic "game in town," conflict over the distribution of rents is more important, relative to redistributive conflict over non-resource wealth or income.

I develop these claims below in the context of two simple models. The strategic environment of the models is similar in key respects to the models in Acemoglu and Robinson (2001, 2006a). Politics is defined by the conflict between a relatively small group of elites and a relatively large group of masses whose members act to advance common interests or purposes. The approach is instrumental, in the sense that preferences over policy outcomes drive preferences over political institutions—because institutions allocate political power and thus ultimately help determine policy outcomes. Following a large body of recent work in political economy and comparative politics, I focus on how economic conflict between elites and masses over fiscal policy, and particularly redistributive tax policy, shapes preferences over political regimes (inter alia, Boix 2003; Persson and Tabellini 2000).[3]

[3] Another interesting contribution is the dynamic general equilibrium model of Feng and Zak (1999), who inter alia relate the degree of income inequality to the probability of a democratic transition, working, however, through a different mechanism than the one emphasized in the models developed here. Working independently of me, Morrison (2007) also developed a model, building on Acemoglu and Robinson's (2001, 2006) framework, that analyzes the impact of natural resources and unconditional foreign aid on democracy.

This approach also emphasizes that although political institutions allocate formal political power, groups sometimes have other sources of political influence: in particular, the ability to take power by force. For example, elites may launch or support coups against democracy, while subordinate groups can threaten authoritarian regimes with popular mobilization and, in the limit, with revolution. Crucially, the ability of out-of-power groups to threaten to take control of the state fluctuates over time; opportunities for coups or social revolutions may be transient. This can create powerful incentives for out-of-power actors to exercise their de facto power today: although groups who hold more formal power today may promise to honor policy favors to out-of-power groups tomorrow, such promises may not be credible because empowered groups may renege once de facto threats to their power recede.

Despite these powerful incentives of out-of-power groups to exercise de facto power and take power by force, political regime change has often been relatively non-violent, while empirically social revolutions are rare events (Skocpol 1979). Yet why would groups that dominate the formal polity choose either to moderate policy or willingly to relinquish formal political power, as in the case, for instance, of democratization? Following earlier theoretical work, the approach here emphasizes that the *threat* posed by out-of-power groups to take power by force can induce both policy change and institutional reform (Acemoglu and Robinson 2001, 2006a). For instance, a coup threat from an elite group may induce democratic majorities to moderate policy in favor of the preferences of that elite (see, e.g., R. Collier 1999 on Southern Europe, Wantchekon 1999a on El Salvador, or Londregan 2000 on Chile), whereas authoritarian incumbents faced with mobilization "from below" may democratize in order to avoid an even less palatable "revolutionary" outcome. That the exercise of a threat of a coup or a social revolution is not always (or even often) observed may be precisely because political incumbents have averted this outcome through some combination of policy moderation or institutional reform.

Given this framework, the key contribution of the formal analysis in this chapter is to clarify how resource rents may shape economic conflict between elites and masses and thereby the emergence and persistence of democratic and authoritarian regimes. On the one hand, resources can raise the opportunity cost of being out of power. Taking control of the state, for instance through a coup, allows elites to control the distribution of resource rents; the difficulty that democracies may experience in credibly committing to transfer rents to elites in the future may increase elites' incentives to take power by force today, when they have the power to do so. On the other hand, resources can also reduce the current and future redistributive costs of democracy to elites, by endogenously reducing the extent to which democratic majorities seek to tax elites' non-resource income or wealth. Resources may therefore mitigate a key incentive of elites to stage a coup, which is the fear that the poor will "soak the rich" once the threat of a coup recedes.

I first develop and solve a game of coups against democracy, in which rich elites weigh the costs and benefits of staging a coup against an existing democracy in which the policy preferences of a relatively poor majority are influential; the comparative statics of the model generate hypotheses that may help to explain variation in political outcomes across resource-rich countries. I then turn to the analysis of a game of democratization, in which incumbent elites in an existing authoritarian regime weigh the costs and benefits of responding to a mobilizational threat of revolt "from below" through repression, policy moderation, or democratization. The results of the two analyses are similar, in that the anticipated costs and benefits of democracy drive the strategic interaction of the players in both models. Here, these two dynamic games are analyzed separately, rather than in a fully intertemporal model in which redemocratization may take place after a coup against democracy, or a coup after redemocratization. It is conceptually simple to extend the games in this manner, as I have done elsewhere (Dunning 2006; see also Acemoglu and Robinson 2001, 2006a). However, such an elaboration comes at the cost of significantly more algebraic complexity but perhaps little additional insight into the particular questions of interest here. I therefore focus here on two simpler games in which the intuitions underlying the core analytic claims are more readily apparent. The final section discusses the results and suggests directions for empirical testing in subsequent chapters.

3.1 A Model of Coups against Democracy

3.1.1 The Setting

Consider an infinitely repeated game in a society with a continuum of citizens of mass one. Citizens belong to one of two groups, the "elites" and the "masses" (or, equivalently, the "rich" and the "poor"). These groups are distinguished both by their size and by their level of private income. First, a fraction $\delta \in (0, \frac{1}{2})$ of the population is rich and a fraction $(1 - \delta)$ is poor, so the poor are more numerous. Second, let the fraction of total private, non-resource income accruing to the rich group be θ, with $\theta > \delta$. Total (and average) private, non-resource income (or wealth) is $\bar{y}$, so the income of each rich individual is $y^r = \frac{\theta}{\delta}\bar{y}$, while the income of each poor individual is $y^p = \frac{(1-\theta)}{(1-\delta)}\bar{y}$. Thus, $y^r > \bar{y} > y^p$.

Citizens derive utility from private consumption and from public spending. In each period t of the game, the instantaneous utility of individual i is given by

$$U_t^i = c_t^i + V(g_t^i), \tag{3.1}$$

where c_t^i is the (post-tax) consumption of individual i at time t, g_t^i is per-capita public spending that is targeted at time t toward the group of which individual i is a member, and V is a concave function with $V'(\cdot) > 0$, $V''(\cdot) < 0$, and $V(0) = 0$. All citizens seek to maximize the (discounted) infinite-horizon sum of their instantaneous utilities, $\sum_{t=0}^{\infty} \beta^t U_t^i$, where $\beta \in (0, 1)$ is the common per-period discount factor.

Private consumption is just private, non-resource income net of taxes, so

$$c_t^i = (1 - \tau_t)y^i, \tag{3.2}$$

where τ_t is a proportional tax on income adopted in period t. In fact, the tax policy τ_t may be thought of more broadly as *any* potentially redistributive policy over which citizens' induced preferences will differ—for instance, land reform, exchange rate manipulations, and so on.[4] For simplicity, however, and without loss of generality, I refer here to τ_t as a tax on income.

Public spending comes from two sources: tax revenue and resource rent. Tax revenue is collected from citizens by the central government and disbursed through public spending. Resource rent, on the other hand, flows directly into the public coffers, without any need for collection of private income from citizens. The government budget constraint in each period is given by

$$g_t^r + g_t^p = \lambda_t[H(\tau_t\bar{y}) + R] + (1 - \lambda_t)[H(\tau_t\bar{y}) + R], \tag{3.3}$$

where λ_t is the proportion of total spending targeted to the rich group in period t, $\tau_t\bar{y}$ is total tax revenue in period t, and R is the per-capita value

[4] The case studies in Chapters Five and Six, for instance, consider a range of redistributive policies beyond simply a tax on non-resource income.

of resource rents. This reduces to

$$g_t \equiv H(\tau_t \bar{y}) + R, \tag{3.4}$$

where $g_t \equiv g_t^r + g_t^p$ gives total per-capita transfers and $H(\cdot)$ is a concave function with $H'(\cdot) > 0$, $H''(\cdot) < 0$, and $H(0) = 0$. Using equation (3.1), the utility of the rich and the poor can therefore be written as

$$U_t^r = (1 - \tau_t)y^r + V(\lambda_t(H(\tau_t \bar{y}) + R)) \tag{3.5}$$

and

$$U_t^p = (1 - \tau_t)y^p + V((1 - \lambda_t)(H(\tau_t \bar{y}) + R)). \tag{3.6}$$

Note that V and H are both concave functions, but the concavities have different interpretations in each case. The concavity of V captures diminishing marginal utility of public spending as well as inefficiencies involved in the provision of goods and services valued by the public. On the other hand, the concavity of H models the specific distortions associated with collecting taxes and other sources of public revenue, *relative* to resource rents. Higher taxes on private income may reduce output, through effects on investment and labor supply, or they may increase tax evasion; the concavity of H can be thought of as capturing these effort, investment elasticity, or tax evasion effects in a reduced-form way. The claim is certainly not that the collection of resource rents by the government does not also lead to such distortionary effects; however, as discussed in Chapter Two and in a large literature on natural resource-rich rentier states, natural resource sectors tend to be relatively easily taxable, as the heavy sunk costs involved in the extraction of many natural resources create a revenue base that is immobile and relatively inelastic and that can provide the government with multiple opportunities for appropriating rent (Hirschman 1977; Madhavy 1970; Mommer 2003; Monaldi 2002a). The concavity of V can be thought of as reflecting inefficiencies or distortions on the spending side of the fiscal balance while the concavity of H captures inefficiencies on the revenue-collection side. The assumption is that whatever its source, revenue is converted into public spending via the same (diminishing returns) technology, while on the revenue-collection side, the generation of revenue from taxes on citizens generates relatively more distortions than the collection of resource rent: unlike resource rents, tax revenues cannot be converted unit-by-unit into public spending.

There are two choice variables in the model, the allocation decision λ_t and the tax rate τ_t. Clearly, because utility is increasing in the proportion of public spending that is targeted to one's group, the unconstrained ideal policy for the rich in any period must involve $\lambda_t = 1$, and the ideal policy for the poor must involve $\lambda_t = 0$. These ideal allocation policies of the rich and poor are denoted by λ_t^r and λ_t^p, respectively.

Given the implementation of the ideal allocation policy λ_t^i for group i, the ideal tax rate of individuals of that group is given by

$$\arg\max_{\tau_t}(1 - \tau_t)y^i + V(H(\tau_t \bar{y}) + R).$$

Thus, the following first-order condition implicitly defines this ideal tax rate of individuals of group i:

$$V'(H(\tau^i \bar{y}) + R) = \frac{y^i}{H'(\tau^i \bar{y})\bar{y}}, \tag{3.7}$$

where τ^i is the tax rate preferred by the group with private income y^i, given that the allocation of public spending is set at group i's ideal point. (For simplicity, I abstract from time subscripts because, as we will see, the ideal tax rate of each individual or group of individuals will be the same in every period.) Since $y^r > y^p$, the concavity of V and H implies that the rich prefer lower taxes and less public spending than the poor. That is, $\tau^r < \tau^p$.

I now turn to defining the structure of the strategic game. Before doing so, however, two comments about the primitives of the model may be in order. First, the assumption that public spending is targeted to specific groups of citizens may seem unnecessarily strong; after all, spending on public goods such as national defense may benefit all citizens. An alternative is to posit g_t^i=g_t for all i; that is, spending is not targeted to one group or the other. Two points about this alternative may be useful to make at the outset. On the one hand, the main results developed below persist to this alternative specification (see Dunning 2006). On the other hand, however, the targeting of public spending is important because, in the existing literature, the control of political incumbents over the allocation of resource rents is one of the sources of the alleged authoritarian effect of rents. It is therefore important to allow political incumbents to control the allocation of rents in the model and, in particular, to target spending toward their own group.[5]

Second, a key idea of the analysis is that the political regime type allocates political power to individuals of one or the other group. Under

[5] We will see that notwithstanding the targeting of spending, a democratic effect of rents will persist. I therefore begin with an assumption that *privileges* the authoritarian effect of resource rents and show that nonetheless there is a democratic effect of rents.

authoritarianism, for example, elites are assumed to hold political power and therefore to choose policy. On the other hand, democracy is assumed to implement the preferences of the poor majority; in the background, there is an unmodeled process of Downsian political competition, in which democracy leads to convergence on the policy preferred by the median voter (as in, e.g., Wittman 1995).[6] The underlying conception of democracy, however, is Schumpeterian; the maintained hypothesis is that democratic contestation and participation will lead to political power for the poor majority, *relative* to authoritarianism. Needless to say, this assertion does not imply that the "masses" exercise political power to the exclusion of elites in any real-world democracy: constitutional rules (Beard 1913; Persson and Tabellini 2000), lobbying (Grossman and Helpman 2001), electoral competition in multi-dimensional policy spaces (Roemer 1998), and other factors can all undercut the influence of a democratic majority. Instead, the assertion should be understood primarily as a *comparative* statement about the ability of masses to influence policy under democracy, *relative* to a modal authoritarian system, and as a useful building block in a theory of the emergence and persistence of democratic and authoritarian regimes. The analytic results developed below would be robust to a similar model in which, say, electoral rules or party systems undercut the political influence of a poor democratic majority—as long as the masses generally have *more* influence under democracy than they do under authoritarianism.

3.1.2 Timing of the Coup Game and Definition of Equilibrium

The timing of the stage game is as follows. Under a democratic regime:

- **(D1)** Nature determines the realization of a random variable $\varphi_t \in \{\varphi^L, \varphi^H\}$, which is observed by both groups.
- **(D2)** The poor majority makes an allocation decision, $\tilde{\lambda}_t^D \in [0, 1]$ and sets a tax rate, $\tilde{\tau}_t^D \in [0, 1]$.
- **(D3)** The rich decide whether to stage a coup, at an exogenous cost φ_t.[7]
- **(D4a)** If the rich stage a coup, there is a transition to authoritarianism: the rich make a new allocation decision $\tilde{\lambda}_t^A \in [0, 1]$ and set a new tax

[6] As will be clear below, there exists a Condorcet winner on the policy space (λ, τ).

[7] The sources of this cost are unmodeled, but they could involve the risks to the rich of staging an unsuccessful coup. In Venezuela, for example, coup plotters who had deposed Hugo Chávez for 48 hours in April 2002 were exiled or imprisoned after his return to power, a cost paid by similarly unsuccessful conspirators in any number of historical instances.

rate $\tilde{\tau}_t^A \in [0, 1]$, instantaneous utilities of both groups are realized, the period ends, and the political regime is authoritarian in the next period.[8]

(D4b) If the rich do not stage a coup, the allocation $\tilde{\lambda}_t^D$ and tax rate $\tilde{\tau}_t^D$ set by the poor in (D2) are implemented, utilities are realized, and the game moves to the next period under a democratic regime.

On the other hand, if society is authoritarian, then in each period

(A1) The rich make an allocation decision $\tilde{\lambda}_t^A \in [0, 1]$ and set a tax rate $\tilde{\tau}_t^A \in [0, 1]$, instantaneous utilities are realized, and the period ends.

I assume $\varphi^L \to \infty$, so that coups are only feasible in some periods of the game. The notation may be somewhat confusing: as in Acemoglu and Robinson (2001, 2006a), the idea is that only when $\varphi_t = \varphi^H$, so that the realization of the random variable φ is "high," does the rich group have the collective-action capacity necessary to threaten the democratic order. The intuition is that opportunities for coups may be transient and only available to the elite at some times. The impermanence of opportunities for coups will play an important role in shaping the strategic calculus of elites. In any democratic period, $\varphi_t = \varphi^H$ with probability p and φ^L with probability $(1 - p)$, so the distribution is stationary across periods. Each period of the infinite-horizon game is thus characterized by a "state of the world" that has two characteristics: first, whether the regime is democratic or authoritarian; second, under democracy, whether economic conditions or some other unmodeled factor have allowed the rich to overcome collective-action problems and thus credibly threaten a coup against democracy. The state space of the game can therefore be denoted $S = \{\{D, \varphi^H\}, \{D, \varphi^L\}, \{A\}\}$, with "*D*" for "democratic" and "*A*" for "authoritarian." Note that here, authoritarianism is an "absorbing state," in that once the regime becomes authoritarian, it remains so forever. As discussed above, it is conceptually straightforward but more algebraically complex and space-intensive to analyze a model in which redemocratization may take place after a coup; such an analysis gives results that are similar in their implications for the impact of resource rents on the political equilibria. Thus, in this chapter the analysis is restricted to the simpler case.[9]

[8] One might instead assume that a coup only succeeds probabilistically. However, the underlying strategic dynamics of the game would be similar, and the effects of resource rents on the persistence of democracy would be invariant to the elaboration of such a richer model, qualitatively speaking.

[9] See Dunning (2006) for an analysis of the fully intertemporal model with regime-switching.

The structure of the game and the distribution of φ are common knowledge. Because the distribution of φ_t is stationary across periods, I sometimes drop the time subscript. The equilibrium concept is Markov-perfect equilibrium, which has an important implication in the current context: because strategies in every period are contingent on the current state of the world and, in particular, are not conditioned on the history of play, both groups will have a limited capacity to commit to future policies (for discussion, see Fudenberg and Tirole 1991).[10] The formal definition of equilibrium is as follows. When the political regime is democratic, the action set of the poor consists of an allocation decision $\tilde{\lambda}^D : \{\varphi^L, \varphi^H\} \longrightarrow [0, 1]$ and a tax rate $\tilde{\tau}^D : \{\varphi^L, \varphi^H\} \longrightarrow [0, 1]$, while the action set of the rich consists of a coup decision $\phi : \{\varphi^L, \varphi^H\} \times [0, 1] \times [0, 1] \longrightarrow \{0, 1\}$, with $\phi = 1$ indicating a coup. When the political regime is authoritarian, the action set of the rich consists of an allocation decision $\tilde{\lambda}^A : \{A\} \longrightarrow [0, 1]$ and a tax rate $\tilde{\tau}^A : \{A\} \longrightarrow [0, 1]$, that is, a mapping from the authoritarian state to a policy pair. A strategy profile for the poor is then defined as $\sigma^p\{\tilde{\lambda}^D(\cdot), \tilde{\tau}^D(\cdot)\}$, while a strategy profile for the rich is defined as $\sigma^r\{\phi(\cdot), \tilde{\lambda}^A(\cdot), \tilde{\tau}^A(\cdot)\}$. A Markov-perfect equilibrium is a strategy combination, $\{\tilde{\sigma}^p, \tilde{\sigma}^r\}$, such that $\tilde{\sigma}^p$ and $\tilde{\sigma}^r$ are mutual best-responses for all states.

3.1.3 *Solving the Coup Game*

Assume without loss of generality that the state in the initial democratic period is "low"; that is, $\varphi_0 = \varphi^L$. Because a coup is prohibitively costly for the rich in this state, the poor can set their ideal allocation policy and tax rate in the current period, unconstrained by the threat of a coup. The instantaneous utilities of the rich and the poor in this period will therefore be defined at λ_t^p and τ^p, and society will remain democratic in the following period. However, the indirect utility of individuals of each group, evaluated at this allocation decision and tax policy, will depend not just on current policy but also on what individuals expect to happen in the future. In particular, individuals of both groups know that with probability p, the state tomorrow will be $\{D, \varphi^H\}$, in which case the rich may want to stage a coup (or, the poor may want to set an allocation decision and tax rate different from their ideal point, in order to avoid a coup). On the other hand, with probability $(1 - p)$, the state tomorrow will be $\{D, \varphi^L\}$.

[10] Although restriction to Markovian equilibria simplifies the analysis, allowing history-dependent strategies may not eliminate intertemporal commitment problems in dynamic stochastic games such as the game developed here, as Powell (2004) has recently shown.

Applying the principles of dynamic programming, the following Bellman equations define the value functions of each group in the state $\{D, \varphi^L\}$:

$$U^r(D, \varphi^L) = (1 - \tau^p)y^r + \beta[pU^r(D, \varphi^H) + (1 - p)U^r(D, \varphi^L)] \quad (3.8)$$

and

$$U^p(D, \varphi^L) = (1 - \tau^p)y^p + V(H(\tau^p \bar{y}) + R) + \beta[pU^p(D, \varphi^H) + (1 - p)U^p(D, \varphi^L)]. \quad (3.9)$$

The first term or terms on the right-hand side of each equation give the instantaneous utility of each group in the present period, defined at the tax rate τ^p. For example, in equation (3.8), $(1 - \tau^p)y^r$ is the instantaneous utility of the rich, who have income y^r, defined at the allocation decision λ_t^p and the tax rate τ^p. (Recall that since $\lambda_t^p = 0$, the rich do not receive any public spending under the ideal policy of the poor, so the term of the utility function of the rich that involves public spending drops out; see equation 3.5.) Similarly, in equation (3.9), $(1 - \tau^p)y^p + V(H(\tau^p \bar{y}) + R)$ is the instantaneous utility of the poor at their ideal policy. Next, the set of terms in brackets is the continuation value of living under democracy tomorrow, which is discounted by β (because it occurs tomorrow). This continuation value is the weighted sum of the value of living under democracy when $\varphi = \varphi^H$ and living under democracy when $\varphi = \varphi^L$, where the weights are the probability p that $\varphi = \varphi^H$ tomorrow and the probability $(1 - p)$ that $\varphi = \varphi^L$ tomorrow.

To define the value functions in equations (3.8) and (3.9), however, we must in turn define $U^r(D, \varphi^H)$ and $U^p(D, \varphi^H)$, the continuation values to the rich and poor of living under democracy when the state is $\{D, \varphi^H\}$ (and the rich may therefore want to stage a coup). To pin down these functions, first suppose the poor follow a strategy of setting a spending allocation $\tilde{\lambda}^D$ and a tax rate $\tilde{\tau}^D$ in any period in which $\varphi = \varphi^H$ such that the rich do not stage a coup, given this allocation policy and tax rate. Then the payoffs to living under democracy when the state is $\{D, \varphi^H\}$ will be

$$U^r(D, \varphi^H; \tilde{\lambda}^D, \tilde{\tau}^D) = (1 - \tilde{\tau}^D)y^r + V(\tilde{\lambda}^D(H(\tilde{\tau}^D \bar{y}) + R)) + \beta[pU^r(D, \varphi^H; \tilde{\lambda}^D, \tilde{\tau}^D) + (1 - p)U^r(D, \varphi^L)] \quad (3.10)$$

and

$$U^p(D, \varphi^H; \tilde{\lambda}^D, \tilde{\tau}^D) = (1 - \tilde{\tau}^D)y^p + V((1 - \tilde{\lambda}^D)(H(\tilde{\tau}^D \bar{y}) + R)) + \beta[pU^p(D, \varphi^H; \tilde{\lambda}^D, \tilde{\tau}^D) + (1 - p)U^p(D, \varphi^L)]. \quad (3.11)$$

On the other hand, rather than accept the policy pair $(\tilde{\lambda}^D, \tilde{\tau}^D)$ that the poor offer, the rich may prefer to stage a coup. What is the payoff to a coup? Define $U^r(A; \tilde{\lambda}^A, \tilde{\tau}_t^A)$ to be the payoff to the rich under any authoritarian period in which the rich propose the policy pair $(\tilde{\lambda}^A, \tilde{\tau}_t^A)$. This payoff is simply the discounted stream of instantaneous utilities of the rich evaluated at $\tilde{\lambda}^A$ and $\tilde{\tau}_t^A$. Because authoritarianism is an absorbing state, it must always be optimal for the rich to set their unconstrained ideal allocation policy and tax rate in every authoritarian period; that is, $\tilde{\lambda}_t^A = \lambda^r$ and $\tilde{\tau}_t^A = \tau^r$ for all t. Now note that the payoff to the rich under authoritarianism is identical to the payoff to the rich of staging a coup, net of the cost of a coup, as in both cases the rich can set their unconstrained preferred tax rate for one period and society is authoritarian in the following period. So, the payoff to a coup is simply the payoff to the rich in any authoritarian period, net of the (one-period) cost of the coup: that is, $U^r(A; \lambda^r, \tau^r) - \varphi^H$.

Putting this discussion together, the continuation values $U^r(D, \varphi^H)$ and $U^p(D, \varphi^H)$ in equations (3.8) and (3.9) are defined as follows:

$$U^r(D, \varphi^H) = \max_{\phi \in \{0,1\}} \phi[U^r(A; \lambda^r, \tau^r) - \varphi^H] + (1 - \phi)U^r(D, \varphi^H; \tilde{\lambda}^D, \tilde{\tau}^D) \tag{3.12}$$

$$U^p(D, \varphi^H) = \phi[U^p(A; \lambda^r, \tau^r)] + (1 - \phi)U^p(D, \varphi^H; \tilde{\lambda}^D, \tilde{\tau}^D), \tag{3.13}$$

with $\phi = 1$ indicating that a coup takes place. If staging a coup maximizes the utility of the rich in equation (3.12), then $\phi = 1$ and $U^r(D, \varphi^H) = U^r(A; \lambda^r, \tau r) - \varphi^H$. On the other hand, if the rich are better off not staging a coup and accepting $(\tilde{\lambda}_t^D, \tilde{\tau}^D)$, then $\phi = 0$ in equation (3.12) and $U^r(D, \varphi^H) = U^r(D, \varphi^H; \tilde{\lambda}_t^D, \tilde{\tau}^D)$. I assume that if the rich are indifferent between these options, $\phi = 0$, there is no coup and society remains democratic. Equation (3.13) gives the utility of the poor in any democratic period in which the state is "high" as a function of the coup decision of the rich.

It will be useful to know when the poor must adopt some policy other than their ideal policy pair if they want to attempt to avoid a coup. Let the *coup constraint* be binding in any period in which $\varphi = \varphi^H$ if the rich prefer staging a coup at the exogenous cost φ^H to living forever under a democracy in which the poor always set $\lambda_t^D = \lambda^p$ and $\tilde{\tau}^D = \tau^p$, regardless of the future realization of φ. The coup constraint therefore binds if

$$U^r(A; \lambda^r, \tau^r) - \varphi^H > U^r(D, \varphi^H; \tilde{\lambda}_t^D = \lambda^p, \tilde{\tau}^D = \tau^p). \tag{3.14}$$

Clearly, if the poor set $\lambda_t^D = \lambda^p$ and $\tilde{\tau}^D = \tau^p$ whenever $\varphi = \varphi^H$, they will also do so when $\varphi = \varphi^L$. (No other tax rate is credible in the "low" state.) Thus, the instantaneous utility of the rich in every democratic period will simply be $(1 - \tau^p)y^r$. The discounted value to the rich of receiving this instantaneous utility forever, beginning in period t, is therefore

$$U^r(D, \varphi^H; \tau^p) = \sum_{t=0}^{\infty} \beta^t[(1 - \tau^p)y^r] \tag{3.15}$$

$$= \frac{(1 - \tau^p)y^r}{1 - \beta}, \tag{3.16}$$

which gives the right side of (3.14). On the other hand, $U^r(A; \lambda^r, \tau^r)$ on the left side of (3.14) is defined analogously as

$$U^r(A; \lambda^r, \tau^r) = \frac{(1 - \tau^r)y^r + V(H(\tau^r \bar{y}) + R)}{1 - \beta}; \tag{3.17}$$

that is, the discounted stream of the instantaneous utilities of the rich evaluated at their ideal policies λ^r and τ^r. Using equations (3.16) and (3.17) to substitute into equation (3.14), the coup constraint will bind if

$$\varphi^H < \frac{(1 - \tau^r)y^r + V(H(\tau^r \bar{y}) + R) - (1 - \tau^p)y^r}{1 - \beta}. \tag{3.18}$$

If this inequality holds, the poor cannot set their ideal tax rate in all periods without incurring a coup.

Consider first the situation in which the coup constraint does bind. In this case, if the poor want to avoid a coup, they will have to set $\tilde{\lambda}^D \in (0, 1]$ and/or $\tilde{\tau}^D \in [\tau^r, \tau^p)$ whenever $\varphi = \varphi^H$. A tax-and-spending policy pair that will make rich elites just indifferent between a coup and no coup, given that the realization of φ equals φ^H, is an allocation $\tilde{\lambda}^{D*}$ and the tax rate $\tilde{\tau}^{D*}$ that satisfies the equality

$$U^r(A; \lambda^A, \tau^A) - \varphi^H = U^r(D, \varphi^H; \tilde{\lambda}^{D*}, \tilde{\tau}^{D*}). \tag{3.19}$$

Clearly, it is optimal for the poor to avoid a coup (if possible) by setting a spending allocation $\tilde{\lambda}^{D*}$ and a tax rate $\tilde{\tau}^{D*}$ such that the equality in equation (3.19) is satisfied—because avoiding a coup allows the poor to retain political power and therefore set $\tilde{\lambda}^D = \lambda^p$ and $\tilde{\tau}^D = \tau^p$ in the future periods in which $\varphi = \varphi^L$, whereas a coup implies an allocation of λ^r and a tax rate of τ^r in the current and all future periods. Of course, the policy pair $(\tilde{\lambda}^{D*}, \tilde{\tau}^{D*})$ that satisfies equation (3.19) with equality will generally not be unique: the poor might appease the rich by cutting taxes, by increasing the allocation of spending to the rich, or both. This will not limit our ability to characterize the equilibrium outcomes of the game below.

An important question, however, is whether the poor will be *able* to avoid a coup by setting $\tilde{\tau}^D \neq \tau^p$ whenever $\varphi = \varphi^H$. If the poor will ever be able to induce the rich not to stage a coup, it will be by setting the policy pair $(\tilde{\lambda}^D, \tilde{\tau}^D)$ at the ideal point of the rich, that is, at (λ^r, τ^r), whenever threatened by a coup. Note that the poor cannot make the rich any better offer than by the ideal policy pair of the rich when threatened by a coup, and they cannot credibly commit to set any policy pair other than (λ^p, τ^p) in future periods in which they are not threatened by a coup. So the best they can do to induce the rich not to stage a coup is to offer a policy pair (λ^r, τ^r) whenever $\varphi = \varphi^H$. If the poor will ever be able to avoid a coup, they will therefore be able to do so by a strategy of setting $\tilde{\lambda}^D = \lambda^r$ and $\tilde{\tau}^D = \tau^r$ when $\varphi = \varphi^H$ and setting $\tilde{\lambda}^D = \lambda^p$ and $\tilde{\tau}^D = \tau^p$ when $\varphi = \varphi^L$.

Suppose that the poor follow this latter strategy. The rich will nonetheless stage a coup whenever $U^r(A; \lambda^r, \tau^r) - \varphi^H > U^r(D, \varphi^H; \tilde{\lambda}^D = \lambda^r, \tilde{\tau}^D = \tau^r)$. We can therefore define a threshold value of φ^{H*} such that the rich are just indifferent between staging a coup in a high period and living under democracy at this value. This "critical coup cost" will satisfy the equality

$$U^r(A; \lambda^r, \tau_t^A) - \varphi^{H*} = U^r(D, \varphi^{H*}; \tilde{\lambda}^D = \lambda^r, \tilde{\tau}^D = \tau^r). \tag{3.20}$$

The left-hand side of equation (3.20) is the value to the rich of imposing authoritarianism, net of the critical coup cost φ^{H*} at which equation (3.20) is satisfied. The right-hand side of equation (3.20), on the other hand, is the value to the rich of living under democracy when the poor follow the strategy of setting $\tilde{\lambda}^D = \lambda^r$ and $\tilde{\tau}^D = \tau^r$ when $\varphi = \varphi^H$ and setting $\tilde{\lambda}^D = \lambda^p$ and $\tilde{\tau}^D = \tau^p$ when $\varphi = \varphi^L$. Note that if the left-hand side of equation (3.20) is greater than the right-hand side, the poor will *never* be able to induce the rich not to stage a coup when the realization of φ gives the rich the chance to do so. Thus, the poor cannot avoid a coup for any $\varphi^H < \varphi^{H*}$.

We can now solve for the critical coup cost in equation (3.20). $U^r(A; \tilde{\tau}_t^A)$ is given by equation (3.17) above. $U^r(D, \varphi^{H*}, \tilde{\tau}^D = \tau^r)$, on the other hand, is the value function of the rich under democracy given that the poor set $\tilde{\lambda}^D = \lambda^r$ and $\tilde{\tau}^D = \tau^r$ when $\varphi = \varphi^H$ and set $\tilde{\lambda}^D = \lambda^p$ and $\tilde{\tau}^D = \tau^p$ when $\varphi = \varphi^L$. Note that equations (3.8) and (3.10), with $U^r(D, \varphi^H) = U^r(D, \varphi^H; \tilde{\lambda}^D = \lambda^r, \tilde{\tau}^D = \tau^r)$, constitute a system of two equations in the two unknowns $U^r(D, \varphi^L)$ and $U^r(D, \varphi^H; \tilde{\lambda}^D = \lambda^r, \tilde{\tau}^D = \tau^r)$. Solving equation (3.8) for $U^r(D, \varphi^L)$, substituting into equation (3.10), and manipulating terms gives

$$U^r(D, \varphi^H; \tilde{\tau}^D = \tau^r)$$
$$= \frac{(1-\beta(1-p))[(1-\tau^r)y^r + V(H(\tau^r\bar{y}) + R] + \beta(1-p)[(1-\tau^p)y^r]}{1-\beta}. \tag{3.21}$$

It is straightforward to show that this expression gives the optimal tax-and-spend policy pair (from the point of view of the rich) to which the poor can credibly commit themselves over time. Intuitively, this is because the poor cannot credibly commit to set a spending allocation other than λ^p or a tax rate other than τ^p when $\varphi = \varphi^L$; and setting the policy pair at (λ^r, τ^r) when $\varphi = \varphi^H$ is clearly optimal for the rich, by the definition of (λ^r, τ^r) as the solution to the maximization problem of the rich.

Now, substituting equations (3.17) and (3.21) in equation (3.20) gives the critical coup cost at which the rich are indifferent between staging a coup and not staging a coup (and thus by assumption do not stage a coup), given that the poor will choose a tax strategy that is optimal from the perspective of the rich from among the set of credible strategies. This critical coup cost is

$$\varphi^{H*} = \frac{[\beta(1-p)]\,[(1-\tau^r)y^r + V(H(\tau^r y) + R) - (1-\tau^p)y^r]}{(1-\beta)}. \tag{3.22}$$

The discussion above establishes the following proposition.

Proposition 1 *The unique Markov-perfect equilibrium outcome of the coup game developed above is as follows:*

(1) *If the coup constraint in equation (3.18) does not bind, or if the coup constraint binds but $\varphi^H \geq \varphi^{H*}$ as defined in equation (3.22), society remains democratic forever.*
(2) *If the coup constraint binds and $\varphi^H < \varphi^{H*}$, the rich stage a coup against democracy in the first period in which $\varphi = \varphi^H$, and society thereafter remains authoritarian forever.*

I focus on the unique Markov-perfect equilibrium outcome of the game in the proposition above because the focus below is on how resource rents influence the incidence of democracy, and characterizing the unique equilibrium outcome will be sufficient for this purpose. Note, however, that the following strategies will support this unique equilibrium outcome:

The poor: if the coup constraint does not bind or if $\varphi^H > \varphi^{H*}$, set $\tilde{\lambda}^D = \lambda^p$ and $\tilde{\tau}^D = \tau^p$ in all democratic periods; otherwise, set $\tilde{\lambda}^D = \tilde{\lambda}^{D*}$ and $\tilde{\tau}^D = \tilde{\tau}^{D*}$ such that equation (3.19) holds whenever $\varphi = \varphi^H$ and set $\tilde{\lambda}^D = \lambda^p$ and $\tilde{\tau}^D = \tau^p$ whenever $\varphi = \varphi^L$.

The rich: in every democratic period, solve the maximization problem in (3.12), and set $\tilde{\lambda}^A = \lambda^r$ and $\tilde{\tau}^A = \tau^r$ in all authoritarian periods.

However, these equilibrium strategies are not, of course, unique. For example, there may be many policy pairs $(\tilde{\lambda}^{D*}, \tilde{\tau}^{D*})$ such that equation (3.19) holds: to avoid a coup, the poor could either limit redistributive taxation, *or* they could increase the allocation of spending to the rich (or both).[11] However, variations on the equilibrium strategies will all support the same unique equilibrium outcome stated in the proposition above. Because the goal is to characterize how the equilibrium outcomes vary as a function of exogenous parameters (such as the level of resource rents), it is adequate for our purposes to summarize the equilibria of the game in this fashion.

3.1.4 Comparative Statics

I now turn to the core question of analytic interest: how do resource rents influence the incidence of coups against democracy in this model? Notice from Proposition 1 that the incidence of coups depends critically on the threshold value φ^{H*}. Indeed, because a period in which $\varphi = \varphi^H$ will eventually be reached with probability one (recall that p, the probability of a "high" state, is strictly positive), a coup will occur with probability one whenever $\varphi^H < \varphi^{H*}$. Thus, any factor that increases φ^{H*} will *increase* the incidence of coups against democracy because coups will take place over a wider part of the parameter space: elites will find it in their interest to stage coups even when coups are relatively "expensive."[12] One can then investigate the impact of resource rents on the incidence of coups by performing comparative statics analysis—in particular, by asking how the critical coup cost φ^{H*} varies as a function of resource rents R.

[11] Note that although the policy space is two-dimensional, actors have *intermediate preferences* over policies: all rich individuals want lower τ and higher λ than poor individuals. Thus, the preferences of voters over the two-dimensional policy space can be projected onto a unidimensional space in which voters may be ordered by their type (i.e., rich or poor). See Grandmont (1978) or Persson and Tabellini (2000: 25–6).

[12] Readers may note that in any given game, φ^H is fixed. However, the thought experiment of interest involves imagining a sequence of games in which φ^H varies: for instance, the cost of a coup (and other parameter values) may differ across different countries.

As a preliminary to this analysis, it is useful to rewrite the critical coup cost given by equation (3.22) in a more intuitive manner. Notice that the numerator of the right-hand side of the equation simply gives the difference between the instantaneous utility of members of the rich group, evaluated at their ideal policy pair (λ^r,τ^r), and the utility of the rich evaluated at the ideal policy pair (λ^p,τ^p) of the poor. Let

$$U^r(\tau^r(R), \lambda^r, R) = (1 - \tau^r)y^r + V(H(\tau^r \bar{y}) + R) \tag{3.23}$$

be the utility of the rich at their ideal tax and spending allocation policy, and let

$$U^r(\tau^p(R), \lambda^p, R) = (1 - \tau^p)y^r \tag{3.24}$$

be the utility of the rich at the ideal policy of the poor. (Here, in writing $U^r(\tau^r(R), \lambda^r, R)$ and $U^r(\tau^p(R), \lambda^p, R)$, I have made the dependence of the ideal tax rate on R explicit. The unconstrained ideal allocations λ^r and λ^p do not depend on R, as they are always at a corner.) Then, substituting into equation (3.22), the critical coup cost can be written as

$$\varphi^{H*} = \eta[U^r(\tau^r(R), \lambda^r, R) - U^r(\tau^p(R), \lambda^p, R)], \tag{3.25}$$

where $\eta = \frac{\beta(1-p)}{(1-\beta)}$. Expressing the critical coup cost in this manner makes it clear that the incidence of coups against democracy will depend on the difference between the instantaneous utility of the rich evaluated at their ideal policy and at the ideal policy of the poor.

Why does the critical coup cost depend on this difference between the utilities of the rich group at the policy pairs (λ^r,τ^r) and (λ^p,τ^p)? Under democracy, the poor will always be able to impose τ^p in the state $\{D, \varphi^L\}$, which occurs with probability $(1 - p)$; under authoritarianism, on the other hand, the rich can impose τ^r. As rich elites decide whether to undertake a coup, they consider the difference between their payoff under authoritarianism and their payoff under democracy, discounted by the probability that they will be able to threaten a coup in future democratic periods and thus induce a change in policy from the democratic majority. The impact of resource rents on the incidence of coups will therefore depend on how rents influence this difference between the utilities of the rich at their own ideal policy and at the ideal policy of the poor.

How do resource rents influence the critical coup cost in the model? Taking the derivative of the critical coup cost with respect to R and applying the chain rule gives

$$\frac{d\varphi^{H*}}{dR} = \eta\left[\frac{\partial(U^r(\tau^r(R), \lambda^r, R) - U^r(\tau^p(R), \lambda^p, R))}{\partial R} + \frac{\partial(U^r(\tau^r(R), \lambda^r, R) - U^r(\tau^p(R), \lambda^p, R))}{\partial \tau} \cdot \frac{\partial \tau}{\partial R}\right]. \quad (3.26)$$

According to equation (3.26), resource wealth has two effects on the critical coup cost and therefore on the incidence of coups. The first term in brackets on the right-hand side of the equation is the "direct" effect of resource rents: it captures how an increase in R directly affects the difference between the utility of the rich at their ideal point and at the ideal point of the poor. On the other hand, the second term in brackets is the "indirect" effect of resource rents. The effect is indirect because it works through the effect of R on the tax rate τ, which in turn directly affects the difference in the utility of the rich at their ideal point and at the poor's ideal point.

As I now show, the first, direct effect of resource rents is *positive*: that is, it drives up the critical coup cost and therefore *increases* the incidence of coups against democracy. However, the second, indirect effect of R is *negative*: that is, it drives down the critical coup cost and thus *decreases* the incidence of coups against democracy. In the model, resource rents therefore have competing effects on the incidence of coups. Whether the "authoritarian" or "democratic" effect will tend to dominate—and thus determine whether the total effect of resource rents on the incidence of coups is positive or negative—depends on the values of exogenous variables in the model, as I will describe further below. First, however, I turn to further analysis of the dual authoritarian and democratic effects of rents in the model.

The Authoritarian Effect of Rents What is the source of the direct, "authoritarian" effect of resource rents? Substituting from equations (3.23) and (3.24) above and taking partial derivatives gives

$$\frac{\partial(U^r(\tau^r(R), \lambda^r, R) - U^r(\tau^p(R), \lambda^r, R))}{\partial R} = V'(H(\tau^r \bar{y}) + R) > 0. \quad (3.27)$$

Equation (3.27) implies that that the direct effect of resource rents *increases* the incidence of coups against democracy; the positive sign follows because V is an increasing function. Why does this effect arise in the model? Control over the state brings control over the *distribution* of the rents; a marginal increase in rents increases the marginal benefit of being in power and thereby being able to target spending to one's own group. For this reason, rents make political power more valuable to the rich and thus increase their incentives to take power through a coup. As emphasized by the long literature on resource rents and authoritarianism, a resource boom increases the incentives of would-be authoritarians to take power even through antidemocratic means.

Clearly, the authoritarian effect of resource rents in this model is somewhat "reduced form." Other contributors to the literature on natural resource politics have suggested a wealth of mechanisms through which resource rents might increase both the incentives and the capabilities of elites to take and hold onto power through authoritarian means (see Chapters One and Two). This model captures this authoritarian effect of rents in a very simple way. However, the virtue of this simplicity is that it will allow us to compare below the authoritarian and democratic effects of resource rents in a transparent way and thereby build a theory to explain variation in political outcomes across resource-rich countries.

The Democratic Effect of Rents Let us then turn to the indirect, "democratic" effect of resource rents in the model. Again using equations (3.23) and (3.24), we have

$$\frac{\partial(U^r(\tau^r(R), \lambda^r, R) - U^r(\tau^p(R), \lambda^p, R))}{\partial \tau} \cdot \frac{\partial \tau}{\partial R} = \frac{\partial \tau^p}{\partial R} y^r < 0. \tag{3.28}$$

Here, I have applied the envelope theorem, which implies that $\frac{\partial U^r(\tau^r(R), \lambda^r, R)}{\partial \tau^r} = 0$ because τ^r is the tax policy that maximizes $U^r(\tau(R), \lambda^r, R)$. To pin down the sign of equation (3.28), we only need the sign of $\frac{\partial \tau^p}{\partial R}$ (since $y^r > 0$). Note that by the first-order condition in equation (3.7) with $i = p$,

$$-y^p + V'(H(\tau^p \bar{y}) + R)H'(\tau^p \bar{y})\bar{y} = 0.$$

Implicitly differentiating this expression with respect to R and rearranging terms gives

$$\frac{\partial \tau^p}{\partial R} = \frac{-V''(H(\tau^p \bar{y}) + R)H'(\tau^p \bar{y})\bar{y}}{[V''(H(\tau^p \bar{y}) + R)(H'(\tau^p \bar{y})\bar{y})^2 + V'(H(\tau^p \bar{y}) + R)H''(\tau^p \bar{y})(\bar{y})^2]} < 0. \tag{3.29}$$

Both terms in the denominator are negative (by the concavity of V and H), and the term in the numerator is positive, so the preferred tax rate of the poor depends *negatively* on resource rents. Consistent with a large empirical literature on the negative relationship between resource rents and taxation (see Chapter Two), an increase in resource rents in this model *decreases* the ideal tax rate of the poor. Thus, because $\frac{\partial \tau^p}{\partial R}$ is negative, the right-hand side of equation (3.28) has a negative sign.

What is the interpretation of equation (3.28)? One way to think about the democratic effect of resource rents in this model is as follows. When threatened by a coup, the poor would like to induce the rich not to stage a coup against democracy, by promising to implement the ideal policy pair of the rich. However, the poor face an intertemporal commitment problem because in any period in which $\varphi = \varphi^L$, it will be optimal for the poor to set $\tilde{\lambda}^D = \lambda^p$ and $\tilde{\tau}^D = \tau^p$. In other words, if the rich do not stage a coup against democracy, the democratic majority retains its political power and can impose its preferred policy in any period of the game in which the rich cannot threaten a coup. This is costly to the rich because not only do the rich not benefit from public spending that is targeted to the poor, but the rich would also like a lower tax rate than the poor because of their greater private wealth. The prospect of redistributive taxation thus increases the incentives of the rich to stage a coup, and intertemporal commitment problems prevent the poor from credibly promising to limit their taxation of the rich.

The democratic effect of resource rents helps to mitigate the commitment problem, however, because resource wealth endogenously affects tax policy: resource rents *decrease* the redistributive tax burden that the poor place on the rich. In other words, resource rents allow the democratic majority to make a credible commitment to reduce the rate at which it redistributes wealth away from rich elites and thereby reduce the incidence of coups against democracy. Although, as discussed above, the desire to control the *distribution* of resource rents increases the incentives of elites to stage coups in the model, the mitigation of *redistribution* of non-resource wealth or income reduces the economic cost of democracy to elites and thereby decreases their incentives to stage coups.

The source of the democratic effect of rents in the model thus has to do with the interaction between resource rents and the non-resource sectors of the economy: the concavity of the function H, which captures the relative difficulty of raising revenue in the non-resource sectors (relative to resource rents) plays a key role. As discussed later, the size of resource rents relative to the total economy, as well as the extent of redistributive conflict in the *non-resource* sectors of the economy, also can contribute to strengthening or weakening the democratic effect of resource rents and thereby help condition the overall impact of resource rents on the incidence of democracy.

3.1.5 *Explaining Variation*

In this model, resource rents have both authoritarian and democratic effects. I now turn to what is perhaps the more interesting social-scientific question: when might we expect resource wealth to promote authoritarianism, and when might we expect it to promote democracy? That is, how can we explain variation in political outcomes across resource-rich countries?

Answering this question involves another comparative statics exercise. In a sense, there is a horse race in the model between two competing forces: the direct, authoritarian effect and the indirect, democratic effect of resource rents. As alluded to earlier in the chapter, explaining variation across resource-rich countries will thus depend on analyzing how different variables contribute to the relative strength of the democratic and authoritarian effects. In the discussion that follows, I emphasize the role of two important variables: inequality of *non-resource* private income and the extent of resource dependence (i.e., the ratio of R to the total size of the economy $R + \bar{y}$).[13]

The Role of Inequality Inequality of non-resource income plays an important role in this model. As in the models of Acemoglu and Robinson (2001, 2006a) and Boix (2003), greater inequality may increase the incentives of elites to stage coups against democracy (or to resist democratization away from an existing authoritarian regime): put simply, inequality gives elites more to lose from redistributive taxation and therefore heightens the future cost of living under democracy. However, the *interaction* of resource rents and inequality has a very different effect.

To explore the argument formally, recall that the fraction of total private (non-resource) income accruing to the rich group is θ, with $\theta > \delta$. Now consider the critical coup cost defined in equation (3.22) above. Substituting $y^r = \frac{\theta}{\delta}\bar{y}$ gives

$$\varphi^{H*} = \eta \left[(1 - \tau^r)\frac{\theta}{\delta}\bar{y} + V(H(\tau^r \bar{y}) + R) - (1 - \tau^p)\frac{\theta}{\delta}\bar{y} \right], \tag{3.30}$$

[13] In Dunning (2006), I consider a third factor: when H is more concave, so the distortionary costs introduced by taxation of citizens are greater, the political impact of resource rents may be more pronounced. Because the shape of H can be interpreted as a measure of "state capacity," this may help explain the apparently moderate impact of resource rents in countries with well-developed bureaucratic apparatuses, e.g., Norway (Karl 1997). This interpretation is not pursued further here.

where $\eta = \frac{\beta(1-p)}{(1-\beta)}$. Implicitly differentiating this expression with respect to θ, using the envelope theorem to simplify, and substituting terms,

$$\frac{d\varphi^{H*}}{d\theta} = \eta\left[\frac{\bar{y}}{\delta}(-\tau^r) + \frac{\partial \tau^p}{\partial \theta}y^r - (1-\tau^p)\frac{\bar{y}}{\delta}\right] > 0. \tag{3.31}$$

The inequality follows from $\tau^p > \tau^r$, $y^r > y^p$, and the fact that the preferred tax rate of the poor is increasing in inequality, which is straightforward to show. Equation (3.31) says that inequality, by driving up the critical coup cost, increases the incentives of elites to stage coups, just as in the models of Acemoglu and Robinson (2001, 2006a) as well as Boix (2003).

However, as shown above, the indirect effect of resource wealth is to *decrease* the difference between the utility of the rich at their ideal point and at the ideal point of the poor. One might therefore conjecture that resource rents mitigate the impact of inequality on the critical coup cost. The sign of the cross-partial derivative of the critical coup cost $\hat{\varphi}^{H*}$ with respect to R and θ will tell us how resource rents affect the impact of inequality on the critical coup cost. Implicitly differentiating equation (3.31) with respect to R gives

$$\frac{d^2\varphi^{H*}}{d\theta dR} = \eta\left[\left(\frac{\partial \tau^p}{\partial R} - \frac{\partial \tau^r}{\partial R}\right)\frac{\bar{y}}{\delta} + \frac{\partial^2 \tau^p}{\partial R \partial \theta}(y^r)\right] < 0. \tag{3.32}$$

Unfortunately, at the level of generality at which the model has been developed thus far, the final inequality in equation (3.32) cannot be verified analytically. However, the sign of the cross-partial derivative can be determined by putting further structure on the shapes of $H(\cdot)$ and $V(\cdot)$ and by assuming realistic parameter values that are consistent with the suppositions of the model. For instance, in the simulation results presented below, the third derivatives of $H(\cdot)$ and $V(\cdot)$ are assumed to be positive on $\mathbb{R}_{++}$, as is the case with many common concave functions.

What is the interpretation of equation (3.32)? Recall from the discussion above that the sign of $\frac{d\varphi^{H*}}{dR}$ is, in general, ambiguous: there is an "authoritarian" effect that makes $\frac{d\varphi^{H*}}{dR}$ more positive but also a "democratic" effect that makes $\frac{d\varphi^{H*}}{dR}$ more negative. In general, a marginal increase in resource rents may either increase or decrease the incidence of coups against democracy. However, the negative sign on the cross-partial derivative in equation (3.32) implies that as inequality of non-resource income increases, the impact of resources on the critical coup cost becomes less positive (more negative).

In other words, the democratic effect of resource wealth is stronger where inequality of non-resource income is greater.

What is the source of this counterintuitive result? As just discussed, a marginal increase in resource rents has two effects. On the one hand, it makes political power more valuable to elites because control of the government brings with it the capacity to target rents to one's own group. Thus, conflict over the distribution of the rents can increase the incentives of elites to stage coups against democracy. On the other hand, a marginal increase in resource rents also diminishes the extent to which democratic majorities will tax the non-resource income or wealth of elites and redistribute it through public spending. In other words, resource rents mitigate the threat of redistribution of non-resource wealth and thereby decrease the incentives of elites to stage coups. In the horse race between the two competing effects of resource rents, the mitigation of redistributive conflict is more important when there is high inequality of non-resource income. And, because inequality makes the impact of resources on the critical coup cost less positive (more negative), at high enough levels of non-resource inequality, on the margin resource rents will eventually decrease rather than increase the incidence of coups.

This effect is most easily investigated through numerical calibration of the model. Consider the following concave functions: $V(x) = x^{\frac{1}{2}}$ and $U(x) = x^{\frac{1}{2}}$. Assume that the rich comprise 10 percent of the population ($\delta = 0.1$) and that $R = 1.25$ and $\bar{y} = 3.75$, so that $\frac{R}{R+\bar{y}} = 0.25$. Thus, resource rents comprise 25 percent of total economic output $R + \bar{y}$ (call this sum "GDP"). Figure 3.1, which depicts results of a computer simulation based on these parameter values and functional forms, shows visually how the impact of resources on the incidence of coups varies with the measure of inequality θ. For further discussion of the construction of the simulation, see this book's Appendix.[14]

Notice several key features of Figure 3.1. First, when society is completely equal, so that the share of non-resource income of the rich is equal to their proportion of the population (i.e., $\delta = \theta$), the total derivative $\frac{d\varphi^{H*}}{dR}$ is positive: on the margin, here resource rents *increase* the incidence of coups against democracy. However, when society is completely unequal, so that $\theta = 1$ and the rich have all the non-resource wealth, the total derivative

[14] In conducting the simulation in Figure 3.1 and the figures below, I ignore the constant $\eta = \frac{\beta(1-p)}{(1-\beta)}$ (see equation 3.30). All simulations reported in this chapter were conducted in Mathematica.

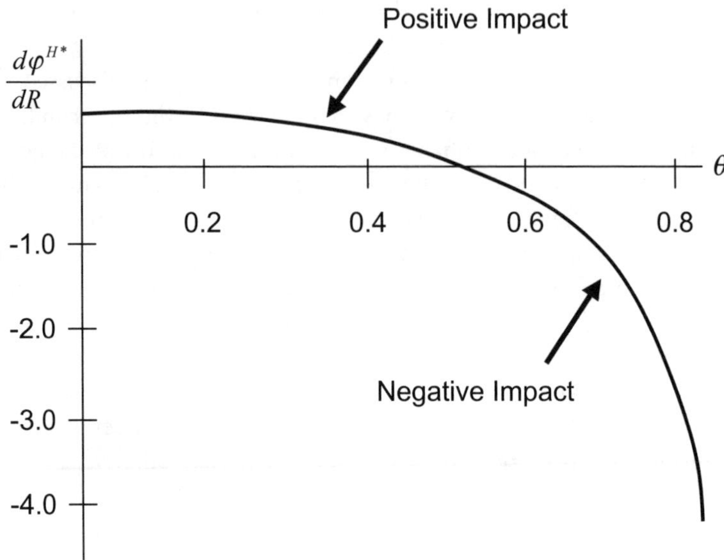

Figure 3.1 The impact of resource rents on the incidence of coups ($\frac{R}{R+\bar{y}} = .25$).

$\frac{d\varphi^{H*}}{dR}$ is negative: then, resource rents decrease the incidence of coups. The threshold value of θ at which the effect of resource rents becomes democratic is not so important, as this will depend on the specific parameter values and assumed functional forms. However, because of the negative sign of the cross-partial derivative in equation (3.32), we will see the same general pattern in all simulations with parameter values and functional forms that are consistent with the assumptions of the model: at lower levels of non-resource inequality, resource rents will tend to have an authoritarian effect, while at higher levels of inequality they will tend to have a democratic effect.

It may be useful to break down the comparative statics suggested by Figure 3.1 into two parts. First, Figure 3.2 plots the "authoritarian" effect of rents (equation 3.27) and the value of the "democratic" effect of rents (the value of the right-hand side of equation 3.28) as a function of the level of resources, holding average income constant as above. In this simulation, inequality is low ($\theta = 0.3$); Figure 3.1 suggests an authoritarian effect of rents in this part of the parameter space. Indeed, in this simulation the authoritarian effect (dashed line) as shown in Figure 3.2, is larger in absolute

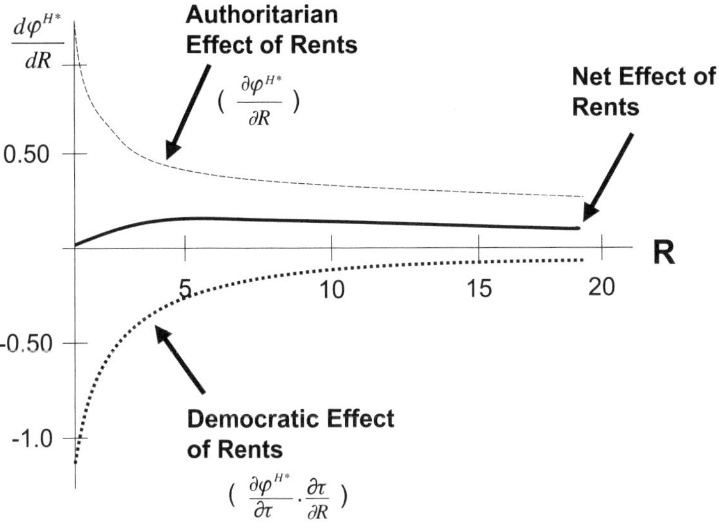

Figure 3.2 A net authoritarian effect of rents: the low inequality case.

value than the democratic effect (dotted line), for all levels of the resource rent. Thus, the net effect is authoritarian.

Note that both of the functions drawn in Figure 3.2 are non-linear in R. In the case of the authoritarian effect, this is because $V'(\cdot)$ has a positive third derivative on the positive real numbers; also τ^r depends on R, and $H(\cdot)$ is non-linear (see equation 3.27). In the case of the democratic effect, $\frac{\partial\tau^p}{\partial R}$ is non-linear in R because of the non-linearities of both $V(\cdot)$ and $H(\cdot)$.

Second, however, Figure 3.3 plots the same simulation but now with high inequality ($\theta = 0.8$). In this part of the parameter space, as Figure 3.1 suggests, there is a net democratic effect of resource rents. Indeed, here the democratic effect of resource rents (dotted line) is larger in absolute value than the authoritarian effect (dashed line) for all levels of the resource rent.

The key idea emphasized by Figures 3.2 and 3.3 is that there are always both authoritarian *and* democratic effects of rents in this model. The core claim, however, is that one or the other effect may dominate, thus engendering net authoritarian or democratic effects, and which effect dominates depends on parameter values such as the level of inequality.

I will subject the hypotheses suggested by Figures 3.1, 3.2, and 3.3 to empirical scrutiny below. However, it is worth underscoring two points

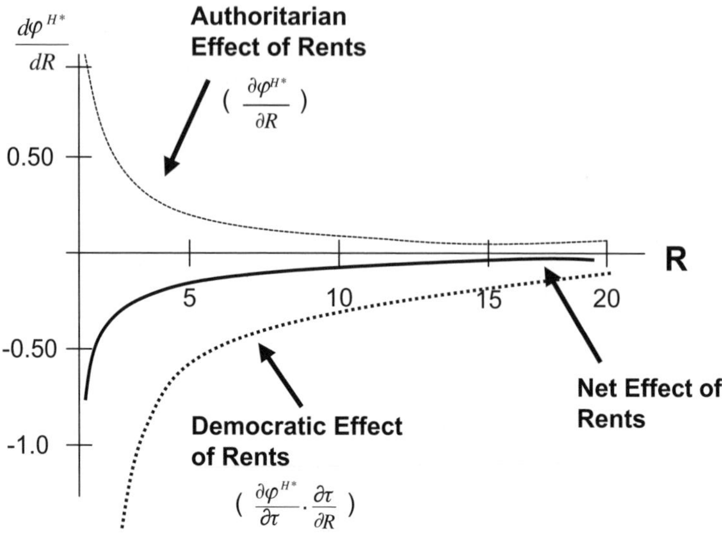

Figure 3.3 A net democratic effect of rents: the high inequality case.

about the result. First, the role played by inequality in this model clearly differs from previous work on resource-rich countries. In the work of Boix (2003), for example, immobile assets like oil and other minerals—which are assumed to be owned by the rich—are easier to tax than other kinds of assets and therefore create incentives for elites to resist the introduction of democracy. Fearon (2005) also suggests that oil may influence political outcomes such as civil war by increasing inequality. It is therefore important to be clear about the interpretation of the measure of inequality in this model: the parameter θ is a measure of the share of private, *non-resource* income that accrues to the rich. In particular, it is independent of R, the level of the resource rent. Moreover, unlike the model developed by Boix, in this model natural resources have a *negative* relationship to taxation, consistent with the empirical literature on the rentier state; this drives the main difference between his results and the results presented here. Second, although the parameter θ has a clear and precise interpretation in the model—conceptually, it should perhaps be thought of as pre-tax and pre-transfer inequality—operationalizing this variable for purposes of empirical testing will raise important measurement issues, as I will discuss further in the next section.

The Role of Resource Dependence This analysis of the horse race between the authoritarian and democratic effects of resource rents leads to

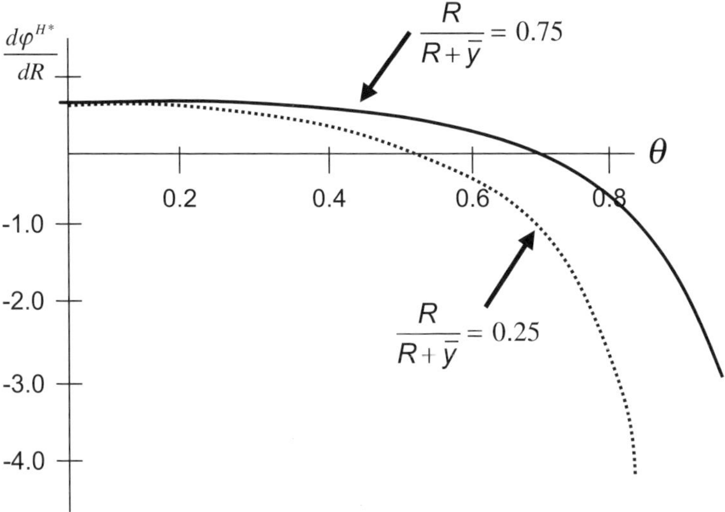

Figure 3.4 Rents and coups: the role of resource dependence.

an additional conjecture: the ratio of resource rents to the total size of the economy—namely, the extent of economic dependence on natural resources—may be expected to play an important role in determining which effect is predominant. For instance, when resource rents comprise a greater proportion of economic activity—that is, when capturing resource rents is the major economic "game in town," as is plausibly the case in many countries of the Persian Gulf and some African states—the direct, authoritarian effect of resource rents may become relatively more important. In resource-dependent countries, though rents may continue to mitigate redistributive conflict over non-resource wealth and thereby reduce incentives to stage coups against democracy, this indirect, democratic effect of rents is less important: the distribution of income or wealth in non-resource sectors of the economy plays a lesser role in shaping the economic incentives of political actors. The overall marginal effect of resources may therefore be to promote authoritarianism to a greater extent than in less resource-dependent (but still resource-rich) countries.

Simulation results support the idea that the extent of resource dependence mediates the relationship between resource rents and the political regime. Figure 3.4 depicts results of a simulation similar to that above but now assuming greater resource dependence. As in the simulations depicted in Figure 3.1, the sum of resource rents R and total private income $\bar{y}$—that is, "GDP"—is held constant at 5 and functional form assumptions are as above. Now, however, $R = 3.75$ and $\bar{y} = 1.25$, so $\frac{R}{R+\bar{y}} = 0.75$ and thus R is 75 percent of GDP. As above, inequality is the share of private income of the richest 10 percent.

The solid line traces the marginal impact of resource rents on the critical coup cost as a function of non-resource inequality, given that resource rents now constitute 75 percent of GDP; results from Figure 3.1 are included for purposes of comparison (dotted line). Comparing the solid and dotted lines, the simulations suggest that when resource dependence is higher, a marginal increase in resource rents decreases the incidence of coups against democracy only at higher levels of non-resource inequality. In other words, resource dependence widens the part of the parameter space over which the authoritarian effect takes place.

This result suggests a plausible reinterpretation of previous evidence presented in support of an authoritarian "resource curse." In the leading empirical studies, typical measures of the independent variable are not measures of resource wealth per se but are in fact measures of resource dependence: for example, the ratio of fuel or non-fuel mineral exports to GDP (Ross 2001), or the fuel export share (Barro 1999). Yet, because such measures tap the size of the resource sector relative to the non-resource economy rather than the size of the resource sector per se, they may overstate the authoritarian impact of resource rents. For example, in the paradigmatic authoritarian rentier states—such as many countries of the Persian Gulf, where oil rents may reach well upwards of 70 percent of GDP—resource dependence is pronounced. Yet resource dependence is much less substantial in many resource-rich democracies, such as Venezuela, where oil rent is typically around 20–25 percent of GDP (Baptista 1997), or even the United States, Canada, or Norway. The simulation results in Figure 3.4 may therefore suggest one way to reconcile the empirical evidence of a robust relationship between resource dependence and authoritarianism with the observation that democracy has flourished in resource-rich countries that, despite high levels of resource wealth per capita, are less resource dependent. I will subject this hypothesis to empirical scrutiny in the next chapter (see also Dunning 2006).

3.2 A Model of Democratization

The game of coups developed above suggests that the anticipated economic costs of democracy play an important role in shaping the incentives of elites to stage coups against democracy. Resource rents enter the picture in two ways. On the one hand, resource rents increase the opportunity cost of foregoing a coup, because a coup implies control over the distribution of the rents. On the other hand, rents also decrease the cost of democracy that stems from the potential for redistribution of non-resource income. In this way there are both authoritarian and democratic effects of rents.

The fact that I analyzed a game of coups against democracy in the section above might seem to suggest that the argument developed here applies only to existing democracies. As discussed previously, however, this is not the case. Indeed, similar strategic calculations may well shape the incentives of incumbent elites in authoritarian regimes, who, faced with mobilization and a threat "from below," consider democratization from among their menu of political options. How resource booms may shape the *anticipated* costs of democracy to elites—for instance, the allocation of resource rents under democracy, or the degree of redistributive taxation—is a key question to consider. The analysis therefore has implications for the potential for democratization in resource-rich authoritarian regimes as well.

In this section, I develop a simple game of democratization in which the goal is to analyze the impact of resource rents on the incentives of authoritarian incumbent elites to democratize. The setting is similar to the game of coups against democracy developed above: the relevant actors, their utility functions, the government budget constraint, and the technologies for raising tax revenues and for converting revenues into public spending are all as above. I therefore move directly to a discussion of the timing of the game.

3.2.1 Timing of Democratization Game

In any authoritarian period, the stage game has the following timing:

- **(A1)** Nature determines the realization of a random variable $\mu_t \in \{\mu^L, \mu^H\}$, which is observed by both groups. The transition probability that $\mu = \mu^H$ is q, while the corresponding probability that $\mu = \mu^L$ is $(1 - q)$. This distribution is stationary across periods.
- **(A2)** The rich, who are in power, decide whether to repress the poor, at a cost of repression ξ. If the rich repress the poor, they make an allocation decision $\tilde{\lambda}_t^A \in [0, 1]$ and set a tax rate, $\tilde{\tau}_t^A \in [0, 1]$, utilities are realized, and the period ends. The next period then begins under an authoritarian regime.

- **(A3)** If the rich do not choose to repress the poor in (A2), the rich then have two choices:
  - **(i)** They can make an allocation decision $\tilde{\lambda}^A \in [0, 1]$ and set a tax rate, $\tilde{\tau}_t^A \in [0, 1]$.
  - **(ii)** They can instead democratize, which gives political power to the poor in the current period. If the rich democratize, the poor make an allocation decision $\tilde{\lambda}^D \in [0, 1]$ and set a tax rate, $\tilde{\tau}_t^D \in [0, 1]$, utilities are realized, and the next period of the game begins under democracy.
- **(A4)** If the rich did not democratize or repress the poor but instead chose to make an allocation decision $\tilde{\lambda}^A$ and set a tax rate, $\tilde{\tau}_t^A$ as in (A3)(i), then the poor decide whether to mount a revolution.
  - **(i)** If the poor revolt, they control political power for the rest of the infinite-horizon game, and they set the tax rate in the current and every future period.[15] However, revolution also carries a cost μ_t, as described below.
  - **(ii)** If the poor do not revolt, the tax rate $\tilde{\tau}_t^A$ set in (A3)(i) is implemented, utilities are realized, and the game moves to the next period under an authoritarian regime.

In any democratic period, the stage game has the following timing:

(D1) The poor make an allocation decision $\lambda_t^D \in [0, 1]$ and set a tax rate $\hat{\tau}_D \in [0, 1]$, instantaneous utilities are realized, and the period ends. The next period begins with a democratic regime.

In any authoritarian period, the action set of the poor is either null (if the rich have repressed) or consists of a revolution decision $\eta : \{\mu^L, \mu^H\} \times [0, 1] \times [0, 1] \longrightarrow \{0, 1\}$, with $\eta = 1$ indicating a revolution; the action set of the rich consists of a repression decision $\zeta : \{\mu^L, \mu^H\} \times [0, 1] \times [0, 1] \longrightarrow \{0, 1\}$, with $\zeta = 1$ indicating repression, an allocation-cum-tax rate $(\tilde{\lambda}^A, \tilde{\tau}^A)$, and a democratization decision, $\psi : \{\mu^L, \mu^H\} \times [0, 1] \times [0, 1] \longrightarrow \{0, 1\}$, with $\psi = 1$ indicating democratization. In any democratic period, the action set of the poor consists of an allocation decision $\tilde{\lambda}^D : \{D\} \longrightarrow [0, 1]$ and a tax rate $\tilde{\tau}^D : \{D\} \longrightarrow [0, 1]$, that is, a mapping from the current democratic state to a policy pair. A strategy profile for the

[15] As with the coups in the game above, one might instead assume that revolutions succeed only probabilistically. This would not greatly alter the strategic dynamics of principal interest, however, and the impact of resource rents on the emergence of democracy would be similar in such a richer model.

poor is then defined as $\sigma^p\{\eta(\cdot), \tilde{\lambda}^D(\cdot), \tilde{\tau}^D(\cdot)\}$, while a strategy profile for the rich is defined as $\sigma^r\{\zeta(\cdot), \tilde{\lambda}^A(\cdot), \tilde{\tau}^A(\cdot), \psi(\cdot)\}$. A Markov-perfect equilibrium of this democratization game is a strategy combination, $\{\tilde{\sigma}^p, \tilde{\sigma}^r\}$, such that $\tilde{\sigma}^p$ and $\tilde{\sigma}^r$ are mutual best-responses for all states.

3.2.2 *Analysis*

To characterize the equilibria of this democratization game, it is necessary to write down the payoffs to the elites and the masses under authoritarianism, under democracy, and after a revolution. The latter two payoffs are easiest to define, because both democracy and revolution are absorbing states in this model. I begin by defining the value functions of the rich and poor after a revolution.

The payoff of revolution to the poor will simply be

$$U^p(R, \mu; \tilde{\lambda}^R, \tilde{\tau}^R) = \frac{(1-\tau^p)y^p + V(H(\tau^p\bar{y}) + R) - \mu}{1-\beta}, \tag{3.33}$$

where $\tilde{\lambda}^R$ and $\tilde{\tau}^R$ are the policies set by the poor after the revolution. These policies, of course, will be $\tilde{\lambda}^R = \lambda^p$ and $\tilde{\tau}^R = \tau^p$, as the poor are (in this simple model where democracy is an absorbing state) unconstrained by the threat of a coup.[16] Equation (3.33) expresses the payoff to the poor when the poor set their unconstrained ideal policy in each period forever, net of the cost of revolution, which is $\mu \in \{\mu^L, \mu^H\}$. The value of μ depends on the current state in the period in which revolution takes place; I assume that $\mu^L \to \infty$, so that, as in the case of coups, revolution will only be possible in some periods of the game. Note that by equation (3.33), revolution is costly not just today but also in future periods. The idea is that although revolution allows the poor to set policy as they like for the rest of the game, it also destroys a part of economic output permanently (perhaps by encouraging economic flight by the rich).

For the rich, revolution is assumed to be the costliest possible outcome because after a revolution they no longer exert any influence over policy.[17]

[16] Again, as discussed above, it is conceptually simple to build a fully dynamic game in which a coup may occur after democratization, and redemocratization after a coup; see Acemoglu and Robinson (2001, 2006a) or Dunning (2006) for examples. However, developing the fully dynamic game comes at the cost of significant algebraic complexity and perhaps little in the way of added intuitions for the particular substantive issues analyzed in this book.

[17] It seems reasonable to assume that revolution is the costliest outcome for the rich. As will be clear below, this will imply that revolution is also off the equilibrium path in this model: it is the *threat* of revolution that will induce a change in the policies adopted by the rich.

To model this idea, the payoff to the rich of revolution is normalized to zero, that is,

$$U^r(R, \mu) = 0. \tag{3.34}$$

Next, it is necessary to characterize the payoffs of each group under a democratic regime. Because democracy is an absorbing state in this model, and because the poor set policy in every democratic period, it will clearly be optimal for the poor group to adopt its ideal policy pair (λ^p, τ^p). The payoffs to each group under democracy are therefore

$$U^r(D; \tilde{\lambda}^D, \tilde{\tau}^D) = \frac{(1-\tau^p)y^r}{1-\beta} \tag{3.35}$$

and

$$U^p(D; \tilde{\lambda}^D, \tilde{\tau}^D) = \frac{(1-\tau^p)y^p + V(H(\tau^p\bar{y}) + R)}{1-\beta} \tag{3.36}$$

for the rich and poor groups, respectively.

Now, in order to begin to characterize the incentives of the rich and the poor under authoritarianism, it is necessary to know the condition under which a revolutionary threat will constrain the tax policy adopted by the rich. Let $\tilde{\lambda}^A$ and $\tilde{\tau}^A$ be the allocation and tax rate chosen by the rich in any stage game under authoritarianism, and suppose that the rich set $\tilde{\lambda}^A = \lambda^r$ and $\tilde{\tau}^A = \tau^r$ in every period, whether the state is high or low. Then the value function of the poor in a period in which the state is "high" will be

$$U^p(A, \mu^H; \tilde{\lambda}^A = \lambda^r, \tilde{\tau}^A = \tau^r) = \frac{(1-\tau^r)y^p}{1-\beta}. \tag{3.37}$$

The *revolution constraint* will bind in the state μ^H when

$$U^p(R, \mu^H; \tilde{\lambda}^R, \tilde{\tau}^R) > U^p(A, \mu^H, \tilde{\tau}^A = \tau^r) \tag{3.38}$$

or, using equation (3.33),

$$\mu^H < (1-\tau^p)y^p + V(H(\tau^p\bar{y}) + R) - (1-\tau^r)y^p. \tag{3.39}$$

If the inequality in (3.39) holds, the rich may want to avoid a revolution if possible by choosing an allocation $\tilde{\lambda}^A \in [0, 1)$ or a tax rate $\tilde{\tau}^A \in (\tau^r, \tau^p]$, that is, by offering an allocation and/or a tax rate that is better for the poor than the ideal policy pair of the rich. Averting a revolution through such policy moderation will clearly be optimal for the rich, as the payoff to revolution is normalized to zero, and continued authoritarianism will allow the rich to set their ideal policy pair in every period in which the realization of μ is μ^L.

A key question is therefore whether the rich will be *able* to avoid a revolution simply by offering an allocation $\tilde{\lambda}^A \in [0, 1)$ or a tax rate $\tilde{\tau}^A \in (\tau^r, \tau^p]$. To answer this question, suppose that the state is "high" and the rich set $\tilde{\lambda}^A = \lambda^p$ and $\tilde{\tau}^A = \tau^p$; that is, policy is set at the ideal point of the poor. Clearly, in any Markovian equilibrium the rich will always set $\tilde{\lambda}^A = \lambda^r$ and $\tilde{\tau}^A = \tau^r$ whenever $\mu = \mu^L$, as in such periods the poor cannot mount a credible revolutionary threat, so it will be optimal for the rich to set policy at their ideal point. Let $U^p(A, \mu^H, \tilde{\lambda}^A = \lambda^p, \tilde{\tau}^A = \tau^p)$ be the continuation value of authoritarianism to the poor, given that the rich follow this strategy. Then whenever $\mu = \mu^H$, the poor will be indifferent between a revolution and accepting the offer $(\tilde{\lambda}^A = \lambda^p, \tilde{\tau}^A = \tau^p)$ at the *critical revolution cost* μ^{H*} such that $U^p(A, \mu^{H*}; \tilde{\lambda}^A = \lambda^p, \tilde{\tau}^A = \tau^p) = U^p(R, \mu^{H*})$.

The latter term is given by equation (3.33) with $\mu = \mu^{H*}$. Note, however, that $U^p(A, \mu^H; \tilde{\lambda}^A = \lambda^p, \tilde{\tau}^A = \tau^p)$ is not the same as equation (3.37) because now, in every period in which $\mu = \mu^H$, the rich will set $\tilde{\lambda}^A = \lambda^p$ and $\tilde{\tau}^A = \tau^p$. Thus, in order to define the critical revolution cost, we must develop an expression for $U^p(A, \mu^H; \tilde{\lambda}^A = \lambda^p, \tilde{\tau}^A = \tau^p)$. This expression is

$$\begin{aligned} U^p(A, \mu^H; \tilde{\lambda}^A = \lambda^p, \tilde{\tau}^A = \tau^p) = {} & (1 - \tau^p)y^p + V(H(\tau^p \bar{y}) + R) \\ & + \beta[q U^p(A, \mu^H; \tilde{\lambda}^A = \lambda^p, \tilde{\tau}^A = \tau^p) \\ & + (1 - q)U^p(A, \mu^L; \lambda^p, \tau)^r], \qquad (3.40) \end{aligned}$$

where the first set of terms on the right-hand side of the equation gives the instantaneous utility of the poor at the allocation λ^p and the tax rate τ^p and the second set of terms defines the continuation values to the poor of continuing to live under an authoritarian regime. The payoff to the poor in a low period is defined analogously as

$$\begin{aligned} U^p(A, \mu^L; \lambda^r, \tau^r) = {} & (1 - \tau^r)y^p + \beta[q U^p(A, \mu^H; \tilde{\lambda}^A = \lambda^p, \tilde{\tau}^A = \tau^p) \\ & + (1 - q)U^p(A, \mu^L; \lambda^r, \tau^r)]. \qquad (3.41) \end{aligned}$$

Equations (3.40) and (3.41) constitute a system of two linear equations in the two unknowns $U^p(A, \mu^H; \tilde{\lambda}^A = \lambda^p, \tilde{\tau}^A = \tau^p)$ and $U^p(A, \mu^L; \lambda^p, \tilde{\tau}^A = \tau^r)$. One can solve for $U^p(A, \mu^L; \lambda^p, \tau^r)$ in equation (3.41) and substitute this expression into equation (3.40) to obtain an explicit expression for $U^p(A, \mu^H; \tilde{\lambda}^A = \lambda^p, \tilde{\tau}^A = \tau^p)$. Equating this explicit expression to equation (3.33) with $\mu = \mu^{H*}$ defines the critical revolution cost,

$$\mu^{H*} = \beta(1 - q)[(1 - \tau^p)y^p + V(H(\tau^p \bar{y}) + R) - (1 - \tau^r)y^p]. \qquad (3.42)$$

This is just the difference between the utility of the poor at the policy pairs (λ^p, τ^p) and (λ^r, τ^r), multiplied by the (discounted) probability $(1 - q)$ that there is no revolutionary threat tomorrow and the rich can therefore set $\tilde{\lambda}^A = \lambda^r$ and $\tilde{\tau}^A = \tau^r$. Note that for any $\mu^H < \mu^{H*}$, the rich will be unable to avoid a revolution through an allocation $\tilde{\lambda}^A = \lambda^p$ and temporary redistribution at the tax rate $\tilde{\tau}^A = \tau^p$ in the state μ^H. Suppose that $\mu^H < \mu^{H*}$, so that the rich cannot avoid a revolution by changing spending and tax policy. Clearly, the rich would prefer to democratize rather than incur a revolution (because the payoff to revolution is here normalized to zero). The interesting question in this model is whether, given a cost of revolution less than the critical revolution cost ($\mu^H < \mu^{H*}$), the rich will prefer to repress the poor or to democratize. Analogous to the analysis above of coups against democracy, I will derive a critical repression cost at which elites will be indifferent between repression and democratization. I can then investigate how resource rents influence this threshold in the model.

Note that repression allows the rich to set $\tilde{\tau}^A = \tau^r$ in every period, whether the state is high or low, but it carries a cost of ζ in periods in which the state is high. Thus, the payoff to the rich of following a strategy in which they repress the poor in every period in which the realization of μ is μ^H is given by

$$\begin{aligned} U^r(O, \mu^H; \zeta, \lambda^r, \tau^r) = {} & (1 - \tau^r)y^r + V(H(\tau^r \bar{y}) + R) - \zeta \\ & + \beta[q U^r(O, \mu^H; \zeta, \lambda^r, \tau^r) \\ & + (1 - q)U^r(O, \mu^L; \lambda^r, \tau^r)], \end{aligned} \qquad (3.43)$$

where the notation "O" stands for "oppression" (since I already used "R" for revolution). What is the interpretation of equation (3.43)? As with the other Bellman equations, the first term captures the instantaneous utility, here the utility of the rich evaluated at τ^r, net of the cost of repression. The final terms capture the continuation value to the rich. With probability q, the state tomorrow is also μ^H, and the revolution constraint will bind tomorrow as well. Now, if the rich found it optimal to repress in a Markovian equilibrium today, they will find it optimal tomorrow. However, with probability $(1 - q)$, the state tomorrow is μ^L, and the poor cannot threaten a revolution. The rich will not pay the repression cost ζ in this case, yet they will set $\tilde{\lambda}^A = \lambda^r$ and $\tilde{\tau}^A = \tau^r$. Thus, the continuation value in the low state will be

$$\begin{aligned} U^r(O, \mu^L; \lambda^r, \tau^r) = (1 - \tau^r)y^r + V(H(\tau^r \bar{y}) + R) \\ + \beta[q U^r(O, \mu^H; \zeta, \lambda^r, \tau^r) \\ + (1 - q)U^r(O, \mu^L; \lambda^r, \tau^r)]. \end{aligned} \tag{3.44}$$

I can then solve for $U^r(O, \mu^H; \zeta, \lambda^r, \tau^r)$ by substitution:

$$U^r(O, \mu^H; \zeta, \lambda^r, \tau^r) = \frac{(1 - \tau^r)y^r + V(H(\tau^r \bar{y}) + R) - (1 - \beta(1 - q))\zeta}{1 - \beta}. \tag{3.45}$$

The interpretation of this expression is as follows. Because the elite are here following a strategy of always repressing when faced with a threat of revolution from the poor, they set their preferred tax policy in any period (whether $\mu = \mu^H$ or $\mu = \mu^L$). However, they will only need to pay the repression cost ζ in periods in which $\mu = \mu^H$, which occurs with probability q. So the present discounted value of playing the repressive strategy in any high period is not the payoff to imposing τ^r minus the repression cost ζ, divided by $1 - \beta$, but rather the payoff to imposing τ^r minus the smaller quantity $(1 - \beta(1 - q))\zeta$, divided by $1 - \beta$. That the numerator is larger than the payoff to τ^r minus the repression cost stems from the fact that the rich will not have to pay the repression cost in all periods. Note that as $q \to 1$, so that the rich pay this cost in nearly all future periods (in expectation), the numerator of equation (3.45) simply approaches the payoff to imposing τ^r minus the repression cost ζ.

Using equations (3.35) and (3.45), the repression cost at which elites are indifferent between repression and democratization can now be defined. Equating (3.35) and (3.45) and rearranging gives

$$\zeta^* = \frac{(1 - \tau^r)y^r + V(H(\tau^r \bar{y}) + R) - [(1 - \tau^p)y^r]}{(1 - \beta(1 - q))}. \tag{3.46}$$

Whenever $\mu^H < \mu^{H*}$, elites cannot prevent a revolution even by setting policy at the ideal policy pair of the masses. Thus, elites will choose between repression and democratization (as revolution represents the worst possible outcome from the point of view of elites). This analysis shows that given a "high" state, elites democratize for any repression cost greater than the critical repression threshold; that is, when the state is μ^H, elites will democratize for any $\zeta > \zeta^*$. Thus, any factor that tends to *decrease* the critical repression threshold ζ^* will *increase* the incidence of democratization in the model.

At this point in the analysis, all the elements necessary to investigate the equilibrium impact of resource rents on democratization are in place. Note, however, that in the part of the parameter space in which the revolution constraint binds but $\mu^H \geq \mu^{H*}$, elites can avert a revolution through policy moderation, rather than regime change—but they may prefer to repress the masses rather than engage in policy moderation such as temporary redistribution. For the sake of completely specifying equilibrium strategies and outcomes of the game, it is necessary to consider the behavior of elites in this part of the parameter space.

Suppose that elites propose an allocation $\tilde{\lambda}^A \in [0, 1)$ and a tax rate $\tilde{\tau}^A \in (\tau^r, \tau^p]$. What is the value function of the masses in the high state, given that elites propose this spending-allocation-cum-tax-rate in every high state (and set $\tilde{\lambda}^A = \lambda^r$ and $\tilde{\tau}^A = \tau^r$ in every low state, as no other policy pair can be optimal for the elite in that state)? Using equation (3.41) to solve explicitly for this value function $U^p(A, \mu^H; \tilde{\lambda}^A, \tilde{\tau}^A)$, and equating it to the payoff to the poor of revolution (given in equation (3.33) with $\mu = \mu^H$) gives the revolution cost at which the poor are just indifferent between accepting $(\tilde{\lambda}^A, \tilde{\tau}^A)$ and revolting (in which case it is assumed that they do not revolt). This critical value is

$$\begin{aligned}\hat{\mu}^H = {} & [(1 - \tau^p)y^p + V(H(\tau^p \bar{y}) + R)] \\ & - [1 - \beta(1 - q)][(1 - \tilde{\tau}^A)y^p + V(\tilde{\lambda}^A((H(\tilde{\tau}^A \bar{y}) + R)] \\ & - [\beta(1 - q)][(1 - \tau^r)y^p]. \end{aligned} \tag{3.47}$$

Some algebra shows easily that $\hat{\mu}^H$ is less than the value of μ^H given in equation (3.39) at which the revolution constraint binds, but it is greater than or equal to the critical revolution cost μ^{H*} given in equation (3.42). This is quite obvious, as μ^{H*} is defined as the cost of revolution at which the masses are just indifferent between revolting and not when they are offered their ideal point in every "high" state; for them to be indifferent between revolting and not when offered something less than their ideal point, it must be the case that revolutions are relatively costly, so $\hat{\mu}^H \geq \mu^{H*}$. (Of course, when $\tilde{\lambda}^A = \lambda^p$ and $\tilde{\tau}^A = \tau^p$, $\mu^H = \mu^{H*}$; this is by definition of μ^{H*}.)

The question that remains to be analyzed is whether elites will *want* to avert a revolution by proposing an allocation $\tilde{\lambda}^A \in [0, 1)$ and a tax rate $\tilde{\tau}^A \in (\tau^r, \tau^p]$ such that equation (3.48) holds with equality. Elites might instead prefer to repress the masses, if repression is cheap enough. The payoff to elites of offering a policy pair $(\tilde{\lambda}^A, \tilde{\tau}^A)$, given $\mu = \mu^H$, is

$$U^r(A, \mu^H; \tilde{\lambda}^A, \tilde{\tau}^A) = (1 - \tilde{\tau}^A)y^r + V(\tilde{\lambda}^A[H(\tilde{\tau}^A\bar{y}) + R]) \\ + \beta[qU^r(A, \mu^H; \tilde{\lambda}^A, \tilde{\tau}^A) \\ + (1 - q)U^r(A, \mu^L; \lambda^r, \tau)^r]. \qquad (3.48)$$

It is straightforward to develop a second Bellman equation for $U^r(A, \mu^L; \lambda^r, \tau)^r)$, solve explicitly for $U^r(A, \mu^L; \lambda^r, \tau)^r)$, and plug this expression into equation (3.48); doing so and rearranging terms gives

$$U^r(A, \mu^H; \tilde{\lambda}^A, \tilde{\tau}^A) = [1 - \beta(1 - q)][(1 - \tilde{\tau}^A)y^r + V(\tilde{\lambda}^A[H(\tilde{\tau}^A\bar{y}) + R])] \\ + \beta(1 - q)[(1 - \tau^r y^r + V(H(\tau^r\bar{y}) + R)]. \qquad (3.49)$$

Now, equating (3.45) and (3.49) gives the cost of repression ζ at which the rich are indifferent between always repressing and redistributing at the level $(\tilde{\lambda}^A, \tilde{\tau}^A)$ whenever the state is μ^H; call this cost $\hat{\zeta}$. Some algebra shows that

$$\hat{\zeta} = [(1 - \tau^r)y^r + V(H(\tau^r\bar{y}) + R) - (1 - \tilde{\tau}^A)y^r - V(\tilde{\lambda}^A H(\tilde{\tau}^A\bar{y}) + R)]. \qquad (3.50)$$

For any $\zeta \leq \hat{\zeta}$, the rich will prefer to repress the poor in high periods rather than redistribute to the poor at the policy pair $(\tilde{\lambda}^A, \tilde{\tau}^A)$.[18]

A comparison of equations (3.46) and (3.50) shows that $\zeta^* > \hat{\zeta}$. This is intuitive: ζ^* gives the repression cost at which elites are indifferent between democratizing or repressing in all authoritarian periods, while $\hat{\zeta}$ gives the repression cost at which they are indifferent between *temporarily* redistributing at the rate $(\tilde{\lambda}^A, \tilde{\tau}^A)$—when faced with a revolutionary threat in high periods—and repressing. Because the latter strategy allows elites to retain political power (and to set policy at their ideal point whenever $\mu = \mu^L$), it is natural that the critical repression cost should be relatively cheap in the latter case. Put differently, for elites to be indifferent between *democratizing* and repressing, repression must be relatively expensive; otherwise, elites would prefer to repress rather than to permanently give up political power.

[18] Of course, the policy pair $(\tilde{\lambda}^A, \tilde{\tau}^A)$ at which equation (3.50) holds will not in general be unique: the elite could raise taxes or spend more on the poor in order to neutralize the threat of revolution. For purposes of characterizing the equilibrium outcomes of the game and analyzing the impact of resource rents on the equilibrium, however, this is not problematic, for the same reasons as in the model of coups.

We can now characterize the equilibrium outcomes of this democratization game.

Proposition 2 *The unique Markov-perfect equilibrium outcome of the democratization game is as follows:*

(1) If the revolution constraint in equation (3.39) does not bind, or if the revolution constraint binds but $\zeta \leq \zeta^*$ as defined in equation (3.46), society remains authoritarian forever.

(2) If the revolution constraint binds and $\zeta > \zeta^*$, elites democratize in the first period in which $\mu = \mu^H$, and society thereafter remains democratic forever.

As in the game of coups, although the equilibrium outcome is unique, there are various strategies that support the equilibrium. One example of strategies that support this equilibrium is as follows:

The poor: In any authoritarian period, if the revolution constraint in equation (3.39) does not bind, set $\eta = 0$, that is, do not revolt. If the revolution constraint binds but $\mu^H \geq \mu^{H*}$, set $\eta = 0$ (do not revolt) if elites set $(\tilde{\lambda}^A, \tilde{\tau}^A)$ in every high period such that $\mu^H \geq \hat{\mu}^H$; otherwise, revolt ($\eta = 1$) in every "high" period (whenever $\mu = \mu^H$). Finally, if $\mu^H \leq \mu^{H*}$, set $\eta = 1$ in every "high" period. In any democratic period, set $\tilde{\lambda}^D = \lambda^p$ and $\tilde{\tau}^D = \tau^p$.

The rich: In any authoritarian period, if the revolution constraint in equation (3.39) does not bind, set $\tilde{\lambda}^A = \lambda^r$ and $\tilde{\tau}^A = \tau^r$ in all periods. If the revolution constraint binds but $\mu^H \geq \mu^{H*}$, then: (i) if $\zeta \leq \hat{\zeta}$, repress in every "high" period and set $(\tilde{\lambda}^A = \lambda^r)$ and $(\tilde{\tau}^A = \tau^r)$ in every "low" period; (ii) if $\zeta > \hat{\zeta}$, set $(\tilde{\lambda}^A, \tilde{\tau}^A)$ such that (3.48) holds with equality in "high" periods and set $\tilde{\lambda}^A = \lambda^R$ and $\tilde{\tau}^A = \tau^R$ in every "low" period. Finally, if $\mu^H < \mu^{H*}$, then (i) if $\zeta \leq \zeta^*$, set $\tilde{\lambda}^A = \lambda^r$ and $\tilde{\tau}^A = \tau^r$ in every "low" period and repress in every "high" period; (ii) if $\zeta > \zeta^*$, set $\tilde{\lambda}^A = \lambda^r$ and $\tilde{\tau}^A = \tau^r$ in every "low" period and democratize in every "high" period (i.e., choose $\psi = 1$).

3.2.3 Comparative Statics

As in the game of coups, the incidence of democracy in the model will depend crucially on a critical threshold—in this case the critical repression cost ζ^*. Indeed, society will eventually democratize with positive probability (and then, with probability one) if and only if $\mu^H < \mu^{H*}$ in equation (3.42) and $\zeta > \zeta^*$. Note that $\mu^H < \mu^{H*}$ is a necessary but not sufficient condition for democratization in the model. It is necessary because, if $\mu^H \geq \mu^{H*}$, elites will either engage in repression or they will "buy out" the masses through temporary redistributive spending in periods in which $\mu = \mu^H$. However, it is not individually sufficient because if $\mu^H < \mu^{H*}$, it may still be the case that $\zeta \leq \zeta^*$. In this case, elites will prefer to repress rather than democratize, even though they cannot buy out the masses through temporary redistribution. Democratization therefore occurs only when $\zeta > \zeta^*$.

The key question of analytic interest, which is how resource rents influence the incidence of democratization in the model, can therefore be answered by comparative statics analysis on the critical threshold ζ^*. Because democratization occurs when $\zeta > \zeta^*$, any factor that tends to *decrease* ζ^* will widen the part of the parameter space over which democratization takes place. The comparative statics exercise of greatest interest thus involves the derivative of ζ^* with respect to R.

For convenience, I replicate equation (3.46), which gives the critical repression cost:

$$\zeta^* = \frac{(1-\tau^r)y^r + V(H(\tau^r \bar{y}) + R) - [(1-\tau^p)y^r]}{(1-\beta(1-q))}. \tag{3.51}$$

Compare this expression with equation (3.22) in the model of coups against democracy. With respect to expressions that are endogenous to R, the right-hand sides of equations (3.51) and (3.22) are identical—in other words, they will have the same response to changes in R. Indeed, taking derivatives of equation (3.51) with respect to R and applying the envelope theorem gives

$$\frac{\partial \zeta^*}{\partial R} = \eta \left[V'(H(\tau^r \bar{y}) + R) + \frac{\partial \tau^p}{\partial R} y^r \right], \tag{3.52}$$

where here $\eta = \frac{1}{(1-\beta(1-q))}$. As in the model of coups, the first, positive term is an "authoritarian" effect of resource rents: it reflects conflict over the *distribution* of rents themselves. The second, negative term, however, is a "democratic" effect of rents: resource rents drive down the preferred tax rate τ^p of the poor and thereby mitigate the threat of *redistribution* of non-resource income, reducing the incentives of elites to block democratization through repression.

It is intuitive that there should be similar, ambiguous effects of resource rents on the incidence of democracy in this model as in the model of coups. This is because there is a strong symmetry between the incentives of elites in both models. Here, as in the model of coups, authoritarianism allows elites to implement their preferred policy pair with at least some positive probability: namely, in periods when elites are not threatened by mobilization "from below," they can limit redistribution of non-resource wealth and also transfer the resource rent to themselves. Democracy carries an economic cost, both because it allows the masses to target spending away from elites and also because it allows the relatively poor majority to set taxes on non-resource income at levels higher than elites would like. A marginal increase in resource rents has offsetting effects: it increases the opportunity cost of democracy (because of the foregone rent) even as it decreases the redistributive cost to non-resource income. Because elites anticipate these effects as they weigh the costs and benefits of repression, resource rents will have much the same effects (in the model) as they do when elites weigh the costs and benefits of a coup against an existing democracy.

In addition, because equation (3.52) has precisely the same form as the corresponding threshold in the model of coups, the comparative statics with respect to inequality of non-resource income and with respect to resource dependence will go through in this model as well. In other words, the explanation for variation in political outcomes across resource-rich states is *not* merely an explanation for why natural resources may consolidate existing democracies in some places rather than others. It is also a candidate explanation for why some authoritarian, resource-rich countries would be more likely to democratize than others.

3.3 Discussion and Interpretation

Leading studies in political science have argued that resource wealth promotes authoritarianism. This analysis does not contradict these claims. In the models developed in this chapter, resource rents increase the incentives of elites to block democratization or to stage coups against existing democracies. The presence of resource rents increases the payoff to controlling power because the group that holds political power controls the distribution of the rents. The dynamic nature of politics and attendant commitment problems further increase the opportunity cost of staying out of power in a resource-rich country: the group that holds power can appropriate the entirety of the resource rent whenever it is unconstrained by a threat from the out-of-power group, and it is unable credibly to promise otherwise. Thus, conflict over the current and future distribution of rents can increase the incentives of elites to stage coups or block democratization. In line with many arguments about the political effects of resource wealth (see Boix 2003; Bueno de Mesquita et al. 2003: 94–5; Ross 2001), the direct effect of resource wealth in these models is to promote authoritarianism.[19]

Yet, there is also an indirect effect of resource wealth, which is indirect because it works through the effect of resource wealth on the preferred tax rate of the poor. Democracy in these models allows the poor to implement their ideal tax policy, in any period in which they are unconstrained by a threat of a coup from the rich, and this elevates the economic cost of democracy to the rich; the poor majority cannot commit not to redistribute income away from the rich in future periods. Yet, resource rents endogenously moderate the extent to which this poor majority wants to soak the rich by taxing non-resource income. This indirect effect of resource wealth therefore makes democracy less costly for the rich: resources decrease the difference between the utility of the rich at their ideal tax policy and the utility of the rich at the ideal tax policy of the poor. In this sense, the political empowerment of a relatively poor majority is less costly to rich elites in resource-rich societies.

A central contribution of the formal analysis is to identify this democratic effect of resource rents and to investigate the conditions under which it tends to become more important. The democratic effect tends to obtain under two conditions: when the private (non-resource) economy is more inegalitarian, and thus elites capable of mounting a coup against democracy or blocking democratization are most concerned with redistributive pressures; and when the economy is less resource-dependent (i.e., when rents comprise a smaller part of overall economic product). These testable predictions of the model will be put to empirical scrutiny in subsequent chapters.

Several comments about the results and predictions of the model are useful to make in conclusion to this chapter. First, in these models the political consequences of the negative relationship between resource wealth and taxation clearly differ from previous work. As discussed in Chapters One and Two, this negative relationship has been interpreted as a source of authoritarianism in resource-rich societies by other scholars (Ross 2001). For

[19] Scholars have noted a range of mechanisms through which resource rents may promote authoritarianism, from the promotion of an incumbency advantage that causes democratic institutions gradually to erode (Lam and Wantchekon 2004; Wantchekon 2002) to the formation of predatory authoritarian states (Acemoglu and Robinson 2006a; Robinson 1997) to the long literature, discussed above, on the reduced need for rulers to strike "representative bargains" with citizens in resource-rich countries, and the model captures only some of the richness of these mechanisms.

instance, echoing a common view advanced by scholars of the Middle East, Beblawi (1987: 53–4) argues that "with virtually no taxes, citizens are far less demanding in terms of political participation."[20] From the perspective of the models developed here, however, the absence of taxation in resource-rich societies is a central cause of a democratic effect of resource wealth: resource wealth displaces taxation of non-resource income or taxation, but this *reduces* the incentives of elites to stage coups or repress the poor. The political effects of the reduced tax burden in rentier states are ultimately an empirical question, one that I seek to address elsewhere in this book. Yet, the model provides a compelling theoretical reason to think that the conventional wisdom on the role of reduced taxation in driving authoritarianism in resource-rich countries may be wrong, or at least highly incomplete.

Second, as noted above, it is important to underscore that the role played by inequality in this model also differs from previous work on resource-rich countries. For example, in the work of Boix (2003), immobile assets like oil and other minerals—which are assumed to be owned by the rich—are easier to tax than other kinds of assets and therefore create incentives for elites to resist the introduction of democracy. Wantchekon (1999b, 2002) argues that resource abundance increases income inequality and thereby the consolidation of dictatorial regimes. Fearon (2005) also suggests that oil may influence political outcomes such as civil war by increasing inequality. In these accounts, rather than mitigating social conflict, the link between resource rents and inequality heightens the authoritarian or conflict-producing effects of resource wealth.

It is therefore important to be clear on what "inequality" means in the model developed here. The connection between resource wealth and inequality posited by Boix (2003), Wantchekon (1999b, 2002), Fearon (2005), and other authors clearly depends on the *distribution* of the rents: for instance, oil rents are captured by politically powerful elites, and this increases

[20] In a different but related argument, Bueno de Mesquita et al. (2003: 94–5) suggest that in natural-resource rich countries with small "winning coalitions" supporting leaders, "leaders do not have to rely on the economic activity of residents to provide the resources they need to reward their supporters as much as when resources are absent. Without the need to hold in check their desire to appropriate income, leaders dependent on small winning coalitions can attempt to seize all of the pie." Bueno de Mesquita et al. (2003: 94) also note, however, that in *large* winning coalition systems—that is, where leaders must compete for the support of a relatively broad cross-section of society, as in a democracy—"the addition of rents from natural resources enables leaders to provide . . . public goods and cut taxes." The latter is the closest statement I have found in the existing formal literature to the democratic mechanism I emphasize here.

inequality (as in Wantchekon) or creates incentives for elites to hold on to power because oil-based wealth is easily expropriated (as in Boix). In contrast, the concept of inequality as developed here does *not* depend on the distribution of the rents. The parameter θ is a measure of the share of private, *non-resource* income that accrues to the rich; in particular, it is independent of R, the level of the resource rent. Inequality should perhaps be thought of as pre-tax and pre-transfer inequality. This disaggregation of inequality into two components, one based in the resource sector of the economy and the other in non-resource sectors (manufacturing, agriculture, and so on), then allows us to ask and answer questions about the interaction of these two broad sectors of the economy.

This conceptual disaggregation of the sources of inequality—the distribution of resource rents versus the redistribution of non-resource income—implies a different predicted interaction between rents and inequality in shaping the regime type. Unlike the model developed by Boix, here the redistributive pressure on elites under a democratic regime has an inverse relationship to the level of the resource rent, and this drives the main difference between his results and the results presented here. The empirical evidence presented elsewhere in this study suggests that indeed, there is a negative relationship between resource rent and the tax burden. On the other hand, the model is designed to analyze the politics of rentier states, in which resource rents tend to flow directly into the coffers of the state. In other settings, because of the kind of resource being exploited or the structure of ownership in the resource industry, resource rent may flow into private hands without the mediation of the state. The political role of the tin barons in pre-revolutionary Bolivia (*la Rosca*, as the barons were known), discussed in Chapter Six, provides an empirical demonstration: there, the flow of rent directly into the hands of an elite may well have played a different kind of political role. In Chapter Seven, I discuss theoretical questions raised by the role of private resource ownership and propose an extension to the model developed in this chapter.

Over the medium term or the long run, of course, there may be an important relationship between the distribution of rents and private inequality. For example, Chaudhry (1997: 175–7, italics in the original) describes the impact of the oil boom in Saudi Arabia as follows:

> From a context in which private property was not a recognized institution in much of the country, Saudi Arabia had, by the end of the 1970s, one of the most unequal land distributions in the world.... By 1981, through state grants and purchase, 82 percent of private land was held by 16.2 percent of the *landowning* population ... by

> the end of the 1980s the government owned virtually no land. A key property right had been allocated.... [In] an attempt to buy support, as the main recipients of the land grants were large merchants, influential officials, heads of tribes, and so on.

There thus may be important feedback from resource booms to private inequality. Nonetheless, drawing the distinction between resources and private wealth or income, as in the models of this chapter (where R is independent of private income $\bar{y}$), is useful. For example, one implication of my argument would be that to the extent a landed elite with significant non-resource economic interests was created in the wake of the Saudi oil boom of the 1970s, as Chaudhry argues, a new resource boom would make Saudi Arabia somewhat more likely to democratize today than it would have been in the 1970s.

One other point about inequality might be raised as well. The models in this chapter, and the argument in the book more generally, tend to elide inequality of wealth and income in the non-resource sectors. The idea is that democracies may put some measure of redistributive pressure on both the wealth and the income of elites, and both kinds of redistributive pressure may raise the economic cost of democracy to elites. Yet assets and income differ; and it is at least possible that elites react differently to the redistribution of wealth (asset stocks, property) and the redistribution of income (taxation on the flow). For instance, redistribution of wealth in some contexts—for example, land reforms in Latin America—might threaten elites' very status as elites, while taxation of income might not. A richer model might consider these issues. Still, the substantive bet here is that the qualitative tendencies of redistributive pressures on wealth and income will be similar, even if redistribution of wealth raises a greater degree of resistance on the part of elites.[21]

Third, it may be useful to say something further here about resource dependence. In the thought experiments afforded by the models of this chapter, I asked how the marginal impact of an increase in resource rents depends on the extent of "resource dependence," or the ratio of resource wealth to overall GDP. As discussed above, the effect of resource rents on the regime type may be conditional on resource dependence: in the simulations, resource dependence widens the part of the parameter space over which the authoritarian effect of rents takes place (see Figure 3.4).

[21] In the empirical work in Chapter Four, the measure of inequality is largely a measure of income inequality: payments to capital owners of manufacturing value-added as a proportion of total manufacturing value-added.

In these simulations, however, the question regards the impact of a resource boom, leaving fixed the level of private income. In reality, there may be feedback from resource booms to the level of private income, as the literature on the economic resource curse would suggest (Isham et al. 2003; Karl 1997; Sachs and Warner 1995). One mechanism may be the celebrated Dutch Disease: appreciation of the real exchange rate during a resource boom may cripple other tradeable sectors, such as agriculture or other sectors. At least over the medium term, a rise in resource wealth may affect the extent of resource dependence not just because it raises R but also because it lowers $\bar{y}$; if natural resource booms cripple the non-resource tradeable sectors, as Dutch Disease arguments suggest, then natural resource wealth may lead to natural resource dependence, augmenting the authoritarian effects of rents. On the other hand, resource booms might also promote economic development under other circumstances (see Herb 2005; Schrank 2004), setting up a virtuous cycle as resource dependence is lessened; then resources might produce a democratization effect for standard modernization reasons.[22] The feedback effects may therefore cut both ways: resource booms may lead to resource dependence, augmenting the authoritarian effects of rents, yet they might also promote non-resource economic development, thereby enhancing the democratic effects of rents.

The wager here is that such feedback mechanisms are somewhat second-order concerns; they do not belie the utility of the analytic approach taken in this chapter. If resource booms lead to resource dependence through the additional channels suggested in the previous paragraph, this may simply heighten the authoritarian effects of resource rents; in terms of the model, the part of the parameter space over which the authoritarian effect takes place may simply be wider. Yet, the underlying comparative statics of the model will be similar; there will be both democratic and authoritarian effects of rents. These issues are discussed further in Chapter Seven.

Finally, it is worth underscoring that in these models, taxation is not targeted at groups; there is a single proportional tax rate and a lump-sum transfer. Why, hypothetically, might the poor under democracy not only appropriate distributional control over resource rents but also tax the rich as much as they would under democracy in a resource-poor country? For instance, with no distortionary costs to taxation, the relatively poor median voter might set the tax rate at unity, with or without resource rents. Because

[22] It is clearly not the case empirically that all resource-rich countries become highly resource-dependent over time: witness the United States, Canada, the United Kingdom, or Australia.

the negative relationship between rents and taxation is a crucial part of the argument here, this question is important to consider. There are at least two reasons this constitutes less of a concern than it otherwise might. First, as long as there are some output or investment elasticity effects of taxing private income (captured by the function H in the models above), relative to the effects of capturing rent, the negative relationship between rents and taxation of elites persists; and, for reasons discussed earlier, it seems reasonable to assume that taxation of non-resource income will be more costly than capturing rents. Even with targeted taxation, the results remain robust. A second reason is empirical: as the evidence reviewed in Chapter Two and elsewhere suggests, there does appear to be a negative relationship between resource rents and the tax rate. Even if the models developed in this chapter do not capture the precise mechanism through which this effect occurs (i.e., it could stem from output or investment elasticities, tax evasion effects, or other sources), the models may remain valid for assessing the political effects of this negative relationship between rents and taxes—and that is the key analytic payoff of developing the models.

The next three chapters of this study turn to the empirical evidence. Two central issues will demand attention. First, is there evidence for a general democratic effect of resource wealth, and is the variation in political outcomes across resource-rich countries consistent with the hypotheses developed in this chapter? In Chapter Four, I turn to the statistical analysis of cross-section time-series data on a global estimation sample to help provide answers to these questions. A second and equally vital question is whether the theoretical framework developed in this chapter helps to capture the *mechanisms* through which resource rents can promote democracy. Although the statistical analysis of Chapter Four helps to some extent (by assessing the extent to which observed variation across resource-rich countries is consistent with the claims advanced here), the primary purpose of turning to extended analyses of the Venezuelan case (in Chapter Five) and briefer analyses of Chile, Bolivia, Ecuador, and Botswana (in Chapter Six) is to probe the extent to which "causal-process observations" (Collier et al. 2004) support the mechanism that produces the democratic effect of resource rents in the model. I discuss issues of case selection further in those chapters.

4

Statistical Tests on Rents and the Regime

Do oil and other natural resources promote democracy? The compelling evidence presented in recent cross-national quantitative studies suggests not (Boix 2003; Jensen and Wantchekon 2004; Ross 2001). The positive and apparently robust empirical association between natural-resource wealth (actually, as I emphasize below, resource *dependence*) and authoritarianism, documented by previous studies, may seem to falsify the claim that oil or natural resources can have a democratizing effect. It is therefore crucial to evaluate the theoretical claims advanced in this study through analysis of the available cross-national data. I turn in this chapter to this task.

Recall that the theoretical analysis developed in Chapter Three and elsewhere does not contradict the idea that natural resource wealth may promote authoritarianism. Instead, the thesis advanced in this book is that natural resource wealth can have both authoritarian and democratic effects: resources have a *conditional* impact on the political regime. According to the theory, greater private inequality and lower resource dependence (i.e., greater development of non-resource sectors of the economy, given the level of resource rents) should tend to promote the democratic effect of resource rents, at the expense of the authoritarian effect. These are, of course, *ceteris paribus* claims; though the theoretical model of Chapter Three is deterministic, the world may not be. If the thesis is correct, however, we should be able to detect such a conditional effect of resource rents in time-series cross-section data.

I take several approaches to the statistical testing of these hypotheses in this chapter. The first set of tests, regarding the mediating impact of inequality, is relatively direct: I posit a series of interaction models that are suggested by the comparative static results of Chapter Three and fit these models to time-series cross-section data for 154 countries from 1960–2001.

I find evidence that supports a main hypothesis to emerge from the model of Chapter Three: inequality conditions the political impact of resource rents. Consistent with the previous quantitative literature, I find that when private inequality is at (or lower than) its average value in the data, resource rents have a positive and significant relationship to authoritarianism. However, when non-resource inequality is higher, resource rents are instead positively and significantly related to democracy. These results help to reconcile the findings of past quantitative studies with my claim that resources may have a democratic effect: on average, the empirical relationship between resources and democracy is negative, yet given particular values of the conditioning variables, the unconditional relationship between resource rents and democracy may instead be positive. As I discuss below, the results are robust to a variety of ways of operationalizing "democracy" (including both dichotomous and graded measures) and to different measures of the key independent variables.

The results are also robust to different statistical modeling strategies for testing the predictions of the formal theoretical model. For instance, as I discuss later, the theory carries implications for the level of democracy in resource-rich countries, despite my theoretical focus on "change" variables such as coups and democratic transitions; because of my desire to compare our results to previous studies (where the level of democracy is the dependent variable), I present results of least-squares analyses using a graded measure of the level of democracy as a dependent variable. Nonetheless, I also estimate a series of dynamic probit models, similar to the empirical approach in Boix (2003) and also Przeworski et al. (2000). These statistical models allow me to test my hypotheses about the impact of resource wealth on coups against democracy and transitions to democracy in ways that are perhaps more faithful to the theoretical framework of Chapter Three.

I also pursue several alternative approaches that complement the main econometric strategies. One relatively indirect method is to drop the direct measure of the conditioning inequality variable and to restrict the estimation sample to Latin American cases; I describe the theoretical motivation for this empirical approach in more detail below. Using cross-section time-series data for eighteen Latin American countries, I show that measures of oil rents and also total resource rents (a measure that includes non-oil minerals) are positively and significantly related to *democracy*, a result that persists to inclusion of country and time fixed effects and to the exclusion of Venezuela from the sample. Because previous analysis of the Venezuelan case helped to generate the puzzle that in part motivates this study, the fact that the results persist to the exclusion of this case is particularly illuminating; this might be considered an out-of-sample test that lends validity to the general insights contributed by the model of Chapter Three. Thus, I find that in a region of the world in which the theory predicts a relatively democratic effect of resource wealth, resource rents are indeed associated with democracy. Clearly, mechanisms other than those posited in this study might account for the difference between the relationships in the Latin American data and those in the global sample; the case studies of Chapters Five and Six will help provide evidence on the mechanisms through which the observed relationship between rents and democracy could have been produced. Yet, in the absence of a theory like the one developed in this study, this finding on the Latin American data is not easily reconciled with previous claims that resource rents only promote authoritarianism.

Finally, I also conduct tests on the global data set that seek to distinguish the effects of resource dependence from the effects of rents per se; I find support in the data for the claim that the apparent authoritarian effects of resource rents is in part a function of the relationship between resource *dependence* and the political regime, rather than resource wealth per se. That is, the strong relationship between resource wealth and authoritarianism found by the previous literature is at least in part a function of the fact that measures of resource *reliance* have in fact been used. These last results are important because along with inequality, they may help to reconcile the apparent relationship between oil and authoritarianism in heavily rent-dependent countries of the Middle East—where oil rents can reach up to 75 percent of GDP—with the apparent relationship between oil and democracy in Venezuela—where oil rents reach no more than 20–25 percent of GDP.

There may clearly be some limits to the interpretability of the results presented in this chapter, however. One of the difficulties, as I discuss further in this chapter, involves the validity and reliability of cross-national indicators of private inequality in the *non-resource* sectors of the economy, though I construct the best available indicator to try to measure this key concept in the formal model. Perhaps more important, in regressions with inequality as a right-hand-side conditioning variable, is the possibility of endogeneity bias arising from the reciprocal relationship between inequality and the regime type. Indeed, the theory of Chapter Three explicitly suggests such a relationship, because according to the theory, the regime type itself influences the extent of (post-tax) private inequality. Estimating the impact of inequality on the regime type in a cross-national sample, and perforce the interactive effect of inequality and resource rents on the regime, is perhaps impossible in the absence of some instrument.[1] (The mixed results of previous empirical studies on, e.g., the relationship between democracy and redistribution may attest to the empirical difficulties involved.[2]) The dynamic probit models and other strategies described in this chapter help somewhat with these issues, because here the impacts of resource rents and other variables are conditioned on the values of those observable variables in the previous period (here, the previous year); indeed, this is precisely the modeling approach taken by previous work in comparative politics that has grappled with the difficulty of designing cross-national quantitative tests of the relationship between inequality and the political regime (Boix 2003: 71–5; see also Przeworski et al. 2000).

However, absent more convincing empirical strategies for overcoming these important threats to valid inference, I view the results of the tests reported in this chapter as being supportive of the claim that descriptive variation in the data is consistent with the hypotheses advanced in this study—that is, consistent with the claim of a conditional effect of resource rents on the political regime. This is clearly not the same as estimating a causal effect, in the sense that (say) an experimental research design would allow. Yet, the importance of showing even a conditional association between resource rents and the regime type should not be too quickly discounted, given the apparently unqualified results of previous cross-national quantitative work on the impact of resource wealth on the political regime. The evidence presented here suggests that far from a few democratic outliers, both the democratic and the authoritarian effects of resource wealth may be quite general. This evidence therefore motivates the attempt in

[1] Even in the counterfactual case in which there was some cross-nationally available indicator that could serve as a valid instrumental variable—i.e., a variable empirically correlated with inequality but independent of the error term in the statistical models presented in this chapter—the interpretation of the estimated coefficients may be complicated. See Dunning (2008) for discussion.

[2] For empirical work on the relationship between inequality, redistribution, and the political regime, see inter alia, Boix (2003), Bollen and Jackman (1985), Lindert (1994, 2000), and Przeworski et al. (2000: 120–2). From the perspective of the theory developed here or in Acemoglu and Robinson (2001, 2006a) or Boix (2003), estimating the relationship between inequality and redistribution among democracies can raise serious sample selection issues because according to the theory, potential redistribution under democracy affects the propensity of countries to become democratic in the first place. (To complicate matters further, the theoretical relationship between inequality and the emergence of democracy is non-monotonic, as in, e.g., Acemoglu and Robinson 2001.)

subsequent chapters to probe further the mechanisms through which resource rents may have a democratic effect.

The rest of the chapter is organized as follows. I begin by discussing measures of key concepts: resource rents, resource dependence, private inequality, and democracy. I then turn to the analysis, fitting a series of statistical models to the data and assessing the extent to which the results are consistent with theoretical predictions. Last, I discuss the relationship of my results to previous findings in the literature.

4.1 Concepts and Measures

4.1.1 Resource Rents

Testing the theory of Chapter Three will require an empirical indicator of "resource rents," my key independent variable. However, the previous quantitative literature has employed what, for my purposes, are clearly imperfect measures of this concept. Two indicators have been most commonly used: oil or other natural resource exports as a percentage of total merchandise exports, and oil or other natural resource exports as a fraction of GDP. The major problem with these measures is that they tap not just the value of rents produced in the resource sector but also the size of these rents relative to the total economy. In fact, these are measures not of resource wealth per se but rather of resource *dependence*, that is, of economic reliance on resource wealth.[3] Indeed, the terms "resource wealth" and "resource dependence" are often used interchangeably in the cross-national statistical literature on the political and economic effects of resources; it is often not clear whether resource wealth per se or instead resource dependence is the key independent variable.[4]

In the theory developed in this book, however, resource dependence is a variable that may *condition* the impact of resource rents. For this reason alone, it is crucial to disaggregate resource rents from the overall size of

[3] In terms of the model of Chapter Three, they are measures not of R but of $\frac{R}{R+\bar{y}}$, i.e., the ratio of resource rents to the total size of the economy.

[4] For example, Ross (2001) refers to "oil," "oil wealth," and "oil reliance"; his empirical measure is the proportion of oil and other mineral exports in GDP. Jensen and Wantchekon (2004: 817, 823) investigate the "political implications of resource abundance" using an ordinal measure of resource dependence that ranges from 1 (countries with less than 25 percent of merchandise exports from fuel and minerals and metals) to 4 (countries with more than 75 percent).

the economy, by developing a more direct indicator of resource rents. A more conceptually valid measure for present purposes comes from the data set originally developed by the environmental economists Hamilton and Clemens (1999).[5] These authors subtract an estimate of the unit production cost and a "normal" return to capital (generally of 15 percent) from the unit world price (or composite of world prices) by year for a large number of natural resources, including oil and gas and many non-fuel minerals.[6] The authors then multiply the ensuing measure of "unit rent" by production quantities for 154 countries from 1970–2001. This approach therefore provides an estimate of the value by year of production of a wide range of natural resources, net of production costs and a return to capital, giving at least a first-order approximation of the size of the rents available for public spending. In principle, this measure, which has been employed by other analysts researching the effects of natural resources on a range of political phenomena (see Ross 2006), gives us the most direct available cross-national measure of the concept of resource rents in the formal model of Chapter Three.

In order to obtain temporal coverage that will more fully allow me to compare my results with the previous quantitative literature on the authoritarian "resource curse," I extended the time series of the Hamilton and Clemens data on oil and gas rents back to 1960, using production data from British Petroleum (2005) and Humphreys (2005).[7] I then divided this measure by population data, creating a per capita measure of rent that is appropriate to the per capita value R in the formal model. This allowed me to obtain a measure, *Oil rents per capita*, for 154 countries from 1960–2001.[8]

5 Updated data are available through 2002 at http://www.worldbank.org/environmentaleconomics. See also Bolt et al. (2002) on the calculation of resource rents in this data set.

6 In most cases, the unit cost is based on a single observation in the 1990s; costs for other years are obtained using a GDP deflator. This clearly must be a source of measurement error in the estimates of resource rents, yet the measure remains superior to other existing indicators. See Bolt et al. (2002) for a description of the construction of the data set.

7 Humphreys (2005) gives petroleum production per capita in dollars per barrel, which I converted to dollars per ton, the metric used in the Hamilton and Clemens data, using a conversion factor of $\frac{1}{7.3} \doteq 0.137$. I then subtracted unit costs by extending Hamilton and Clemens' data on unit costs and took price data from the BP statistical review. This is similar to the practice used by Hamilton and Clemens to create the original data set; see Bolt et al. (2002).

8 Ross (2006) extends the Hamilton and Clemens data set in a similar fashion.

Using Hamilton and Clemens' data, I also constructed another measure, *Total resource rents per capita*, which includes not just oil and gas but also many non-oil rent-producing minerals, including, for example, copper, for 154 countries from 1970–2001.[9] Because there is little conceptual difference between oil and gas and other natural resources capable of producing rents for the state (as discussed in earlier chapters), it will be useful to test these claims using this broader measure of natural resource rents as well.

These direct measures provide more valid indicators of the concept of "resource rent" used in this study than any other available measure.[10] However, because one goal is to make the results reported here as comparable as possible to previous results in the literature, I have also estimated the statistical models described below using other measures of resource wealth, including the (gross and net) export value per capita of fuel and non-fuel mineral exports from the World Bank as well as the per capita oil production data.[11] Using these alternative measures, I have found broadly similar results to those reported below; where differences exist, I have noted them in footnotes.[12]

4.1.2 *Resource Dependence*

The concept of resource dependence, as I have discussed elsewhere in the book, is relatively straightforward. Assessing the extent of resource

[9] I did not extend the time series for this indicator back to 1960 because of missing unit cost and production data for different minerals, which were readily obtained in the case of oil and gas but much more difficult to obtain for the many minerals in the Hamilton and Clemens (1999) data set.

[10] Another possibility would be to attempt to measure yearly government revenues from oil or other resources. The main reason I do not take this approach here is simply the lack of data availability, but this may be possible in future research (see Haber and Menaldo 2007; Herb 2005).

[11] The indicator of export value was obtained by multiplying the fuel export share (and the non-fuel mineral export share) by the size of fuel (non-fuel mineral) exports, using data from the World Bank's World Development Indicators (which are downloadable by institutional subscribers at http://devdata.worldbank.org/dataonline), and normalizing by population.

[12] Somewhat surprisingly, the bivariate correlation between the measure of oil and gas rents per capita that I constructed by extending the Hamilton and Clemens (1999) data back to 1960 and World Bank data on fuel exports per capita is relatively weak (0.30), as is the correlation between the Hamilton and Clemens measure and the Humphreys (2005) oil production data (0.24). The correlation between the World Bank export data and Humphreys' production data is stronger (0.73).

dependence involves comparing the size of resource rents to the size of the total economy, including both resource and non-resource sectors: in terms of the model of Chapter Three, this is given by the fraction $\frac{R}{R+\bar{y}}$. The ratio of resource rents to gross domestic product therefore provides a straightforward and credible operationalization of resource dependence. As I discuss later, there are important theoretical issues related to the functional *form* of the relationship between resource dependence and the other variables in our model. However, because these issues relate to model specification rather than conceptualization and measurement of resource dependence itself, I postpone them for later discussion.

4.1.3 Private Inequality

Testing the predictions of my theory with cross-national quantitative data will also require a measure of what I have called "private" inequality, which has a precise meaning in the formal model developed in Chapter Three. Recall that the parameter θ was defined in that chapter as the share of private (non-resource) wealth or income that accrues to the rich group; in particular, this parameter is independent of the level of the resource rent R. We might therefore want a measure of "pre-tax-and-transfer" inequality of asset ownership or income in sectors of the economy *not* linked to the rent-producing resource sector—for instance, an indicator of asset or income inequality in the manufacturing or agricultural sectors.

Conceptually, the partition of the economy into resource and non-resource sectors is relatively straightforward. Recall from Chapters One and Two a key feature of resource-rich rentier states: because of the relative absence of "forward" and "backward" linkages between natural resource enclaves and the rest of the economy (Hirschman 1977), non-resource economic sectors tend to have an important degree of autonomy from the rent-producing resource sector (though this autonomy is never, of course, absolute). The geographic concentration of mineral production, the low proportion of the population typically employed in the resource sector, and other factors then imply that natural resource rents influence the domestic political economy primarily through their influence on patterns of public revenue generation and spending.

The distinction between these economic sectors is therefore conceptually unproblematic. However, it is more difficult to operationalize a distinction between, on the one hand, inequality of private, non-resource assets and income—that is, the parameter θ in the model—and, on the other, inequality that stems from the *distribution* of the rent R itself. Consider one candidate measure, the widely used Gini coefficient.[13] As is well known, existing measures of inequality such as Gini coefficients suffer from comparability and coverage issues because the definition of income or wealth varies from country to country and from survey to survey; in addition, data on many countries of the Middle East are especially scarce, which presents special difficulties for testing the interactive effect of oil rents and inequality on the regime type.

Even more crucially for present purposes, however, Gini coefficients may conflate unequal allocations of assets or income in non-resource sectors of the economy with the unequal distribution of resource rents. For purposes of testing my theory, this is problematic because, if elites seek to appropriate resource rents, inequality that stems from the distribution of resource income may be both an outcome of and a raison d'être for the emergence and persistence of authoritarian regimes. Indeed, in my data set the Gini coefficient is positively correlated with oil rents among authoritarian regimes, while it is negatively correlated with oil rents among democratic regimes. The problem with using the Gini coefficient is not just that putting inequality measures on the right-hand side of a regression equation to predict regime type may introduce endogeneity problems, though, as discussed above, this may certainly be a concern with any measure of inequality. The problem is also that using an inequality measure that reflects the distribution of rent—such as, plausibly, the Gini coefficient—may weaken and even reverse the posited conditional relationship among resource rents, inequality, and the political regime. For instance, if control over the distribution of the rent increases both the incentives and the capability of rulers to hold onto political power by authoritarian means, as the previous literature has suggested, and if my measure of inequality reflects the unequal distribution of the rent, then we might expect the positive relationship between resource rents and authoritarianism to be even *more* pronounced, not less pronounced, when inequality is high.[14]

[13] The Gini coefficient is a measure that runs from 0 to 1; at 0, there is complete equality, while at 1, all income is concentrated in a single individual.

[14] Wantchekon (1999b, 2002), e.g., suggests that resource abundance increases income inequality and thereby the consolidation of authoritarian rule, and Boix (2003) assumes that immobile, easy-to-tax assets like oil are owned by the rich, which increases elites' incentives to resist the introduction of democracy; see Chapter Three.

The Gini coefficient is thus clearly an inadequate measure for my purposes.[15] A measure of θ that does not as clearly reflect the unequal distribution of rent itself is therefore preferable. The best available indicator for my purposes is provided by cross-national data on the share of capital in manufacturing value-added, compiled by Rodrik (1999) and Ortega and Rodríguez (2006). In the empirical analyses of the determinants of democracy in this chapter, following analysts such as Przeworski et al. (2000: 121–2) and Acemoglu and Robinson (2006a: 58–60), I use capital shares as the indicator of private inequality.[16]

In the rest of this subsection, I first describe the capital shares measure and then discuss why it provides a particularly useful indicator of inequality. The data come from the United Nations Industrial Development Organization (UNIDO), which sends annual questionnaires to the statistical offices of countries with an industrial-level survey or census. UNIDO reports yearly country-level data on aggregate value-added and wages and salaries by industry for 136 countries since 1963 (Ortega and Rodríguez 2006: 8). Rodrik (1999: 710, 721) uses these data to construct cross-section time-series measures of the factor share of labor income in manufacturing GDP, which is the ratio of average wages and salaries in the manufacturing sector to manufacturing value-added per worker.[17] However, whereas Rodrik (1999) provides a summary measure for each country (or country-year), Ortega and Rodríguez (2006) estimate capital shares by industry within each country, at the 3-digit (since 1963) or 4-digit (since 1985) ISIC level.[18] The Ortega and Rodríguez (2006) data set provides a particularly useful extension to Rodrik (1999) for my purposes: because capital shares are given at the industry level, this data set allows me to remove from the indicator the average capital shares in resource sectors, such as petroleum and other

[15] In Dunning (2007), I conduct a series of empirical tests similar to some of those reported below, using Gini coefficients as well as the capital share as an inequality measure. As discussed there, results using the Gini coefficient are similar but less robust, a fact that may well reflect the conceptual inadequacy of the measure.

[16] Przeworski et al. (2000: 121–2) and Acemoglu and Robinson (2000) both use the labor share of value-added in manufacturing as indicators of inequality. The capital share measure I use here, which is just one minus the labor share, provides an increasing rather than decreasing indicator of inequality.

[17] One minus the labor share (i.e., one minus the ratio of wages and salaries to manufacturing value-added) then gives the capital share in manufacturing.

[18] I am grateful to Francisco Rodríguez for sharing these data with me.

mineral commodity sectors.[19] After removing these resource sectors, I take decade averages of industrial capital shares for four decades (1960–1969, 1970–1979, 1980–1989, and 1990–2003), giving a total of 3,913 observations.

Why does the industrial capital share provide a useful indicator of inequality for my purposes? While in many countries a relatively poor majority obtains most of its income from labor, capital income tends to accrue to a relatively small elite (Acemoglu and Robinson 2006a: 58–9). To some extent, this observation may be predicated on at least some limits to the flow of goods, services, and capital across borders, as international trade tends to narrow cross-national gaps in goods and factor prices. Then, as a logic based on the Heckscher-Ohlin model would predict, locally abundant factors (such as labor in many developing countries) will command a lower price in the absence of international trade, while locally scarce factors such as capital receive a higher return; according at least to classical theory, international trade tends to reduce inequality between workers and the holders of capital (Magee, Brock, and Young 1989; Rogowski 1989; Stolper and Samuelson 1941). Yet, even in the absence of trade considerations, capital's share of industrial value-added should provide a useful proxy for the degree of inequality (see Acemoglu and Robinson 2006a: 59–60). A higher share of capital in industrial value-added should therefore correspond, *ceteris paribus*, to a higher degree of inequality.[20]

A key virtue of the adjusted capital share measures I use here, as discussed earlier, is that they comprise only industrial (manufacturing) sectors of the economy and do not, perforce, include the primary commodity extractive sector. This is a tremendous advantage for purposes of proxying the

[19] I removed capital shares for the following industries from my aggregate measure: ISIC 353 (Petroleum refineries), ISIC 354 (Miscellaneous petroleum and coal products), and ISIC 369 (Other non-metallic mineral products).

[20] To be sure, capital ownership is relatively widespread in some advanced industrial countries, at least relative to developing countries; and inequality in such countries increasingly stems from wage inequality (Roemer 2006), which might lead capital share measures to understate the true degree of inequality. Ortega and Rodríguez (2006), in fact, show a significant negative correlation between national income and capital shares in their data, countering the previous claims of Gollin (2002) and Bernanke and Gúrkaynak (2002) that the inclusion of income from the self-employed creates an upward bias in traditional economy-wide estimates of capital shares drawn from national account statistics; see also Caselli (2005). Yet, conditioning on the level of national income (as I will do in the regression specifications in this chapter), there is nonetheless substantial cross-national variation in average capital shares.

income distribution in non-resource sectors of the economy. In contrast to Gini coefficients, which may pick up transfers and subsidies to household income associated with the distribution of resource rents, average capital shares across industries are less likely to be less endogenous to the allocation of rents. Indeed, the correlation between oil rents per capita and the capital share in my data set (−0.005) is not statistically different from zero, suggesting that the industrial income distribution is independent of the distribution of the resource rent—just as in the formal model of Chapter Three.[21] This contrasts with the case of Gini coefficients and thus suggests that at least relative to Gini coefficients, capital shares provide a more valid measure of the parameter θ in the models of Chapter Three, which is assumed independent of R.

Of course, there remains the possibility that the regime type itself shapes capital shares.[22] In this chapter, I discuss further the possibility of endogeneity of capital shares to the regime type, which could pose problems for interpreting the results of our econometric models. However, it is noteworthy that the unconditional relationship between the regime type and capital shares is weak: in 51.8 percent of the country-years for which I have average capital share data, the political regime is authoritarian, and in these authoritarian countries, the mean capital share is 0.575 (s.d. 0.117). In 48.2 percent of the country-years for which I have capital share data, the regime is democratic, and in these countries, the mean capital share is 0.613.[23] This contrasts with the case of Gini coefficients, where there is a stronger unconditional relationship with the regime type. The capital share measure is imperfect from other perspectives as well. Like data on Gini coefficients, the capital share data suffer from missing values (which are in all likelihood not missing even conditionally at random), though the cross-sectional and intertemporal coverage of the data is better than for the Gini coefficents; and there always remains the possibility of the endogeneity of capital shares to the regime type, as I discuss later.

Nonetheless, capital shares represent the best available cross-national indicator of private inequality; it comes closest to measuring θ in the theoretical model of Chapter Three. If the predictions of the model are to

[21] The correlation between "total" resource rents per capita and labor share is somewhat stronger (−0.021), but still not significantly different from zero.

[22] Indeed, Rodrik (1999), whose main argument is that democracies pay higher wages, makes precisely this claim.

[23] To stratify on the political regime here, I use the dichotomous "regime" variable found in Cheibub and Gandhi's (2004) update to the Przeworski et al. (2000) data set.

be tested empirically on a large-N data set—as the previous quantitative literature on rents and authoritarianism certainly necessitates—then using capital shares as the empirical indicator of inequality represents the best possible "direct" route.[24] Elsewhere in this chapter, however, I discuss alternate emprical strategies that may allow the capture of the conditioning effects of private inequality without entering a direct measure of inequality into the regression specification.

4.1.4 Democracy

Finally, I turn to measures of the dependent variable. Recall that one goal of the analysis in this chapter is to make the results as comparable as possible to the earlier quantitative literature on the authoritarian political effects of resource rents (e.g., Ross 2001). Thus, following this literature, I begin by using as our indicator of democracy a graded measure, the Polity2 scores from the Polity IV data set (Marshall and Jaggers 2002). This measure combines information about the competitiveness of and constraints on executive recruitment with information about the extent of political competition. Again following the earlier literature on resource rents and democracy, I recode the measure to run from zero to 10 with higher scores indicating greater levels of democracy.[25]

Two points are in order about the use of this indicator in the current context. First, the conceptualization of democracy in the theory advanced in Chapter Three is Schumpeterian, in that it accepts a procedural minimum definition of democracy; the maintained hypothesis is that participation and contestation in free and fair elections will give the "poor majority" greater political power than will the modal authoritarian regime. Thus, using standard indicators of liberal democracy or polyarchy is consistent with the overall theoretical approach. Although the Polity measure has been recently criticized (see, e.g., Treier and Jackman 2005), it remains one of

[24] An even better measure of inequality for my purposes might be cross-section time-series data on the distribution of land, which may tend to change rather slowly and in any case may not be too greatly affected by patterns of rent distribution, at least in the short term (but see Chaudhry 1997: 156–63 on rising inequality of land distribution in Saudi Arabia during the oil boom of the 1970s). Yet, good cross-section time-series data on the distribution of land do not appear to exist.

[25] The indicator is the sum of Polity's democracy score, which runs from 0 to 10, and the autocracy score, which runs from 0 to −10. Hence, the resulting measure runs from −10 to 10; a simple linear transform creates a variable that runs from 0 to 10.

the most widely used cross-national indicators of democratic institutions.[26] Second, the formal model of Chapter Three might seem to suggest the use of a dichotomous measure of the dependent variable (together with a possibly non-linear regression model for binary choice). However, it is in fact conceptually simple to extend the formal approach to allow for graded measures of democracy, with little difference for the underlying analytics. For example, as mentioned in Chapter Three, one might hypothesize that political outcomes under democracy are a weighted average of the preferences of rich elites and the poor majority, where the weights are measures of the political power of the respective groups.[27] The underlying results of the model in Chapter Three will carry through as long as the poor group has relatively *more* political power in more democratic regimes; I do not adopt this approach in the formal model above because the model is already quite complex, and there is in fact little analytic payoff to extending the two-regime model. The main point is that it matters little, for the comparative statics of interest, whether in the formal model democracy is conceptualized in a dichotomous or graded fashion.

However, it is also certainly the case that the models of Chapter Three focus on "change" variables, such as coups and democratic transitions. Notwithstanding the fact that the apparent disconnect between the dichotomous conceptualization in the formal model and the graded operationalization in our first empirical tests is theoretically inconsequential, it may be more satisfying to test theoretical predictions in a context in which the statistical model "looks like" the formal model to a greater extent. As discussed in this chapter, I therefore estimate a series of dynamic probit models in which the linear predictors are specified as in the previous models, employing a dichotomous measure of democracy as the dependent variable (using an updated version of the Przeworski et al. 2000 data set compiled by Cheibub and Gandhi 2004). I find results that are similar in their main implications to those reported using least-squares analysis of the graded measure of democracy.

[26] Indeed, the criticisms of Treier and Jackman (2005) may be more relevant to the use of the Polity indicator as an independent variable, in which case measurement error may induce bias in estimates of the parameters of the regression model, than in the present context, as the linear regression model is developed explicitly to account for measurement error in the dependent variable.

[27] Acemoglu and Robinson (2006a: 361–7) develop such a model.

4.2 *Rents and the Level of Democracy*

4.2.1 *A Direct Test*

Having discussed the key concepts and measures, I now turn to the statistical tests. As suggested by the simulations depicted in Chapter Three, one testable hypothesis to emerge from the formal model is that inequality of *non-resource* wealth (or income) conditions the political impact of resource wealth—in particular, that private inequality increases the *democratic* effect of resource rents. A relatively direct approach to testing this hypothesis is to posit the following interaction model:

$$D_{it} = \alpha + \beta_1 R_{it} + \beta_2 \theta_{it} + \beta_3 (R_{it} * \theta_{it}) + \mathbf{X}_{it} \gamma + \varepsilon_{it}. \tag{4.1}$$

According to the model, the level of democracy D in country i in year t is a linear-in-the-parameters function of resource rents R_{it}, inequality of non-resource wealth (or income) θ_{it}, the interaction of these two terms, a row vector $\mathbf{X}_{it}$ of control variables, and a mean-zero random error term ε_{it}, where the ε_{it} are assumed independent of the independent variables. The model will be estimated with feasible generalized least squares (fGLS); the error terms are assumed to be heteroscedastic across panels and to follow an AR1 autoregressive process within panels.[28]

What are the expected signs of the coefficients? The marginal impact of a unit increase in resource rents in country i and year t is $\beta_1 + \beta_3 \theta_{it}$. According to the theory, the sign of β_1 (i.e., the impact of resources on the regime type in a country-year with zero inequality) is negative; the sign of β_3 is positive; and the sign of the overall marginal impact of resource rents on democracy may be either positive or negative (because this also depends on the values of other parameters in the model).[29]

[28] With 154 countries and only 43 years, it is not possible to estimate contemporaneous correlation of the errors as well as panel heteroscedasticity. This also implies that estimating the model with OLS and calculating "panel-correct" standard errors (Beck and Katz 1995) is not feasible.

[29] The expected sign of β_2 (the impact of inequality on democracy in a country-year with zero resource rents) is positive. However, in the formal model developed here (as in the models of Acemoglu and Robinson 2001, 2006a) there is a non-monotonic relationship between inequality and democracy. As discussed later, I include a squared measure of inequality in the vector of control variables to capture this possible non-monotonicity.

Table 4.1. *Resource Rents, Inequality, and the Level of Democracy (fGLS estimates of interaction model) Dependent Variable: Polity Scores*

Variable	Expected Sign	Coefficient Estimate (standard error)	Coefficient Estimate (standard error)
Oil rents per capita (in hundreds of real US$)	Negative	−0.2040 (0.0399)	−0.2111 (0.0465)
Capital share (in percentages)	–	−0.0091 (0.0239)	0.0209 (0.0312)
Oil rents*Capital share (Interaction term)	Positive	0.0033 (0.0007)	0.0033 (0.0008)
Capital share squared	–	0.0000 (0.0002)	−0.0002 (0.0002)
Log real GDP per capita	–	0.1033 (0.0189)	0.1492 (0.0214)
British colony	–	–	(0.2325) (0.1652)
Ethnolinguistic fractionalization	–	–	0.8209 (0.3537)
Percent Catholic	–	–	0.0111 (0.0027)
Percent Muslim	–	–	−0.0112 (0.0040)
N	–	3,107	2,352
Log likelihood	–	−3880.5	−3276.6

Note: Constant term estimated but not reported.

Table 4.1 reports the results.[30] The estimates support the hypothesis that inequality mediates the political impact of resource wealth. As predicted above, the estimate of the "direct" effect of rents, β_1 in equation (4.1), is negative and highly signficant: resource rents can promote authoritarianism. Yet, the estimate of the "indirect" effect of oil rents, β_3 in equation (4.1), is highly signficant and *positive*. Figure 4.1 plots the marginal impact of oil rents on the level of democracy, as a function of inequality, using the regression results depicted in Table 4.1; as the figure shows, the

[30] In Table 4.1, I focus on a measure of oil rents per capita for reasons of space. However, I have estimated the model in equation (4.1) using a measure of total resource rents per capita, which includes a range of non-fuel minerals in addition to oil; see Hamilton and Clemens (1999). The results are similar to those reported in the table.

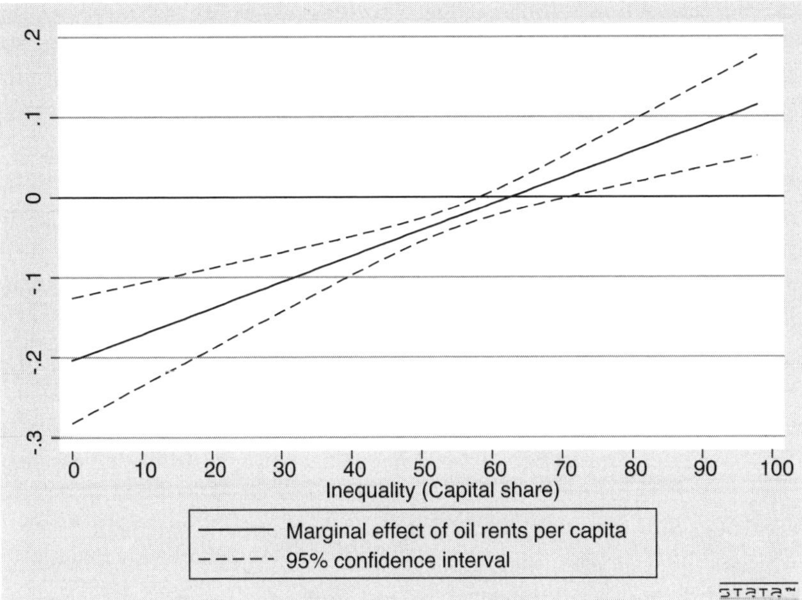

Figure 4.1 The effect of oil on democracy as inequality varies (fGLS estimates of interaction model).

unconditional marginal effect of oil on democracy may be either negative or positive.[31] Thus, according to these results, the overall marginal impact of oil rents may be to increase or decrease the level of democracy, depending on the value of other variables.[32]

To get a sense of the size and interpretation of the effects, imagine increasing oil rents per capita by $500 in real terms, in a country in which capital is paid 50 percent of value-added in non-resource manufacturing sectors. In the specification reported in the first column of Table 4.1, the estimated coefficient on β_1 is -0.2040, while the estimated coefficient on

[31] I used Stata code written by Matthew Golder to implement the marginal effects plot in Figure 4.1; see http://homepages.nyu.edu/~mrg217/interaction.html. I am grateful to Bill Clarke for pointing me to the code.

[32] An earlier version of this book featured a figure similar to Figure 4.1 with, however, slightly different estimated thresholds for the positive and negative effects of resources on democracy. The difference is due to the fact that previous estimates were based on measures of the industrial capital share that had not been adjusted by removing resource sectors such as oil and non-oil minerals, as they have been in Figure 4.1. See the discussion in section 4.1.3.

β_3, the interaction term, is 0.0033; both estimates are significant at the 0.001 level. The results imply that the expected change in the Polity score is (−0.2040)*(5)+ (0.0033)*(5)*(50) = −0.195: that is, if oil rents per capita are increased by $500 dollars in real terms, the Polity score will decrease by 0.195 points, and the political regime will become less democratic.[33] Because the Polity variable is measured on a scale from −10 to 10, a decrease of 0.195 points on average may well indicate a non-trivial difference in regime outcomes.

In addition, this estimate is comparable in size to estimates in the previous empirical literature on the authoritarian "resource curse." Ross (2001: 341, table 3), for example, finds that a percentage point increase in fuel exports as a percentage of GDP is associated on average with a decrease in Polity scores of 0.0346 points. Suppose per capita GDP in a given country is $10,000. Then an increase of $500 in rents (stemming from fuel exports) implies a 5 percent increase in the fuel export share of GDP and thus, according to Ross's estimates, a drop in the Polity score of about 0.173—which is about the same magnitude drop that I estimate for a country where the capital share is 50 percent (i.e., just under the mean capital share in our data). This is why, in the neighborhood of the empirical mean of the inequality variable, the estimate is comparable in size to Ross's, even though I use a measure of resource rents rather than oil exports as a percentage of GDP.

However, estimating the model in equation (4.1), rather than a model that posits an unconditional effect of rents, also allows us to see that the total impact of resource rents combines two effects that have much larger absolute values but that are of opposite signs. Depending on the degree of inequality, the total impact of resource rents on the level of democracy may be either negative or positive because resource rents have both "authoritarian" and "democratic" effects. Imagine a country with extreme inequality—say, a country in which the capital share is 75 percent, so that labor is paid just 25 percent of manufacturing value-added. Then the expected impact on the Polity score of an increase of $500 in per capita oil rents is (−.2040)*(5) + (0.0033)*(5)*(75) = 0.218; that is, there is a *positive* relationship between oil rents and Polity scores. The key result is therefore as follows: at higher levels of private inequality, as measured by the

[33] Note that oil rents per capita are measured here in US$100, so, e.g, the "direct effect" of increasing rents by $500 is (−0.2040)*(5), not (−0.2040)*(500).

non-resource capital share, an increase in resource rents is expected to increase the level of democracy rather than decrease it.[34]

Note that these results do not extrapolate from the data, in the region in which the point estimate for the marginal effect of resources on democracy is positive. Eleven countries in the data set have average scores of at least 80 on the capital share variable, out of the 103 countries on which capital share data exist; six of these eleven countries are in Latin America. Moreover, there are twenty-eight more countries that have scores of at least 70, eight of which are in Latin America. (As will be seen in the next subsection, the fact that there is such high inequality in Latin America will help to motivate another, complementary empirical approach.) Thus, in the part of the parameter space where the estimate of the conditional impact of oil rents on democracy is positive and significant—namely, where the capital share exceeds around 70 percent—there are nearly forty cases in the data set.

Before turning to alternate tests of these key hypotheses, I close this subsection by discussing the robustness of these results to alternate assumptions and measures. First, notwithstanding the conceptual superiority of the direct measure of oil rents for our purposes, I explored alternate measures of the independent variable, including oil production per capita data (taken from Humphreys 2005 and British Petroleum, various years) as well as the fuel share of exports and of GDP; the results are largely robust to these alternate measures, and they are also robust to the use of a measure of total resource rents, which includes non-oil minerals. (Results are available from the author upon request.) The results also persist to the use of dichotomous measures of the dependent variable, as discussed further in this chapter.

Next, I discuss the issue of control variables. The estimates reported in the second column of Table 4.1 involve relatively few controls: the vector of controls is simply two-dimensional, including a measure of GDP per capita in thousands of 1985 U.S. dollars, *GDP per capita*, and the square of the inequality term.[35] Thus, I initially estimate a model with relatively

[34] As mentioned in note 30, similar results obtain when the per capita value of total resource rents is used, rather than just oil rents per capita.

[35] We want to control for GDP because, according to the formal model, the impact of inequality on the impact of resource rents on the regime type is conditional on the size of the non-resource economy. The quadratic inequality term is included because, in the framework of Chapter Three (as in the models of Acemoglu and Robinson 2001, 2006a), there may be a non-monotonic relationship between inequality and democracy: at very low

few control variables.[36] An additional point in this context is that resource rents tend to be allocated at least to some extent by the lottery of natural endowments. Thus, although I clearly need to control for GDP, the need to control for other variables that might be correlated with these endowments and also with the regime type may be significantly attenuated.

Yet, there may well be variables correlated with the conditioning variable of inequality that I should include in the regression specification. Though my ability to deal with sources of bias introduced by unmeasured variables in this observational context, absent an appropriate instrument, may be somewhat limited, in the third column of Table 4.1 I introduce several additional control variables. In addition to logged GDP per capita and the square of the capital share variable, I include an indicator variable for having been a British colony, the widely used ethnolinguistic fractionalization measure constructed from the Atlas Naradov Mira by Taylor and Hudson (1972),[37] the share of the population that is Catholic, and the share of the population that is Muslim (all taken from Cheibub and Gandhi 2004). As expected by the claim that resource endowments reflect in part the influence of a natural lottery, these variables are very weakly correlated empirically with my measure of oil rents per capita, though they are more strongly correlated with inequality (in particular, the measures of ethnic diversity).[38] However, the key results are unchanged by the introduction of these control variables. Indeed, the estimated coefficients on the two variables of greatest theoretical interest are virtually identical; the coefficient on the oil rents variable is

and very high levels of inequality, democracy does not emerge, either because elites in an authoritarian regime are never forced to extend democracy as a way to avoid revolution (the low inequality case; formally, the revolution constraint does not bind) or because the redistributive cost of democracy is so great for elites that they will prefer to repress threats from below rather than democratize (the high inequality case). Only at intermediate levels of inequality might elites prefer to democratize in order to avoid a "revolution."

[36] The models appeal perhaps to Achen's (2002: 445–7) principle of "A Rule of Three" (ART)—i.e., the advice that regressions might ideally not include more than three (theoretically well-specified and understood) variables.

[37] Roughly speaking, this measures the probability that any two individuals chosen at random are from the same ethnic group, as of 1960. I considered an alternative measure of ethnic diversity, which is the largest ethnic group's percentage of the population, taken from Cheibub and Gandhi 2004; results reported in the third column of Table 4.1 are identical in key respects when this variable is used instead.

[38] The correlations between the oil rents measure and log GDP per capita, the British colony dummy, ethnolinguistic fractionalization, and the percentage Muslim, respectively, are as follows: 0.42, −0.03, −0.10, and −0.01. The weak and insignificant correlation between oil rents and percentage Muslim is especially striking; this may effectively underscore the key difference between resource *abundance* and resource *dependence*.

negative and highly significant, while the coefficient on the interaction of oil rents and capital shares is positive and highly significant.

Finally, however, it is also useful to bear in mind several caveats about the results. As statistical models go, equation (4.1) is fairly simple, yet it raises non-trivial issues that merit discussion. First, many elements involved in the specification of the statistical model—for instance, the existence and statistical properties of an additive "error term"—are not countenanced by the game-theoretic model developed above, which is a typical problem involved in assessing the empirical implications of theoretical models. Testing these predictions in the context of a statistical model will therefore involve making important additional assumptions. Second, as discussed above, the assumed independence of the ε_{it} and the matrix of independent variables, which is of course necessary for unbiased least-squares estimation of the model's parameters, might well be suspect. On the one hand, the assumed independence of resource rents and the ε_{it} seems plausible. Democratic and authoritarian leaders alike have incentives to maximize the resource rents accruing to the government, so positing a causal arrow from the regime type to the per capita value of resource rents is uncompelling.[39] On the other hand, the independence of the ε_{it} and inequality is possibly less compelling; for instance, the regime type may well influence the extent of inequality, as indeed implied by my theoretical approach.[40] In principle, there are statistical corrections that might allow one to adjust for some of the potential sources of bias or threats to measurement validity described here, yet these corrections require strong theoretical knowledge about the mechanisms that may produce the bias.[41] Lacking such knowledge, my preferred approach is simply to estimate the model in equation (4.1), applying some obvious corrections to adjust for probable departures from the standard Gauss-Markov assumptions about the statistical properties of the error term. At the least, this approach allows us to assess the extent to which empirical variation in the data is *consistent* with the theory developed earlier.

[39] Note, for instance, that the founding members of OPEC, an international organization that aims to exercise a degree of market power and thereby maximize resource rent, include four countries that were autocracies in 1960 (Iran, Iraq, Kuwait, and Saudi Arabia) and one that was a democracy (Venezuela). The latter country, led by its hydrocarbons minister Juan Pablo Perez Alfonso, was particularly crucial to the founding of OPEC.

[40] Rodrik (1999), however, finds that democracies pay higher wages, indicating possible endogeneity of labor shares as well.

[41] For example, one might apply Heckman-style models to correct for non-ignorable missing data. Yet, successful application of these models requires, at the least, strong theoretical priors about the mechanisms that generated the missing data, which I lack in this case.

Although some caution in interpreting the results is warranted, in light of these inferential issues, the approach discussed in this section provides an important test of the plausibility of the hypotheses advanced earlier: the evidence suggests that the observed variation in political outcomes across resource-rich states is consistent with the theory. It is important to supplement this initial evidence with further tests, however. I now continue with this task.

4.2.2 An Indirect Test

According to my theory, the democratic effect of resource rents should be more pronounced where private inequality is higher, *ceteris paribus*. The evidence presented in the previous subsection supports this claim. However, it is useful to complement the "direct" analysis with a more "indirect" approach to testing the comparative static result on inequality. Here, rather than employ the existing, admittedly imperfect indicators of inequality, as I did earlier, I take a different approach, which is to restrict the statistical analysis to Latin American countries and inquire about the empirical relationship between resource rents and democracy in this region.

What is the theoretical motivation for this empirical approach? The analytic utility of restricting the estimation sample to Latin American countries may be easily misunderstood, so it is important to lay out the theoretical rationale for doing so here.

First, Latin America is the world's most unequal region (IDB 1998). As Table 4.2 suggests, of the three regions in which previous analysts have signaled an especially important political role for natural resource rents—the Persian Gulf, sub-Saharan Africa, and Latin America—the last is the most unequal according to the capital share measure, with the Persian Gulf being the *most* equal and sub-Saharan Africa falling in between. Moreover, as the evidence on capital shares in non-resource sectors suggests, it is also one in which the distribution of *non-resource* wealth and income is thought to be extremely unequal; according to many analysts, the politics of redistribution has played an especially crucial role in the emergence and persistence of different regime types in Latin America (see Acemoglu and Robinson 2006a; R. Collier 1999; Stepan 1985). Thus, recalling Figures 3.1–3.3 in Chapter Three, it is more likely that Latin American countries lie in the part of the parameter space where natural resources would tend to have a democratic effect. Second, even in the most resource-rich countries of the region, well-developed non-resource sectors play an important role in

Table 4.2. *Industrial Capital Shares by World Region (Non-Resource Sectors)*

Region	Average θ*
Western Europe	48.2
Persian Gulf	53.1
Sub-Saharan Africa	59.3
Latin America	70.4

* θ is the (non-resource) industrial capital share, my measure of private inequality.

the economy, and the distribution of wealth and income in these sectors is highly unequal. The low level of resource dependence in the region, even in the most resource-rich countries, therefore suggests that restricting the analysis to Latin America can provide a test of the joint hypotheses about non-resource inequality and resource dependence.[42] Finally, there is substantial cross-sectional and intertemporal (within-country) variation in the value of oil rents per capita in the region, which allows me to assess the empirical relationship between resource rents and democracy.[43] In sum, given high non-resource inequality and low resource dependence in the region, the theory suggests that if we are to observe the democratic effect of resource rents anywhere, we should observe it in Latin America.[44]

Note that in the regression models to be estimated and reported in this subsection, variables such as inequality and resource dependence will not be measured directly, as they were in the models reported in the previous subsection. Here, instead, the idea is to stratify countries on the basis of inequality and resource dependence and then—in an estimation sample of high inequality, low resource dependence cases, where there is nonetheless

[42] Compare, e.g., the extent of resource dependence in countries such as Venezuela and Libya. In both countries, the per capita value of oil rents is historically similar. Yet, in Venezuela, rents constitute around 20–25 percent of the total economy (Baptista 1997), whereas in Libya resource rents have exceeded 90 percent of GDP (author's calculations).

[43] For example, the current value of Ecuador's oil rents per capita has ranged from less than one U.S. dollar, in the 1960s, to a high of $335 in 1980. Mexico's oil rents per capita have ranged from just over $2 in the 1960s up to $546 dollars in 1982; they dropped to under $200 in the 1990s (author's calculations based on Hamilton and Clemens 1999 data).

[44] One might also point out that scholars have identified inequality and the politics of redistribution as an important force in shaping the emergence and persistence of democratic regime types in Latin America during the period under study, when both democracy and authoritarianism were clearly "available" regime types.

Table 4.3. *Rents and Democracy in Latin America Dependent Variable: Polity Score*

	MODEL 1 (OLS with panel-correct s.e.'s)	MODEL 2 (OLS with panel-correct s.e.'s	MODEL 3 (excluding Venezuela)
Oil rents per capita (in hundreds of real US$)	0.1538 (0.0483)	–	0.0955 (0.0533)
Total rents per capita (in hundreds of real US$)	–	0.2732 (0.0823)	–
Log GDP pc	0.8818 (0.0725)	0.5309 (0.1527)	0.8230 (0.0745)
Constant	−1.0298 (0.4155)	0.3854 (0.7298)	−.9069 (0.4071)
N	832	623	792
R^2	0.09	0.08	0.06

cross-sectional and intertemporal variation in the size of resource rents—estimate the relationship between resource rents and democracy. The prediction is that if we should see a democratic effect of rents anywhere, we should observe it in this estimation sample because we will be in the part of the parameter space where the theory predicts a net democratic effect of rents.

In this subsection, I therefore take a simple statistical model to data for eighteen Latin American countries between 1960 and 2001, regressing the Polity measure of the regime type on oil rents per capita and GDP per capita (in one specification) and on total resource rents per capita and GDP per capita (in another specification). The first two columns of Table 4.3 report results for specifications including oil rents per capita and resource rents per capita as independent variables, respectively.[45] The third column excludes Venezuela from the sample for the specification in which oil rents per capita are included. All models are estimated with OLS and panel-correct standard errors (Beck and Katz 1995; White 1980).[46]

45 I also ran the specification reported in the first and third columns with a lagged dependent variable, following the specification of Ross (2001), and found similar results to those reported below.

46 Unlike the models in the previous section, which were applied to time-series cross-section data in which the number of countries well exceeded the number of years, when I restrict the sample to Latin America, there are eighteen countries and 45 years; here it is feasible to estimate contemporaneous correlation of the errors from the data. Moreover, as is well known, fGLS estimates of standard errors may be biased in such settings (Freedman and

In all three specifications reported in Table 4.3, the estimated coefficient on the resource rent variable (either oil rents per capita or total resource rents per capita) is positive and statistically different from zero. The size of the estimated coefficient of oil rents per capita, 0.1538, suggests a large democratic effect of rents. As in the more "direct" test based on the interaction model above, where I found a positive conditional relationship between oil and democracy at high levels of the capital share variable, here we also observe a robust positive relationship between resource rents and democracy in Latin America, the most unequal region of the world.[47]

It may be especially notable that these results persist when Venezuela is excluded from the sample (third column of Table 4.3). Because the Venezuelan case in part helped to generate the observation that oil rents could apparently promote democratic stability, we might learn relatively little that is new from the regression on Latin American data if the results depended heavily on the inclusion of Venezuela in the sample. Instead, variance in political outcomes and the level of resource rents in other countries that have been relatively oil or gas-rich at various times during this period—for example, Bolivia, Ecuador, Mexico, and Peru—contributes to the positive overall relationship between per capita oil rents and democracy.[48]

Tests on Latin American data therefore provide further support for the hypotheses advanced earlier. Of course, one might object that factors besides high inequality or low resource dependence could account for the positive relationship between rents and democracy in the Latin American data. There are at least two answers to such a reasonable and plausible objection. First, the theory developed here predicts a relatively democratic effect of rents in such settings; although the observation of evidence supportive of this prediction does not necessarily support the mechanisms I emphasize, we lack another theory that would suggest how such a relationship would obtain through different mechanisms than those emphasized in this book. Indeed, the prevailing theory about the authoritarian effects of rents would not predict such a relationship (according to that theory, why should Latin America be any different from other regions?). Even absent further

Peters 1984). Estimating the model with OLS and calculating "panel-correct" standard errors may therefore be preferable (Beck and Katz 1995; though see Freedman 2005: 168).

47 I find similar results using alternate measures of the independent variable, including oil rents as a percentage of GDP (as in Ross 2001) and as a percentage of exports.

48 I ran several regressions using alternate measures of rents—e.g., oil production per capita and oil exports per capita as well as non-fuel mineral rents—but omit these results here due to space. The results largely support the argument developed here.

evidence on the mechanisms, the results are therefore interesting in their own right. Second, however, I will use additional statistical tests in the rest of this chapter, and particularly the case-study evidence of the following two chapters, to try to assess the extent to which the mechanisms emphasized in this book can help explain this aggregate quantitative evidence.

4.2.3 Dichotomous Regimes

The formal models presented in Chapter Three involve dichotomous conceptualizations of the regime type (i.e., democracy/no democracy). However, I argued in that chapter that this framework is easily adapted to the analysis of graded measures of democracy. For instance, one could suppose that different groups have different *degrees* of political power under distinct regimes; a given regime might then be thought of as implementing a weighted average of the preferences of these groups, where the weights reflect their political power. Along with my desire to compare the results directly to previous estimates in the quantitative literature on the authoritarian "resource curse" (e.g., Ross 2001), this was my justification in subsection 4.2.1 for using the same graded measure of democracy as has been used in the previous literature (namely, Polity scores).

However, it is useful as a robustness check to look at the relationship of the independent variables to regime change when the dependent variable is instead measured dichotomously. To investigate this question, I use a binary measure of democracy, drawn from an update to the Przeworski et al. (2000) data set (Cheibub and Gandhi 2004). My model specifies that country i undergoes a democratic breakdown in year t if $y^*_{it} \geq 0$, where

$$y^*_{i,t} = \alpha + \beta_1 R_{it} + \beta_2 \theta_{it} + \beta_3 (R_{it} * \theta_{it}) + \mathbf{X}_{it} \gamma + \delta_{it}. \tag{4.2}$$

The random error term $\delta_{i,t}$ is assumed standard normal and independent of the covariates but dependent within countries (i.e., within i); I will thus estimate the asymptotic variance-covariance matrix of the errors assuming intertemporal dependence of the errors. The probability that a country i is democratic in year t is then given by

$$Prob(R_{it} = 1 | R_{it}, \theta_{it}, \mathbf{X_{it}}) = \Phi(\alpha + \beta_1 R_{it} + \beta_2 \theta_{it} + \beta_3 (R_{it} * \theta_{it}) + \mathbf{X}_{it} \gamma), \tag{4.3}$$

where $\Phi(\cdot)$ is the normal cumulative distribution function. The scalar parameters α, β_1, β_2, and β_3, and the vector γ are estimated by maximizing the log-likelihood function,

$$logL = \sum_i \sum_t [R_{it} \cdot Prob(R_{it} = 1 | R_{it}, \theta_{it}, \mathbf{X_{it}}) + (1 - R_{it}) \cdot (1 - Prob(R_{it} = 1 | R_{it}, \theta_{it}, \mathbf{X_{it}})). \quad (4.4)$$

The expected signs of the key coefficients of interest are as in the least-squares model in equation (4.1) above.

Table 4.4 presents the results, both in a pared-down specification (column 2) and in a model in which I include the same controls as in the least-squares specifications above (column 3). I find results similar in their qualitative implications to those found with a graded measure of democracy.

Table 4.4. *Rents, Inequality, and Democracy: Probit Model Dependent Variable: Regime (1 = Democracy)*

Variable	Expected Sign	Coefficient Estimate (robust standard error)	Coefficient Estimate (robust standard error)
Oil rents per capita (in hundreds of real US$)	Negative	−0.1152 (0.0342)	−0.1494 (0.0333)
Capital share (in percentages)	–	2.7130 (1.9789)	−0.4502 (2.7480)
Oil rents*Capital share (Interaction term)	Positive	0.0020 (0.0007)	0.0026 (0.0007)
Capital share squared	–	−0.0002 (0.0002)	−0.0001 (0.0002)
Log real GDP per capita	–	0.02230 (0.0058)	0.0074 (0.0067)
British colony	–	–	0.3799 (0.0760)
Ethnolinguistic fractionalization	–	–	−0.5413 (0.1074)
Percent Catholic	–	–	0.0025 (0.0009)
Percent Muslim	–	–	−0.0135 (0.0014)
N	–	3,109	2,354
Log likelihood	–	−1925.8	−1366.7

Data on regimes: Cheibub and Gandhi (2004), based on Przeworski et al. (2000). Constant term estimated but not reported.

In particular, in both specifications the impact of the "direct" effect of resource rents is positive and highly significant, while the "indirect" impact (the coefficient on the interaction term) is positive and highly significant. This robustness check thus supports my main claim: there is a conditional effect of resource rents on the regime type.

4.2.4 The Authoritarian Effect of Resource Dependence

Finally, before leaving specifications in which I examine the determinants of the level of democracy, I turn to the issue of resource dependence. As I have emphasized in other chapters, previous studies that have found evidence for a positive relationship between resource wealth and authoritarianism have generally used measures of resource *dependence*—for example, the value of fuel exports as a percentage of GDP (Ross 2001) or of total exports (Barro 1999). However, the theoretical results of the analysis in Chapter Three suggest that the impact of resource rents on the regime type may be conditional on the extent of resource dependence: namely, for a given level of non-resource inequality, resource dependence tends to widen the part of the parameter space over which the authoritarian effect occurs, because the direct authoritarian effect of resource rents is strengthened relative to the indirect democratic effect (see, e.g., Figure 3.4). In other words, the empirical relationship between resources and authoritarianism observed by previous studies may at least partially reflect the relationship between the regime type and resource dependence, rather than the relationship between the regime type and resource rents per se.

In the "indirect" test in subsection 4.2.2, I argued that restricting the estimation sample to Latin American cases could provide a joint test of the hypotheses on private inequality and resource dependence. However, it is useful to attempt to examine this issue more directly; I turn in this subsection to that task.

As described above, here I have constructed an explicit measure of resource rents; using this measure and our data on GDP to find the ratio of resource rents to GDP, I can also construct a measure of resource dependence. Although oil rents per capita and the ratio of oil rents to GDP are well correlated in the data (0.77), there is still substantial variation across countries. Consider, for example, the contrast between Ecuador and Angola: in Ecuador, while the average per capita value of oil rents per capita across all years in the data set (1960–2001) was $128.4, oil rents on average constituted just 4.2 percent of GDP. In Angola, on the other hand,

Table 4.5. *Resource Dependence: fGLS Estimates Dependent Variable: Polity Scores*

Variable	Model 1 (Oil rents)	Model 2 (Total rents)
Oil rents per capita (in hundreds of real US$)	0.024 (0.016)	–
Total rents per capita (in real US$)	–	0.031 (0.015)
Oil rent dependence (rents/GDP)	−.2531 (0.0275)	–
Total rent dependence (rents/GDP)	–	−0.2709 (0.025)
Capital share	−0.2561 (0.0060)	−0.2386 (0.0066)
N	3,107	3,340
Log likelihood	−3946.5	−3421.9

Constant term estimated but not reported.

where the average value of oil rents per capita was just $140.5, oil rents constituted 21.1 percent of GDP, on average. Among three oil-rich Latin American countries (Ecuador, Mexico, and Venezuela), oil rents are 5.7 percent of GDP, on average. Other comparisons across countries in the data set suggest similar differences in the extent of resource dependence.

Unfortunately, the formal model does not give strong guidance as to the particular functional form of the relationship among resource rents, resource dependence, inequality, and the regime type. We might simply ask, however, what the relationship is between resource rents and the regime type, once we have controlled for the extent of resource dependence and given the level of inequality. In other words, do the data allow us to distinguish between resource dependence and resource rents per se?

Table 4.5 presents the results of a feasible generalized least-squares regression of Polity scores on our independent variables, using the global data set.[49] I report two specifications, one in which the independent variables are oil rent abundance and oil rent dependence (rents/GDP), and the other in which the independent variables are total rent abundance (i.e., including

[49] The specification assumes first-order panel-specific autocorrelation and panel heteroscedasticity (but not contemporaneous correlation of the errors, for the same reason as above).

non-oil minerals) and total rent dependence (rents/GDP). I also control for private inequality using our capital share measure: this is because the claims about resource dependence derived from the models in Chapter Three are *conditional* on the level of private inequality.[50]

In both specifications, the coefficient on resource rents is positive and significant, while the coefficient on the resource dependence measure (rents over GDP) is negative and significant. Even though the measures of rents and rents to GDP are highly correlated, and given the caveats discussed elsewhere in this chapter, the data do appear to allow us to distinguish between variation in political outcomes associated with resource dependence and variation associated with resource rents per se. The evidence lends support to our claim that resource dependence heightens the authoritarian effects of rents.

4.3 Democratic Transitions and Breakdowns

As discussed above, analyzing the conditional relationship among oil rents, inequality, resources, and the level of democracy constitutes a valid test of the hypotheses derived from the models of Chapter Three. Yet, it would also be useful to build statistical models to study the questions of regime change that are at the heart of our formal approach. In this section, I estimate several models of democratic breakdown and democratic transition that will further help us to test these claims. These models will allow us to provide candidate answers to questions such as these: How does the probability of democratic transition and democratic breakdown depend on the level of oil rents, the degree of private inequality, the interaction of these variables, and other covariates? How does the incidence of coups against democracy depend on these variables?

4.3.1 A Dynamic Probit Model

I begin by estimating a dynamic probit model, an empirical strategy pursued by, among others, Przeworski et al. (2000: 137–9) and Boix (2003: 71–88), who pose similar questions of their data.[51] The approach is to assume that

[50] That is, for a given level of inequality, resource dependence widens the part of the parameter space over which the authoritarian effect of rents takes place; see Figures 3.1 and 3.4 in Chapter Three.

[51] For discussion of this "dynamic probit" model, see Ameyima 1985, chapter 11.

the data follow a first-order Markov process, so that the regime type this year depends only on the regime type in the previous year as well as the values of conditioning variables in the previous year.[52] The matrix of transition probabilities between regimes is

$$\begin{pmatrix} q & p \\ 1-q & 1-p \end{pmatrix},$$

where q is the probability that an authoritarian regime in year $t-1$ becomes democratic at year t, while p is the probability that a democratic regime in year $t-1$ becomes authoritarian at year t. (Thus, $1-q$ is the probability that an authoritarian regime stays authoritarian, while $1-p$ is the probability that a democratic regime stays democratic.)

The model is linked to the data by assuming that the transition probabilities depend on the observables as follows:

$$q_{it} = \Phi(\mathbf{X_{i,t-1}}\alpha) \tag{4.5}$$

and

$$p_{it} = \Phi(\mathbf{X_{i,t-1}}(\alpha+\beta)), \tag{4.6}$$

where $\Phi(\cdot)$ is the standard normal cumulative distribution function and the matrix $\mathbf{X_{i,t-1}}$ takes $R_{i,t-1}$, $\theta_{i,t-1}$, and other covariates as its columns; α and β are vectors. The impact of a marginal increase in some $x_{i,t-1}$ (a variable in $\mathbf{X_{i,t-1}}$) on the probability of a democratic transition is thus, for example,

$$\frac{\partial q_{it}}{\partial x_{i,t-1}} = \phi(\mathbf{X_{i,t-1}}\alpha)\alpha, \tag{4.7}$$

where ϕ is the density of the standard normal distribution.

Let $R_{it} \in \{A, D\}$ be the regime type in country i in year t. Then the probability that the regime type is democratic, given the regime type and the values of the observables in the previous year, is

$$P(R_{it} = D | R_{i,t-1}, \mathbf{X_{i,t-1}}) = q_{it} \cdot I[R_{i,t-1} = A] + (1-p_{it}) \cdot I[R_{i,t-1} = D], \tag{4.8}$$

where I is an indicator variable and q_{it} and p_{it} are given by equations (4.5) and (4.6), respectively. The parameter vectors α and β are estimated by

[52] In this respect, the structure of the empirical model is similar to the structure of the theoretical models of Chapter Three.

Table 4.6. *Democratic Breakdowns and Democratic Transitions: Dynamic Probit Model Dependent Variable: Regime (1 = democracy)*

	Model 1		Model 2	
	$\hat{\alpha}$	$\hat{\beta}$	$\hat{\alpha}$	$\hat{\beta}$
Oil rents per capita (in hundreds of real US$)	−0.1253 (0.0737)	0.3627 (0.1923)	−0.0920 (0.0817)	0.3027 (0.2905)
Capital share	−0.0279 (0.0384)	0.1234 (0.0108)	−0.0010 (0.0531)	0.1566 (0.0200)
Oil rents*Capital share (interaction term)	0.0026 (0.0015)	−0.0065 (0.0032)	0.0019 (0.0017)	−0.0058 (0.0049)
Capital share squared	0.0003 (0.0003)	−0.0010 (0.0002)	−0.0001 0.0004	−0.0011 (0.0003)
Log GDP per capita	0.0077 (0.0141)	0.0133 (0.02185)	−0.0082 (0.0178)	0.0371 (0.0371)
British colony	–	–	0.4092 (0.4092)	−0.5393 (0.3914)
Ethnolinguistic fractionalization	–	–	0.1932 (0.2805)	−1.1129 (0.5400)
Percent Catholic	–	–	0.0079 (0.0026)	−0.0141 (0.0051)
Percent Muslim	–	–	0.0000 (0.0028)	−0.0042 (0.0070)
N	3,108		2,362	
Log likelihood	−452.0		−251.6	

Data on regimes are from Cheibub and Gandhi (2004), based on Przeworski et al. (2000). All independent variables are at 1-year lagged values. Standard errors in parentheses. Constant term estimated but not reported.

maximizing the likelihood function:

$$L = \Pi_{it}[p(R_{it} = D|R_{i,t-1}, \mathbf{X_{i,t-1}})]^{R_{it}}[1 - p(R_{it} = D|R_{i,t-1}, \mathbf{X_{i,t-1}})]^{1-R_{it}}. \tag{4.9}$$

Results Table 4.6 presents the parameter estimates, both for a baseline model with the main independent variables and a richer model adding a set of controls, as in the specifications above. The results are broadly supportive of the hypotheses, though with some important caveats. One issue is that the structure of the capital share data, which uses decade averages, implies an extremely high correlation between the current and lagged values of several of the variables. The resulting multicolinearity implies that coefficients are not very precisely estimated; in my baseline specification, the standard errors are large, and only a few of the coefficient estimates are significant at standard levels. The problem only worsens as I add more variables to the second specification. Thus, even if the model is correctly specified, in most cases it is difficult to say with any confidence whether the coefficients have a positive or negative sign.

However, the evidence is nonetheless suggestive. For instance, following equation (4.7), the marginal impact of an increase in oil rents is given by $\Phi(\cdot)(\alpha_1 + \alpha_3^*$ Capital share). The term in parentheses, which determines the sign of the whole expression, is estimated as $-0.1252 + 0.0026$*Capital share. (Both estimates are individually significant at the 0.10 level.) The impact of resources on the probability of a democratic transition can thus be either positive or negative; it depends on the value of the capital share variable. Thus, the same pattern obtains as in the results above with respect to transitions to democracy. Though I cannot draw strong inferences from the results, they do provide a further piece of evidence on the conditional impact of resource rents and are useful in combination with the other evidence discussed in this chapter.

4.3.2 Coups

Finally, rather than examine the relationship of our independent variables to democratic breakdowns generically, as in the previous subsection, it will be useful to close this chapter by looking directly at the determinants of coups. I construct a measure of coups from several sources. Alesina et al. (1996) construct data on coups from 1960–1982; McGowan (2003) codes both successful and unsuccessful coups in sub-Saharan Africa from 1956 to 2001 (drawing on newspaper reports and various other sources to code unsuccessful coups); and Belkin and Schofer (2003: 608) compile a list of coups from 1960–2000 from a variety of sources.[53] I draw on all of these sources to create a dichotomous variable, *coup*, which takes on a value of 1 if a successful or unsuccessful coup was attempted in country i in year t (and 0 otherwise). The rationale for including unsuccessful as well as successful coups is that the theory I have developed is largely about elite *incentives* to engage in coups; an unsuccessful coup should be taken as evidence that

[53] I am grateful to Nikolay Marinov for sharing various data on coups.

incentives were such that a coup was attempted in the country-year, even if it in fact failed.

I take a simple probit model like that in equation (4.3) to the global time-series cross-section data set; here the dependent variable is the coup variable. I assume intertemporal dependence of the errors within countries and calculate robust standard errors. As above, in one baseline specification, I include the main independent variables; in another, I include a richer set of controls. Here, however, I enter a new control variable into both specifications: the "sum of past transitions to authoritarianism" (STRA) variable from Cheibub and Gandhi (2004; see Przeworski et al. 2000). The idea is that because I am looking at democratic breakdowns (via coups), unobservables that tend to promote this outcome (above and beyond our key variables and measured controls) may be proxied by this variable. (The results, however, are all robust to the exclusion of this variable.) I report results, as above, using the oil rents variable, but the results persist with the measure of total resource rents.

Table 4.7 presents the results. I find that the same general pattern holds as in our analyses above: here there is strong evidence for a conditional relationship between resource rents and the political regime type. The estimated coefficient on the oil rents per capita variable is positive and highly significant; yet the estimate coefficient on the interaction of this variable with the capital share measure is negative and highly significant. Thus, the value of the capital share variable conditions the relationship between resource rents and democracy, in the direction predicted by the theory. This is consistent, in sum, with the claim that oil rents may either promote or hinder democracy.

4.4 Assessing the Large-N Evidence

What light can the empirical analysis in this chapter shed on the findings of previous cross-national statistical studies? A number of recent studies have found a negative, significant relationship between resource dependence and democracy; these studies have substantially aided our understanding of the political effects of resource wealth by generalizing an insight initially found in studies of the Middle East and testing the claim that rents hinder democracy on a broader cross-section of countries. One important contribution of Ross's (2001) study, for example, was that it used cross-regional evidence to find support for an argument initially developed by specialists on the Middle East, where, however, the political effects of oil wealth could not

Table 4.7. *Rents and Coups: Probit Model Dependent Variable: Coups*

	Model 1	Model 2
Oil rents per capita (in hundreds of real US$)	0.5207 (0.0962)	0.3461 (0.1375)
Capital share	0.1198 (0.0285)	0.1330 (0.0490)
Oil rents*Capital share (interaction term)	−0.0092 (0.0016)	−0.0068 (0.0022)
Capital share squared	−0.0009 0.0002	−0.0011 (0.0004)
Log GDP per capita	0.0455 (0.0087)	0.0543 (0.0163)
STRA	0.1639 (0.0559)	0.1657 (0.0849)
British colony	–	0.0271 (0.1267)
Ethnolinguistic fractionalization	–	−4.9056 (0.3819)
Percent Catholic	–	0.0104 (0.003)
Percent Muslim	–	−0.0046 (0.0018)
N		2,354
Log likelihood		−439.6

See the text for discussion of the dependent variable. Robust standard errors in parentheses. Constant term estimated but not reported.

be statistically identified, as many factors that might explain authoritarianism were common to the countries of the region. From the perspective of this evidence, cases such as Botswana, Norway, or Venezuela—where, as I discuss elsewhere in this study, democratic stability *increased* during the petroleum boom of the 1970s—may simply constitute statistical outliers. Might there, however, also be a more general democratic effect of natural resource wealth?

The evidence presented in this chapter suggests that the answer is yes. To be sure, the evidence discussed earlier does not contradict previous empirical work that has found a relationship between natural resource wealth and authoritarianism: as discussed previously, I find that at average values of the conditioning variables in the data set, resource rents may have an authoritarian effect. Yet, the interaction models I estimate suggest that resources may also have a positive conditional relationship to democracy. The data suggest that rents may be associated with either authoritarianism or democracy, and conditioning variables influence whether the relationship between rents and democracy is positive or negative.

Of course, this chapter presents the results of only one set of econometric tests, undertaken after fitting a series of related statistical models to one set of observational data; like all such strategies, the results depend on assumptions about model specification, such as the functional forms of relationships between the variables of interest. Although different permutations of the models may be tried and tested, the inferential leverage from doing so is often diminishing in the number of permutations; to name only one of the important issues, fitting many models to a data set tends to undermine the interpretation of statistical significance tests (see Freedman 2005: 64–5). Here, moreover, there may be substantial concerns about the validity of other core assumptions of the models, like exogeneity: the theory itself suggests the regime type may influence the extent of inequality, a key right-hand-side variable in many of the regressions above. Unfortunately, the ability to confront these problems with refinements to the models or by using different estimation strategies is necessarily limited. For instance, one frequently encountered strategy involves the use of instrumental-variables least-squares regression; yet while some right-hand-side variables in the models presented here might be subject to instrumentation, valid instruments for variables such as the level of inequality are not obvious.[54] For this reason, I have emphasized that the chapter is geared toward assessing descriptive patterns in the data and evaluating the extent to which conditional relationships are consistent with the theory developed here. This is an important task, and certainly an assessment of the large-N evidence is crucial, given the prior belief of many scholars that overwhelming evidence of an authoritarian effect of natural resource wealth undercuts claims of

[54] Other variables, such as the size of per capita rents, might be instrumented; in an interesting paper, Ramsey (2006) develops an instrument for the price of oil based on natural disasters. An interesting extension for future research would involve estimating the models in this chapter with such an instrument. However, the strategy may be less useful if other right-hand-side variables are endogenous; and the size of rents may be the easiest of the independent variables to instrument in the models that are estimated in this chapter.

conditional positive relationships between rents and democracy. The results are compelling enough on their own that absent any other evidence, it would still be worth turning to finer-grained analysis, in the chapters that follow, of the mechanisms through which resource rents may have a democratic effect.

There are other sources of evidence, however, that also help to shed light on the predictions of the theory developed in this book and that, in combination with the analysis in this chapter, both validate the theory at a large-N level and suggest the value of finer-grained empirical analysis of key mechanisms in the theory. In particular, several recent studies have independently contributed to a significantly more nuanced view of the relationship between resource wealth and the regime type in cross-national quantitative data, contributing to a reconsideration of the findings of early quantitative research on this topic. These studies, which tend to be primarily empirical rather than theoretical, are useful to discuss here in some detail.

Haber and Menaldo (2007) ask whether fiscal reliance on natural resource wealth is associated with authoritarianism within countries, and in long time series within matched pairs of countries.[55] Constructing a unique historical data set that dates back to independence (for instance, to 1818 for Chile, or to 1926 for Yemen), Haber and Menaldo ask whether within-case variation in fiscal reliance on resource rents is positively or negatively related to democracy. They also compare the evolution of the democracy in each country to the regional average (say, the average in year *i* is subtracted from the democracy score in Venezuela in year *i*), and the resulting measure is regressed against lagged fiscal reliance on natural resources. Finally, these authors also compare the evolution of democracy in resource-rich countries to a matched country that was broadly similar on a range of historical and institutional dimensions prior to the exploitation of natural resources in the first country but that has largely lacked fiscal reliance on rents (for instance, Venezuela vs. Colombia).

The results are suggestive for current purposes. For example, in a regression of Polity scores on a 1-year lag of their measure of fiscal reliance on resource wealth, using the historical time-series data, the coefficient on fiscal

[55] One key point made by Haber and Menaldo (2007) about the previous large-N literature on the authoritarian effects of natural resources is that these studies tend to privilege cross-sectional rather than within-country variation. Yet, if the theory that natural resources have an authoritarian effect is correct, they argue, then countries should tend to become more authoritarian as they experience resource booms and as natural resources become a more important source of public finance.

reliance is *positive* and significant at standard levels in four out of eleven cases they examine, while there is no significant relationship in the other seven; three of the four positive cases are in Latin America.[56] Countries that are fiscally reliant on resources are also above the regional trend in Latin America (the estimated coefficients for Venezuela and Ecuador are positive and significant), while states that are fiscally reliant in Latin America tend to be more democratic than their matched pairs, though the effect is significant only for a Mexico–Brazil comparison in the specification reported in Haber and Menaldo (2007, table 4). These results do not persist in regressions where independent and dependent variables are first-differenced (instead of measured in levels), and Haber and Menaldo (2007) also suggest that there may be non-stationarity in the time series; reporting results of estimating models that attempt to correct for this and other complications, the authors suggest that one should not conclude that there is a positive relationship between natural resource reliance and democracy, any more than one should conclude there is a negative relationship. It is important to emphasize that these authors attempt to estimate average rather than conditional effects; that is, their tests do not allow the investigation of conditional hypotheses about the conditions under which natural resources might tend to promote or inhibit democracy. An estimated average effect near zero is consistent with no effect of natural resources, but it is also consistent with the idea of different (positive and negative) effects that may net close to zero on average; only by testing conditional hypotheses can we adjudicate between these claims. Yet, the evidence Haber and Menaldo do find, that fiscal reliance and democracy tend to have covaried positively in Latin America (at least in levels), is consistent with the evidence presented above and also with the theory developed in this book.

Wibbels and Goldberg (2007) also contribute to a more nuanced evaluation of the relationship between natural resources and democracy, using data from the U.S. states. These authors produce findings that are qualitatively similar in many respects to those reported in this chapter, finding that resource abundance has a range of different indirect effects working through taxation and asset specificity; although the latter increases incumbent advantage in elections in U.S. states, the negative relationship between rents

[56] These cases are Mexico, Venezuela, and Ecuador. These regressions include a measure of log per capita income and linear and quadratic time trends; without controls, the coefficient on lagged fiscal reliance is positive and significant in six out of eleven cases, while it is negative and significant in one (Nigeria). See Haber and Menaldo (2007, table 1) for details.

and taxation tends to have a *democratic*, not authoritarian, effect. Wibbels and Goldberg (2007: 29) conclude that "the causal story is more complex than standard accounts suggest . . . with weak tax effort and increased inequality contributing to more competitive politics and asset specificity detracting from electoral competition." Like other work by these authors (see Goldberg and Wibbels 2007), this research provides a valuable opportunity to evaluate hypotheses on the political effects of resource wealth on a new set of cases, the U.S. states; the evidence from this out-of-sample test is consistent with the idea that resource wealth has contrasting political effects, with resources strengthening electoral competition through some mechanisms and diminishing it through others.

Other valuable contributions have also recently suggested mixed effects of natural resources on the political regime. For instance, Herb (2005) also finds a more nuanced relationship between these variables, working through different mechanisms than those emphasized in this book, however; according to Herb's (2005) research, the direct effect of natural resource wealth is to increase autocracy, but resources also increase GDP, leading to an indirect positive effect on democracy. Mahon (2007), investigating the broader relationship between different types of revenues and the political regime, notes both negative and positive relationships between rents and democracy in within-country time-series data; he emphasizes that somc of the negative effect may be due to the impact of resource exports on the current-account balance, and that the negative relationship between resources and democracy is substantially attenuated once this is controlled. He concludes that the relationship between natural resource wealth and the political regime may also include effects that cut in several directions.

In sum, the results from several recent large-N studies are largely complementary to the main claims advanced in this chapter: there may be competing effects of natural resource wealth on the regime type, producing a more attenuated relationship between natural resources and autocracy than the early statistical literature on this topic had suggested. Although some scholars have suggested that the net effect of these conflicting forces on the regime type may be near zero, this leaves open the possibility that the size of the positive and negative effects of natural resources on democracy varies in different contexts, so that the net effect of resources may tend to be democratic in some settings and authoritarian in others. Guided by the theory developed in the previous chapter, this chapter has sought to put this idea to the test. Although the results are subject to the important caveats noted above, they do suggest the value of pursuing interactive and conditional hypotheses about the effects of natural resource wealth on democracy; and they show that the descriptive variation in the data is consistent in key ways with the claims advanced in this book. It is therefore crucial to turn to other, complementary sources of evidence in the following chapters to assess the extent to which the mechanisms emphasized in this book can account for the democratic effects of natural resource wealth.

Before closing this discussion of the large-N evidence, it is also worth calling attention to a more specific aspect of the relationship between the results presented above and the previous literature on the authoritarian effects of rents, especially Ross (2001). Ross (2001) seeks to test the prevailing claim in the literature on the authoritarian rentier state that reduced taxation is one mechanism through which resource rents promote authoritarianism—a claim that is obviously in contrast to the theory I advance here. His empirical strategy is as follows. After regressing a measure of democracy (the same Polity measure I use) on measures of resource dependence and controls in his time-series cross-section data, Ross (2001: 347–9, table 5) enters a measure of the percentage share of taxation in government revenue into the model specification. The tax share of revenue is positively and significantly related to democracy, and entering the tax variable in the specification reduces the absolute value of the (negative) estimated coefficient on the oil dependence variable. This presumably occurs because the tax share variable is positively correlated with democracy but negatively correlated with resource dependence (which is in turn negatively correlated with democracy on average).

Although, as Ross (2001) points out, this evidence is consistent with the claim that the reduced tax burden in rentier states is one mechanism through which resource dependence may lead to authoritarianism, it is crucial to note that the theory advanced in this book also predicts a negative correlation between resource wealth and taxes (because resource rents displace taxes) and a positive relationship between the tax share and democracy (because the relatively poor democratic majority prefers a higher tax rate than rich elites, who control political power under authoritarianism). In other words, at least at the large-N level where we are comparing aggregate relationships between these variables, the theory developed in this book has some of the same observational implications for the empirical relationship among rents, taxes, and democracy as does the theory Ross advances.

Adjudicating between these claims is an empirical matter; future research may be able to design sharper large-N statistical tests for discriminating between these competing theories.[57] Yet, there are other kinds of complementary evidence that may be brought to bear to make progress on adjudicating between these claims, or at least in assessing the conditions under which one or the other may be more valid: these theories have different observable implications with respect to the *mechanisms* through which the alleged political effects of resource rents occur, and careful probing of historical and case-study evidence may help to complement the essentially correlational analysis of this chapter. I turn to this task in the following two chapters.

[57] It is of course conceivable that both theories are right: the diminished tax burden associated with resource rents might promote authoritarianism in some contexts, by relieving pressures for representation, while in other contexts it might promote democracy, by reducing elite disincentives associated with democracy. Future empirical research may be able to design sharper tests to evaluate this hypothesis.

5

The Democratic Effect of Rents

In contrast to much recent work on the political effects of natural resource wealth, the argument developed in this study posits the existence of a democratic effect of resource rents. The theoretical approach developed in Chapter Three suggests conditions under which this democratic effect may become more important, relative to the authoritarian effects of resource wealth. The theory therefore generates hypotheses to help explain variation in political outcomes across resource-rich countries.

The statistical evidence presented in Chapter Four broadly supports these hypotheses. Consistent with previous quantitative work on the link between resource wealth and authoritarianism (Jensen and Wantchekon 2004; Ross 2001), my analysis of cross-section time-series data does not contradict the idea of an authoritarian effect of rents; indeed, at average values of conditioning variables in the data set, the net effect of oil rents is to promote authoritarianism. Yet, the evidence also suggests a conditionally positive effect of natural resources on democracy. Although natural resources may have an authoritarian effect, there is also evidence that natural resource wealth can instead promote democracy.

Nonetheless, other theories are conceivably consistent with the evidence presented thus far. As discussed in the previous chapter, the democratic effect of rents might work through other socioeconomic channels than those I emphasize (Herb 2005); various institutional variables might also provide the principal source of variation across resource-rich countries. It is therefore crucial to probe relatively fine-grained case-study evidence. Evidence from detailed analysis of cases may uncover "causal-process observations" that supplement and inform interpretation of the statistical analysis and, especially, provide evidence on the mechanisms through which rents may have a democratic effect (D. Collier et al. 2004). In addition, the case studies will in turn help to extend and enrich the theoretical approach developed in Chapter Three.

5.1 Case Selection: Probing the Mechanisms

Yet which cases should be chosen for in-depth analysis? A working presumption of this study is that the mechanisms through which resource wealth may promote authoritarianism have been previously and extensively studied by political scientists. For instance, case studies of authoritarian politics in rentier states include many analyses of countries in the Persian Gulf, while many fine case studies have also contributed to the analysis of resource wealth and authoritarianism in North and sub-Saharan African countries.[1]

It is crucial to note that these studies, which have nicely illuminated the authoritarian effects of resource wealth, have also largely focused on cases in which the theory developed in this study would predict the authoritarian effects of resource wealth to be relatively important. That is, the countries on which these studies focus tend to be not just resource-abundant but also highly resource-dependent (i.e., the ratio of resources to the overall size of the economy is high); quantitative studies of the African cases have in fact used measures of resource dependence rather than of resource rents per se (e.g., Jensen and Wantchekon 2004; Lam and Wantchekon 2004). They are also not countries in which the redistribution of unequally allocated private income tends to provide a particularly salient dimension of political conflict.[2] We may expect the role of resources in mitigating redistributive conflict to be relatively less important in such cases. In other words, in the resource-rich cases widely analyzed by previous scholars, much or most of the economy is comprised of resource rents, while inequality of

[1] Analyses of Persian Gulf countries include studies of Iran (Beblawi 1987; Mahdavy 1970; Shambayati 1994; Skocpol 1982), Iraq (Batatu 1978; Chaudhry 1994), Kuwait (Crystal 1990), Saudi Arabia (Chaudhry 1997; Entelis 1976; Quandt 1981); studies of the authoritarian effects of resources in Africa include analyses of Algeria (Moore 1976; Quandt 1998), Congo (Clark 1997; Englebert and Ron 2004), Gabon, Libya (First 1980; Vandewalle 1998), and the former Zaire (Young 1983), as well as quantitative studies of the continent as a whole (see Jensen and Wantchekon 2004; Lam and Wantchekon 2004).

[2] For instance, some scholars have in fact emphasized that in many sub-Saharan African countries since independence, measured economic inequality has been relatively low, despite the persistence of severe political inequalities (Acemoglu et al. 2007: 2). Economic inequality in resource-rich African countries, and especially in the Persian Gulf, tends in turn to reflect the distribution of resource rents, as discussed elsewhere in this book.

non-resource income may be relatively modest. Although this may set the stage for important distributive conflict over the rents themselves, and therefore enhance the authoritarian effects of rents, it also undermines the salience of the redistributive conflict in non-resource sectors of the economy—thus limiting natural resource wealth's expected democratic effects.

It therefore makes sense to select cases for which values on key independent variables predict a relatively democratic effect of resource rents. Because such cases are understudied in the literature on resource wealth, analyzing them should allow us to develop a richer understanding of sources of variation in regime outcomes across rentier states. Comparing the results with previous studies of authoritarian resource-rich countries should give us a richer basis for contrasting and understanding the authoritarian and democratic effects of natural resource wealth. As just discussed, two such independent variables emerged in the theoretical and empirical analyses of previous chapters as central: the extent of resource dependence and the degree of inequality in non-resource sectors of the economy. In particular, the previous analysis suggests the value of selecting for intensive case-study analysis those resource-rich rentier states in which resource dependence is low and private, non-resource inequality is high.

In this chapter, I conduct an in-depth analysis of historical and contemporary evidence from Venezuela, where I conducted the most extensive fieldwork; in Chapter Six, I develop complementary analyses of Chile, Bolivia, Ecuador, and Botswana. These cases offer several advantages for my purposes. First and most important, all are resource-rich rentier states and meet the two key conditions of relatively low resource dependence and relatively high private, non-resource inequality. Second, they are also cases in which different natural resources have provided the basis for rentier states, providing cross-case variation in the source of rents (oil in Venezuela; nitrate and copper in Chile; tin and natural gas in Bolivia; oil in Ecuador; and kimberlite diamonds in Botswana). Finally, there has also been substantial over-time variation in the extent to which rents accrued to the state in these cases, allowing insight into how such changes map onto political outcomes (and the key intervening variables such as redistributive conflict) in each case.

Note that four of these five cases are in Latin America; as I discussed in Chapter Four, Latin American cases tend to fall in the part of the parameter space in which, because of relatively low resource dependence and high non-resource inequality, the model of Chapter Three predicts a relatively democratic effect of resource rents.[3] If we are to observe a positive relationship between rents and democracy anywhere, we should observe it in Latin America; similarly, if we want to probe evidence on the mechanisms through which resource rents promote democracy, we ought to look at cases for which we expect these mechanisms to be relatively prominent or important. This in no way implies, however, that resources may bolster democracy only in Latin America or that the mechanisms through which resources have a democratic effect are only relevant to that region. In the next chapter, I extend the purview beyond the Latin American context, discussing case-study evidence from Botswana; in the conclusion, I discuss comparative issues further.

Given the case-selection strategy, the goal in conducting the case studies is not primarily to test the claim that there is a conditionally positive relationship between resource wealth and democracy, which was the objective of Chapter Four.[4] The primary goal in probing the case-study evidence is, instead, to probe the extent to which this evidence is consistent with the mechanisms through which I have argued that resource rents can promote democracy. For example, in a society with important non-resource economic sectors and high levels of private inequality, the theory predicts a decrease in the salience of redistributive conflict in the wake of a resource boom (and a corresponding increase in redistributive conflict during a resource bust). Case-study evidence can help us evaluate the extent to which this and other mechanisms posited by the theoretical approach are in fact consistent with observed outcomes. Put differently, the case-study evidence should help us to evaluate the extent to which causal-process observations (D. Collier et al. 2004) support the claim of a democratic effect of resource rents as well as support the specific mechanism for which this study argues.[5]

3 Note from Table 4.2 in Chapter Four that industrial capital shares in Latin America are higher on average than in any other region of the world (70.4, compared to 59.3 in sub-Saharan Africa, 53.1 in the Persian Gulf, and 48.2 in Western Europe); these figures are for non-resource industries. This accords with the frequent observation that Latin America is the world's most unequal region (IDB 1998).

4 I will, however, exploit the substantial over-time variation in the size of resource rents in some of these cases in order to evaluate the within-case relationship between resource rents and democracy, with an eye to probing further the evidence that rents and democracy may covary positively.

5 D. Collier et al. (2004: 252–3) define a causal-process observation as "an insight or piece of data that provides information about context or mechanism and contributes a different kind of leverage in causal inference.... A causal-process observation may be like a 'smoking gun'... [that] gives insight into causal mechanisms, insight that is essential to causal

My fieldwork undertaken in Venezuela, Chile, Bolivia, and Botswana, in conjunction with analyses of secondary literature on all cases, provided an important source of such causal-process observations. It helped to bolster my understanding of the democratic effects of natural resource wealth while simultaneously discounting several important alternative explanations for the outcomes I discuss in each case.

5.2 Venezuela: The Rise and Demise of Rentier Democracy

In this section, I turn to historical and contemporary evidence from Venezuela, where, in part because of high inequality in the relatively well-developed non-resource sectors of the economy, the theory developed in this study predicts a relatively democratic effect of resource rents. Several initial comments may be in order about further case-selection issues specific to Venezuela. Previous analyses, including studies by Karl (1987, 1997), España (1989), Naím and Piñango (1984), Rey (1989), and Urbaneja (1992), have underscored the important role of oil in promoting democracy in Venezuela, though they have largely emphasized different mechanisms than those I explore here. In assessing the validity of the hypothesis that oil has promoted democratic stability in Venezuela, I am able to take advantage of intertemporal trends in the size of oil rents, as well as new within-case variation in political outcomes not available to these earlier analysts. My review of this new evidence suggests that previous analysts were justified in asserting a positive relationship between oil rents and democratic stability in Venezuela. Unlike many earlier analyses, however, I suggest that secular trends in the size of oil rents can help account not just for the past stabilization but also the more recent *destabilization* of Venezuelan democracy.

However, the value of probing the case-study evidence comes not just from an assessment of the validity of the hypothesis that oil rents have largely had a democratic effect in Venezuela. Because the Venezuelan case helped to generate the apparent contradiction that in part motivates this research, the positive relationship between oil rents and democracy might be of only limited relevance for assessing my general argument about the democratic effect of resource rents. Perhaps more important, the case study allows me to adjudicate between rival mechanisms through which oil rents had a democratic effect in Venezuela. As discussed above, the model developed

assessment and is an indispensable alternative and/or supplement to correlation-based causal inference."

in Chapter Three has observable implications, and an extended inquiry into historical and contemporary evidence from Venezuela can assess the extent to which these implications are in fact observed. In this chapter, I argue that causal-process observations drawn from the Venezuelan case are consistent with the observable implications of the theory. Indeed, I argue that the theory developed in this study may provide the single most consistent explanation for regime outcomes in Venezuela in both historical and contemporary perspective.

The argument I advance is that the growth of oil rents over the middle part of the twentieth century, by reducing the costliness of democracy in a highly unequal society, altered the incentives of elites to block or reverse Venezuela's transition to democracy in 1958. This was not, however, because elites received direct benefits from the distribution of oil rents themselves, as other analysts have suggested (e.g., Rey 1989). Elites did benefit from the distribution of oil rents, yet political control of the state could conceivably have brought them even bigger direct benefits. Instead, the state's ability to extract ever-increasing oil rents from the oil sector nearly eliminated any redistributive demands that the democratic political system put on the Venezuelan economic elite. Compared to earlier, failed instances of democratization—for instance, Venezuela's brief democratic interregnum from 1945–1948, when oil rents were not nearly as important a source of government finance as they would later become—democracy after 1958 was underwritten by oil-financed government expenditures on health care, education, and other public services that were valued by the democratic majority, as well as by policies of wage defense and investment in basic infrastructure. This was particularly true during the oil boom of the 1970s, precisely the decade in which some previous analysts have put Venezuelan democracy at its most stable (Neuhouser 1992: 125–9).

Because public spending was underwritten by oil, however, none of it came at much cost to elites. Oil rents not only reduced the present economic costs of democracy to elites but they also influenced elites' expectations about the redistributive consequences of democracy into the foreseeable future. Whereas the brief democratic period from 1945 to 1948 (the so-called *trienio* period) was characterized by sharp class conflict and polarization, and its breakdown was driven by elites' reaction against redistributive demands from below, Venezuelan democracy after 1958—and particularly in the 1970s—was characterized by a degree of class "compromise" and "consensus" that was highly unusual in Latin American countries during this period (Levine 1978; Neuhouser 1992; also Collier and Collier 2001).

However, I also argue that a more recent decline in the level of oil rents accruing to the central government, a decline that began in the 1980s and deepened in the 1990s, contributed to the destabilization of democracy in ways that are consistent with the theoretical framework of this study. Especially given the emphasis of earlier analysts on the degree of class compromise during the so-called Punto Fijo period that followed the transition to democracy in 1958, the most remarkable feature of contemporary Venezuelan politics is the extent to which this apparently integrative and consensual system has almost totally broken down since the late 1980s. Indeed, perhaps the most salient feature of Venezuelan politics in the last decade has been the politicization of social class (Ellner 2004); although this feature clearly sharpened after the election of Hugo Chávez as president in the late 1990s, the new political salience of class was readily apparent by the beginning of that decade. I argue that the decline of oil rents as a source of public finance produced the social-structural base that was necessary for the politicization of social class in Venezuela and for the emergence of redistribution as a salient dimension of political conflict, in ways that are consistent with the theory. In a society that remained highly unequal, the inability of the state to finance public spending from oil rents helped produce a democratic majority in favor of increased redistribution of non-resource wealth. The increased salience of redistribution as an axis of political conflict in turn raised the perceived economic cost of democratic institutions to Venezuelan elites. The increased redistributive cost of democracy then helps to explain in various ways the destabilization of democratic institutions, including the incidence of an attempted coup that was broadly supported by elites.

Finally, I consider the political influence of oil rents as they have risen in the most recent years, and particularly since the attempted coup of 2002—a story that is still unfolding as of this writing and that is therefore necessarily sketched somewhat tentatively. Despite the extreme social polarization as well as class antagonism that continues to characterize the Venezuelan polity, I suggest that political outcomes in the wake of the renewal of the rentier state are also consistent in important ways with the theory developed in this book. For a range of reasons explored below, the size of oil rents accruing to the central government was relatively small during the first years of the Chávez administration; it was in this context that a range of economic decrees were passed at the end of 2001 that provoked elite concern about the redistributive consequences to which a continuation of the Chávez government would lead. Since the coup of 2002, however, the size of oil rents accruing to the Venezuelan government has sharply increased. Notwithstanding the redistributive political discourse that has characterized the Chávez administration, and despite the adoption of some measures that threaten to impose a redistributive cost on Venezuela's economic elite, the extent of actual redistribution imposed on this elite has been relatively moderate as of the time of this writing—certainly relative to the redistributive language that characterizes contemporary political discourse in Venezuela and, especially important, relative to the redistribution that might ensue in the *absence* of high levels of oil rents, a counterfactual claim that over-time evidence drawn from the Chávez period also helps to sustain. I elaborate this argument and discuss its political consequences more fully in this chapter.

Clearly, alternative explanations exist for regime outcomes in each of the main historical periods on which I will focus: the breakdown of the democratic interregnum from 1945 to 1948, the democratic period after 1958, and the more recent destabilization of democracy as well as the rise of Chavismo as a political phenomenon. Comparing Venezuela's democratic stability after 1958 to the more common cases of democratic breakdown elsewhere in South America, for example, many analysts have emphasized the special character of the democratic institutions established in Venezuela's "pacted" transition to democracy in 1958 and the Constitution of 1961 (e.g., Levine 1978; see also Coppedge 1994). Others have combined a focus on institutions with an emphasis on the structural economic changes associated with the rise of the oil economy (Karl 1987; also Coronil 1997). As I elaborate below, such explanations should certainly be seen as complementary to the argument I advance here; for purposes of evaluating this study's general argument about the democratic effect of rents, the main point is merely that rather than undermining democratic stability, as a Friedmanesque argument about the "law" of authoritarian petropolitics would have it, oil rents helped to produce democratic stability in ways that are consistent with the theoretical framework elaborated here. However, I also argue that explanations focused on the special character of Venezuela's democratic institutions have a difficult time accounting for the decline of democratic stability without highlighting the changes wrought by the decline of oil rents as a source of public finance. Nor do explanations that emphasize long-term structural change in the economy help to explain the particular character of democratic destabilization that accompanied the decline in oil rents in the 1980s and 1990s. In contrast, the framework developed here helps to illuminate the specific relationship between oil rents and the rise of social and class polarization, as well as the implications of class polarization for democratic stability, and it can account not just for the emergence and stabilization of Venezuelan democracy but also its destabilization. To be sure, oil rents are clearly just one causal factor shaping regime outcomes in Venezuela in historical and contemporary perspective. Nonetheless, unlike many other accounts, the approach advanced here does provide a consistent explanation for cycles of authoritarian and democratic regimes in Venezuela over the course of the twentieth century.

I develop these arguments in more detail in the following sections. After a brief overview of long-term trends in the extent of oil rents in Venezuela, I begin the argument by way of contrast, exploring the initial transition to democracy and the character of its breakdown in 1948. I then describe the foundations and the consolidation of a "democratic rentier state" after 1958. I also link the demise of this democratic rentier state, beginning in the mid-1980s, to a decline in the size of oil rents and ensuing changes in patterns of public finance; and I trace the re-emergence of redistributive conflict as a salient dimension of politics in Venezuela and link it to the ultimate destabilization of democracy in Venezuela. Finally, I briefly consider the implications of this argument for understanding Venezuelan politics in most recent years, before closing by comparing my argument to alternative explanations for the development of the political regime in Venezuela.

5.2.1 The Rise of the Democratic Rentier State

Viewed in historical perspective, oil revenues have provided a highly variable source of income for the Venezuelan government. Figure 5.1 plots the per capita value of Venezuelan central government revenues stemming from the oil sector between 1921 and 2002, in constant 1984 U.S. dollars. As the figure suggests, oil has provided a highly uneven source of revenue for the Venezuelan government. Although revenues more than doubled in real terms between the mid-1940s and the mid-1950s, before leveling off during the 1960s, the oil price shocks of the 1970s brought the most extreme spike in government oil revenues. This intertemporal pattern was similar, of course, to revenue trends in the world's other major petroleum exporters, though in Venezuela, as I will detail later, this secular pattern has been shaped not just by world market price trends but also by changes in the extent to which the government extracted rents from the oil sector in percentage terms.

Together, secular changes in the world market price of Venezuela's basket of crude oil and changes in the percentage take of the government have

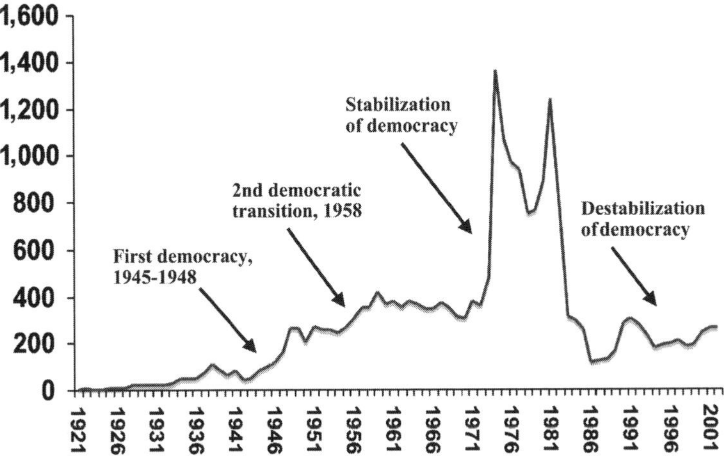

Figure 5.1 Venezuelan central government's revenues from oil 1921–2002, per capita (1984 US$). *Source:* Author's calculations based on Ministry of Energy and Mines, *Petróleo y otros datos estadísticos*, various years, and Baptista (1997).

implied significant variation in the extent to which oil rents accrued to the government budget. Measured in constant U.S. dollars, as in Figure 5.1, the fall in the value of central government oil revenues looks somewhat steeper (and comes earlier in the 1980s) than it would if revenues were measured in the domestic currency, because a major devaluation of the *bolívar* in 1983 and other adjustments in subsequent years boosted the domestic purchasing power of the government's dollar-denominated rents from oil.[6] Yet, the main contours of the pattern traced in Figure 5.1 are similar, whether the government's oil revenues are measured in the domestic currency or in dollars.

Figure 5.1 also displays key moments in the evolution of Venezuelan democracy. The pattern certainly is consistent with the claim that there is a positive link between oil rents and democratic stability—and appears on its face to belie the "first law of petropolitics," according to which the price of oil and the "pace of freedom" move in opposite directions (Friedman 2006).

[6] This raises the interesting question of whether government oil rents are more appropriately measured in terms of their international or domestic purchasing power. In the statistical analyses in Chapter Four, I use the dollar value of rents, as these data are available cross-nationally. According to the models of Chapter Three, however, what matters is the ability of the government to provide goods and services domestically, and so perhaps measuring the domestic purchasing power of rents is most appropriate. I am grateful to Gustavo García, Professor at the *Instituto de Estudios Superiores de Administración (IESA)*, for his comments on this point; interview, Caracas, May 6, 2005.

By the 1970s, at the height of its oil boom, Venezuela appeared to enjoy a consolidated democracy; indeed, as democracy after democracy fell victim to coups in South America, the country appeared a regional democratic oasis. It was often repeated that Venezuela was a "refuge for all democrats in Latin America."[7] Yet, is the qualitative evidence on the mechanisms through which democracy was introduced, toppled, and reintroduced consistent with the claims of the approach adopted here? Did oil rents in fact help to stabilize democracy, and did they do so through the mechanisms elaborated elsewhere in this study? And, how can we explain the subsequent destabilization of democracy in Venezuela?

Some initial insights come from comparing the democratic interregnum from 1945–1948 (the so-called *trienio* period) to the decades following redemocratization in 1958. The brief democratic period from 1945 to 1948 was characterized by an atmosphere of intense class conflict. Popular mobilization prior to 1945 had played a crucial role in forcing the emergence of democratic rule in Venezuela.[8] Under the repressive dictatorship of General Gómez (1908–1935), quiescence was forced upon the population at a relatively low cost: with the exception of an important student protest in 1928 (Betancourt 1956) and a relatively few scattered strikes (Bergquist 1986), Gómez governed almost unperturbed by popular mobilization. However, Gomez's death unleashed collective protest on an unprecedented scale. Unions were formed in a number of sectors, and new political parties made universal suffrage and the extension of other political rights among their primary demands. The authoritarian regimes that followed Gómez confronted this popular mobilization and demands for democratization with a combination of policy moderation and repression. Gómez's handpicked successor, López Contreras (1935–1941), initially promised to enact a broad agenda of labor, health, and education-related reforms but then turned abruptly toward a more repressive policy (Collier and Collier 2001: 251–5). The authoritarian regime of Medina Angarita (1941–1945) adopted a more moderate stance, legalizing some opposition parties, which allowed them to gain influence. The military junta that toppled Medina then invited the labor-based party Acción Democrática (AD) to join the government, and in 1947 AD's Rómulo Betancourt was elected president in national elections with universal adult suffrage.

[7] Alfredo Torres Uribe, political consultant; interview, Caracas, February 17, 2005.

[8] This point was emphasized to me by Ramón J. Velasquez, who was interim president of Venezuela from 1993–1994. Interview, Caracas, May 12, 2005.

Yet, if popular mobilization and opposition helped to force elites to consider the option of democratization in the first place, the prospect of democratic majorities controlling economic policy clearly proved extremely threatening to elites after 1945. The new Constitution of 1947 enshrined a compendium of political, social, and economic rights, including the right of labor to unionize and strike, the right of equal pay for equal work, the right to social security and health care, and many other provisions that had not appeared in any previous Venezuelan constitution (Kornblith and Maignon 1985). Betancourt and AD promoted what were radical policy reforms in the context of mid-twentieth-century Venezuela: especially, an incipient but assertive program of land reform; a program of massive investment in public works and education; and a vigorous policy of promoting real wage increases (Betancourt 1956: 319–42). Acción Democrática mobilized and organized actively among lower sectors in both the cities and the countryside, raising the concern among AD opponents that this popular party was on the verge of monopolizing political power. In elections for a Constituent Assembly in 1946, AD won 137 of 159 seats; the party's presidential candidate, Rómulo Gallegos, took nearly 75 percent of the vote in the elections of 1947; and in the new Congress, AD had 83 out of 110 deputies and 38 out of 46 Senators (Betancourt 1956: 224–33). As Urbaneja (1992: 168–70, translation mine) puts it, "The lower classes rose abruptly, to the consequent inconvenience of the upper classes . . . a tidal wave of sindicalist, agrarian, and educational reforms . . . generated a climate of apprehension among those we could call—as they called themselves—the decent people."

Most analysts therefore concur that the coup of November 24, 1948, was intended to counter the political power of mass majorities under a democracy with universal adult suffrage and, in particular, to block the redistributive reforms proposed by the leading labor-based party Acción Democrática. Myers (1986: 122) argues that AD interpreted its electoral success in 1946 and 1947 "as a mandate to increase the pace of social change," thereby alienating landowners, manufacturers, and other powerful groups. Hellinger (1984: 49) suggests that the coup occurred in part because the "Venezuelan bourgeoisie . . . was not prepared to accept the institutionalization of labor unions." According to Levine (1978: 92), "the overthrow of AD . . . stemmed ultimately from the threat its continued rule had come to pose to a wide range of social interests."[9] Urbaneja (1992: 168) suggests

[9] Unlike the other authors quoted in this passage, however, who clearly give priority to the role of class conflict, Levine's (1978) emphasis is in part on religious conflict and the anticlericalism of the *trienio* government.

that the reforms implemented by AD necessitated "a vigorous correction that would reestablish...respect for certain social hierarchies inhabited from the past." Indeed, AD's policies provoked a "climate of apprehension" (Urbaneja 1992: 170) about the outcomes to which democracy might lead; consistent with the theory developed earlier, the Venezuelan elite was concerned not just with the current but also the future redistributive consequences of the democratic regime. That the coup of 1948 was undertaken in order to block redistribution from below is underscored by the policies of the authoritarian regime of Pérez Jiménez (1948–1958) that followed the coup: the number of unions fell from around 1,000 in 1948 to only 387 in 1951 (Bergquist 1986: 268); labor's share of national income fell sharply; and lands taken during the agrarian reforms of 1945–1948 were returned to their owners (Neuhouser 1992: 122). It is therefore clear that class and particularly redistributive conflict played an important role in engendering support among the elite for a coup against democracy.

The years after the breakdown of democracy in 1948, however, brought a qualitative change to the fiscal basis of the state. Although Venezuela had been an important oil exporter since the 1920s (see Figure 5.1), the contribution of oil rents to the Fisc had been relatively modest in real terms during the *trienio*, certainly relative to later periods.[10] However, during its brief tenure in power, the AD-led government after 1945 made the capture of increased oil rents a major part of its policy platform (Betancourt 1979).[11]

[10] By 1928, Venezuela was the world's leading oil exporter and was second in production only to the United States. However, hydrocarbons did not yet constitute anywhere near the overwhelmingly important fiscal resource that they later would become. To be sure, General Gómez (1908–1935) and his associates personally profited from oil: Gómez granted or sold land to various political allies who then sold land to the oil companies, in the process greatly enriching both themselves and Gómez, who became Venezuela's richest man (Coronil 1997). By 1924, however, oil contributed no more than 6 percent of the state's fiscal revenue, and by the end of the 1930s, petroleum still provided just 30 percent (Urbaneja 1992: 88, 95).

[11] According to the historiography advanced by Rómulo Betancourt and other AD leaders, the "*entreguista*" regimes of Gómez and the authoritarian leaders to follow allowed foreign oil companies to pay neglibible royalties and practically to write the legislation that governed taxation of the oil sector. For example, in his *The Petroleum Pentagon*, Juan Pablo Pérez Alfonso (2003 [1967])—who was Minister of Development during the *trienio*, Minister of Mines and Hydrocarbons under Rómulo Betancourt (1959–1964), and who played the leading role in the founding of OPEC—argues that while the democratic *trienio* government took measures that led to the "improving [of] the country's participation in the exploitation of its fundamental collective wealth...in 1949, the Republic was again defenseless under the power of an [sic] usurping dictatorship, a naturally propitious circumstance for another onslaught of the foreign interests" (Pérez Alfonso 2003: 8). The flavor of this statement is

In particular, the *trienio* government set in motion important policy changes that would allow subsequent governments to capture ever-increasing levels of oil rent.[12] For example, the *trienio* government deepened the revenue impact of the new hydrocarbons law of 1943 by raising the income tax from 12 to 28.5 percent in 1945, established the principle of a "50–50 split" of profits between oil companies and the state (through a decree in 1945 and further legislation in 1948), and began to formulate a policy of "no more concessions" to the companies—though these latter two policies would only become firmly entrenched after 1958 (Pérez Alfonso 2003).[13] In 1947, when AD's Rómulo Gallegos was elected president, the central government took in 1,085 *bolívares* per capita in oil revenue, measured at 1984 prices. By the time that the overthrow of the authoritarian government of Pérez Jiménez in 1958 brought redemocratization, the central government took in 2,343 *bolívares* per capita, also measured at 1984 prices.[14] Thus, the central government's revenue from oil more than doubled in real terms between 1947 and the return of democracy in 1958. The democratic government that was installed in 1958 thus had at its disposal a much more important source of rents than it had between 1945 and 1948.

After the return to democracy in 1958, these trends in the collection of rents by the state only increased.[15] As Figure 5.1 indicates, the real value of the central government's oil revenues more than tripled between 1958 and its peak in 1974. This increase was partly a function of trends in the oil markets—particularly, of course, the price boom of the 1970s that followed the Arab oil embargo of 1973 and then the Iranian hostage crisis in

matched by countless others throughout Rómulo Betancourt's 900-page testimony on the topic, *Venezuela, Pólitica y Petróleo* (1979 [1956]).

[12] For example, the "Fair Share" was one of the five "angles" of Pérez Alfonso's so-called pentagon, which he said should anchor Venezuelan policy toward the oil sector. During the *trienio*, the Fair Share was operationalized to mean that the Venezuelan state should receive not less than 50 percent of the profits of the oil companies—the famous "50–50 split" (see Betancourt 1979 and Pérez Alfonso 2003).

[13] Many concessions were due to revert to the state in 1983 under the terms of the Hydrocarbons Law of 1943, which was actually legislated under the comparatively "soft" authoritarian regime of Medina Angarita. Although advocacy and pressure from opposition AD legislators played the key role in bringing about this legislation (Betancourt 1956), in the end, AD leaders had opposed the law of 1943 as insufficiently radical.

[14] Author's calculations, based on Ministry of Energy and Mines, Petroleo y Otros Datos Estadísticos, various years, and Baptista (1997).

[15] As Pérez Alfonso (2003 [1967]: 7) says, "In its first period (October 18, 1945-November 24, 1948), the democratic government hardly had time to begin to define a Fair Share and to formulate its basic principles."

1979—and partly a function of the ability of the government to take advantage of the increasing power of oil-producing countries relative to the multi-nationals and thereby to extract a continually greater portion of rents from the oil sector.[16] This process was, of course, highly discontinuous: during the 1960s, in fact, soft world oil markets somewhat weakened the government's fiscal position. However, increased production by the companies and an increased percentage take by the state helped to offset this trend and eventually contributed to the boom in value of oil revenues in the 1970s.[17] When Rómulo Betancourt and AD had first come to power in 1945, the central government appropriated around 25 percent of total revenues in the oil sector, and this figure remained below 40 percent until the end of the 1950s. The creation of OPEC, the growing oil nationalism of petroleum-producing countries around the world, and new legislation in Venezuela regarding hydrocarbon concessions all led foreign companies to anticipate the eventual nationalization of their properties in Venezuela. With this limit on their time horizons, foreign oil companies increased current production (at the expense of new investment), even as the Venezuelan central government was able to greatly increase its percentage "take" of revenues in the oil sector through new legislation raising the fiscal contribution required of the companies. By the time the law nationalizing the Venezuelan oil sector was passed in 1975, the percentage of oil revenues that accrued to the central government had surpassed 80 percent.

Oil revenues became in consequence a much more important part of the overall budget: whereas by the end of the 1930s petroleum provided just 30 percent of the government's total fiscal revenues (Urbaneja 1992: 88, 95), by 1958 this figure had reached nearly 60 percent, and by 1974 it would rise to a peak of 86 percent (author's calculations based on Ministry of Energy and Mines, various years). Thus, the effects of the positive price shocks of the 1970s, which dramatically increased the market value of Venezuela's oil exports, together with the greater proportion of oil revenue appropriated by the state, sharply distinguish the 1960s and especially the 1970s from earlier periods in Venezuelan history. By the 1970s, Venezuela was truly a rentier state—a "petrostate" of the first order.

[16] The implications for my argument of the evolution of oil policy and of the state's "take" in percentage terms are discussed further below.

[17] In 1948, Venezuela produced 490 million barrels of oil a year (more than 1.3 million per day); in 1958, this figure had climbed steadily to 951 million barrels (2.6 million per day), while it reached its peak in 1970 at 1.35 billion barrels a year (3.7 million barrels per day).

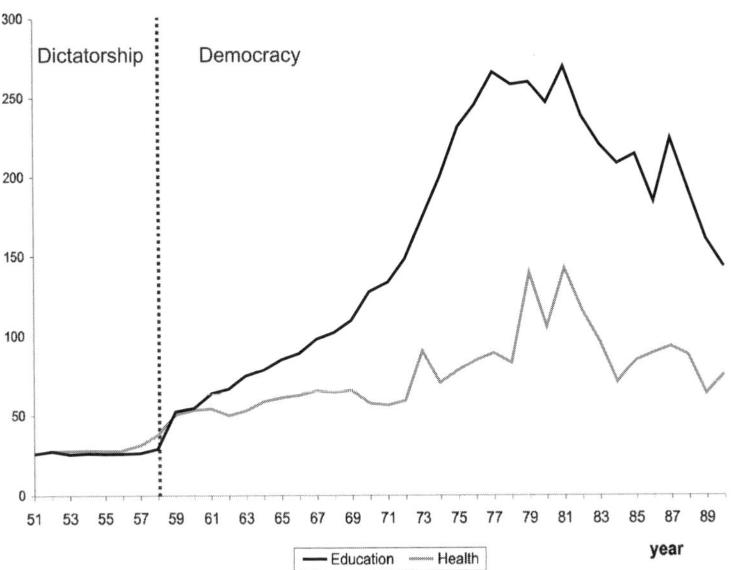

Figure 5.2 Real education and health spending in Venezuela, 1951–1990.

How did increased oil rents contribute to the evolution of political institutions? I argue here that the oil rents available to the state after the return to democracy in 1958, and particularly during the 1970s, helped to underwrite a degree of class compromise and consensus that contrasted sharply with the first democratic period from 1945–1948. Two factors were key in allowing oil rents to underwrite class compromise after the return to democracy in 1958. First, increased revenue from oil rents allowed for massive public spending on government services valued by the relatively poor majority. Inflation-adjusted spending on education increased by a factor of more than 20 between 1958 and 1980, while real spending on health increased by a factor of nearly 5; as a percentage of total government spending, the budget of the education ministry rose from just over 6 percent to nearly 19 percent over the same period (Kornblith and Maignon 1985). Many medical services were subsidized and remained completely free until the 1980s (España 1989: 168), and domestic fuel price subsidies made Venezuelan gasoline among the cheapest in the world. By the end of the 1960s and beginning of the 1970s, public spending had succeeded in meeting a wide range of popular demands (see Figure 5.2, based on a graph prepared by Mario Chacón).[18]

[18] The data are from Zambrano y España (1991).

Second, however, none of this new public spending came at much cost to elites. A notable feature of the post-1958 period was the hostility of elites to new taxation, which contributed to the total failure of the very few proposals (in 1966, 1971, 1975, 1986, and 1989) that were floated that would have increased taxes even modestly. For example, in 1966, members of Acción Democrática proposed a tax reform project that would have raised personal income taxes by 1.8 percent on the upper 6.6 percent of income earners, and corporate income taxes by 4 percent on the most profitable enterprises.[19] Reaction from elites was hostile. A spokesman for a newly formed group, consisting of leading private-sector elites and calling itself the "Committee for the Protection of the Middle Class," commented: "The conclusion is clear. The [tax reform] laws submitted to Congress will take Venezuela directly into Communism" (Tugwell 1975: 91). In 1971, Acción Democrática itself rejected another proposed tax reform, preferring instead to raise a new tax on petroleum companies (Gil Yepes 1978: 191). In 1989—when non-petroleum personal and corporate income taxes were just *2 percent* of non-petroleum gross domestic product—the president of the influential business association, FEDECAMARAS, reacted to a small proposed tax increase in the following manner: "In a country such as Venezuela, which receives such a large rent from petroleum, I am certain that empresarios . . . should not have to pay taxes in the excessive quantities that they do today" (Rodríguez Balsa 1993, translation mine). Not until the 1990s, after the precipitous decline in the level of oil rents that accrued to the Fisc, was a tax reform successfully pushed through, and this reform did not raise personal or corporate income taxes on the upper brackets but instead established a value-added tax (VAT).[20]

However, the resistance of elites themselves to new taxes did not much matter because—crucially for the argument advanced in this study—oil rents clearly moderated the extent to which the political representatives of democratic majorities themselves sought to tax the elite. Not only were

[19] That is, the businesses above the 83rd percentile in terms of profitability (Tugwell 1975: 90–1).

[20] Some analysts suggest this VAT is lightly regressive, while others suggest it is neither a regressive nor progressive tax (see García et al. 1998 for a discussion of the Venezuelan VAT). Note, however, the argument of Engel et al. (1999), who suggest that the best way to redistribute in Latin American countries (Engel et al. focus on the Chilean case) is to increase the VAT, rather than raise progressive income taxes, and then to direct revenues toward spending on the poor. Indeed, as in the models of Chapter Three, the unequal distribution of private income implies that a proportional tax is redistributive, even without any spending bias. I am grateful to Mariano Tommasi for comments on this point.

modest personal or corporate income tax increases on the rich vigorously opposed by elites, but they were also largely rejected by the labor-based party Acción Democrática itself, as in their response to the tax reform project of 1971. In place of taxation, leaders of AD preferred to find new ways of capturing petroleum rents. Indeed, as far back as the authoritarian regime of Medina Angarita, opposition leaders from AD emphasized that demanding increased payments from the foreign oil companies could take the place of foreign borrowing, close budget deficits, and, especially, pay for education and other social programs (Betancourt 1979: 141; see also Coronil 1997: 102). Under the guidance of Juan Pablo Pérez Alfonso, architect of OPEC and oil minister under Betancourt after 1958, the democratic government was able to force increased contributions upon the companies throughout the 1960s. Consistent with the idea that resource wealth reduces the redistributive demands placed on a rich elite under democracy, Coronil (1997: 94) suggests that "the idea that [the] state's programs could be financed at least in part by citizens' taxes was simply absent."

To be sure, the moderation of class conflict and the stability of the democratic system itself were arguably more pronounced during the 1970s than during the 1960s. Politics in the years immediately after 1958 resembled the instability of 1945–1948 in some respects: there were several coup attempts after 1958 that could have imperiled the new democracy (Urbaneja 1992), and there was also an important guerrilla movement led by disaffected members of AD as well as Communists that was not pacified until the end of the 1960s; and several coup attempts. Here too, however, the availability of oil rents played a crucial role. The land reform program undertaken after 1958 was comprehensive, compared to other agrarian reforms in Latin America (Goodwin 2001: 231); yet full compensation was paid for expropriated land. Hellinger (1991: 107) suggests that "enough peasants received land and other benefits to forestall widespread support for guerrillas." Thus, oil-financed spending played an important role in reducing the demand for greater redistributive policy "from below."

Neuhouser (1992), in fact, argues convincingly that only in the 1970s was the post-1958 Punto Fijo democracy stabilized, a fact that he likewise attributes to the role of oil rents.[21] Yet, this only further supports the argument here that oil rents contributed to democratic stability, as the 1970s

[21] Neuhouser's (1992) argument, which focuses on the period from the democratic transition until the 1970s, emphasized the moderation of class conflict at the expense of "elite pacts," which had been a dominant interpretation of the sources of democratic stability

were precisely the period in which oil rents were accruing to the Venezuelan state at the greatest levels. As Neuhouser (1992) also notes, this also seems to belie claims that the particular nature of Venezuelan democratic institutions, established through an elite-led "pacted" transition to democracy in 1958 and enshrined in the Constitution of 1961, accounts for the stability of democracy—as these factors were roughly constant over the period in consideration, while both oil rents and the degree of "consensus" and "compromise" varied.

I discuss in more detail later alternative explanations that have been proposed to explain the stabilization of democracy in Venezuela during this period. Some such explanations have emphasized the important role of political institutions and of the particular "pacted" nature of the transition to democracy in 1958: the Pact of Punto Fijo, in particular, has been singled out as an important explanation for Venezuela's later democratic stability.

In conclusion to this section, I note that almost all analysts of Venezuelan democracy after 1958 have emphasized the degree of class compromise that characterized the integrative system (e.g., Levine 1978; also Collier and Collier 1991), and they have attributed to this "consensus" the stability of democracy. By the 1970s, a democratic system had consolidated in which two parties, AD and COPEI, had rotated several times in the executive office; compared to countries of Latin America's Southern Cone, where coups in the 1960s and 1970s installed authoritarian regimes, Venezuela seemed a model for democracies all over Latin America and a leading regional exemplar of democratic stability (Coppedge 1994). The key points of debate have centered on the causal sources of this class compromise and consensus. Before returning to this question further, it will be useful to consider the course of politics during the 1980s and 1990s.

5.2.2 The Demise of the Democratic Rentier State

The ability of the state to finance public spending from oil rents was severely undermined in the 1980s and especially 1990s. By the mid-1980s, the real value of the government's oil revenues, measured in constant U.S. dollars, had fallen *below* its level in 1945, when AD was first brought to power and Venezuela's first experience with democracy was initiated. Measured in domestic currency rather than U.S. dollars, the fall is somewhat less brutal, and comes somewhat later, than suggested by the pattern depicted

in Venezuela. This is perhaps the closest thesis in the extant literature to the argument developed here.

in Figure 5.1: in particular, the government's devaluation of the *bolívar* in 1983 increased the domestic purchasing power of oil rents and thereby arguably allowed the perpetuation of a democratic rentier state through at least the end of the 1980s. For instance, as García, Rodríguez, and de Figueroa (1998: 5, translation mine) note:

> The monetary instability that began in 1983 altered the fiscal contribution of the petroleum industry in favor of the central government. The devaluation permitted the decline in dollars (of 56 percent) to result in a smaller decline in constant *bolívares* (45 percent). During the period of multiple exchange rates (1983-1988), diverse opportunites were established for a lower [tax] rate for petroleum exports, with the goal of creating profits for the Central Bank and then for the central government, once the profits were transferred to the national treasury. The introduction of indexing for inflation in the ISLR [income tax] reduced the fiscal effects of the devaluation, since the volume of external debt contracted by PDVSA affected the determination of taxable income, through its effect on the liabilities of the industry. Nonetheless, throughout the period, the exchange adjustment undoubtedly permitted a compensation for the decline of the petroleum rent in dollar terms."[22]

Nonetheless, no matter how oil rent is measured, the pattern in terms of government revenues from oil is similar: a peak in the level of oil rents in the 1970s was followed by a steep fall in the 1980s and a further decline in the 1990s. Two factors contributed to the demise of the Venezuelan rentier state. First, and most important, the effects of the negative world oil price shocks in the 1980s contributed markedly to the fall in the real value of central government oil revenues, as in the world's other major oil exporters. Second, however, the Venezuelan central government itself also began to receive a smaller percentage share of total revenues in the oil sector, especially in the late 1980s and the 1990s. However, it is not necessary to establish the sources of this secular trend in order to document that beginning in the 1980s, the central government received oil rents at levels far below the boom years of the 1970s; at least by the mid-1990s and probably well before, the Venezuelan rentier state had entered a state of significant decline.

How did the demise of the Venezuelan rentier state contribute to the evolution of class conflict and of the political regime during the 1980s and the 1990s? As noted above, most analysts of the Punto Fijo period that followed Venezuela's democratization in 1958 emphasize the degree of "compromise" and "consensus" that characterized the integrative Venezuelan democratic system (Levine 1978; also Collier and Collier 2001). Thus, the most remarkable feature of recent Venezuelan politics is the extent to which

[22] See also note 6 in section 5.2.1, regarding Figure 5.1.

this apparently integrative and consensual system has almost totally broken down since the late 1980s. Along with the near-complete loss of electoral support for the traditional political parties, AD and COPEI, the most salient feature of Venezuelan politics has been the emergence of "class" conflict as the basis for a politically salient cleavage (Roberts 2004). Although this politicization of class in Venezuela has certainly been most prominent since the election of Hugo Chávez as president in 1998, it dates at least from the late 1980s. As an important party leader of COPEI put it, "As long as there were resources from petroleum, health care and education reached the people.... But when the role of petroleum fell in real terms, that was the beginning of the discontent of which Chávez [later] took advantage. The large parties [AD and COPEI] started to lose" support.[23]

I argue here that the decline in oil rents, combined with high levels of inequality, produced the structural base necessary for the politicization of class in Venezuela. Class conflict in turn made Venezuelan democracy significantly more costly to elites, raising the specter of redistribution through the ballot box, and ultimately contributed to the destabilization of democracy—as, for example, with the attempted coup of 2002. I develop this argument in further detail in the rest of this section.

One central explanatory factor is that the ability of the state to finance public spending from oil rents was severely undermined in the 1980s and 1990s.[24] Faced first with the effects of the oil price shock in the mid-1980s and then with the fiscal effects of a reduced percentage take of oil revenues in the late 1980s and 1990s (Mommer 2003), the state received a dwindling share of a shrinking pie. This dramatically affected spending patterns and helped to transform the social-structural base of the Venezuelan political economy. In 1993, per capita social spending was 40 percent below its 1980 level, including "real cuts of greater than 40 percent in education programs, 70 percent in housing and urban development, 37 percent in health care, and 56 percent in social development and participation" (Roberts 2004: 59). García Larralde (2000) estimates that spending on education and health care fell even further, from 1,100 *bolívares* per capita in constant 1984 prices to about one-third of that amount during the Caldera administration (1994–1999). The prolonged economic crisis was generalized, as gross domestic

[23] Interview, Gustavo Tarre Briceño, member of the national executive committee of COPEI; Caracas, May 23, 2005.

[24] Another important factor was the need to service debt taken on during the expansionist 1970s. Baptista and Mommer (1988) note that by 1986, 75 percent of rents went to service principal and interest on the debt.

product fell nearly 20 percent from the late 1970s to the mid-1990s (Crisp 2000; Karl 1997), yet the impact fell particularly heavily on lower-income groups. Between 1984 and 1995 the proportion of the population living below the poverty line increased from 36 to 66 percent, while the purchasing power of the minimum wage dropped by more than two-thirds between 1978 and 1994.[25] Real industrial wages plummeted, reaching by the late 1990s less than 40 percent of their 1980 levels, while the percentage of workers employed in the informal sector rose from around 35 percent in 1980 to 53 percent in 1999.[26] Inequality may have increased moderately as well (though levels of inequality have been constantly very high throughout the twentieth century).[27] The fall in public spending thus contributed to a marked shift in the social-structural base of the Venezuelan political economy.

This shift contributed to a new politicization of class in Venezuela.[28] For example, popular mobilization, some of it more "organized" than others, took on sharply defined class tones. The most well-known incident involved the protests that broke out in Caracas in February 1989, after bus drivers promised to pass on to consumers a planned reduction in fuel price subsidies announced by the newly elected government of Carlos Andrés Perez. The protests were brutally suppressed by the national guard and armed forces (Norden 2004: 96) and hundreds were killed (the exact numbers are still debated); journalists referred to this "Caracazo," as the protests came to be called, as "the day the shantytowns came down from the hills" (P. Márquez 2004: 201). Yet, many other popular protests, which totaled more than 5,000 from 1989 to 1992, occurred, and these were concentrated in poorer areas of Caracas and other cities (Ellner 2004). The attempted coup of 1992 led by Chávez and other disaffected military officers (though perhaps not as

[25] I am grateful to Luis Pedro España, Director of the Instituto de Investigaciones Económicas y Sociales of the Universidad Católica Andrés Bello, for discussion of these points. Interview, Caracas, March 11, 2005.

[26] Alfredo Padilla, Instituto de Altos Estudios Sindicales, Confederación de Trabajadores Venezolanos (CTV); interview, Caracas, April 25, 2005. See also Roberts (2004: 59).

[27] CEPAL (1999: 63), for example, found that the income share of the poorest 40 percent shrank from 19.1 percent in 1981 to 14.7 percent in 1997, whereas the income share of the wealthiest 10 percent grew from 21.8 to 32.8 percent (see also G. Márquez 1993). Most notably, all but the wealthiest 20 percent of Venezuelans lost relative income shares over the decades of the 1980s and 1990s (CEPAL 1999: 63).

[28] Bartolini and Mair (1990: 213–20) propose a three-dimensional concept of political cleavages, emphasizing social-structural, organizational, and normative/ideological elements as the concept's constitutive features. Venezuela has experienced a profound political reorientation along all three of these dimensions.

closely linked in the public mind to class politics as it might have been, had more been known at the time about its protagonists) enjoyed wide support among the popular sectors.[29] During the late 1980s and 1990s, popular mobilization and protest increased dramatically and were linked to class politics in a qualitatively different way than during the previous post-1958 democracy.[30]

In addition, and perhaps more germaine to the theory developed here, voting behavior became much more tightly linked to class. The multi-class and integrative components of the party system in Venezuela were almost completely transformed, as the traditional parties almost completely lost electoral support. At the time of the transition to democracy in 1958, Acción Democrática drew its core support base from lower sectors, including especially the rural and urban workers that it had previously organized and mobilized electorally during the *trienio* government of 1945–1948 (Collier and Collier 2001). COPEI, on the other hand, drew greater support from urban middle sectors and traditional elites.[31] Nonetheless, there was considerable convergence over time in the constituencies of AD and COPEI, and both became multi-class "catch-all" parties, though AD retained an organizational advantage in the labor movement (Collier and Collier 2001). Both AD and COPEI had substantial degrees of penetration of the "popular sectors," via the parties' organization of "grassroots committees" (*Comités de Base*) that served as important vehicles for clientelist distribution of public spending to the poor.[32] Party leaders in each district (*parroquia*) and each neighborhood (*barrio*) distributed scholarships, helped constituents obtain public employment or ever-scarce hospital beds, and assisted those who

[29] See the useful discussion of the ideological roots of the coup of 1992 in class politics, as well as anti-establishment sentiment, in Marcano and Barrera Tyszka (2005).

[30] The extent of the change in patterns of popular mobilization can be overstated: in one recent revisionist interpretation, Lopez-Maya and Lander (2006), for example, find that popular protests were more frequent in the earlier period of "stable" democracy than previous analysts had suggested. Yet, they also find an important shift in the purpose of mobilizations, with those in the earlier period after the transition to democracy focused more on political and civic rights and those in the latter period focused on economic issues.

[31] A third party, URD, was more progressive than COPEI but drew support from groups formerly associated with the authoritarian regime of Medina Angarita, while the small Communist Party rivaled AD for support among some labor unions.

[32] Gustavo Tarre Briceño, who was a member of COPEI's national executive committee (and perforce an important party leader or *cogollo* under the old party system; see Coppedge 1994) and later the president of the Finance Commission of the National Assembly during Caldera's second presidency, described the "Comités de Base" to me as important mechanisms for clientelism. Interview, Caracas, May 23, 2005.

wished to avoid military service.[33] The support of AD and COPEI among the popular sectors was roughly equal.[34]

However, the integrative nature of the party system was shattered during the 1990s. Indeed, the party system itself collapsed, as AD and COPEI eventually lost near-total electoral support. This decline was preceded by a generalized weakening of voters' party identifications in the face of a declining economy, voters' perceptions of corruption among officials, and other factors (Seawright 2006), yet the role of social class was also central. In the 1988 Congressional elections AD and COPEI won 48 percent and 33 percent, respectively, of seats in the Chamber of Deputies, for a combined share of 81 percent, and 46 percent each of seats in the Senate, for a combined share of 92 percent (Villasmil et al. 2004, table 1). In the 1993 Congressional elections, AD took only 27 percent of seats and COPEI took 26 percent of seats in the Chamber of Deputies, for a combined share of just 53 percent; in the Senate, the figures were 32 percent and 28 percent, for a combined share of 60 percent (Villasmil et al. 2004, table 2). By the legislative and regional elections of 1998, which were held separately from the presidential elections for the first time in the post-1958 democracy, AD gained around 24 percent and COPEI just around 11 percent of the Congressional vote, and AD won only 35 percent of governorships (Villasmil et al. 2004). In place of the traditional parties rose an array of smaller parties as well as "anti-system" candidates. Even Caldera, who was reelected as president in 1993, ran as an independent backed by a coalition of many smaller parties, rather than as COPEI's candidate. The collapse of the AD-COPEI duopoly and the rise of many smaller parties are underscored by the growth in the vote shares of smaller parties in legislative elections: the effective number of parties in the Chamber of Deputies rose from 2.6 in 1988 to 4.7 in 1993, then reaching 6.1 by 1998.

The failure or inability of the traditional parties to adapt to the new electoral reality constitutes an important puzzle and not one I entirely resolve here. The traditional parties, and especially AD, had strong ties to the formal labor movement, for instance, through the Venezuelan Workers' Confederation (Confederación Venezolano de Trabajadores, CTV). Yet,

[33] Military service was obligatory but many exceptions were made: for instance, students, only children, and people with certain medical conditions (e.g., "flat-footed" people or *piesplano*). This opened many avenues for clientelism toward the popular sectors on the part of both AD and COPEI. Interview, Gustavo Tarre Briceño, Caracas, May 23, 2005.

[34] Tarre Briceño, ibid. COPEI traditionally had more support in the west of the country, while AD had more in the east.

although the relative decline of the formal economy and the rise of economic informality clearly posed a challenge to the organizational basis of the traditional parties, the parties also did not lack ties to the informal sector. In the 1990s, for instance, street vendors in Caracas were required to be part of an association (*gremio*) to apply for permission from the mayor or city council to set up street stalls. As one labor leader emphasized to me, this not only strengthened organizational ties between the traditional parties and the informal sector (AD in particular had strong links to the street vendors' associations) but, especially, generated an important degree of clientelism in the informal sector.[35]

The informal economy and the popular sectors in general could therefore conceivably have been much more successfully cultivated by the traditional parties (as they have been by the Chávez government more recently and especially since 2003; see below). The key constraint seems not to have been organizational nor so much on the spending side but rather on the revenue side. To be sure, in the wake of the Caracazo, attempts were made by the Pérez administration, and later by the Caldera administration, to put into place compensation schemes targeted toward the popular sectors. Pérez, for example, initiated education scholarships (*derecho escolar*), health care (*farmacia popular*), food security (*beca alimentaria*), and day-care (*hogares de cuidado diario*) programs. One COPEI leader told me that the major difference between these programs and the *Misiones* later put into place by the Chávez government (discussed later) was simply that Pérez's programs were run through government ministries and the oil Parastatal Petróleos de Venezuela (PDVSA) was not directly involved in administering the programs.[36]

Yet, the other major difference is obvious: compared to the oil boom of the 1970s (or the more recent boom that began in 2003–2004 in Venezuela), the amount of rents available for such distributive programs was miniscule. Caldera, coming to office in the wake of the impeachment of Pérez and the interim presidency of Ramon J. Velasquez, signed a "letter of intent with the Venezuelan people" (in parody of the letters of intent signed by his predecessor and other Latin American leaders with the International Monetary Fund), in which he pledged more social spending. Yet, the banking crisis of 1994–1995, among other factors, limited his ability to do so.

[35] Alfredo Padilla, Instituto de Altos Estudios Sindicales, Confederación de Trabajadores Venezolanos; interview, Caracas, April 25, 2005.

[36] Gustavo Tarre Briceño. Interview, Caracas, May 23, 2005.

Given low oil prices, and absent more redistribution of non-oil income, the meager distributive programs initiated by Pérez and Caldera clearly could not fill the gap between popular demands "from below" and the supply of spending "from above."[37] One alternative might have been greater redistribution of non-oil income, yet the traditional parties did not pursue this path themselves, for reasons my framework does not entirely elucidate.[38]

What is most important for my argument, however, is that although the electoral fortunes of the traditional parties declined precipitously among Venezuelans of all social strata during the late 1980s and 1990s, backing for the new parties and candidates that emerged to replace the traditional parties broke down notably along class lines. Alternative political movements such as Causa R and, later, Hugo Chávez's Movimiento Quinta República (MVR), sought to mobilize lower sectors to the near exclusion of upper-income groups (Ellner 2004: 19–20; López Maya 2004: 77–8). Though Chávez had a very low level of support in opinion polls when he launched his campaign for the presidential elections of 1998, he rapidly gained a following as the only candidate who did not seem to represent, if not the traditional parties, then at least an elite segment of Venezuelan society.[39] Indeed, Chávez garnered disproportionate support from the poorest Venezuelans in the presidential elections of 1998 (Lander and López Maya 2005), and the opposition to Chávez came disproportionately from upper-income groups. Surveys shortly before the election of 1998 found support

[37] Villasmil (2005: 51–2) and Villasmil et al. (2004) emphasize the gap between the high voter expectations for public spending that were engendered during the rise of the democratic rentier state, especially during the boom of the 1970s, and the ability of the state to finance that spending in the wake of the decline of oil rents. Other analysts routinely stress the importance of the idea that in the wake of the decline of oil, members of the popular sectors perceived the country as rich (in oil) but perceived themselves as poor.

[38] More controversially, another alternative might have involved a reorganization of the fiscal regime in the oil sector; according to Bernard Mommer, Vice-Minister of Energy and Mines during a portion of the Chávez administration, if Caldera had enjoyed the same fiscal regime as in the 1970s, his administration would have obtained US$17.5 billion more for spending than it had; interview, Bernard Mommer, Caracas, May 10, 2005. This counterfactual is complicated, however, because of the possible effects of a tighter fiscal regime on investment and production in the oil sector; see the later discussion.

[39] Among other candidates, Irene Sáez, the mayor of Chacao, an upper-income municipality in Caracas, "offered the prospect of an antiparty candidacy consistent with the middle class's desire to participate in a globalized capitalist economy" (Hellinger 2004: 39), while Henrique Salas Römer, a former member of COPEI and a Yale-educated business leader, proposed "a 200-day program of shock therapy... deregulation of prices, fiscal austerity, reductions in the public bureaucracy, and a review of Venezuela's membership in OPEC" (Buxton 2004: 124).

for Chávez among 83 percent of lower-income groups but just 32 percent among the middle and upper classes (Roberts 2004: 66). This tendency became even more pronounced in the elections of 2000 and 2004.[40] Consistent with the theory developed in this study, the dramatic voter realignment during the 1990s was driven in part by an important "change in voter preferences" (Monaldi et al. 2005); in particular, the preferences on economic policy of richer and poorer voters diverged significantly (Hellinger 2004: 35, table 2.1). Thus, class played an important role in the almost complete transformation of electoral politics.[41]

In a highly unequal country with a majority of poor voters, the preferences of the poor proved most influential at the ballot box. After his election in 1998, Chávez implemented his campaign promise to hold elections for a constituent assembly that would rewrite the constitution; taking advantage of Chávez's political popularity as well as electoral rules that deemphasized proportional representation, Chávez's coalition won 125 out of 131 seats (Norden 2004: 101) and drafted the new Constitution of 1999.[42] Chávez's presidency was then ratified in the "mega-elections" of 2000, as required by the new Constitution, and elections to the new unicameral National Assembly gave the Chavista coalition and Chávez himself enormous power to shape economic policy.

However, early in his adminstration, Chávez in fact moved cautiously on redistributive policy, even as world oil prices remained relatively low through 1999 in the wake of the Asian financial crisis. Yet, with limited fiscal resources, Chávez did not seem to be delivering on promised benefits to the poorest section of the population, and his popularity ratings had fallen sharply by late 2001 (Buxton 2004: 130). It was at this point that Chávez began to implement economic policies that seemed concretely to

[40] Chávez was elected president in 1998, stood for election again in the "mega-elections" of 2000 (as required by the new Constitution of 1999), and then defeated a referendum seeking to recall him from office in August 2004.

[41] A few revisionist studies have suggested that class was not as important a factor in shaping support for Chávez as this discussion would suggest, particularly in the elections of 1998; such studies have pointed to some measure of support for Chávez in relatively "elite" or middle-class neighborhoods, e.g., Chacao in Caracas. However, these districts are themselves quite socially heterogeneous. On economic voting in the 1998 elections, see Weyland (2003).

[42] Norden's (2004) figure is 121 out of 131 because 121 legislators were elected from the so-called Chavista "Kino." However, another three legislators were Chavistas from indigenous districts and one (who later became a Chavista governor from Portuguesa) was a Chavista elected outside of the Kino. The popular vote was roughly 58% for Chávez's coalition and 42% for opposition candidates.

threaten the interests of the private-sector elite. For instance, the passage of several decrees (enabling laws) at the end of 2001 set a ceiling on the size of agricultural estates and subjected proprietors who failed to use more than 80 percent of their land to an "inactivity" tax. This law promised to fall particularly heavily on the 3 percent of proprietors who owned 70 percent of agricultural land (Buxton 2004: 129).[43] In addition, influenced by critics of the previous evolution of Venezuelan oil policy during the 1990s, Chávez also began to move to reassert the central government's control over the state-owned oil company PDVSA—for example, nominating new presidents of PDVSA who were outside the tight inner circle at the company and thereby, in the view of executives at the company, shattering the tradition of "meritocracy" that governed promotions at the state-owned company.[44] For an important section of elites, Venezuela under Chávez would soon follow the path of Fidelismo in Cuba, and the perceived threat of redistribution as well as state control over the economy raised renewed opposition to Chávez among economic elites. Consistent with the emphasis of the model of Chapter Three that actors seek to influence political institutions because institutions allocate future as well as current power, expectations of elites about where Chavismo would *lead* played an especially critical role in arousing opposition to the regime—because, notwithstanding the decrees at the end of 2001, actual redistributive measures remained relatively muted at the time.

The threat of redistribution played an important role in shaping elite support for an attempted coup against Chávez, who was deposed on April 11, 2002, by a group of military conspirators linked to leaders of the largest business association, FEDECAMARAS—only to be brought back to power 48 hours later. Among its actions during its exceedingly brief window in power, the group of business elites who deposed Chávez appointed the head of FEDECAMARAS as interim president, named a new president of PDVSA, and suspended the Constitution of 1999 and dissolved the National Assembly. To be sure, among both the Chavistas and the anti-Chavistas demonstrating and fighting in the streets of central Caracas were members of different economic strata of Venezuelan society, yet Chávez clearly drew his support from the poorest Venezuelans—while the patrician

[43] An agricultural census taken by the Instituto Nacional de Estadísticas (INE) estimated that 5% of the proprietors owned 75% of the land.

[44] Rodrigo Penso, Executive Secretary, Confederación de Trabjadores de Venezuela (CTV); interview, Caracas, May 26, 2006. Ramón Espinasa, former Chief Economist, PDVSA; interview, Caracas, February 24, 2005.

faces of the triumphant coup plotters on national television suggested to some that the traditional Venezuelan elite had been returned to power.

Thus, by 2002 Venezuelan democracy had been both transformed and destabilized, largely in the ways that the general framework developed in this study would predict. The decline in oil rents provided the social-structural basis for the politicization of class and led to a sharp increase in redistributive conflict. Although the politicization of class intensified after the election of Chávez in 1998, it clearly preceded this election by around a decade, a development that was all the more striking in light of the apparent class compromise that characterized the Punto Fijo democracy after 1958 and particularly in the 1970s. The character of democratic institutions themselves evolved during the 1990s, yet this evolution largely *followed* the social-structural transformation of the Venezuelan political economy and the growth of class-based politics. Political movements such as Causa R and, later, the MVR gained substantial support on the basis of class-based platforms during the 1990s, while the intensification of redistributive conflict after the election of Chávez—and particularly after the decrees of 2001, which promised increased redistribution even as low oil prices inhibited the administration's ability to renew the public spending desired by the relatively poor democratic majority—contributed to substantial opposition among elites to the Chávez administration. Ultimately, opposition to the redistributive platform advanced at the end of 2001 contributed to support among important segments of the elite for the attempted coup of 2002. Echoing in striking if inexact ways the breakdown of democracy at the end of the *trienio* period, when elite concern about the monopolization of political power by Rómulo Betancourt and AD contributed to support for the coup of 1948, erstwhile committed democrats supported a military reversal of the economic policy trends initiated after the elections of 1998 and especially at the end of 2001.

To be sure, however, there are many elements of Venezuelan politics during the 1990s and up to the attempted coup of 2002 that the general framework proposed in this study may be less useful for illuminating. One such element, perhaps, is the left-leaning coup attempt of 1992, led by Chávez and other disaffected military officers. On the one hand, the emergence of class as a salient dimension of politics prior to the coup attempt—for example, as reflected by the character and greatly increased number of popular mobilizations after 1989—is consistent with the framework of this study, which predicts an increase in the redistributive preferences of the relatively poor "median voter" as oil rents decline. Rather than responding to the new political reality as oil rents fell, the traditional parties and particularly AD under the second administration of Carlos Andrés Pérez instead adopted the austerity measures as part of the neoliberal package of 1989. The coup attempt of 1992 clearly responded to and attempted to take advantage of the changing preferences of the mass electorate, as retrospective evaluations of the ideological roots of the coup attempt have made clear (see Marcano and Barrera Tyszka 2005); support for the coup was widespread among the popular classes, and even some members of the political class pointed out the new political reality to which the coup attempt seemed to respond.[45] However, without a somewhat ad-hoc reinterpretion of the coup attempt of 1992 as an incipient "revolution from above" in response to a political system that was unwilling or unable to adapt, one is clearly somewhat hard pressed to explain this event within the general framework advanced here.

Another related issue that this framework does not appear to illuminate is the question of why the traditional parties in fact failed to adapt more successfully to the changed electoral atmosphere in the late 1980s and particularly the 1990s. Voting behavior clearly became more tightly linked to class in response to the decline in oil rents while the relatively poor "median voter" was clearly in favor of greater public spending—yet the traditional parties did not respond by spreading the burden of adjustment to economic elites. There *were* some proposals for tax reform initiated as the Venezuelan rentier state waned, most notably the reforms floated in 1989 as a part of Pérez's IMF-backed austerity package, which would have included the adoption of a VAT, modifications to the law on income tax, and further reforms of the tax code. Congress, however, rejected the VAT in 1990, while a modest reform of the income tax was approved in 1991, after 2 years of discussion.[46] Some of the changes to the income tax, however, "had a negative impact on tax collection but were necessary for reasons of economic efficiency. It was hoped that they would have a positive impact in

[45] In a famous address to the legislature the day after the attempted coup of 1992, Rafael Caldera appeared to some to be an apologist for the coup, asking how the masses could maintain their faith in Venezuelan democracy given the recent decline in their social and economic fortunes (see Villasmil et al. 2004). His speech outraged much of the political class but probably contributed to his election as president 2 years later.

[46] As mentioned above, there was also an earlier partial reform of the income tax (*impuesto sobre la renta, ISLR*) that was attempted in 1986. Rodríguez Balsa (1993: 13) reports that the reform, "instead of simplifying and making more efficient the process of tax payment, complicated it to the point that collection of taxes fell more than 25 percent in real terms in the five years after the reform was approved."

the long run, once the elimination of distortions improved the economic environment. But many proposals were modified by Congress under pressure from economic and legislative groups who demanded 'relief from the tax burden for the middle class.' The result was a law that reduced some distortions and simplified various procedures but that augmented the possibility of erosion" of the tax base (García et al. 1998: 5–6, translation mine; see also Villasmil et al. 2004). Revenues from the income tax (*impuesto sobre la renta*, *ISLR*) in fact fell in 1991 and 1992 to their lowest historical levels. In fact, because the reforms allowed for adjustment of assets and liabilities for inflation by firms and creating new exemptions, "the impact [of the reforms] on horizontal and vertical equity was distortionary and regressive" (García et al. 1998: 10, translation mine). The VAT was eventually approved in 1993, under the interim presidency of Ramon J. Velásquez that followed the impeachment and removal from office of Carlos Andrés Pérez, and it had important effects on the collection of tax revenue—though the VAT was hardly a progressive and was probably a lightly regressive tax in the Venezuelan context.[47] Indeed, in his successful campaign for the presidency in 1993, Rafael Caldera campaigned against the VAT "on the grounds of the perverse effect of indirect taxation on the poor" (Villasmil et al. 2004).

At least in the early 1990s, reforms did not move toward spreading the burden of adjustment. Some of this may have reflected the spike in world oil prices as a result of the first Gulf War, which allowed a temporary recovery of public and social spending (see Figures 5.3 and 5.4) and perhaps made the need to adjust less immediately pressing. Nonetheless, as the Caldera administration, which took office in 1994, sought to prioritize social spending even as fiscal resources plummeted, increasing the redistributive tax burden was not the response proposed by the democratic system. As García et al. could write as late as 1998, "excluding revenues from petroleum, Venezuela has one of the lowest levels of taxation in the world. The majority of industrialized countries have a level [of tax revenues] between

[47] There is substantial debate on the regressivity or neutrality of the VAT in Venezuela; see García et al. (1998). Governments throughout Latin America adopted the VAT during the 1980s and 1990s; indeed, there appeared to be substantial consensus that VATs offered not only the most efficient means of tax collection but also the most feasible form of redistribution (Engel, Galetovic, and Raddatz 1999). From this perspective, the focus on VATs at the expense of progressive direct taxes may be less of a puzzle for the framework developed here than it initially appears. I am grateful to Mariano Tommasi for his comments on this topic.

30 and 40 percent of gross domestic product; and the majority of developing countries, between 15 and 20 percent. In 1994, non-petroleum taxation in Venezuela reached 11 percent of gross domestic product" (1998: 5, translation mine). The failure to spread the burden of adjustment to elites might well lie in the particular nature of the Venezuelan party system, which gave elites themselves substantial control over the introduction of policy reforms (Coppedge 1994), in the rise of presidents without strong ties to parties in the 1990s (Corrales 2002), or in other factors (see Villasmil et al. 2004).[48] Further consideration of these factors constitutes an important topic for future research.

Finally, it may be useful to conclude this section with a more systematic examination of the sources of the rise and decline of oil rents in Venezuela. As discussed above, two factors contributed to the demise of the Venezuelan rentier state during the 1980s and 1990s. The first and by far the most important variable was the negative world oil price shocks in the 1980s, which contributed markedly to the fall in the real value of central government oil revenues, as in the other major oil exporters. This was the major factor behind the secular decline in government oil revenues that began at the start of the 1980s and is depicted in Figure 5.1. Second, however, the Venezuelan central government itself also began to receive a smaller percentage share of total revenues in the oil sector, especially in the late 1980s and the 1990s. As described earlier, the central government's share of revenues had increased during the first democratic government (from 1945 to 1948) and then rose much more markedly during the 1960s. Ironically, however, the percentage take of the central government began to decline *after* nationalization, and especially during the 1990s, as foreign multi-nationals were invited to invest in servicing "marginal" oil fields and in production of "extra-heavy" oil located in Venezuela's Orinoco Belt.[49] As described below, these multi-nationals were given very favorable tax and royalty treatment, as was allegedly necessary to attract this investment; combined with

48 For example, the framework developed here predicts that the democratic system might fail to adopt redistributive reforms due to fear of a coup from the right—i.e., that there might be an endogenous moderation of democratic policy in anticipation of a coup threat. I am not aware of evidence on this point from the Venezuelan case, however.

49 Extra-heavy oil has higher viscosity and specific gravity and is much more costly and capital-intensive to extract and bring to market than lighter crudes, as it requires special refineries. Venezuela has the largest heavy-oil reserves in the world; including the heavy oil of the Orinoco Belt in the calculation of Venezuela's crude reserves would imply a level of reserves greater than Saudi Arabia. See inter alia Mommer (2003).

other factors, this implied a decline in the share of total gross revenue in the oil sector that was appropriated by the central government.[50] By 2000, the percentage of total revenues appropriated by the state had declined to around 20 percent—that is, to levels not seen since the 1930s, *before* Venezuela's first democratic transition. Beginning in the 1980s, the central government received a dwindling share of a shrinking oil pie.[51]

The decline in the central government's share of total revenues in the oil sector is controversial because, according to critics of the company during the 1990s, PDVSA's executives made conscious efforts to shield fiscal revenue from the central government's fiscal coffers (see Baena 1999; Mommer 2003). Though other observers suggest that the need to attract foreign investment on the upstream production side and to secure markets for Venezuelan heavy oil on the downstream side motivated PDVSA's management during this period, there was clearly disagreement between the managers of the state-owned (but legally profit-making) enterprise and some actors at the center about the extent to which PDVSA should retain revenues for its investment budget.[52] Particularly after a nearly 3-month strike in 2002–2003 that was concentrated in the oil sector, the Chávez administration would make an issue of the apparently "subversive" actions of PDVSA executives who sought to reduce the extent of the company's fiscal contributions to the central government (Mommer 2003).

I focus on these considerations here because they might seem to raise important issues for the general approach to rents and to rentier states developed in this book. The central government's struggle to control revenues might suggest that oil rents fall like something less than "manna from heaven" into the fiscal coffers of the state. Indeed, it is almost certainly

[50] One such factor, according to Mommer (2003), was the purchase by PDVSA in the 1990s of heavy-oil refineries and retail interests, through its subsidiary CITGO, in the United States and Europe. PDVSA itself effectively became a multi-national company during this period: by the end of the 1990s, around 20 percent of PDVSA's consolidated assets were held outside of Venezuela, foreign holdings were valued at around $7–8 billion, and PDVSA was the third largest refiner of oil in the United States, behind only Exxon Mobil and BP Amoco (Monaldi 2002b: 26–7). According to the company's critics, this effectively allowed the parastatal to pass its profits to relatively low-tax jurisdictions abroad and import costs for accounting and fiscal purposes. See also Boué (1997) and Baena (1999).

[51] I am grateful for comments on this topic from Luis Lander and Dick Parker, Facultad de Ciencias Económicas y Sociales (FACES) of the Universidad Central de Venezuela (UCV). Interview, Caracas, February 22, 2005.

[52] Indeed, the former Chief Economist of PDVSA characterized this as a "distributive struggle within the State" over control of PDVSA's earnings. Interview, Ramón Espinasa, Caracas, February 24, 2005.

correct, as I already emphasized in Chapters One and Two, that rents are not "manna" in any absolute sense: despite the high-sunk costs and other aspects of resource industries that allow the state to appropriate rents relatively easily, resource sectors also share the characteristics of many other industries in market-oriented economies, such as the need to attract investment. However, the idea that rents are like "manna" is intended as a *relative* statement: resource rents are easy for the state to extract, *relative* to other sources of revenue and in particular relative to taxation of the private income of citizens. For reasons I detail elsewhere, this must almost certainly be true on average (see Chapter Two). In fact, the presence of an apparent distributive struggle over rents does nothing to undercut the validity of the basic contrast between rents and other sources of revenue.

Assuming that this alleged distributive struggle between the parastatal and the central government was in fact a salient cause of the decline in rents during the 1990s, a much more problematic issue for our approach might be the following charge: the level of resource rents is itself endogenous to the *regime type*. Perhaps democracies or autocracies, respectively, have a more difficult time extracting rents—and thus what I treat as an exogenous independent variable is in fact endogenous.

Yet, this claim is belied by evidence from the Venezuelan case itself, for the democratic period since 1958 witnessed the greatest *rise* in the central government's rent extraction, in both absolute and relative terms, as well as its greatest decline. In fact, it was the authoritarian government of Medina Angarita that in 1943 passed hydrocarbon legislation raising taxes and royalties on the foreign companies operating in Venezuela and setting the basic legislative structure for governing the industry that would endure until nationalization in 1975.[53] Yet, the growth of the percentage take of the central government after 1945, and especially during the 1960s, reflected the influence of the democratic leaders of Acción Democrática who had long made the capture of greater oil rents one of the party's main policy platforms (Betancourt 1956). During the *trienio* government of 1945–1948, income tax on the companies (the *Impuesto sobre la Renta*, ISLR) was raised from 12 percent to 28.5 percent, and royalty payments were set at 16.67 percent. The *trienio* government also moved toward establishing the later principle of a fifty-fifty split of profits between companies and the state, first via a decree in 1945 and then by a reform of the tax code in 1948, and

[53] Note, however, that AD leaders ended up opposing the legislation as insufficiently radical (Betancourt 1956: 182–7).

promoted a policy of "no more concessions" of oil exploitation rights to private companies (Betancourt 1956: 242–5).[54] After the return to democracy in 1958, with the founder of OPEC, Juan Pablo Pérez Alfonso, at the helm of oil policy, taxes on the companies were raised from 28.5 percent to 47.5 percent, which contributed to achieving a government–company split of sixty-forty of on profits (the so-called *Decreto Sanabria*; see Pérez Alfonso 2003), and then to 52 percent in 1967 and 60 percent in 1970.[55] These trends, however, were common to the major oil exporters during this period: changing world market conditions enabled substantially more bargaining power on the part of the world's oil-producing states, a process pushed forward by the founding of OPEC in 1960.

I argue here that it is not the regime type per se that causes trends in state "take" but rather a complicated set of factors involving evolutions in the structure of the world oil market, the different basis of the relationship between the central government and foreign multi-nationals and between the central government and state-owned companies, and other factors. Although these factors are rich, complex, and quite interesting, they ultimately simply form a background for the main argument advanced in this chapter. Indeed, a central premise here is that politicians in both democratic and authoritarian regimes have strong incentives to maximize rents through any means possible. It is perhaps telling that among the founding members of OPEC, an organization explicitly designed to maximize the rents of oil-producing states, there were four authoritarian countries (Iraq, Iran, Saudi Arabia and Kuwait) and one democracy (Venezuela)—and the leader, Juan Pablo Pérez Alfonso, came from the democratic regime. Rent may not fall

[54] The two main mechanisms for collecting revenue from the oil industry in Venezuela, as in other states, are royalty payments—a percentage of the gross value of production at current prices—and taxes on profits. Other related mechanisms—e.g., requiring companies to value exports at a "price" set by the government, for purposes of royalty payments (the so-called *valor fiscal de exportación*)—contributed to raising the percentage take of the state, as did other levies.

[55] Other mechanisms that reinforced the control of the central government over the oil sector included the Constitution of 1961, which made new concessions subject to the approval of Congress, thus enshrining the policy of "no new concessions" first advanced during the *trienio*; the so-called fiscal export value (*valor fiscal de exportación*) according to which companies would value exports at a price set by the government, chiefly as a way to avoid the practice of transfer pricing through which multi-nationals sold cheap oil to their subsidiaries abroad; and, in 1971, the so-called Reversión Law ("*Ley sobre bienes afecto a la reversión*"), which governed the return of oil production infrastructure to the state at the end of the forty-year concessionary period foreseen in the 1943 hydrocarbons law, i.e., in 1983.

into the fiscal coffers of the state precisely like manna, yet it is also less costly for states to extract than citizens' taxes—and leaders at the helm of both democratic and authoritarian states have strong incentives to extract rents.

5.2.3 The Renewal of the Democratic Rentier State?

"Socialism in a petro-state can temporarily dispense with blood and fire." From a newspaper editorial by an academic commentator associated with the Venezuelan opposition to Hugo Chávez (Romero 2005).

In recent years, and particularly since 2002, a number of factors have restored the central role of oil rents in the Venezuelan fiscal budget. First, and most important, world oil prices rose dramatically in response to the possibility and, eventually, the reality of the U.S.-led invasion of Iraq, as well as other developments in the world oil markets. At the beginning of December 2002, a barrel of Venezuelan Tia Juana Light (31° API) sold on the spot market for US$24.13; at the beginning of the same month in 2003, 2004, 2005, 2006, and 2007, the per-barrel spot price was at $28.10, $42.26, $50.25, $56.47, and $84.63 (US-EIA 2008). Prices for other grades of Venezuelan petroleum, including the heavy crude oil produced in the country's Orinoco Belt, experienced a similarly sharp upward trajectory between 2002 and 2006, and especially beginning in 2004. Second, tensions between the executive branch and the management of the state-owned oil company, PDVSA, led to a showdown in the failed oil strike of December 2002–February 2003; the executive branch emerged victorious from this showdown, as described further in this chapter, which led to a substantial reconstruction of the central government's fiscal relationship to the oil sector.[56] Third, increased payments to the Fisc from foreign operators of Venezuelan oil fields contributed as well to the renewed role of oil rents as a source of public finance.

Collectively, these factors have caused oil rents to accrue to the central government at staggering levels since 2003 and especially 2004. Though the level of oil rents is not yet quite as enormous in real terms as during the boom of the 1970s, it is clearly appropriate to suggest that rents have been restored as the fiscal basis of the state since 2003. In other words, Venezuela is again a rentier state in the midst of an oil boom. Yet, what are the political effects of this boom?

[56] Alvaro Silva Calderón, former Secretary General of OPEC and Minister of Energy and Mines. Interview, Caracas, February 28, 2005.

The framework developed in this study would predict that, even if the new boom has some authoritarian and some democratic effects, the renewal of the Venezuelan rentier state since 2003 would—as in earlier episodes of rentierism in Venezuela—have a net democratizing effect. Evaluating this prediction raises a host of complicated issues, however. First, few issues are as polarizing for Venezuelans (as well, perhaps, as for scholars of contemporary Venezuelan politics) as the sources and nature of the contemporary Chávez administration, and so an evaluation of the evidence must wade through many competing claims—most notably, of course, about the extent to which the contemporary Venezuelan regime should be considered democratic. Of course, it is also important to separate evaluations of the nature of the regime type—that is, the value for this case on the dependent variable—from the question of interest here, which is the impact or causal effect of oil rents on the regime type. Second, the recency of this period means that data with which to evaluate predictions are not yet fully available; the evolution of Venezuelan politics in the most recent years is clearly an unfolding and as-yet-unfinished story as of the time of this writing. It is important to emphasize that nothing in the broader argument I make depends on resolving these complex issues here.

Nonetheless, I take up the implications of the most recent period in this section of this chapter. I argue that the theoretical model developed in this study is consistent in important respects with the evidence from Venezuela in the wake of its most recent oil boom, even as it is less helpful for explaining other aspects of recent developments. First, the oil boom has prompted a dramatic and remarkable growth in public spending on goods and services valued by the relatively poor majority—especially, social spending on health, education, subsidized basic foods, and other items. Second, as in earlier booms, this growth of public spending has thus far come at remarkably little redistributive cost to Venezuelan elites—a fact all the more remarkable in light of rhetorical attacks on the "squalid oligarchy" by Venezuelan president Hugo Chávez and a move toward statism and a more "socialist" economic model. As I discuss later, this is not to imply that Chavismo has been uncostly for elites; it is instead to assert that the dramatic rise in public and social spending has come at less redistributive cost to Venezuelan private elites than would very plausibly be the case in the counterfactual case of low oil prices. The key is to assess the political consequences of these economic developments. Here, the evidence appears more mixed. On the one hand, consistent with this book's framework, there also appears to be some evidence of diminished polarization and reduced

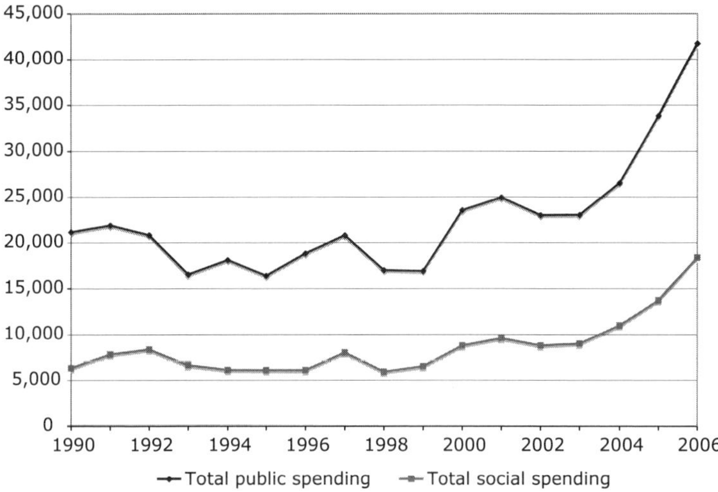

Figure 5.3 Total and social expenditures in Venezuela, 1990–2006 (billions of 2000 *bolívares*).

elite incentives to oppose a populist democracy through anti-democratic means, relative to the period of low oil prices between the election of Chávez and the renewal of the rentier state that began in 2003. On the other hand, various threats to Schumpetarian democracy, including decreased electoral competition and an important degree of incumbent advantage, are also very plausibly due to the renewed accrual of oil rents to the state. These necessarily tentative observations are probed further in this subsection.

Class Polarization, Public Spending, and the Political Trajectory of Chavismo First, and most uncontroversially, the state's renewed access to oil rents has clearly allowed public and especially social spending to rise at a remarkable rate. Figure 5.3 shows total real public and social spending since 1990; as the figure suggests, the growth has been particularly sharp since 2003–2004.[57] Per capita public spending as a whole has grown at an average annual rate of nearly 7 percent since 1998. Social spending, which includes education, health, housing, social security, and other categories, has risen sharply as well.[58]

[57] The source of data is the Ministerio de Planificación y Desarrollo—Sistema Integrado de Indicadores Sociales para Venezuela (MPD-SISOV). After 2003, direct social spending by PDVSA is included.

[58] Arturo Tremont, Deputy and member of Social Development Commission, National Assembly. Interview, Caracas, April 15, 2005.

The general increase in public spending has been disproportionately concentrated in various kinds of social spending as well: between 1998 and 2004, real social spending per capita grew more than 50 percent (MPD-SISOV 2005), rising more than 20 percent between 2003 and 2004 alone.[59] As a percentage of GDP, social spending was at a low point of 7.1 in 1996 but rose steadily to 12.3 percent in 2004. Increases in social spending have in turn been concentrated on public education and social security provision.[60] For example, real per capita spending on public education grew more than 75 percent between 1998 and 2004, rising from 3.2 to 5.3 percent of GDP. Health care spending has also grown, though somewhat less markedly: real per capita expenditures on health care grew nearly 40 percent from 1998 to 2004.[61] For each of these categories of social spending, the sharpest increases have come since 2002 and particularly between 2003 and 2004. Figure 5.4 shows real spending on both health care and education since 1990 and makes the increase in the last few years very clear.

The relationship of oil rents to these recent increases in public and social spending is direct and widely advertised by the central government in Venezuela. An important portion of oil revenues is now deposited in a Fund for Economic and Social Development of the Country (*Fondo para el Desarrollo Económico y Social del País*, FONDESPA) that is administered at the National Economic and Social Development Bank (BANDES) and that is to be used for infrastructure and other public works, agricultural activities, health, and education. In addition, a proportion of petroleum revenues, instead of being exchanged into *bolívares* at the Central Bank as previously required since 1982, is now deposited by PDVSA directly into a National Development Fund (Fondo de Desarrollo Nacional, FONDEN); like the FONDESPA, this fund has as its objectives the financing of productive projects, education, and health care services (Parra Luzzardo, 2005).

Direct social spending by the oil parastatal PDVSA itself has also increased greatly, much of it going to fund the ever-increasing number of

[59] It may be most appropriate to discuss the path of social spending since 2003 because this was the year in which the new oil boom began; on the other hand, economic indicators fell sharply at the start of 2003 as a result of the general strike in 2002–2003. The general time trend of the indicators discussed here can be seen in Figures 5.3 and 5.4.

[60] The focus on education and social security seems to have come partially at the expense of spending on housing (MPD-SISOV, figures not presented here).

[61] The lower relative share of health care expenditures may partially reflect the nature of one of the new health care delivery programs, the so-called *Misión Barrio Adentro*, which relies in part on the low-cost medical services of more than 11,000 Cuban doctors.

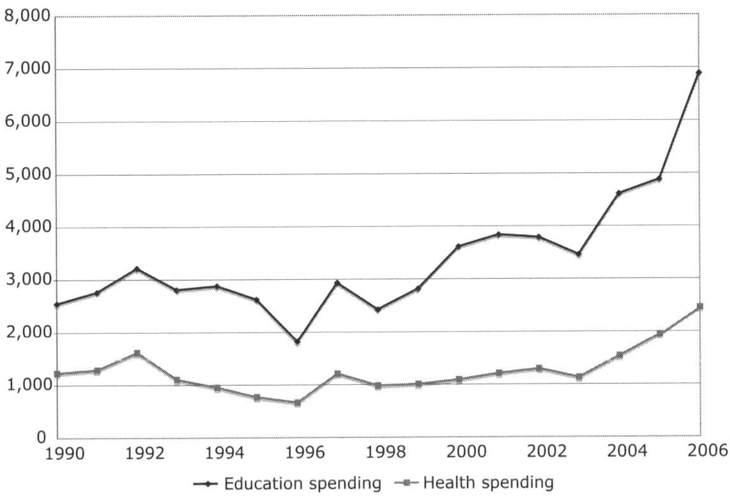

Figure 5.4 Education and health spending, 1990–2006 (billions of 2000 *bolívares*).

Missions (or *Misiones*), which are service delivery programs set up in poor urban neighborhoods and rural areas to provide health care, education, and other social services, as well as to subsidize food through a public supermarket chain, Mercal.[62] PDVSA reports having transferred Bs. 916 billion (around US$486 million, at the official exchange rate for 2004) to the Ribas Mission, which funds secondary education; Bs. 197 billion (US$105 million) as of May 2005 to *Misión Barrio Adentro* (Mission Neighborhood Within), the primary health care mission[63]; Bs. 179 billion (US$95 million) to the Mercal Mission (*Misión Mercal*), the subsidized supermarket chain; and other funds for a technical education mission (*Misión Vuelvan Caras*), for a mission that has registered previously unregistered voters (*Misión Identidad*), for a mission that provides assistance to indigenous communities (*Misión Guaicaipuro*), and for the construction of the Bolivarian University of Venezuela (UBV) as well as scholarships for students at the university. Other sources report PDVSA's total social expenditures in recent years at more than US$7 billion. The central government assigned Bs. 634 billion

[62] According to PDVSA, "The state subsidy to [basic food items] is 40%, and in cases of extreme poverty, the distribution is totally free. In less than a year since its founding, the Mercal Mission had reached nearly 75% of Venezuela's poor." See www.pdvsa.com, accessed January 2008.

[63] As mentioned above, this mission is jointly financed by Venezuela and Cuba and sends Cuban doctors to Venezuela to serve as primary care physicians in poor neighborhoods.

(US$301 million, at the exchange rate for 2005) to the Mercal supermarket chain and many other billions of *bolívares* to the other Missions.[64]

A sizable percentage of the Venezuelan population reports having benefited from the Missions. An AP-IPSOS poll taken in 2006, like many other public opinion surveys, found that voters had benefited from the *Misiones* and particularly from the missions focused on health care and education as well as the subsidized supermarket chain Mercal. Indeed, nearly 60 percent of respondents reported that they or family members have benefited from Mercal, while 42 percent reported benefiting from *Barrio Adentro* (the health care Mission that has brought Cuban doctors to Venezuela). Substantial though smaller percentages also report benefiting from such programs as the *Misión Ribas* (a program that provides scholarships to help adults finish high school), *Misión Robinson* (a literacy program), and *Misión Habitat* (a housing program), along with other Missions (AP-IPSOS 2006).[65]

In sum, the connection of oil rent to the delivery of social spending that reaches significant sections of the Venezuelan population is direct and broadly proclaimed by the government itself, and the rent has clearly been widely distributed. As a widely seen propaganda ad on the state-owned station, Venezuela de Televisión, has put it, "Now oil has many Missions."[66]

The second point to make about the recent boom in oil rents is that it appears to have diminished the redistributive cost of Chavismo to elites in Venezuela. The point is not that Chavismo has been uncostly in economic terms to elites in Venezuela, although the relative lack of overt redistribution to date, for which I discuss evidence in this section, is particularly striking in light of Chávez's public discourse, which has often contained sharp criticisms of the so-called squalid oligarchy. The point instead rests on a counterfactual claim: redistribution under Chávez would very likely be more costly for elites in the case of low rather than high oil prices.

There are several kinds of evidence that help sustain this claim. One type comes from comparing redistributive policies under Chávez to those

64 The spending figures for PDVSA and the central government reported in the previous two sentences are given at www.pdvsa.com, accessed January 2008.

65 Note that these are self-reports from surveys; the interest here is not in the effect, for example on literacy, of receiving funding or scholarships, which has been widely discussed (see Ortega et al. 2006), but rather on whether Venezuelans report having benefited from such programs; this seems to be the crucial question for gauging the political impact of the spending.

66 The essential role of oil in this political project was also underscored to me by Bernard Mommer, Vice-Minister of Energy and Mines: "There is no Chavista program without petroleum." Interview, Caracas, May 10, 2005.

proposed or carried out by earlier, relatively radical regimes, during periods of lower oil rents in twentieth-century Venezuela: namely, the *trienio* government of 1945–1948 and also the government elected after the second transition to democracy in 1958. Another comes from over-time evidence from the Venezuelan case itself, that is, from comparing redistributive policies under Chávez when oil rents were relatively low, as in the first years of the administration, to redistributive policies during the boom. The perhaps surprising conclusion drawn from such a comparison is that even as the regime has radicalized both discourse and policies in many arenas, the direct redistributive cost to elites remains quite moderate during the current oil boom.

For instance, the current land reform is arguably less extensive than either the agrarian reform that was initiated during the *trienio* of 1945–1948 or that which in fact followed redemocratization in 1958—and almost certainly is not more extensive than these other agrarian reforms. With respect to the *trienio*, reform was among the first initiatives announced after the Revolutionary Government Junta took power in 1945, in a speech given by Rómulo Betancourt in December of that year, and the reform commenced with two decrees issued in December 1945 and February 1947 (Betancourt 1956: 391, 397). Betancourt reports that by 1947 nearly 6,000 peasants had already benefited from the distribution of government lands, while another 25,000 had benefited from extensive credits to peasant associations and tens of thousands more from credit and land granted to newly created agricultural communities (Betancourt 1956: 397–8). Article 69 of the new Constitution of 1947 then codified the agrarian reform, requiring the state to realize:

> a systematic and planned action oriented towards transforming the national agrarian structure, rationalizing agricultural production, organizing and distributing credit, improving the conditions of rural life, and [ensuring] the progressive economic and social emancipation of the peasant population. A special law will determine the technical conditions... in accordance with the national interest, necessary to make effective the right that the national recognizes to peasant associations and individuals capable of agricultural work, who lack workable lands or do not possess them in sufficient quantities, to be granted these and the means necessary to make them productive (Betancourt 1956: 401–2, translation mine).

This new agrarian reform law required by the Constitution, was passed in October 1948, just over a month before the coup removed the AD government from power; the National Agrarian Institute created by the law was endowed with 100 million *bolívares* and would have received annual contributions of 2 to 4 percent of the central government's budget (Betancourt 1956: 402). In all likelihood, the program would have involved a quite radical restructuring of land-tenure relations in the countryside, as a reading of Betancourt's (1956: 381–404) own account makes clear. This agrarian reform, however, was cut short by the coup in November 1948.

The agrarian reform law of 1961, on the other hand, adopted after the return to democracy, was actually implemented and therefore entailed a more extensive restructuring of land-tenure relations in the countryside. By 1968, the AD regime had established more than eight hundred agricultural settlements with a "full panoply of coordinated [government] services" that "directly affected the lives of as many as 100,000 peasant families, bringing them slowly into the main channels of the national economy" (Powell 1971: 110). Goodwin (2001: 231) estimates that by 1975 more than a quarter of rural households in Venezuela benefited from the land reform. Other estimates suggest that between 1960 and 1998, 11.5 million hectares were distributed to 230,000 families (Instituto Nacional de Tierras, 1998). To be sure, for some observers the actual amount of land distributed through the agrarian reforms begun in the 1960s seemed insufficient. At the same time, elites were surely hostile to these reforms, though oil rents helped finance the compensation paid for expropriated lands; still, oil rents were not as important a source of state finance as they would be in the 1970s—or after 2002.[67] Goodwin, in his study of revolutionary movements, scores the Venezuelan case after 1961 as one of the few that successfully implemented agrarian reforms in Latin America; citing Paige (1997: 136), he (2001: 231) calls the Venezuelan reform "the third most extensive nonsocialist agrarian reform in Latin America, after the Bolivian and Mexican reforms associated with the revolutions that took place in those countries."

Compared to the agrarian reforms of 1945–1948 and 1961, the current Venezuelan land reform to date appears perhaps surprisingly modest; at the very least, it is certainly not thus far any *more* radical than these prior reforms.[68] As discussed above, the Land Law passed by decree at the end of 2001 set an upper limit on the size of agricultural estates and promised to levy an "inactivity" tax on proprietors who failed to use more than 80 percent of their land. The decree, which particularly appeared to threaten the

[67] Recall that in the 1960s democracy was not as stable as it would later be in the 1970s; for instance, there were several failed coup attempts, and the extensive land reform of the early 1960s surely contributed to motivating support for these coups.

[68] See the *La ley de terras de desarrollo agrario.*

interests of the 3 percent of proprietors who owned 70 percent of agricultural land (Buxton 2004: 129), clearly helped to precipitate the atmosphere that led to the coup attempt of 2002.[69] Since the recovery of oil production and world oil prices after the end of the oil strike in December 2002–February 2003, although the Venezuelan land reform has continued to be a polemic issue, actual redistribution of lands appears relatively slight. The stated intention of the government is to regularize titles to property, and the major direct redistributive action is to move against some estates of more than 5,000 hectares (the definition of a *latifundio*) in which the propietor allegedly cannot prove title to the land. One such target of the land reform, singled out in early 2005, was the El Charcote ranch in western Cojedes state, owned by the British firm Vestey. In fact, concentration of land in the hands of foreign firms has clearly been targeted; as the report of a special commission created by the President of the Republic put it, "Parallel to the land reform [begun in the 1960s], a strong expansion of an empresarial kind has occurred, primarily in public lands, in which the presence of foreign capital is quite worrisome" (translation mine). In addition, the resolution of the standoff with Lord Vestey, the British beef magnate, in early 2006 is typical of conflicts with domestic owners as well: "the Vestey Group handed over two cattle ranches covering 56,000 hectares, in return for keeping another eight totalling 258,000 hectares, in an agreement that has been presented as a model within the agrarian reform process underway" (H. Márquez 2005). As the president of the Venezuelan subsidiary of Vestey put it, the company did not feel "it has lost anything, rather it has gained confidence in its future, and the country has gained, because we have contributed not only land, but also production" (H. Márquez 2005).

While such a statement no doubt reflects the weak negotiating position of this foreign firm vis-a-vis the government, the contemporary "land" reform in fact appears less focused on land redistribution than on alleviating rural poverty through health and education programs as well as subsidies to agricultural inputs. In principle, according to the Land Law of 2001, these rural poverty programs are supposed to be financed with a tax on idle or underutilized lands, as defined in that law. In practice, the taxes are extremely costly to collect (agricultural lands are dispersed, and "underutilization" must be defined, measured, and audited), and oil rents have clearly contributed to the rural health and education programs (as described

[69] Especially, the Decree with Force of Law for Land and Agrarian Development (*Decreto con Fuerza de Ley de Tierras y Desarrollo Agrario*) No. 1546 of 2001.

above in the Missions). Actual redistribution of lands thus appears relatively muted—especially when contrasted to the combative and redistributive political discourse of the government. At a ceremony in early 2005, Chávez stated that "the war against the agricultural estate [*el latifundio*] is the essence of the Bolivarian Revolution," a comment echoed in various ways throughout the year.[70] Because oil rents have paid substantially for rural health and education program as well as for credits to rural associations, one might well ask the counterfactual question of the extent of redistribution in which the government might be engaged in the *absence* of oil rents. Clearly, for purposes of evaluating the causal impact of oil rents on the redistribution of private income, this appears to be the relevant question.

Aside from the land reform, the extent of redistribution in other non-oil sectors of the economy also appears to be quite remarkably modest, again, especially given the degree of overtly redistributive political discourse. The Chávez administration in fact eliminated a tax on bank transactions, and, strikingly, the tax collection agency decided to eliminate the estate tax in 2006. The elimination of the estate tax may be offset by a small new proportional tax on assets, and enforcement of the collection of the sales taxes has been stepped up by the tax collection agency, SENIAT, in perhaps surprisingly effective ways. Of course, sales taxes are generally not progressive and may indeed be lightly regressive; conversely, as discussed in footnote 47, raising the VAT and biasing spending in a pro-poor direction may be one of the most effective ways to redistribute income in the Latin American context (Engel et al. 1999).[71] Yet, even the enforcement of the VAT, a surprising outcome during the boom period, has appeared to mitigate recently; as part of an anti-inflationary package, in 2007 the VAT was reduced from 14 to 11 percent, with a scheduled further reduction to 9 percent.

It is therefore arguably the case that direct redistributive action has been relatively constrained since Chávez defeated the recall referendum of 2004 that would have removed him from office, even as discourse and policies have radicalized along a range of other dimensions. Greatly increased oil rents have allowed for a dramatic rise in public and social spending in the most recent years of the Chávez administration without, however, requiring the regime to incur the full extent of the distortionary costs that would

[70] This was Decree No. 3,408, January 10, 2005.

[71] The distributional effects of the VAT have been debated in Venezuela; see García et al. (1998) for a discussion.

clearly be involved in "soaking the rich." The disconnect between the redistributive political discourse and the redistributive reality is therefore striking. Perhaps the spirit of this argument is captured best by a commentator associated with the opposition, quoted in the epigraph earlier, who put the point as follows: "Socialism in a petro-state can temporarily dispense with blood and fire" (A. Romero 2005, translation mine).

What have been the political effects of this moderation of direct redistributive conflict? Evaluating the causal impact of the recent rise in oil rents on the political regime as a whole remains a complicated issue that raises a number of controversial questions, particularly in light of developments in Venezuela at the time of this writing (in the wake of the rejected constitutional reforms of December 2007). I take these difficult questions up later in the chapter. Here, however, I first emphasize that between the recall referendum of August 2004 and the presidential elections in December 2006, several aspects of Venezuelan politics appear consistent with the theoretical predictions of the book. In particular, even as social class remained the best predictor of support for or opposition to the government, there is some evidence of both a moderation of elite resistance "from above" and of redistributive demands "from below," in ways that are consistent with the theory. In other words, although the Venezuelan polity remained deeply polarized with respect to approval of Hugo Chávez, and even as the discourse of the government remained quite redistributive, many elites appeared to reconcile themselves to aspects of Chavismo even as the base of the Chávez movement appeared to reject moving farther along the path toward what the government has called the "socialism of the twenty-first century."

This evidence for these claims is necessarily tentative yet bears discussion here; I make several main observations. First, I suggest that business elites who had backed the attempted coup of 2002 began to reconcile with the administration in certain ways, as high oil prices brought profits and also seemed to reduce the likelihood of direct redistribution. Second, I discuss evidence from public opinion surveys suggesting that elite resistance to Chávez, and particularly elite disapproval of economic policies, moderated during this period from 2004 to 2006. Third, I describe the way in which a substantial current of the political opposition, instead of boycotting elections as it had in the legislative elections of 2005, favored going to the polls to contest the presidency in 2006; strikingly, in doing so, this more "moderate" wing of the opposition to Chávez even adopted significant elements of the Chavista rent-based public spending program as its own, underscoring that this distribution of oil rents posed a rather limited threat to elite interests. Finally, I discuss the implications of the failure of Chávez's constitutional reform project, rejected by Venezuelan voters in December 2007, for the argument developed here.

First, there are indications that between 2004 and 2006, important sectors of the private sector were reconciled to the administration in ways that are consistent with the argument advanced here. According to at least some observers, in August 2004, a week before the recall referendum that would (as opinion polls had made clear) ratify Chávez's rule, one of the country's richest businessmen allegedly met privately with Chávez. This member of the business elite, who had also allegedly provided financing and/or logistical assistance for the attempt to remove Chávez from power, told the president that he recognized him as Venezuela's president, purportedly reporting that he was "losing lots of money, and wanted economic peace."[72] Though this account remains unconfirmed, the desire of some segments of the elite to get on with life under Chávez may well reflect the economic opportunities (and lack of redistributive cost) posed by the petroleum-led boom. Of course, this is not to suggest that substantial resistance of the most hostile kind did not persist among elites during this period, in a Venezuelan polity that remained highly polarized; it most certainly did. For some segments of this elite, any approximation or conciliation with the Chávez regime suggested a "collaboration" with an illegitimate regime. Moreover, anecdotes such as these are only suggestive, and they can be hard to interpret: for example, in reconciling themselves in certain respects to Chávez's economic platform, were elites reacting to a reduced redistributive threat in the wake of the oil boom or simply accommodating themselves to a political equilibrium in which Chávez had clearly become the predominant political force?

Such questions suggest the utility of looking at other sorts of evidence, which takes us to a second point: public opinion data suggest that elite resistance to Chávez, and particularly elite disapproval of economic policies, moderated during this period from 2004 to 2006. Survey data from Greenberg Quinlan Rosner (GQR) support the claim not only that the Chávez

[72] Paraphrased by Margarita López Maya, sociologist, Universidad Central de Caracas. Interview, Caracas, July 26, 2006. I have not found independent confirmation of the meeting. This businessman allegedly also played a key role in the election of Chávez to the presidency in 1998, providing him with campaign financing and free access to media advertising. However, Chávez's campaign manager told me that the campaign had not received such payments. Interview, Luis Miquilena, Caracas, August 2006.

administration has enjoyed increased general popularity since 2004 but also that, on the matters of economic policy of particular interest here, support has increased most markedly among the upper social strata.[73] Among upper-income groups—those classified among the "A, B, or C plus" income strata, using the system of the Venezuelan national statistics institute—Chávez's general job approval rating (the percent of respondents who strongly or somewhat approve of his performance) rose from 20 percent in March 2004 (1 month before the recall election) to 48 percent in May 2006.[74] Conversely, his general approval rating also rose from 51 percent of respondents in March 2004 to 75 percent in May 2006 among the poorest Venezuelans (the E group), while the corresponding change was from 49 percent to 73 percent among the D group and from 33 to 69 percent among the C group. This evidence again suggests the strong relationship between social class and support for Chávez (with job approval ratings much higher among lower-income groups), yet it also suggests a roughly symmetric increase in job approval ratings among all groups during this time period.[75]

More useful for present purposes is an investigation of public views on economic policy. With respect to Chávez's handling of the economy, there was an appreciable but somewhat modest increase from March 2004 to October 2005 in the approval rating among the poorest respondents, from

[73] I am grateful to Stan Greenberg and Mark Feierstein of GQR for facilitating my access to data reported in this and the following paragraph.

[74] There are two ways to use the GQR data to investigate changing political views by social class. One is to use education as a proxy for class: here, respondents are stratified by highest level of education received (primary, secondary, technical, or university/post-graduate). Another is to use the income stratification system used by the Venezuelan national statistics institute (*Instituto Nacional de Estadística, INE*), which classifies citizens into income strata designated as A, B, C, D, or E, with A being the wealthiest group and E being the poorest. The GQR data to which I gained access in turn collapse the system used by the INE into four categories: "A, B, or C plus"; "C"; "D"; and "E." In the seven surveys administered by GQR in 2004, 2005, and 2006, the "A, B, or C plus" strata comprises between 4 and 6 percent of respondents; including the "C" group as well brings the group to between 17 and 19 percent of respondents. Meanwhile, those who have received university or post-graduate education comprise between 13 and 16 percent of respondents. Thus, the "A, B, or C plus" category may provide a credible proxy for upper-income groups, while including the "C" group or using university/post-graduate education as an alternate proxy may provide a measure of upper and upper-middle income groups.

[75] Chávez's approval ratings among respondents who identify with the opposition party "Primero Justicia" rose from 5 percent in March 2004 to 16 percent in May 2006. Identification with this party grew somewhat over the period, from 5.7 to 8 percent of respondents, but it is unlikely that the changing composition of party members would account for this shift.

47 percent to 56 percent among E strata respondents, from 46 to 55 percent among D strata respondents, and from 37 to 55 percent among C strata respondents.[76] In addition, substantial numbers of respondents from these groups continued to disapprove of economic policy, however: in October 2005, 27 percent of E strata respondents strongly disapproved and 15 percent somewhat disapproved of Chávez's handling of the economy, while the corresponding figures for D strata respondents were 29 and 14 percent, respectively. In contrast, the increase in approval rates among upper-income groups was much more marked. In the "A, B and C plus" strata, those who strongly or somewhat approved of Chávez's handling of the economy rose from 16 to 45 percent of respondents between March 2004 and May 2005; in this period, the percentage of upper-income respondents who strongly disapproved of economic policy fell from 71 to 34, while the percentage who approved somewhat rose from 8 to 23 percent and the percentage who approved strongly rose from 8 to 22. The number of respondents in the "A, B and C plus" strata, who constitute between 4 and 6 percent of the sample in different surveys, is relatively small, making these estimates subject to large sampling variability. However, the pattern is similar among the larger group of respondents who have received university or post-graduate education (around 18 percent of respondents): in this group, approval ratings for economic policy rose from 26 to 53 percent over this period, compared to a rise of 50 to 58 percent among those who have received only primary education, 48 to 55 percent among those who have received secondary education, and 36 to 51 percent among those who have received technical education. Rather remarkably, by October 2005, approval ratings for economic policy did not differ sharply by education levels. These public opinion results are perhaps unsurprising, for the political economic reasons discussed: Chávez increasingly moderated his rhetoric and has reached out to the middle class, giving Christmas bonuses to public servants a month early in 2006 and thus preceding the elections of December 3 (S. Romero 2006a). Public spending *grosso modo* had risen to almost 40 percent of GDP, roughly double the level when Chávez took office in 1999 (S. Romero 2006b; see also Table 5.3).

Third, however, there is evidence that a more moderate and engaged section of the Venezuelan opposition to Chávez gained some ascendancy during the period under consideration. While there had been a complete

[76] Unfortunately, data on approval ratings for economic policy are not available from GQR through May 2006, only through October 2005.

opposition boycott of legislative elections in 2005, which left the National Assembly entirely in the hands of the Chavista coalition, several credible opposition candidates emerged to contest the presidency in the elections of December 2006: Julio Borges, Teodoro Petkoff, and Manuel Rosales. After a planned intra-opposition primary (which would have been unprecedented in Venezuela) was scrapped at the last minute, negotiations led to a relatively united opposition supporting the candidacy of Rosales, the governor of the oil-producing state of Zulia and a longtime Chávez opponent.[77] The presidential elections of 2006 were thus contested by a credible, single opposition candidate, who garnered nearly 40 percent of the vote. To be sure, there remained an important section of the opposition that maintained that any "engagement" with the administration, including engaging in electoral politics, amounted to legitimizing an administration that (in their eyes) was patently illegitimate. Yet the period between 2004 and 2006 also witnessed moderation in this view among substantial sections of the opposition. That Rosales, who was publicly implicated in the failed coup attempt of 2002, opted to challenge Chávez through the electoral route in 2006 may itself be telling.

Of course, Rosales and the opposition faced an uphill fight. Public opinion surveys taken just before the presidential election of December 3, 2006, support these conclusions. An Associated Press-IPSOS poll released on November 24 of 2,500 registered voters (including 1,500 likely voters) found a vote intention of 59 percent for Chávez among likely voters, compared to just 27 percent for Manuel Rosales.[78] There was strong popular backing for the current path of Venezuela, for Chávez himself, and to a lesser extent for the MVR and other parties associated with the government: among likely voters, 62 percent said Venezuela is on the right track; 49 percent approved strongly (and 15 percent more approved but less strongly) of Chávez; and of the 62 percent of likely voters who said they had an affinity for a political organization, 69 percent said they had an affinity for the MVR (while another 5 percent indicated other parties in the government coalition).[79] Sixty-three percent of likely voters said that presidents should

[77] Rosales was also implicated in the failed coup attempt of 2002.

[78] Among registered voters, the respective percentages were 58 and 27 percent. For most questions, percentages are very similar across likely and registered voters; thus, I only report percentages for likely voters in the text. The poll's sampling error was plus or minus 2.2 percentage points for registered voters and plus or minus 2.9 percentage points for likely voters.

[79] The question read, in the Spanish, "*Hay alguna organización de su simpatía en estos momentos?*"

be able to govern more than two consecutive terms, and when read two alternatives (pro-government/Chavista and anti-government/anti-Chavista), 57 percent of likely voters said they considered themselves Chavista (AP-IPSOS 2006). The chances of Rosales competing and winning in the electoral competition of 2006 were thus undeniably slim.

For present purposes, however, what is perhaps most striking about the presidential election of December 2006 is the extent to which the Rosales campaign appeared to lift pages out of Chávez's political-economic book. Rosales advocated the creation of a banking card that he baptized "*Mi Negra*"—loosely, "my dark-skinned woman" or, alternately, "my dear"—that would transfer oil rents directly to the poor. The cards would transfer the cash equivalent of $280 to $460 a month to around three million of the poorest Venezuelans, something akin to the direct payments of oil rent made by the U.S. state of Alaska to its residents (S. Romero 2006a). That the leading candidate of the opposition—a longtime Chávez opponent who was implicated in the coup of 2002—would adopt such a rent distribution platform at the height of the oil boom may only underscore the lack of direct threat that such an economic program in fact poses to private elites.

Finally, it is worth discussing the rejection of the constitutional reform package, initially proposed by Chávez and a coterie of close advisors and then amended and expanded by the National Assembly. The reforms contained in the package, which were voted on in a popular referendum in December 2007, would have amended key articles of the Constitution adopted in 1999; key measures included an extension of the presidential term from 6 to 7 years, the removal of term limits on the presidency (but not other offices), the strengthening of local "communal councils" (*consejos comunales*) at the expense of mayors and governors, and the creation of a social security fund for workers in the informal sector.[80] The reforms would have not only had the effect of helping to entrench Chávez in power, through the removal of term limits and extension of the presidential term but also through the removal of checks on presidential authority at intermediate (mayoral, gubernatorial) levels of government; they would also have had the effect of deepening the social and economic Bolivarian revolution and paving the path toward the still ill-defined "socialism of the twenty-first century."

[80] In the referendum, Venezuelan voters were asked to vote "yes" or "no" on two different "blocks"; the first block A would have amended forty-six articles of the Constitution of 1999, while the second block B, added by the National Assembly, would have reformed an additional twenty-three articles.

The Democratic Effect of Rents

The narrow rejection by voters of the constitutional reform package in December 2007 was widely understood not so much as a rejection of Chávez's mandate as a rejection of the radicalization of the Bolivarian revolution's broader political, social, and economic program. According to the official tallies by the National Electoral Council (CNE), the "yes" option on the Block A reforms received 49.3 percent of the vote, compared to 50.3 percent for the "no"; the "yes" option on the Block B reforms received 48.9 percent, while the "no" received 51.1 percent. The government announced that it would respect results of this referendum several hours after the polls closed, averting a near-certain crisis in the country. Chávez's own approval ratings remained high even after the failure of the recall referendum.[81] Yet, even some core Chávez supporters, many of whom appeared to stay home rather than turn out to vote on the reforms, seemed uncomfortable about the more radical changes portended by the reforms.[82]

The rejection of the constitutional reforms not only augured well for the continuation of Schumpetarian democracy in Venezuela (the acceptance of negative results by the government had not been predicted by many observers); it may also suggest an interesting degree of policy moderation on the part of voters. It is conceivable and consistent with a range of evidence that this moderation owes at least some of its origin to the influence of oil rents. After all, rents are being supplied and spent at a remarkably rapid clip in Venezuela, much of it on goods and services valued by the popular majority; more fundamental restructuring of social relations along the lines envisioned by Chávez may seem unnecessary to say the least to the median voter, in a way consistent with the prediction of Chapter Three that the availability of rents moderates that voter's redistributive demands. Of course, this claim is extremely difficult to evaluate at present, given among other factors the recency of events in Venezuela; the observations on this most recent period sketched above are thus necessarily tentative, and only time will tell how they are borne out by ensuing events.

81 Recognizing perhaps that the failure of the reform package reflected voters' unease about a radicalization of the Bolivarian Revolution rather than a rejection of his mandate, Chávez announced soon after the failure that he would consider a more limited reform in the coming years that would be focused on removing term limits to the presidency.

82 Turnout was a key factor in the defeat of the referendum. According to CNE records, there were 8,883,746 valid ballots cast on block A (with 4,379,392 for the reform and 4,504,354 against it). By contrast, in the presidential election of December 2006, there were 11,790,397 valid votes, with 7,309,080 cast for Chávez. In other words, Chávez's vote total in the presidential election just a year before brought him nearly 3 million more votes than were cast for the constitutional reform.

What does the discussion in this subsection imply for the larger argument, both in this chapter and in the book as a whole? As noted in the introduction to this chapter, the question of interest is not so much the state of democracy in Venezuela today but rather the impact of oil on the state of democracy today. Nonetheless, it is also obviously crucial to have some sense of the quality of democracy itself in contemporary Venezuela, in order to evaluate arguments about the causal impact of oil on the regime. I turn to this question before offering concluding observations on the impact of oil on the regime type in the most recent period.

On the one hand, power is concentrated in the executive to a substantial extent in contemporary Venezuela. This is not necessarily a new phenomenon in Venezuela, nor is the potential role of oil in promoting the power of the state more generally.[83] Yet, it is clear that in contemporary Venezuela, judicial and legislative checks are weak, to say the least. After the approval by voters of the new Constitution in 1999 and the enlargement of the number of justices on the highest bench, it is credible that there is little judicial oversight.[84] The boycott of legislative elections by the opposition in 2005 left the National Assembly entirely in the hands of the Chavista coalition. Chávez himself has made announcements that augur extremely poorly for the longevity of Schumpeterian democracy; for example, after triumphing in the elections of 2006, he announced that prior to the next elections in 2012, he would consider holding a popular referendum on whether the president should be elected for an "indefinite" term. Thus, the claim that there has been a breakdown of liberalism and of checks-and-balances in the Venezuelan system seems credible, while electoral competition and participation could eventually erode as well. At the time of this writing, there is no guarantee that Venezuela will remain a democracy, in a procedural minimal or even in an "electoralist" sense (Karl 1990).

On the other hand, electoral competition and participation have remained fairly robust over the last several years, despite the boycott of legislative elections by the opposition in 2005. Chávez himself has faced the voters in 1998, 2000, 2004 (a recall referendum), and 2006, while constitutional reforms were put directly to the voters in 1999 (when they were

[83] As one labor leader from the political opposition to Chávez told me, the "behavior of Chávez enabled by petroleum is old news ['de vieja data']; it didn't start with Chávez, though it worsened with Chávez." Alfredo Padilla, Instituto de Alto Estudios Sindicales, Confederación de Trabajadores de Venezuela (CTV); interview, Caracas, April 25, 2005.

[84] Historically, of course, judicial oversight of the executive, e.g. during the first Pérez administration, has been weak in Venezuela.

approved) and 2007 (when they were rejected). A year prior to the recall referendum in 2004, there was a substantial probability that the government would lose the recall, as Chávez's popularity ratings had plummeted; the initiation of and heightened funding of the *Misiones* undoubtedly aided in the recovery of Chávez's popularity and his eventual electoral triumph. Corrales and Penfold (2007) note an increase of political competition during the Chávez period, even as they also highlight the decline in institutions of accountability. The 2006 elections were contested by a credible candidate. Even the U.S. Assistant Secretary of State for the Western Hemisphere, Thomas A. Shannon, Jr., was quoted after the presidential elections of 2006 as saying, "Political battle that is unfolding within Venezuela is now conducted through democratic institutions" (S. Romero 2006b, quoted in El País).[85]

In this sense, political outcomes since the failed coup of April 2002 and especially the failed strike of 2004 are arguably consistent with the general theoretical framework advanced in this study. Up to this moment, it is difficult in my view to credibly assert that Schumpeterian democracy has not survived in Venezuela (though not all experts agree). The Chávez presidency was ratified in the failed recall elections of 2004, which were certified by the Carter Center and other international monitors; allegations of widespread fraud in the recall elections that have been advanced by some members of the opposition appear unsubstantiated.[86]

85 Public opinion in Venezuela seems to support this impression as well. A 2005 Latinobarometro survey found that "satisfaction" with democracy in Venezuela was the second highest in Latin America, after Uruguay, and Venezuelans gave a higher ranking of the "democraticness" to their country than respondents in any other Latin American country. In an AP-IPSOS poll, when asked whether their vote really made a difference or not, 95 percent of likely voters said it did, and 71 percent of likely voters said they were "very" or "somewhat" confident that votes would be correctly counted. On the other hand, fully 55 percent of likely voters pronounced themselves "very" or "somewhat" worried that people could suffer repercussions due to their vote in the presidential elections (AP-IPSOS 2006).

86 The Carter Center audited paper ballots in a number of *mesas* or polling stations that were selected randomly. One allegation is that members of the National Election Commission sympathetic to the government knew the seed of the random number generator in advance and thus could alter ballots in polling places that they knew would not be audited. While this hypothesis itself is difficult to assess, there is apparently no credible claim that the audited polling places were not (quasi-)randomly selected. The proportion of the vote for Chávez (i.e., a "no" vote on the recall referendum) among audited ballots should thus provide an unbiased estimate of the proportion of the vote for Chávez in the population of ballots; indeed, the sample estimate is identical up to sampling error as the reported vote for Chávez in the population, around 58% (see Carter Center 2004; Hausmann and Rigobón 2004 provide an argument for fraud that does not, however, dispel the idea that the sampled districts were in fact selected quasi-randomly).

At the time of this writing, then, the political regime remains democratic in the Schumpetarian sense: the right to rule is acquired by means of a competitive struggle for the peoples' vote (Schumpeter 1976). Yet, there is no guarantee that Schumpetarian democracy will continue into the indefinite future. The opposition is extremely weak after withdrawing candidates from recent elections for the National Assembly and losing the presidential elections of 2006, though it appears to have rebounded somewhat with the defeat of the constitutional reform in 2007. Chávez has announced that he may consider a future, more limited constitutional reform aimed only at the removal of term limits. The future of Schumpetarian democracy in Venezuela seems unclear at the time of this writing.

Yet, my main goal here has not been so much to assess or code the democraticness of the contemporary Venezuelan regime as to assess how *oil* has contributed to the degree of democracy. How can we assess the political influence of oil in the most recent period? For some observers, the prevailing arguments in the literature on the authoritarian "resource curse"—for example, the argument that resource rents can create a strong "incumbency advantage" that erodes electoral competition and leads to authoritarianism (e.g., Lam and Wantchekon 2004)—may do more to elucidate current Venezuelan politics than the framework developed here (Corrales 2006). For some analysts, the recent fall in the degree of de facto electoral competition has clearly brought into question the extent to which the current regime is a democratic one (e.g., Corrales 2006), and the disbursement of oil rents has clearly contributed to Chávez's strength at the polls and to his current popularity. For example, as discussed above, some analysts attribute the disbursement of funds to the social Missions prior to the recall election of 2004 to Chávez's strong performance in that election.

On the other hand, it seems highly plausible that the economic cost of Chavismo to elites is substantially lower than it would be in the counterfactual case of low oil prices today. Indeed, analysts from the political opposition have concurred that the greatest threat to democratic stability in Venezuela may come when oil prices eventually *fall*, not when they are high. Pedro Palma, a leading economist, noted that "there could be a very dramatic crisis" if oil prices fall; Eduardo Fernandez, a former presidential candidate, told Reuters that "if petroleum prices decline then authoritarianism will increase" (Wade 2006). The recency of the period and absence of data certainly make it quite difficult to adjudicate between these claims. Yet, I have presented evidence that supports the counterfactual argument that oil rents serve to limit, not further, redistributive conflict—and that this effect of oil rents helps to stabilize democracy, even as oil rents also have had authoritarian effects through other mechanisms. The main argument advanced in this chapter, of course, does not rise or fall on how one views the influence of oil rents on political developments in Venezuela in the most recent years, as these will surely be the subject of debate for many years. Instead, the main focus is on the role of oil rents in stabilizing democracy after the transition of 1958 as well as its more recent destabilization. For this purpose, the theoretical model I develop in this study provides a coherent prediction not only of the emergence of a stable democracy in Venezuela but also of its destabilization. In particular, the theoretical model helps elucidate the relationship of oil rent to redistributive conflict, tax policy, patterns of public spending, and the evolution of social polarization over time. Clearly, as noted above, there are important questions for which this theoretical framework may be less helpful—for example, understanding why the traditional Venezuelan parties failed to adapt to the changed electoral reality of the 1990s. Although the rise and fall of oil rents cannot explain everything about Venezuelan political development in the second half of the twentieth century—it would be foolish to imagine that it might—this is a factor of crucial importance both to understanding the stabilization and destabilization of Venezuelan democracy, in ways that the theory I develop in this study helps illuminate.

5.2.4 Alternative Explanations

It is useful to close this chapter by discussing alternative explanations for democratic stability over the relatively *longue durée* in Venezuela, by way of contrast with the argument developed here. I take up two classes of explanations: first, those that have emphasized the role of oil in fostering democratic stability but have emphasized different mechanisms; second, those that have focused instead on the role of "pacting" or electoral institutions or the party system in fostering democratic stability. In many ways, as we will see, these could be considered not so much alternative explanations so much as complementary. Yet, I argue that without a focus on the role of oil rents in mitigating class and redistributive conflict, each alternative explanation has some difficulty accounting for *both* the stabilization and the destabilization of Venezuelan democracy in a single framework. A focus on these alternative explanations thus highlights the importance of oil rents as a causal factor undergirding democratic stability in Venezuela, in contrast to prevailing views about the authoritarian effects of natural resource rents.

Oil and Democratic Stability The claim that oil rents advanced the stability of democracy after 1958 is found throughout the existing literature on Venezuela, sometimes in ways that appear close to the argument advanced here. Urbaneja (1992), for example, suggests that the presence of a large economic sector such as oil, that "didn't belong to anybody" but that could provide an important source of fiscal revenues, allowed the post-1958 regime to pay for investments in education, health, industrial development, agrarian reform, and other measures without unduly threatening the economic interests of the rich, and many other accounts allude to the idea that oil eased the economic conflict between different social groups. Naím and Piñango (1984) early on emphasized the "illusion of harmony" that oil rents had fostered. Most analysts in this vein have asserted that oil rents created a "positive-sum" game, that is, a political arena with no losers (especially Rey 1989; also España 1989; Karl 1997; and recently, Buxton 2004: 115).

Though these arguments are consonant with the flavor of the thesis advanced here, the theoretical basis for the claim that rents create a positive-sum game seems somewhat thin—as it is not at all clear as a theoretical proposition why the presence of a big "prize" such as oil rents should either limit conflict or promote democracy. If political control of the state brings control of the rents, then oil rents should presumably raise the benefits of, say, a coup d'état, without affecting the costs. It is plausible that oil rents should then, on the margin, increase the incentives for a coup. In the general framework developed in this book, by contrast, there *are* losers—for example, the direct effect of rents can increase the opportunity cost of democracy to elites because political control of the state could confer benefits from the distribution of the resource rent. However, even as the direct effect of resource rents raises the benefit of a coup, the mitigation of redistributive conflict reduces the costliness of democracy—not because oil engenders a positive-sum game (democracy *is* costly to elites here) but because the endogenous effect of oil on the taxation of other forms of income allows democratic majorities to commit to low levels of future redistribution under democracy. As I have emphasized, this latter effect is all the more important in political economies in which high inequality in relatively well-developed non-resource sectors of the economy makes the redistribution of non-resource wealth a salient basis for political conflict. Formulating the theoretical proposition that oil makes democracy better for all groups because it makes politics a "positive-sum" game does not clarify this mechanism, and, indeed, it cannot help us distinguish in comparative perspective why oil should create a "positive-sum" game in some places but more conflict over a bigger "prize" elsewhere.

Perhaps the best-known and most sophisticated argument that oil promoted democracy in Venezuela is the analysis by Karl (1987; also 1997), who combines a focus on the structural economic changes induced by the rise of the oil economy with a focus on the process of political "pacting" that preceded the transition to democracy in 1958. On the structural side of the equation, according to Karl, the growth of the oil economy in the first half of the twentieth century decimated the landed cacao- and coffee-growing aristocracy, in part because real exchange rate movements disadvantaged non-oil tradables (1987: 68–9), and it provoked a dramatic process of rural-to-urban migration among former peasants (1987: 69–70). Perhaps most important, it also created a counter-elite, namely, a new bourgeoisie that had an economic "interest" in democracy: this counter-elite "began to see that the political and economic platform of a party like Acción Democrática might hold some future advantages" (1987: 74). Echoing Barrington Moore (1966), Karl (1987) argues that these structural changes in the economy proved propitious for democracy. Although these factors are different from those I emphasize here, they could certainly be seen as complementary explanations, particularly as explanations for the stabilization of democracy after 1958. At the same time, they are perhaps somewhat less compelling as explanations for the later destabilization of democracy. For one, although oil may well have facilitated the transition to democracy by easing "the virulence of landlord-peasant disputes, providing a permanent 'exit' from the land" (Karl 1987: 70), such an emphasis elucidates neither the strong reaction against land reform by elites during the *trienio* government of 1945–1948 (see Urbaneja 1992: 164–71) nor the continued salience of agrarian reform as a political issue in contemporary Venezuela. For another, although other analysts have echoed Karl's claim that the oil-based economy created a bourgeoisie with an interest in the perpetuation of democracy (España 1989), private-sector elites formed the backbone of support for the coup attempt against Chávez in 2002. The support of these erstwhile convinced democrats for a military coup d'état against a democratically elected government (albeit one that many in the opposition saw as governing in an "undemocratic" fashion) suggests an interpretation with a different emphasis: oil did not create an "interest" in democracy for these elites so much as it limited their disincentives to accept a democratic regime, in a highly unequal society in which a large democratic majority had economic interests opposed to those of the small private elite.

From the perspective of the argument developed here, however, Karl's (1987) most interesting and important contribution may be her emphasis on the relationship between the oil economy and the role of industrialization in the period following the Second World War. Indeed, Karl suggests that industrialization helped to mediate the impact of oil rents on the regime type, because oil "initially served to buttress regime arrangements" (1987: 67) under the authoritarian rule of Gómez (1908–1935), while it later contributed to the stability of democracy after the growth of import-substituting industrialization in the post-war period. The theoretical framework advanced here underscores why this may be so. Industrialization helped to create wealth in the non-resource private sector of the economy that was also highly unequally distributed. To the extent that political pressure under democracy, absent oil, would have produced demands for greater redistribution of this wealth, the democratic effect of oil on easing redistributive conflict in non-resource sectors of the economy could well have become more important over time, as Venezuela industrialized and private income grew. Of course, as pointed out above, the fiscal basis of Venezuela's rentier state was also qualitatively transformed after the breakdown of democracy in 1948 and during the first years of the new democratic regime after 1958. Nonetheless, temporal variation in the extent of industrialization may well contribute to the strengthening of the democratic effect of rents over time, underscoring Karl's assertion that oil rents had different effects on the regime at different points in time within the Venezuelan case.

"Pacts," Institutions, and Democratic Stability In the literature on Venezuela, predominant explanations for democratic stability during the post-1958 period emphasize several factors besides the role of oil rents. One prominent argument focuses on the role of political "pacting" prior to the transition to democracy, as well as the political "learning" that took place among leaders of AD and other parties as a result of the breakdown of democracy in 1948 (Levine 1978; also Karl 1987). Another leading explanation focuses on the role of electoral rules, such as closed party lists, in contributing to the emergence of a stable two-party system, albeit one that reinforced the power of a small group of party leaders and limited the space for alternative agendas to emerge (Coppedge 1994). In general, I view my argument as largely complementary to, rather than competitive with, these explanations. Yet, I find that theories that emphasize such features of

Venezuelan democracy also have difficulty explaining democratic destabilization without making reference to the decline in oil rents.

The literature on political pacts, in particular, appears to suffer from both empirical and theoretical problems. According to this important argument, the "pacts" struck by leaders of AD, COPEI, and a third party (URD) prior to the transition to democracy in 1958 allowed these competing parties to limit conflict by promising to share the spoils of power (including cabinet posts) with electoral losers as well as to enact a common basic economic and development agenda that, especially, would respect the sanctity of private property (Karl 1987: 82–6).[87] In this view, the spirit of these pacts was also institutionalized in the Constitution of 1961, which fashioned electoral laws so as to constrain party competition. In addition, analysts have underscored that repeated interaction between political leaders within the context of a centralized and concentrated party system fostered policy consensus (Monaldi et al. 2005). As Neuhouser (1992: 123–5) and others have argued, however, this argument faces important empirical difficulties. The power-sharing arrangements agreed to by AD, URD, and COPEI in the Pact of Punto Fijo in fact unraveled soon after the transition to democracy: URD defected from the first AD government of Rómulo Betancourt, while COPEI refused cabinet posts in the second AD government of Raul Leoni from 1964–1968. For most of the 1960s, in fact, the party system was characterized by a high degree of fractionalization, relative to the essentially two-party system that had solidified by the 1970s. The argument that pacts agreed to by party leaders before the elections of 1958 helped to produce policy consensus and limit party competition thus seems empirically flawed.

A related theoretical problem, which may also help to explain the empirical difficulties, is that the literature on pacting does not explain why such pacts should have been credible commitment devices. In other words, as political conditions changed, what mechanism ensured that party leaders would not defect from the "pacts" of the immediate pre-transition period? The argument I develop above, like the literature on pacts, suggests that the ability to limit polarization and moderate conflict, particularly over

[87] These agreements, which were signed by the leaders of each party prior to the holding of the first elections and outlined in very broad terms their commitment to consensus, were called the Pacto de Punto Fijo and the Declaración de Principios y Programa Mínimo de Gobierno (Karl 1987: 82).

economic issues, helped to underwrite democratic stability. Yet, in the view I advance here, the ability of parties to commit to limit future redistribution arose endogenously, as a result of the effect of oil rents on the extent of redistribution preferred by the political parties—particularly AD, which historically had represented the interests of the popular classes who would have benefited the most from redistribution, absent oil rents. The fact that policy consensus and institutional stability were weaker in the 1960s than in the 1970s is only further empirical corroboration for this argument, as oil rents increased dramatically during the boom years of the 1970s.[88]

The literature on the role of electoral rules and the evolution of party systems also makes an important contribution to the understanding of democratic stability after the transition of 1958. Yet, this literature is less useful for understanding the destabilization of democracy in the contemporary period. If these institutions promoted democratic stability after 1958, why did they fail to do so in the more recent period? True, there was important institutional evolution in Venezuela during the late 1980s and early 1990s, for instance, increasing decentralization and the direct election of governors (see Monaldi et al. 2005 for a perceptive and lucid discussion). Nonetheless, the basic institutional framework established by the Pacto de Punto Fijo and the Constitution of 1961—the same framework that accompanied Venezuela through at least two decades of solid democratic stability—was still in place in the 1990s. These factors were thus relatively constant, at least relative to the pace of change in the political-economic equilibrium that I have argued underwrote democratic stability. Thus, institutional factors, although clearly complementary to the variables I have emphasized here, cannot alone account for the scope of democratic stabilization in the 1960s and 1970s, nor can they alone explain the destabilization of democracy in the 1990s.

In contrast, the advantage of a focus on the fiscal basis of the democratic rentier state is therefore that such a focus can simultaneously help account both for the stabilization *and* the destabilization of Venezuelan democracy. The theory elaborated here—which, like all theories, is a simplification of a complex reality—nonetheless helps to provide a consistent account of patterns of regime change over the relatively *longue durée* in Venezuela.

Thus, the Venezuelan case largely supports the claim of a democratic effect of resource rents, and "causal-process observations" from the case largely validate the specific mechanism for which I have argued here. Still,

[88] See Neuhouser (1992) for a related argument.

not withstanding the statistical evidence presented in Chapter Four, doubts may linger about the generality of this mechanism. Perhaps Venezuela really is an outlier, in statistical parlance, or perhaps other mechanisms explain the more general association between rents and democracy uncovered in the statistical chapter. In the subsequent chapter, I therefore turn to probing case-study evidence on the democratic effect of resource rents in comparative perspective.

6

Rentier Democracy in Comparative Perspective

The theoretical argument developed in this study, in contrast to recent work on the political effects of natural resource wealth, posits the existence of a democratic effect of resource rents. The theory also suggests conditions under which this democratic effect may become more important, relative to the authoritarian effects of resource wealth, and thereby generates hypotheses to help explain variation in political outcomes across resource-rich countries. The statistical analysis of cross-section time-series data presented in Chapter Four is broadly consistent with these hypotheses, and the Venezuelan case study developed in the previous chapter suggests not only that resource rents have had a democratic effect in Venezuela—a country with a highly unequal distribution of wealth in the relatively well-developed, non-resource sectors of the economy—but also that the mechanisms emphasized in this book can help explain both the stabilization and the destabilization of Venezuelan democracy.

Nonetheless, as discussed earlier, other theories might conceivably be consistent with the evidence presented so far, particularly with respect to the cross-national variation uncovered by the statistical analysis; moreover, Venezuela provides just one case (albeit a rich and informative one) with which to evaluate the theory empirically. In this chapter, I therefore analyze evidence from Chile, Bolivia, Ecuador, and Botswana, leaving detailed examination of other cases to future work. (Several other cases, including cases for which the theory would predict an authoritarian effect of rents, are considered in the concluding chapter.) Chile, Bolivia, and Ecuador can each be considered resource-rich, at least relative to many other Latin American countries; in each country resource rents have provided a significant source of government revenue—although there is also substantial within-case (over-time) variation in the extent to which this is so, which will usefully provide leverage for purposes of evaluating the theory. As a percentage of GDP, however, resource rents have been consistently lower in all three cases, and particularly in Ecuador and Chile, than in typical resource-rich countries of the Persian Gulf and sub-Saharan Africa; thus, these are cases that are resource-rich without being highly resource-dependent, as the latter concept is used in this study. Similarly, as discussed below, Botswana is substantially less resource-dependent than other resource-abundant African states. All four cases are also countries that share a high degree of inequality in non-resource sectors of the economy. According to many scholars, in high-inequality Latin American countries, the politics of redistribution of non-resource wealth (as in, e.g., land reforms) has played an important role in the emergence and persistence of democracy; as discussed below, Botswana exhibits an extremely high degree of inequality as well. These cases therefore provide an additional opportunity to evaluate the causal mechanisms emphasized in this study and, in particular, allow a chance to assess the democratic effect of resource rents in comparative perspective.

How can each of these cases contribute to enriching (and confirming or disconfirming) our understanding of the democratic effect of resource rents? First, Chile is one of Latin America's oldest rentier states, though two different resources (sodium nitrate and copper) have provided substantial rents to the government in different historical periods. Prior to the coup of 1973, Chile was also one of Latin America's oldest and most stable democracies. I argue here that the theory developed here helps to illuminate in new ways the sources of Chile's democratic stability, though my framework is certainly only complementary to other approaches. Yet, Chile also seems to provide a challenge for the theory, in the sense that a famously anti-redistributive coup d'état interrupted democracy in 1973. As I discuss further in this chapter, a closer look at the evidence suggests that many of the observable implications of the theory developed here in fact appear supported by the case-study evidence, notwithstanding the occurrence of the coup. Causal-process observations drawn from this case suggest an important political role for resource rents, in ways perhaps underappreciated by many previous analyses of Chilean democracy.

Next, Bolivia presents a particularly interesting and theoretically enriching case. Prior to the Bolivian Revolution of 1952, by which time tin had supplanted silver as Bolivia's dominant export, the country's tin mines were owned by an extremely small domestic oligarchy, epitomized by the tin baron Simón Patiño. This oligarchy—*la Rosca*, as it was known—exerted a powerful and largely anti-democratic influence on Bolivian politics; for this elite, tin rents very plausibly played a crucial role in *increasing* rather than reducing the disincentives associated with democracy. During the pre-revolutionary period, for reasons I discuss in this chapter and in Chapter Seven, a theoretical perspective similar to that promoted by Boix (2003) may be useful for understanding the influence of resource rents on the incentives of the rich. As I describe in this chapter, however, the destruction of the power of this oligarchy laid the foundations for a democratic rentier state in Bolivia. Although the capacity of tin rents to underwrite democracy in this highly unequal country was exhausted a little more than a decade after the Revolution, other instances of rentierism—most recently, with the rise of natural gas exports—provide a useful opportunity to test observable implications of this book's theory. On the whole, evidence from this case both supports the claim of a democratic effect of resource rents and confirms that the mitigation of redistributive conflict can be an important mechanism through which this effect occurs. While it supports the theory, however, fine-grained historical and contemporary evidence from Bolivia also suggests new extensions for future work—for example, theoretical extensions that consider the form of resource ownership, a challenge I take up further in Chapter Seven.

Third, I turn to the Ecuadorian case. This case provides an important challenge for the theory of the authoritarian resource curse: massive oil deposits were produced in the Ecuadorian Amazon, mostly after a military coup in 1972 whose plotters had as at least one part of the raison d'être the blocking of the rise to national power of a left-wing populist mayor from Guayaquil. The academic literature from the mid-1970s reads in many respects like the literature on the authoritarian "resource curse": oil rents went in important portions to pay for the military budget and other prerogatives of the autocrats' political power. Yet, Ecuador redemocratized in 1979 and, as I suggest here, oil rents played an important role in this process, in ways that are consistent with our view of the democratic effect of rents. Intertemporal variation in political outcomes supports the idea of a democratic effect of resource rents—even as it is at odds with the predictions of the literature on oil rents and authoritarianism. The Ecuadorian case therefore suggests that, far from simply stabilizing incument regimes, oil rents may play an active and important role in promoting democratic transitions.[1]

Finally, I turn to the Botswanan case. Botswana is both a diamond-rich rentier state and a nearly unique political and economic success story among

[1] I am grateful to Jorge Domínguez for comments on this point.

the countries of post-colonial, sub-Saharan Africa (Acemoglu et al. 2003; Dunning 2005). Particularly when contrasted with the many resource-rich sub-Saharan African countries that are poorer today than they were at independence and/or that have long histories of authoritarianism in the post-colonial period, Botswana appears to constitute an important exception to the idea of a political or economic "resource curse." Although some aspects of the Botswana case make it anomalous from the perspective of the theory I have developed here, I argue that our framework provides insights that, together with complementary explanations, can help explain why diamond rents in Botswana have plausibly had a democratizing effect. In sum, the four cases examined in this chapter support key elements of the general claims advanced in this book about the democratic effects of resource rents—even as they also suggest new directions for theoretical and empirical inquiry.

6.1 Chile: Class Conflict in a Rentier Democracy

Chile is perhaps the longest-standing rentier state in post-independence Latin America. However, two different natural resources—sodium nitrate and copper—have at various historical moments provided the central government with its major source of rent. Between the War of the Pacific (1879–1883), in which Chile appropriated nitrate-rich territories from its neighbors Peru and Bolivia, and the mid-1920s, duties and taxes on the largely British-controlled nitrate mines constituted Chile's most important source of government revenue. This source of rents was eventually eclipsed by the invention of synthetic substitutes and an eventual dip in world demand for sodium nitrates; consistent with the theory of this book, the decline of the nitrate sector contributed to major social upheavals in the mid-1920s and a crisis of important dimensions that was characterized by intense redistributive conflict in this highly unequal country. However, nitrates were soon replaced as a source of rents by the rise of a North American-dominated, capital-intensive, and geographically concentrated enclave copper mining sector, which allowed the perpetuation of a classic rentier state model in Chile. After the Second World War, copper constituted from 60 to 80 percent of exports and a substantial portion of government revenue, although it made up a smaller proportion of the total economy (from 10 to 20 percent) than in more resource-dependent countries. As in other resource-rich rentier states, rents from both nitrate and copper shaped the domestic political economy in Chile chiefly through their influence on patterns of public revenue generation and spending.

The argument developed in this study would suggest that in Chile—a highly unequal country in which redistribution of non-resource wealth was clearly a salient dimension of political conflict—rents from sodium nitrate and copper should have had a democratizing effect. Does evidence from the Chilean case support or belie this hypothesis? On the one hand, prior to 1973, Chile was one of Latin America's oldest and most stable democracies, even if the extent of the suffrage was extremely limited through the first several decades of the twentieth century; and it was one in which as a rule coups against democracy had played a limited role.[2] On the other hand, on September 11, 1973, Chile also became the site of Latin America's most well-known and explicitly anti-redistributive military interventions into democratic politics—namely, the coup that General Augusto Pinochet led against the government of Salvadore Allende, a Socialist who was elected president in 1970. Indeed, redistributive conflict was perhaps the most pronounced characteristic of democratic politics under the administration of Allende, and elite resistance to redistributive reforms, such as the land reforms first promoted by the Christian Democratic administration of Eduardo Frei (1964–1970) and then deepened under Allende's government, contributed to support for Pinochet's coup. One might therefore conceivably claim that the Chilean coup contradicts the argument that resource rents contributed to democratic stability in Chile by mitigating redistributive conflict.

In fact, such a claim would misunderstand the basic causal argument advanced in this study. I have argued that the democratic effect of resource rents stems from rents' role in mitigating redistributive conflict in the rest of the economy, and that this effect will be more important in countries in which the threat of redistribution of non-resource wealth is potentially more political salient. Nothing in this claim, however, suggests that a particular resource-rich country for which the theory might predict a democratic effect of resource wealth will, in fact, be a democracy.[3] The existence of the

[2] As Valenzuela (1976: 9) noted just after the coup of 1973, "Coup d'etats and military rule, common in other Latin American countries, have been practically absent since the 1830's." One exception, as discussed below, was the coup and period of military rule in the 1920s that followed the decline of the nitrate rentier state.

[3] This is true even without drawing a distinction between deterministic and probabilistic theories of causality: even a deterministic reading of the theory implies only that, for a country in which variables such as non-resource inequality or the extent of resource dependence predict a democratic effect of resource rents, resource rents will make the country more democratic than it would have been, in the absence of resource rents.

Chilean coup raises an important methodological issue: what does it mean to use the case study to assess (and further develop) the theory developed in this study, and how can probing evidence from the Chilean case support or cast doubt on the mechanisms emphasized here? Fearon's (1991) discussion of the use of counterfactuals in hypothesis-testing is useful here. Counterfactual reasoning seeks to assess the causal impact of a variable *X* by asking, what would outcomes look like if, instead of *X*, we had "not *X*"—and we were able to hold all else "constant," or imagine a "most similar world" in which only the absence of *X* marked a difference from the world we actually observe (Brady 2002). As Fearon (1991) points out, such a thought experiment is crucial to many attempts to investigate causality using case studies.

In the Chilean case, the relevant counterfactual involves imagining the level of redistributive conflict, and its implications for democratic stability, in the *absence* of resource rents. As I argue below, the baseline level of redistributive conflict was extremely high in Chile at the moment of the 1973 coup. Yet, it would conceivably have been even higher in the absence of copper rents. A range of evidence explored below suggests that resource rents did contribute to moderating redistributive conflict—indeed, that elites understood that resource rents could play this role and that they turned to the resource sector of the economy for this purpose, particularly at moments when the threat of redistribution was particularly strong. By contrast, I have not found evidence to suggest that resource rents instead promoted redistributive conflict; nor have I found evidence that resource rents help to explain the incidence of the coup itself through other mechanisms.[4] Notwithstanding the coup of 1973, the evidence reviewed below suggests that natural resource rents did help to mitigate redistributive conflict and thus, through the mechanisms I have emphasized, very plausibly promoted democratic stability in Chile.

6.1.1 The Rentier State and Democracy in Chile

Episode One: Nitrates Chile's first episode of rentier statism, which dates roughly from around 1880 until around the mid-1920s, centered on the

[4] While this book's theory would suggest that such mechanisms may exist—namely, that the desire to control the distribution of rent could have motivated Chile's coup plotters—it also suggests that such an effect would tend to be overridden in a country such as Chile by the democratizing effects of rents. As far as I am aware, nowhere in the literature on Pinochet's coup is the assertion that the desire to control copper rents played an important role in incentivizing the coup plotters.

export of sodium nitrate, a mineral that was used in the production of dynamite and other explosives as well as fertilizer.[5] As a result of the War of the Pacific (1879–1883), Chile appropriated from Peru and Bolivia the northern provinces of Tarapacá and Antofagasta, which were rich in nitrate (particularly Antofagasta). British capital played the most important role in the capital-intensive mining of nitrate in the late nineteenth century.[6] Together with the relative geographic isolation of the sector—nitrate deposits were located in less populous northern Chile whereas the government's spending of nitrate rent was concentrated disproportionately in the Central Valley—these characteristics meant that during the nitrate period, Chile would conform to classic patterns of the rentier state: nitrate rents came to influence the Chilean political economy primarily through their impact on patterns of revenue generation and public spending.

By 1889, nitrate contributed more than 45 percent of government revenues (Blakemore 1974: 43–4), rising to more than 50 percent in 1900, and nitrate rents would continue to provide the most important source of foreign exchange and government revenues until after the First World War.[7] At a time of booming world demand for nitrate, the mineral replaced copper as Chile's leading export (Blakemore 1974: 8), and the nitrate mines came to constitute a quintessential rent-producing enclave and a predominant source of revenue for the Chilean Fisc. As Hurtado (1988: 34, translation mine) appropriately notes, "The economic situation in Chile after the War of the Pacific was very similar to that which characterized that petroleum-exporting countries at the beginning of the 1970s."[8]

[5] Prior to the rise of nitrate, the Chilean state extracted substantial revenues from taxes on small-scale Chilean copper mines, owned largely by domestic producers (Zeitlin 1984: 38, citing Segall 1953: 43). However, the small-scale Chilean copper mines of the nineteenth century produced levels of rent an order of magnitude smaller than the nitrate sector after 1880. The nitrate sector conforms to a much greater extent to the classic pattern of a rent-producing enclave sector; see Chapter Two for further discussion.

[6] Bauer (1975: 208–9; see also Blakemore 1974), e.g., notes that the participation of Chilean capital in mining declined sharply after the seizure of the nitrate-rich territories in the war (though previous studies may have overestimated the extent of this decline).

[7] According to the figures provided by Mamalakis (1976: 38–9), resource surpluses averaged 14 percent of GDP between 1882 and 1930, while the value of nitrate exports was $217 million and the amount of taxes paid $81 million between 1880 and 1909. In total, some 37.3 percent of the export value went to the Chilean government.

[8] A similar point was emphasized to me by Jorge Arrate, a former president of the Socialist Party in Chile who was a minister in the Allende, Aylwin, and Frei administrations and later Ambassador of Chile to Argentina during the Lagos government. Interview, Santiago, Chile, July 7, 2004.

Rents produced by the geographically isolated enclave nitrate sector in northern Chile were spent on transport, education, urban improvement, and other goods and services demanded by residents in both urban and rural central Chile.[9] Expenditure grew rapidly, particular after the turn of the century: between 1900 and 1913, the average annual growth rate of expenditure was 5.6 percent (Humud 1971: 50). Although infrastructure and particularly the building of railroads received a large proportion of the expenditure, spending on education, health, and other social services was not neglected. According to Humud's (1971: 58, table 13) estimates, social expenditures of the central government—including allocations to the ministries of justice, education, health and social security, and social welfare—accounted for an average of 7.5 percent between 1865 and 1880 but rose to 14.4 percent in 1890 and an average of 12.28 percent between 1890 and 1910. The nitrate boom underwrote both an expansion of the size and scope of the state, providing a source of public spending from which various social groups, in one way or another, benefited.

As in other rentier states, however, this expansion of the state and growth of public spending on infrastructure, education, and public services came at relatively little cost to traditional elites—in this case, the landowning interests of Chile's Central Valley. Taxes on landowners declined sharply during the nitrate boom.[10] For instance, a tax on inheritance and gifts that had been established in 1878 was eliminated in the 1880s, and a tax on assets established in 1897 was transferred to local municipalities after the entry of the nitrate-rich territories into Chilean hands (Humud 1971: 44, note 2).[11] Congress abolished the agricultural land tax, the excise tax, and duties on sales of real property, resulting in sharply declining taxation of non-mining

[9] As Bauer (1975: 212, 217), following Santa Cruz Pinto (1962) and Blakemore (1974), notes, "In Chile, the social and political reflection of mining tended to be one step removed from the activity itself; that is, the government obtained the Chilean share through taxation and channeled this revenue through the public administration into transport, education and urban improvement."

[10] Zeitlin (1984: 38), citing Bauer (1975: 118), comments that "even after the abolition of the *catastro* [land tax] and the enactment of taxes on agrarian income rather than landholdings in 1860, not only were taxes on the large landowners infinitesimal while their burden rested almost entirely on mineowners, but also the 'landowners enjoyed an ever decreasing tax burden.'"

[11] This latter point is discussed extensively by Soifer (2006). Some decline in taxes collected by the central government is due to the turning over to municipalities of tax collection. Yet, the research by Zeitlin (1984) and especially Mamalakis (1976) makes clear the small and diminishing tax burden on Central Valley landowners during the nitrate boom.

sectors (Mamalakis 1976: 21–2).[12] Together with the reduction in tax rates and thus the value of tax receipts from the non-nitrate economy, the rise of nitrate sharply decreased the proportionate share of internal taxes in government revenues: as a share of ordinary revenues, internal taxes fell from 23.1 percent in 1845 to 0.5 percent in 1900 (Humud 1971: 41). After President José Manuel Balmaceda, whose infrastructure projects were enabled by taxes on nitrate production, was defeated in the civil war of 1891 (Zeitlin 1984: 304), rural taxes were reduced even further, and collection was also further turned over to local municipalities where large landowners held significant power (Bauer 1975: 118).[13]

Consistent with the theory developed here, nitrate paid for public spending from which virtually all Chilean social sectors benefited in one way or another, even as it reduced a tax burden that would otherwise have imposed a redistributive cost on landowning elites.[14] As a Chilean newspaper intoned in 1922:

> The War of 1879 gave us a military victory brought about by the vital strength of our race. The succeeding governments converted it into a diplomatic snarl, a disturbing element in the system of Public Finance. What was to be windfall [nitrate taxes], providing income for reserves and investments in public works to stimulate the development of the country was ultimately destined for the elimination of [other] taxes and the destruction of the tributary system.[15]

As in many other rentier states, the nitrate boom in Chile implied a decline in non-resource taxation.

How did the availability of rents from nitrate influence the extent of redistributive demands “from below”? Compared to many mineral sectors, the extraction of nitrate was relatively labor-intensive (Collier and

[12] As Mamalakis (1976: 21–2) puts it, “Taxes on Central Chile and the non-mining sector were not only minuscule throughout the 1840-1924 period but declined after 1880 . . . the large landowners, industry, and most of the service sectors (all of which could afford to pay) escaped except for the minor burden of indirect taxes.”

[13] On the decline of taxes in Chile during the nitrate boom, see also the discussion in Chapter Two of this book.

[14] Consistent with the theory of Chapter Three, Mamalakis (1976: 24) writes that “in the short run the government’s policy [of emphasizing the extraction of nitrate rents at the expense of other sources of revenue] favored all classes and most sectors and was advocated by almost all Chileans; it is difficult to assign responsibility for the problem to any one group, though the landowners may have been more responsible for its introduction and perpetuation than others.”

[15] *La Nacion*, March 5, 1922, quoted in Reynolds (1965: 334).

Collier 2001: 72–5).[16] Some of the literature on this topic attributes incipient worker mobilization in the first decades of the twentieth century to the concentration of a nascent proletariat in the Northern nitrate enclaves themselves.[17] For example, a major protest in the Northern port town of Iquique in 1907 was brutally repressed by the army (Collier and Collier 2001: 74; Deves 2002; also Rivera Letelier 2002), and this period witnessed the formation of a combative proletariat (Bauer 1975: 220–2). Yet, during Chile's first episode as a rentier state, redistributive demands were in fact quite muted, and they posed relatively little threat in particular to rural landowning elites. Nitrate rents financed spending on infrastructure, transport, and particularly social expenditures in central and urban Chile with few consequences for the unequal distribution of non-resource wealth or income.[18] Even the growth of the labor movement—which was extensive compared to other Latin American countries of the period (Collier and Collier 2001: 102, table 4.1)—and other forms of popular mobilization did not pose a strong redistributive threat to the traditional elite during Chile's first nitrate period.

How does the nitrate boom shed light on the theory developed in this book? As discussed above, consistent with this theory, nitrate rents inhibited redistributive taxation even as they stabilized the social order by providing spending valued by various sectors of the population; in the absence of nitrate rents (as later events would bear out; see later in this section), challenges to the elite could have been more substantial. To be sure, Chile's "democracy" during this period was a highly limited one, in which the suffrage was restricted to literate adult males over the age of 21; the electorate ranged between 7 and 15 percent from the 1880s to the 1940s (Valenzuela 1976: 10). Chile remained a country politically dominated by the landowner class (Bauer 1994: 245, translation mine), and the political regime clearly did not fully meet Schumpeterian or procedural minima requirements for democracy (such as elections with full participation and open contestation). Yet, access to power *was* regulated through regular, relatively competitive

[16] Still, following the classic pattern, the nitrate sector employed only a relatively small proportion of the population, as did the copper sector that arose later. The estimated employment share of mining and quarrying averages 4.3 percent across the years analyzed by Mamalakis (1976: 11, Table 1.2).

[17] See, however, DeShazo 1983, who emphasizes instead the importance of worker organization in Santiago and Valparaíso.

[18] As Bauer (1975: 228–9) puts it, "The nitrate fields produced a torrent of wealth but paradoxically this went to fortify an elite whose principal value was still landownership."

elections (albeit with a highly restricted suffrage); especially compared to those other Latin American countries of the period that were also characterized by relatively labor-repressive organization of the agricultural sectors in large landed estates, Chilean politics was relatively inclusive, electoral politics was relatively competitive, and the political arena was relatively stable. That the nitrate period did not bring with it significant challenges to the economic and political power of the large landowners—while the decline of the rentier state *did* witness the rise of more serious challenges from below—is consistent with the thesis advanced here that resource rents decrease the threat of redistribution to elites.

The decline of nitrate, by contrast, was associated with a sharp rise in the salience of redistributive politics in Chile. The fiscal impact of the decline in rents was brutal, as reflected in the percentage contribution of customs (mainly mining) duties to the Chilean Fisc, which decreased from 78.8 percent in 1895 to 48 percent in 1925 and then to 41.3 percent in 1930 (Mamalakis 1976: 19–20). The critical years came in the aftermath of the election of Arturo Alessandri Palma as president in 1920 and, especially, later in the 1920s. In his campaign, Alessandri had challenged a candidate who represented the traditional oligarchy and, in discussing the "social question," attempted to attract some working-class support (Collier and Collier 2001: 110). Although the role of the working class as a voting bloc was reduced by the limited extent of the suffrage, popular mobilization did play an important role in the outcome of the election. Although Alessandri won the election of 1920 in the electoral college (and apparently lost the popular vote with 49.4 percent), Congress seemed ready to use its constitutional ability to annul the victory, as government repression of student and working-class protest took place alongside a possibly "diversionary" mobilization of the armed forces to counter an apparently manufactured threat from Peru in the north.[19] This only sparked further mobilization by the working class, however, and fear of the social upheaval that would result if Alessandri were not inaugurated resulted in his eventual confirmation (Collier and Collier 2001: 111). The decline of the nitrate economy played an important role in these events, bringing as it did an important recession and a large volume of strike activity (Collier and Collier 2001: 112).

The nitrate crash brought a turn to redistributive taxation of the nonmining sectors, as well as to other measures that threatened traditional elites

[19] Formally, Congress had the power to annul the victory of an elector after considering claims of electoral fraud and corruption.

and strengthened mass actors. Alessandri's reform program was stalled in his first term, due in part to the lack of a majority of his Liberal Alliance in Congress; even after congressional elections of 1924, the impasse continued. Yet, the fiscal balance grew increasingly precarious, due to the collapse of the nitrate industry. The growth of ordinary government revenues fell from 5.2 percent a year between 1900 and 1913 to 2.2 percent between 1914 and 1924, yet expenditure growth only slowed from 5.6 percent to 4.4 percent (Humud 1971: 50). Some of the gap was filled by international credit, but the need for new sources of revenue forced a turn to internal taxation. Alessandri enlisted the aid of several military officers, including Major Carlos Ibáñez, who presented a list of demands that included "social security laws, income tax legislation, workers' health and accident insurance, and labor legislation," and he threatened to close Congress and call for a constituent assembly to rewrite the constitution, with the army's support if necessary (Collier and Collier 1991: 176–7). The increasing salience of a threat from below played an important role in the passage of new social and labor laws.[20]

The reforms threatened to impose a theretofore unknown redistributive cost on the traditional oligarchy.[21] Most notably, income taxes were introduced for the first time in 1924, with the heaviest burden falling on real estate income.[22] As a result of the new income tax law, internal taxation contributed $19.9 million to ordinary revenues in 1925, an increase from $12.2 million in 1924, and then rose to contribute $46.9 million in 1930 (Humud 1971: 45–6). The share of internal taxes in government revenues rose from 0.5 percent in 1900 to 3.5 percent in 1910, 8.9 percent in 1920,

[20] As Bauer (1994: 269, translation mine) remarks, "In 1924, under an unexpected political pressure caused in part by the collapse of the sodium nitrate industry and the broad recognition of a serious 'social question,' the Congress passed a series of social and labor laws, which later in 1931 would comprise the Labor Code." In addition to the income tax, new laws established the contract of private salary earners and introduced social security (the *Caja de Previsión*) and other labor legislation (Mamalakis 1976: 19–20, 64).

[21] There had been minor experiments with new taxes in the first two decades of the twentieth century, as nitrate began to falter. For instance, there were new taxes on spirits (in 1902), insurance companies (1905), tobacco and cards (1910), banks (1912), and various levies on gambling and public entertainment (Humud 1971: 45). However, the new income tax law of 1924 promised a qualitatively different extent of taxation and one whose burden would fall squarely on the traditional elite.

[22] Law 3996, which established the income tax in 1924, "created six tax rates: 9 per cent on real estate, 4.5 per cent on the income from capital, 2.5 per cent on profits of industry and commerce, 5 per cent on profits of mining and metallurgy, 2 per cent on salaries, public or pirvate, pensions and funds of widows, and finally 2 per cent on the earnings of professionals" (Humud 1971: 45).

and then to 30 percent in 1930 (Humud 1971: 41; see also Mamalakis 1989). Partly as a result of this new source of revenue, fiscal expenditure soared between 1924 and 1930, growing at an annual rate of 9.6 percent, compared to 4.4 percent between 1914 and 1924, as noted above (Humud 1971: 51). Social expenditures as a share of total central government spending grew from 8.3 percent in 1920 to 14.4 percent in 1925 and 16.4 percent in 1930; the current value of social expenditures grew 167 percent between 1920 and 1930, whereas between 1910 and 1920 it grew by just 20 percent (calculated from figures in Humud 1971: 57, table 12). Thus, new expenditures that were explicitly designed to meet the challenge from below posed by the "social question" were increasingly financed by internal taxes, a burden that fell most heavily on the powerful landowning class.

These developments prompted support among the traditional elite for a military solution, as more conservative senior officers took over the leadership of the junta that was installed in the crisis of 1924. In particular, the threat that further regulation would extend to the rural sector, with even stronger implications for the economic power of landowners, prompted a vigorous reaction from elites.[23] The role of the military in politics after 1924 and until the fall of Ibáñez in 1931 was complicated; it is important to recall that junior reformist officers—especially Ibáñez, who eventually became president and forced through a continuation of the reforms begun under Alessandri—played a key role in initiating and sustaining the reforms that the traditional oligarchy resisted. Yet, the military also acted to enforce a paternalistic control of the legalized labor movement while launching a vigorous anti-Left campaign, banning the Communist Party in 1927 (Collier and Collier 2001: 189–91).[24] In sum, the decline of nitrate rents after the First World War contributed to the intensification of the social question and demands for redistributive measures, including Chile's first income tax, as "the urban masses began gradually to move onto the stage of Chilean politics" (Bauer 1975: 230); and this heightened elite

[23] "The still-powerful landlord faction then dedicated itself, with all its force, to preventing the application of the measures established in this legislation to the countryside" (Bauer 1994: 269, translation mine).

[24] As Collier and Collier (2001: 171) note, after 1925 "the modus vivendi imposed by the authoritarian regime was one in which the reformers, to whom the oligarchy had to cede control of the state, would protect the material interests of the oligarchy. The project of those who came to power was one of social, political, and administrative reform, which would change the nature of the state and displace the hegemony of the oligarchy, but would not attack the economic position of the oligarchy nor leave it without substantial political power."

support for an authoritarian solution that would concede some reforms but that would also keep popular demands in check. Consistent with the theory developed here, resource rents had an inverse relationship to redistributive conflict, and redistributive conflict carried important implications for the stability and persistence of democratic rule.[25]

Episode Two: Copper The full consequences of the decline of nitrate as a source of public finance, however, were perhaps blunted by the rise of a new basis for the rentier state. By the beginning of the Second World War, nitrate had been replaced by another source of rent for the state: copper. After the turn of the century, new technology had made the mining of lower-grade ores increasingly economically viable, and growing world copper demand and the prospect of completion of the Panama Canal project, which would reduce freight rates between Chile and the eastern United States, attracted foreign investment from the increasingly vertically integrated copper industry (Reynolds 1965: 214–15).[26] In the first two decades of the twentieth century, the North American firms Braden, Kennecott, and Anaconda invested in three mines—El Teniente (a mine southeast of Santiago), Chuquicamata (in the northern province of Antofogasta), and another mine in Atacama province—which came to constitute the main pillars of Chile's "Gran Minería," or large-scale mining sector.[27] This entrance of North American conglomerates with the technological know-how and capital necessary to mine lower-grade copper mines would eventually allow the revival of a rentier state model in Chile.

As Reynolds (1965: 219) notes, the three main mines of Chile's Gran Minería epitomized the characteristics of classic enclave economies: capital-intensive and geographically isolated, the mines had relatively little in the way of connection to Chilean input and factor markets. They

[25] None of the above is intended to suggest, of course, that the decline of nitrate was the *only* source of the rise of the social question or the increased salience of redistributive issues beginning in the 1920s. The evidence presented above is merely meant to underscore the ways in which patterns of public finance, shaped by nitrate, very plausibly contributed to the course of redistributive conflict—and, via that channel, to the nature of national politics.

[26] As noted above, in the nineteenth century small-scale copper production had constituted an important sector of the Chilean economy. The decline of the "Pequeña Minería," or small-scale mines, of the nineteenth century had resulted partially from competition from lower-cost producers in North America and Spain, falling world prices, and the inability to mine low-grade ores in Chile, as well as perhaps Chilean economic policy failures (see J. Przeworski 1980 on the latter point).

[27] Eventually, both El Teniente and the mine at Potrerillos in Atacama province came under the control of Kennecott, while Anaconda owned the mine at Chuquicamata (Reynolds 1965: 214–19).

were also, increasingly, an important source of rent to the Chilean state, particularly as the nitrate economy waned and the Chilean state stepped up demands for tax and royalty payments by the copper firms. In a classic pattern characteristic of high sunk-cost industries (Monaldi 2002a, Moran 1974), discussed in Chapter Two, the effective rate of tax on the copper industry rose steeply over time. Reynolds (1965: 226) estimates that between 1913 and 1924, for example, Braden paid just 0.8 percent of the gross values of sales as total taxes. However, a combination of increased taxes, royalties, and the manipulation of multiple exchange rates—such as the requirement established in 1932 that companies must pay local costs in dollars at the official rate of exchange—raised the effective rate of taxation on profits to 18 percent in 1934, 33 percent in 1939, and 65 percent in 1942 (Reynolds 1965: 234–9). The tax share of copper sales rose from 4 to 25 percent between 1925 and 1959.

How did the new availability of copper rents shape the extent and nature of redistributive conflict as well as the salience of class in the political arena? As discussed above, the demise of the nitrate economy after the First World War was followed by a period in which class conflict and the threat of redistribution took a much more central role in Chilean electoral politics. In the 1920s, the "social question" seemed to imperil the viability of even limited democratic rule, as traditional elites sharply resisted the reforms proposed by Alessandri and supported an authoritarian solution. The fall of Ibáñez in 1931 and a return to democracy brought an initial electoral victory for Ibáñez's minister of the interior, who was supported by a center-right alliance; the extremely short-lived ascendancy, via a coup d'état, of Marmaduque Grove's "Socialist Republic"; and eventually, the reelection of Alessandri to the presidency in 1932. In the context of the Great Depression, leftist parties had growing electoral success, epitomized in the election in 1938 of a presidential candidate, Pedro Aguirre Cerda, who had support from a coalition (the Popular Front) that included the Communists and Socialists as well as the center-right Radical Party (Collier and Collier 2001: 374–7). Thus, the period following the end of the nitrate period was marked by a growing electoral role for the working classes and urban masses.[28]

In fact, however, the policies of the elected Popular Front government were more moderate than its campaign rhetoric and initial platforms might have suggested (Collier and Collier 1991: 379). Perhaps most importantly,

[28] "By 1938, with the election of a popular front government, [the] presence and influence [of the urban masses were] apparent to everyone" (Bauer 1975: 230).

the Socialists acquiesced to a ban on rural unionization, reifying a basic pact in which the Left acquiesced to continued Conservative domination of the countryside in exchange for its participation in the government and the protection of the urban working class (Bauer 1975; Loveman 1976). As the traditional historiography on Chile has emphasized, there were certainly many reasons for this policy moderation: especially important was the Conservative opposition's majority in Congress. It is important to note, however, that the policy orientation of the government remained moderate even after the Popular Front parties took control of both houses in the legislature in 1941 (Collier and Collier 2001: 384).

The point I wish to underscore here is the following: although the factors that traditionally have been proposed as explanations for the moderation of the Popular Front were clearly important, copper rents also appear to have played an essential role in allowing the Popular Front government to undertake a range of social and development expenditures while simultaneously pacifying rightist parties and their social base among the traditional landowning elite. For example, the national development corporation (Corporación de Fomento de la Producción, CORFO), which was founded in 1939 under the presidency of Aguirre Cerdo, was financed by a new tax on the copper industry (Reynolds 1965: 237–8), rather than by any new internal taxation on land or assets. Between 1930 and 1940, in the midst of the Depression, public employment roughly doubled in absolute terms, while by the early 1940s, "the public sector accounted for more than 50 percent of all internal investment capital" (Loveman 1976: 259). The point is that copper helped to allow the government to diminish potentially redistributive threats to the landowning elite while simultaneously satisfying the demands of urban middle- and working-class constituents. This important effect of copper rents, however, appears under-explored by the traditional historiography on moderation during the Popular Front period.

In addition, the centrist orientation of Chilean politics continued not only through the two subsequent elections after the death of Aguirre Cerda in 1941, as parties of the Left lost substantial electoral support, but also into the 1950s and 1960s. Notwithstanding the dominant interpretation, in which analysts have emphasized a growing degree of political and social polarization after mid-century (Stallings 1978; Valenzuela 1978), electoral returns in fact seem to suggest the predominance of centrist parties in Chile until at least 1965. In fact, as Collier and Collier (1991: 517–18) show, drawing on data from Valenzuela (1985), "there was a steady growth of centrist parties . . . from about 30 percent [of the vote, in election results for the Chamber of Deputies] in 1932 to 56 or 60 percent" in 1965. Right parties also steadily lost support in percentage terms (partially as a result of the extension of the suffrage). And, although parties of the Left gained support after 1952, they in fact merely regained ground that they had lost after their success during the Popular Front period. Thus, rather than an experience in party polarization, "new experiments to create a viable political center occurred . . . from 1952 to 1970" (Collier and Collier 2001: 509). It is also perhaps notable that the parties of the Left lost substantial support in the late 1940s and 1950s—precisely at a time in which copper rents were providing ever-increasing rents to the state.

During this period of political moderation, the rent-producing copper enclaves contributed to producing economic conditions that facilitated the growth of the state, the provision of public services valued by the working sectors, and wage gains for the working and especially the middle class, all in ways that, at least until the 1960s, did not appear to threaten deeply the economic interests of traditional elites. The enclave copper sector played a crucial role in underwriting the expansion of public spending: for instance, between the end of the Second World War and the fall of the Allende administration in 1973, the value of copper production by the two companies Anaconda and Kennecott alone constituted between 7 and nearly 20 percent of GDP, while tax revenues from copper financed from 10 to 40 percent of annual government expenditures, and copper exports ranged from 30 to 80 percent of foreign exchange earnings (Moran 1974: 6). There were wage gains for both white-collar and blue-collar workers (though gains for the latter appear more modest): the passage of a minimum wage for white-collar employees in 1942 (with an automatic cost-of-living adjustment) contributed to the sharp rise in real incomes for these employees between 1940 and 1953 (Collier and Collier 1991: 394–5, 398). At least some of the public spending in this period, and in the 1960s, therefore stemmed from a classic rent-producing sector that underwrote public spending without necessitating the recourse to redistributive taxation. Indeed, as had nitrate in an earlier period, copper permitted an impressive growth in the size of the state: "the public sector, even before the Allende election, accounted for about 40 percent of the domestic product and 60 percent of all investments. . . . In no other Latin American country did the state play so prominent a role" (Valenzuela 1976: 15–16).[29]

[29] Hirschman (1963, p. 222) famously observed that inflation in Chile provided a sort of substitute for civil war. He might well have mentioned copper rents too.

6.1.2 Redistributive Conflict and the Coup of 1973

Notwithstanding the alleged moderating effect of copper rents, redistributive conflict obviously did play an important and growing political role in Chile in the 1960s and early 1970s, first during the Christian Democratic administration of Eduardo Frei (1964–1970) and then, especially, after the election of Salvador Allende in 1970. The Christian Democrats began an agrarian reform, though the party withdrew support in 1967–1968 when its urban constituency was asked to bear part of the cost (Bauer 1975: 231; Kaufman 1972). As Fourcade-Gourinchas and Babb (2002: 543) put it, "Simmering conflict over how to divide the economic pie . . . ultimately exploded into more overt class warfare, exemplified by the Allende government's nationalization of private assets and the subsequent military coup backed by large business groups" (see also Stallings 1978).

The Chilean coup might therefore seem to belie the theoretical prediction that resource rents should moderate redistributive conflict and thereby promote democracy, particularly since Chile was (and is) a highly unequal country and one that is not as resource dependent as many other resource-rich countries. Yet, there are three important reasons why, despite the observed outcome of the coup, case-study evidence from this period on balance supports the claim of a democratic effect of resource rents.

First, there is strong evidence that politicians *did* attempt to use copper rents to alleviate the class conflict and political polarization that seemed to threaten the stability of democracy in the late 1960s and especially the early 1970s. Particularly striking is the political debate about increased Chilean control over, and eventually nationalization of, the copper sector. During the course of the Christian Democratic administration of Frei (1964–1970), Chile had enacted a series of new taxes as well as a process of "Chileanization" that promised even greater national control over the copper sector as well as a greater percentage take of rents from the industry. These reforms were resisted on ideological grounds by many politicians on the Right, who in Chile as elsewhere in Latin America tended to support the protection of the property rights of foreign investors, in part to defend a principle that could also be used to defend the property rights of domestic elites. The Conservative Party, according to Moran (1974: 204):

> was the group that once again drew the crucial lines of battle: the central issue, according to the official statement of the Conservatives, was the "right of property" as guaranteed in Article 10 of the Constitution of Chile. The North American companies were claiming that they could not invest in Chile, the statement declared, unless

they were given 20-year guarantees of inviolability for their capital. This demand was being written into the Chileanization legislation. Yet the Agrarian Reform bill, which was also pending before the Congress, would allow the government to expropriate landlords' property at the government's discretion and at a possible "damaging" price. Thus, the Conservative Party concluded, the government would be giving guarantees of "inviolability" to the property of foreigners while moving ... to withdraw the Constitutional inviolability of the property of its own citizens. There could be no copper program, the Conservatives declared, without substantial modification in the Agrarian Reform.

In fact, the Right hoped to promote its own interests, particularly its rural interests, at the expense of the foreign companies. As Moran (1974: 205) says, "The Conservative Party, which had the largest constituency of landowners, was most explicit in its strategy of holding the destiny of the copper companies in suspension until modification could be negotiated in the Agrarian Reform." President Frei apparently used the prospect of increased copper rents to convince interests on the Right that land reform could be moderated or made less painful: Moran (1974: 207, note 75) notes that "*El Siglo* reported that Frei made a personal compact with leaders of the Conservative and Liberal Parties in early 1966 that with rising ... prices for copper he would give them a 'good' system of payment for expropriation if they would speed their agreement on the copper program." When the Frei administration sought to obtain a majority holding for Chile in Anaconda's national operations, "Anaconda searched in vain for local support among business, banking, and commercial groups.... Not a single important Chilean business group, legal group, or banking group spoke out in their favor" (Moran 1974: 212–13). At the moment of extreme social and political polarization that surrounded Allende's election as president in 1970, politicians on the Right were prepared to turn to the copper sector as an increased source of rents, in the hope that nationalization of the copper sector would be the lesser of evils. As one interviewee put it, in a quote that underscores the perceived tradeoff between taxing the copper companies and redistributing income from domestic elites, "In that revolutionary setting [of the early 1970s], no one on the Right was not going to offer up [the copper companies] to the gods."[30]

Soon after taking office, Allende introduced legislation for complete nationalization of the copper sector, with compensation to the companies that was formally to be paid over a 30-year period but that was de facto

[30] Joseph Ramos, Dean of the Facultad de Ciencias Económicas y Administrativas of the Universidad de Chile. Interview, Santiago, Chile, June 16, 2004.

offset by deductions for "excessive profits" accrued since 1955. On July 16, 1971, in a Congress dominated by the opposition, the nationalization of the copper sector was approved *unanimously* (with only one abstention) as a constitutional amendment (Moran 1974: 147, 215). That many on the Right, including Conservatives, voted for nationalization suggests the extent to which they were prepared to sacrifice the principle of private property protection, if copper rents could be used to alleviate the threat of domestic redistribution.[31]

Second, however, there is also evidence that the *capacity* of the copper sector to provide the rents necessary to moderate redistributive conflict had been somewhat weakened by the time of the 1973 coup. As Moran (1974: 32–5) notes, the oligopoly power of the international copper conglomerates was steadily diluted after the Second World War, due to the continuing discovery of large new sources of copper, the growth of smaller copper companies (due to the availability of credits from fabricators and consumers of copper), and the diversification of non-resource companies into investment in the upstream copper mining sector. These factors contributed to a long-term secular decline in the real price of copper (Moran 1974: 36; see also Shafer 1983).[32] In Chile as in other producing countries, however, these trends were offset during the 1950s and 1960s by the increasing take of the government in percentage terms. In what Moran (1974: 17–49) terms the "obsolescing bargain," the classic pattern in negotiations between multi-national firms and host-country firms in heavy sunk-cost industries is for bargaining power to shift over time to the governments of producing countries, who are able to levy ever-increasing taxes and royalties

[31] A related argument about the role of the domestic elite in Jamaica and Peru can be found in Stephens (1987). Discussing the imposition of a unilateral levy on the foreign-owned bauxite/aluminum industry in Jamaica under Michael Manley and the People's National Party in 1972, for instance, Stephens emphasizes that "action in the mining industry was facilitated . . . by the inability of TNCs [Transnational Corporations] to mobilize influential local allies to oppose state action . . . TNCs attempted to appeal to the local capitalists' interests in the inviolability of contracts. However . . . the local capitalists' concerns with greater availability of foreign exchange outweighed their concerns about the breach of contract vis-a-vis the TNCs, particularly since the government took great pains to reassure them that bauxite was a very special case" (1987: 79). In a footnote, Stephens notes that "even the *Daily Gleaner*, the island's major newspaper, dominated by a conservative section of the capitalist class and strongly opposed to virtually all policies of the Manley government, supported the levy" (1987: 97, footnote 41).

[32] Moran (1974) also presents evidence that profit rates for the major copper-producing companies, including Anaconda, Kennecott, Phelps Dodge, and American Smelting and Refining, had declined since the Second World War.

on the mining sector (see Chapter Two of this book; also Monaldi 2002a; Vernon 1967; Wells 1971).[33] Chile was no exception, as the effective tax rate on the copper companies increased dramatically from next to nothing in the first decades of the twentieth century to upwards of 70 percent in the 1960s, and "Chileanization" during the 1960s and eventual nationalization of the Chilean copper industry in 1971 can be seen as simply natural extensions of this trend. Ironically, however, the nationalizations of foreign companies at the end of the 1960s and beginning of the 1970s in copper-producing countries around the developing world, from Chile to Zambia to Zaire, further weakened the oligopoly power of the large copper corporations (Cobbe 1979; Shafer 1983), undercutting an important economic basis of the rents (a pattern we also observed in the Venezuelan case).

Although declining oligopoly power in the world copper market was offset by the increasing "take" of the Chilean state, and although the nationalizations in copper-producing countries around the world were perhaps too temporally proximate to have a large amount of weight as a causal factor, Valenzuela (1976) concurs that a substantial decrease in the price of copper after 1971 contributed to polarization and conflict in Chile. The ability of the copper sector to underwrite social harmony in Chile and, in particular, to moderate the threat of redistribution therefore was plausibly attenuated at the time of the coup of 1973.

A third and final consideration that may support my claim of a democratic effect of resource rents in Chile—notwithstanding the anti-redistributive coup of 1973—is that there is little evidence that the presence of copper rents *contributed to* the coup, as the theoretical claim of an authoritarian effect of resource rents would suggest. Causal-process observations that would support such an alternative interpretation might include evidence—from interviews or written accounts—that control over the rents themselves helped to motivate the plotters of the 1973 coup. Although it is true that control of the state did bring benefits in the form of copper rents to the Chilean military, including a share of royalties guaranteed by legislation, my interviews with actors involved in Chilean politics during the period did not

[33] Moran noted in 1974 that "over the long term, final consumers have been winning. And primary producers and their host governments have lost. To a large extent, however, the waning power of producers to exact economic rents from consumers has not been apparent to Chile (or Zambia, or Peru, or the Congo) because the ability of the host governments to demand more of a contribution from the foreign companies has been simultaneously increasing" (37).

reveal evidence that the anticipation of these benefits motivated the coup plotters, nor to my knowledge do accounts of the coup in the secondary literature. Moreover, even if the desire to maintain control over copper revenues could have provided an additional incentive for resisting the eventual return to democracy at the end of the 1980s and beginning of the 1990s, the theory developed here simply suggests that in a highly unequal country such as Chile, where the threat of redistribution has played an especially important role, the *net* effect of resource rents should be democratic rather than authoritarian. Analysis of the case-study evidence suggests that this is, very plausibly, the case, in contrast to the prevailing view on the political effects of natural resource wealth.

Thus, the picture that emerges from secular analysis of the Chilean case is one in which resource rents—first from nitrate, then from copper—provided a source of public finance that partially helped to obviate the need to turn to other sources of revenue, including redistributive taxation. Copper rents did not prevent the collapse of democracy in 1973, in an explicitly anti-redistributive coup. Nonetheless, the level of baseline class conflict at the time of the coup of 1973 was extremely high. Chilean politicians, even those on the Right, apparently did turn to the copper sector as a potential antidote to redistributive conflict. It therefore seems likely that copper rents contributed to moderating rather than worsening redistributive conflict. There is also no evidence I have found that the potential to control the distribution of rents itself motivated coup plotters in 1973. It therefore seems most likely that, as predicted by the theory, the causal effect of resource rents in this highly unequal country, in which redistributive conflict formed a primary axis of political conflict, was to promote democracy rather than authoritarianism.

6.2 Bolivia: Rents, Revolution, and Democracy

As in Chile, two distinct sets of natural resources—on the one hand, nonfuel minerals, primarily tin but also silver, and, on the other, oil and especially natural gas—have produced substantial rents in Bolivia during the twentieth century. These resources have also supplied the government with revenue in distinct historical periods, though with somewhat more temporal overlap between episodes of "rentierism" than was the case in Chile: in Bolivia, the heyday of tin and silver rents was reached in the first half of the twentieth century, while oil and especially natural gas have been increasingly important over the second half of the twentieth century.[34] An extremely unequal country in which the political salience of redistributive threats has clearly been great at various moments, Bolivia presents a further opportunity for investigating the political effects of resource rents.

However, Bolivia also presents important contrasts with earlier cases I have considered, especially from the perspective of the theory developed in this study. First, the large tin and silver mines in Bolivia, when in private hands, were owned not by foreign multi-nationals but by domestic elites: prior to the Revolution of 1952, for instance, a small oligarchy popularly known as *la Rosca* appropriated the vast majority of rents produced by the tin mining sector. As we will see, this contributed to a substantially different domestic political dynamic from the one I have described in other cases. Rather than providing rents that flowed into the coffers of the state more or less like "manna from heaven"—at least from the point of view of domestic fiscal politics—natural resources instead constituted a portion of the wealth of rich elites, which carried very different implications both for redistributive conflict and the development of the political regime. In fact, in the period in which tin and silver were the major sources of rent in the Bolivian political economy, Bolivia was *not* a resource-rich rentier state, as that concept has been developed in this study. Because of this, the case does not constitute a challenge to the theory so much as an opportunity to refine it; in Chapter Seven, I extend the model of Chapter Three to examine the political consequences of rents when natural resources are owned by rich private elites. The tin and silver period in Bolivia does raise important questions about how to understand the conditions—whether technological or political—that lead to the emergence of a resource-rich rentier state in the first place, which I addressed in Chapter Two and discuss further in this section.

Second, analysis of the later period in which oil and particularly natural gas, rather than tin, produced the largest rents in Bolivia also provides opportunities to refine our understanding of the political effects of natural resources. In contrast to the heyday of the tin and silver mines, in this period Bolivia *did* constitute a rentier state, and—in this extremely unequal country in which the threat of redistribution has clearly had a marked influence on the political incentives of elites—rents have played a political role consistent with the theory developed in this book. At the same time, the Bolivian case presents previously unconsidered mechanisms through which natural

[34] On the role of resource rents in the Bolivian economy, see Contreras (1993), Crabtree et al. (1987), Dunkerley (1984), Mitre (1993), and Muñoz (2000: 89).

resource rents may influence national politics, in particular, through the effect of oil and natural gas on incentives for regional autonomy or secession. This aspect of natural resources provides an opportunity to broaden the purview of our theory as well. I now turn to discussing these issues in more detail.

6.2.1 *The Rule of* la Rosca *and the Bolivian Revolution*

Among the cases examined in this study, the Bolivian tin sector is unique in that ownership of and control over the sector were exercised by a politically powerful domestic oligarchy in the period before the Bolivian Revolution of 1952. Indeed, during the first half of the twentieth century, the most powerful element of the Bolivian oligarchy, or *la Rosca* as it was popularly known, consisted of the tin barons. Comprised of essentially three family firms, this tin oligarchy controlled 80 percent of an industry that itself accounted for 80 percent of Bolivian exports; up to the end of the Second World War, these companies produced between a quarter and half of the world's tin output (Dunkerley 1984: 7–10). The largest firm was owned by Simon Patiño, who controlled up to 40 percent of national production and, by the early 1950s, 10 percent of world tin output; yet the other two large mining companies—the Aramayo company and a firm owned by Mauricio Hochschild—were major producers as well (Geddes 1972).

The economic power of the tin barons corresponded to an important political influence as well. The enormous influence of the tin oligarchy over the affairs of the state earned it the title of *superestado minero* (mining superstate); faced with a substantial problem of controlling the workforce at the mines, the tin oligarchy resorted to its influence on the state to repress labor organization and protest.[35] The tin companies themselves paid a part of the wages and benefits of soldiers stationed at their mines, underscoring the degree of official connection between the tin oligarchy and the state's repressive apparatus. The response to growing labor militance during the Great Depression and especially during the 1940s underscores the political influence of the tin barons. Local police and military stationed at the major mines, such as Patiño's Catavi mine, put down an increasing number of strikes during the 1940s. In December 1942, after workers at the Catavi

[35] The Bolivian tin industry was comparatively labor intensive, and miners faced terrible working conditions, extremely low wages, and a high likelihood of early death from silicosis, induced from working in the mines (see Nash 1979).

mine went on strike to protest a growing disparity between profits and real wages, Patiño prevailed upon the regime of General Peñaranda to send in troops, and thirty-five unarmed miners were killed.[36] Though none of the tin barons sought political office (and thus this elite remained formally independent of the state), the preponderance of *la Rosca*'s economic power was complemented by its control of various newspapers.[37] A striking feature of the Bolivian case during the heyday of tin was thus the extent to which a domestic oligarchy that owned and controlled the natural resource sector wielded both economic and political power.

This pattern of ownership and control contributed to a substantially different relationship between the resource sector and national politics from that I have analyzed in other cases. To be sure, the tin sector produced a substantial amount of rent, particularly in the 1920s and also throughout the period prior to the Revolution of 1952; in part due to a process of domestic and international integration of the production process, tin producers enjoyed an impressive degree of price-setting power. Yet, much of the rent was captured by the domestic oligarchy itself. By the 1940s, for instance, Patiño's company registered profits of around 30 percent of capital value, while his personal wealth reached an estimated 70 million pounds (Dunkerley 1984: 9). Resource rent did provide the state's most important source of revenue and one that grew over the first half of the twentieth century, but the impositions remained relatively small in percentage terms, and the wealth of the private oligarchy sometimes exceeded that of the state.[38] Though under reformist governments such as that of Major Gualberto Villarroel (1943–1946), the contributions of the sector increased in percentage terms, these increases were vigorously opposed by the tin barons, who threw their support behind authoritarian regimes and opposed reformist approaches. The tin barons' opposition was important both in leading to the downfall of the reformist Villarroel government and,

[36] According to Dunkerley (1984: 14–15), Patiño had increased his revenue by 84 percent while inflation had reached 30 percent in the previous year; the company's real wage bill had grown by less than 5 percent, at a time when an estimated 3 percent of workers earned more than a dollar a day. Workers at Catavi went on strike in demand for wage increases of between 20 and 70 percent.

[37] Aramayo, Hochschild, and Patiño each owned one of Bolivia's three largest newspapers.

[38] In 1906, Patiño's bank had working capital that was "greater than the total revenue of the state, which imposed a meagre four per cent export tax on tin . . . the regime of the Republic Party increased export taxes from 7.5 per cent to nearly 15 per cent the following year" (Dunkerley 1984: 9).

especially, in negating the results of the election of 1951, which the populist party *Movimiento Nacionalista Revolucionario* (MNR) won despite the exile of its two top leaders.

The main point here is that unlike other cases I have considered, in pre-revolutionary Bolivia the state's attempts to capture more rent for the public coffers itself implied a substantial redistributive dynamic in domestic politics. That is, any capture of rent by the state for purposes of greater public spending would tend to redistribute income from the tin oligarchy to the benefit of (some segment of) the rest of the population. To the extent that the incentives of this elite to resist demands for greater democracy stemmed from the redistributive threat democracy could pose—and in Bolivia this was a considerable threat—then rents from tin, far from moderating redistributive conflict and thereby reducing elites' opposition to democracy, could well heighten it, increasing elite support for repressive and authoritarian solutions. In fact, tin barons in Bolivia exerted their substantial political influence to oppose democratizing reforms that might lead to greater redistribution of tin wealth itself.

This political dynamic is reflected in the extent to which popular mobilization prior to the Revolution of 1952 was aimed at attacking the economic and political power of the tin barons themselves. After the massacre at the Catavi mine in 1942, Victor Paz Estenssoro, the leader of the MNR who would later become president after the Revolution, directly denounced *la Rosca*'s use of the apparatus of the state to put down workers (Klein 1969: 364). The MNR used the Catavi massacre to strengthen the party's contact with the labor movement in the mines (Alexander 1982: 70); the national union federation formed by miners in 1944, the *Federación Sindical de Trabajadores Mineros de Bolivia* (FSTMB), was itself perhaps the most critical collective actor in shaping the events that led to the Revolution, aside from the MNR itself.[39] Both the MNR and FSTMB made invectives against the power of the tin barons a major staple of their programs (Klein 1969: 337), both under the Villarroel government (in which the MNR was a junior partner) and in the 6-year hard-line authoritarian regime that followed

[39] Although the FSTMB had a close relationship to the MNR, which at the time of the FSTMB's formation was a junior partner in the reformist regime of Villarroel (1943–1946), the labor federation was never subordinated to the party. The independence and radicalism of the labor movement, which grew out of the mines, are notable features of the Bolivian case.

its downfall. Popular mobilization and reformist governments therefore seemed to pose a direct threat to the tin barons.[40]

In the years leading up to the Revolution, the tin barons continued to vigorously resist democratizing reforms on the grounds of anti-Communism. In 1951, the MNR was allowed to stand candidates in the presidential election (in part because, with several of its leaders in exile, the party appeared to the ruling elite to be in a weakened position). Notwithstanding the exile of its leaders and the repression of the party during the authoritarian period of 1946–1951, the MNR trumphed at the polls, winning a plurality with Víctor Paz Estenssoro and Hernán Siles Zuazo as its candidates. However, President Urriolagoitia declared the election results void, alleging connections between the MNR and the Bolivian Communist Party, and gave power to the junta led by Hugo Ballivián. After this abortive electoral victory, the MNR added a vigorous campaign for democratic rights to its attacks on *la Rosca* and feudal relations in the countryside (Dunkerley 1984: 36–7), gaining substantial popular support. Yet, the tin barons continued to favor a repressive solution over democratization, and it was the revolution in April of the following year that would take power from *la Rosca* by force.

Rather than providing a source of rent that could moderate redistributive conflict, the mining sector was itself at the epicenter of redistributive politics, a fact made all the more salient by the dominant role of mining in the national economy. To be sure, there was also huge inequality in non-mining sectors of the economy, characterized by the large, nearly feudal latifundia system that dated from the colonial period and was expanded during the nineteenth and the twentieth centuries at the expense of communal holdings.[41] Yet, in part because tin rents accrued to the barons, who themselves exerted substantial domestic political influence, resource rents also did not underwrite redistributive conflict in non-resource sectors of the economy. Instead, during the pre-revolutionary period, the tin oligarchy engaged in labor-repressive productive practices in its own mines; used its influence with the state to encourage military repression of miners;

[40] When after a congress in 1946 the FSTMB promulgated its Thesis of Pulacayo, in which it "identified the proletariat as the only truly revolutionary class, called for an alliance under its leadership with peasants, artisans and the petty bourgeoisie ... [and] warned against the dangers of believing in 'worker ministers' appointed by bourgeois governments ... Patiño had the entire Thesis reprinted in *El Diario* as a warning of where the FSTMB was going" (Dunkerley 1984: 17).

[41] For instance, eight hacendados owned 10 percent of cultivated land in 1938; other figures on the unequal distribution of land are given in Klein (1982).

vigorously resisted any attempts to impose a greater fiscal burden on its operations; and exerted active influence over the development of national politics. Tin rent, rather than moderating redistributive conflict, very plausibly heightened it, creating incentives for the elite, or at least a segment of the elite, to block or reverse the introduction of democracy precisely because of the redistributive threat that democracy could pose in the tin sector itself.

What light does the discussion of the pre-revolutionary period in Bolivia shine on the theoretical approach developed in this study? In fact, Bolivia during the pre-revolutionary period was *not* a rentier state in the sense that that concept has been developed here and as it has been used by scholars of the Middle East. Mahdavy (1970), for example, emphasizes the importance of the "external," foreign source of rent; precisely because the source of rent is external, in rentier states the rent flows into the fiscal coffers of the state without demanding the extraction of resources from domestic citizens (see also Beblawi 1987; Chaudhry 1989, 1997). In pre-revolutionary Bolivia, on the other hand, tin rent was eminently "internal" in origin in the sense that the tin sector was privately owned by a powerful domestic oligarchy. As the discussion in this section has indicated, the fiscal politics surrounding the rent-producing sector was thus quite different from the other cases I have analyzed. Rather than providing a source of state revenue that obviated the tax burden of the domestic elite under democracy, rents made the tax burden under democracy potentially more costly to this elite, or at least to a politically powerful segment of this elite.

The case of Bolivia prior to the Revolution of 1952 therefore provides a useful chance to extend the theoretical purview of this study; in Chapter Seven I extend the formal framework developed in Chapter Three to study the effects of private resource ownership. In that framework, when resource rents accrue directly to a private elite—rather than flowing directly into the coffers of state—rent may unambiguously increase the incentives of elites to resist democratization and thus have very different political effects from those for which I have argued. As discussed in Chapter Two, however, this is best considered a theoretical modification and extension rather than a fundamental shift in the theory developed in this book. The reason is that there are, in most resource-producing countries, opportunities for the state to capture rent without confronting a narrow, resource-owning domestic oligarchy; ownership of rent-producing natural resources by a concentrated domestic elite is the exception rather than the rule in resource-rich countries. And, where this form of ownership does exist, it is sometimes broken by a social revolution or disparate encroachments on elites' resource wealth by the state—exactly as in Bolivia. As we will now see in the Bolivian case, once the concentrated ownership of the elite is broken, the theory outlined in the baseline framework of Chapter Three becomes more pertinent.

6.2.2 Rentier Statism after 1952

The Revolution's destruction of the economic and political power of *la Rosca* moved the fiscal basis of the Bolivian government toward that of a classic rentier state. After the Revolution, the MNR under Paz Estenssoro moved toward nationalizing the tin mines. The party was initially more cautious in its approach than the mineworkers' union, the FSTMB, which had long demanded immediate nationalization without compensation and with worker control of the mines, yet nationalization seemed inevitable, given the central role that struggle against the tin oligarchy had played in the Revolution.[42] The formation of the *Central Obrera Boliviana* (COB), which was to possess authority of the entirety of the workers' movement, also helped to spur eventual nationalization. In October of 1952, the mines of *la Rosca* were nationalized by a decree signed at Patiño's Siglo XX-Catavi mines, establishing the state-owned *Corporación Minera de Bolivia* (Comibol), which took control of the holdings previously possessed by Patiño, Hochschild, and Aramaya. Thus, through revolution, the rent-producing sector of the economy passed from the hands of a small domestic oligarchy—which had vigorously resisted democratization in part because of the redistributive consequences this might bring in the tin sector itself—to the hands of the state.

In the post-revolutionary period, tin rents did provide a source of state revenue for public spending in the rest of the economy. In 1956, for example, the new state-owned company Comibol contributed $30 million to the state's development arm, the *Corporación Boliviana de Fomento* (CBF), and $10 million to the state oil company, *Yacimientos Petrolíferos Fiscales de Bolivia* (YPFB) (which itself would later become a major rent-producer for

[42] That the Revolution was understood by many, particularly in the mining proletariat itself, as a confrontation with the interests of *la Rosca* was underscored by the words of Juan Lechín Oquendo, the executive secretary of the FSTMB, speaking at a May Day march in 1952: "The Revolution has only just begun and with the sacrifice of our martyrs we must construct it on the base of an organised and conscious proletariat, the only guarantee of saving it from the Rosca.... So long as we don't nationalise the mines... the Rosca will destroy our Revolution.... Those who are against our programme are against Bolivia because our programme is the programme of the exploited of Bolivia" (quoted in Dunkerley 1984: 56).

the state), at a time when Comibol was itself registering a loss due in part to the requirement that it sell its dollar earnings to the Central Bank at below-market rates. There was clearly an attempt to use rent from the tin sector to contribute to, inter alia, moderating redistributive conflict under the democratic governments that followed the Revolution—for example, by helping to finance the agrarian reform that followed the Revolution and by paying for industrial development.[43]

Ironically, however, the destruction of the economic and political power of the tin barons, which laid the fiscal basis for a rentier state in Bolivia, also coincided with a period in which the capacity of the tin sector to produce rent for the state was markedly in decline (Baptista Gumucio 1985). This was partly a result of secular trends in the profitability of the Bolivian tin industry that in fact dated from the pre-revolutionary period. For one, Bolivian tin became more costly to mine, as "the tin content of Bolivian ore had been dropping consistently (in the case of the key Catavi complex from 6.7% in 1925 to 1.3% in 1950, falling further to 0.5% in 1960)" (Dunkerley 1980: 23–4). For another, beginning in the 1930s there was a long-term secular decline in the real-world price of tin, exacerbated by the large quantitites of tin sold to the United States at preferential rates during the Second World War, which thereafter left the United States with a stockpile of tin that allowed it substantial influence over the world tin price (Dunkerley 1984: 24). In 1950, the real value of tin production was only two-thirds the 1929 value.[44] Even before the Revolution, according to Malloy (1970: 29), "the simple fact was that the great mines were giving out. The companies failed to explore new sources, and the rate of investment in existing plants declined." Dunkerley (1984: 11–12), in fact, attributes the weakening of the rule of *la Rosca* on the eve of the Revolution of 1952 to the secular decline of the tin industry and perturbations in the world tin market during World War Two: "The official New York price index for tin

[43] Public spending at the time also had a clear regional bias, going in disproportionate amounts to the eastern and lowland departments, especially that of Santa Cruz. A new highway constructed to the eastern lowlands from Cochabamba was completed 2 years after the Revolution; between 1955 and 1960 Santa Cruz and other lowland department received 58 percent of credits from the Banco Agrícola, compared to 16.1 percent for the (highland) departments of La Paz, Oruro, and Potosí (see Eaton 2007, also Dunkerley 1984: 94–5).

[44] Malloy (1970: 29–31) dates the beginning of this long-term decline as early as 1929, the year that the value of tin production peaked (in constant 1950 prices), though this claim may be somewhat overstated: despite a secular decline in tin prices, and a decline in production during the Depression, production also rose in the 1940s, so that the value of production nearly reached the level of 1929 in the mid-1940s.

stood static between 1941 and 1945 but the real price actually fell during those years, progressively depriving the Bolivian state of vital tax revenues and reversing the upward trend of the companies' profit margins. (That of Patiño had risen from £80,000 in 1939 to £1.4 million in 1942 but dropped back to £300,000 in 1946).... The companies' response to this situation inside the country was to generate serious political problems."[45]

However, the tin sector declined further after the Revolution. Nationalization of the tin mines, ironically, produced a further decline in the capacity of the sector to produce rent that could be spent in other sectors of the economy (a pattern we also observed in the discussion of nationalizations in Venezuela and Chile). In part, this was because, whereas Patiño and the other tin barons had vertically integrated production in Bolivia with smelting plants outside the country, the link was broken with nationalization (Dunkerley 1980: 24). Thus,

> Comibol's position in the world market was no better and in some aspects discernibly worse than that of the Rosca before it.... The price of tin was anyway on an emphatic downward trend; it did not rise between 1952 and 1961 and only reattained its 1951 level in 1964. Moreover, it was within three months of nationalisation that price levels took their biggest dip: from $1.20 to $0.80 per pound.... Comibol's exports rose somewhat in 1953 but thereafter they fell steadily; in 1958 earnings from tin were less than half those in 1952 (Dunkerley 1984: 59).

Payments to miners, given their crucial role in the Revolution itself, also absorbed an important portion of rent: Comibol's workforce also expanded from 24,000 in 1951 to 35,000 in 1956 (Dunkerley 1980: 25).

Thus, the capacity of the rent-producing sector to underwrite the moderation of redistributive conflict, under the democratic governments established after the Revolution, was substantially attenuated. Bolivia's tin-based rentier state died, perhaps, at birth. Having survived a failed rightist coup attempt in 1953, the MNR pressed forward with an agrarian reform (like nationalization, that had not in fact constituted an important part of the party's program prior to 1952). Peasant mobilization had played a very limited role in revolution, and after the fact, "government leaders expressed a certain confidence in developing limited proposals for change in the

[45] In order to minimize the effect in the short term and meet the very great demand, *la Rosca* maximized production, increased its labor force by 40 percent, and had doubled 1938 production within 4 years. At the end of the war, therefore, substantial deposits of tin had been mined at decreasing profit with the result that the pits were in commercial terms over-manned and badly under-capitalized.

countryside. This was partly determined by pressure from the right wing, which perceived in an agrarian reform implications for property relations in general that were far more dangerous than those evident in the nationalization of the mining companies" (Dunkerley 1984: 65). However, in the wake of the Revolution, the largely indigenous peasantry undertook a growing number of localized rural mobilizations, including attacks on landed estates, that provoked a climate of apprehension among *hacendados* that Klein analogized to the "Great Fear" in revolutionary France (Klein 1982: 233). The leadership of the MNR thus undertook an agrarian reform that would concentrate on providing land parcels to peasants and ending "feudal" labor practices. Development of the *oriente* or lowland Eastern part of the country took a major role, as emigration from the *altiplano* or Western highlands would be encouraged. In fact, the effects of the agrarian reform on the redistribution of land would be relatively modest (Dunkerley 1984: 73–4).

The threat of redistribution therefore clearly shaped the incentives of elites in opposing the revolutionary governments, which had been ratified through democratic elections in 1956, 1960, and 1964—and eventually, in 1964, supporting the military coup that overthrew the government of Paz Estenssoro, recently reelected as president. During the long 12 years that followed the Revolution, the political power of MNR clearly rested in part on its ability to deliver popular benefits and services, particular to the urban popular sectors:

> Nationalization of the big mining companies, agrarian reform and universal suffrage were the three central accomplishments of the MNR and constituted the basis of the national revolution. Yet, the party was to rule for over twelve years on the strength of measures passed in the first 18 months; clearly its success depended on other factors, however popular the core reforms proved to be.... [The MNR's continued success] depended on the MNR's capacity to maintain a following in the urban centers, all of which required not only diligent redistribution of wealth under conditions of increasing crisis—even bankruptcy—but also a sustained populist image and a coherent apparatus that would fulfil the function of ensuring political supremacy and channelling favours (Dunkerley 1984: 75).

Yet, the capacity of tin to produce rents that would help the government deliver public spending without unduly threatening the economic interests of the still-powerful landowning section of the oligarchy was clearly undercut by the decline of the tin sector itself. Within 4 years of the Revolution, the economy was in crisis, in part because "the high costs of compensating the expropriated mine-owners had completely impoverished the revolutionary economy" (Dunkerley 1980: 25): foreign reserves had fallen by 50 percent and price increases were approaching hyper-inflation. In desperation, the government turned in 1956 to the United States and the International Monetary Fund for financial assistance—creating a new source of "rent" through foreign aid but one that, unlike tin, would come with strong strictures on the form and allocation of public spending. Foreign aid also carried other conditions that would limit the foundations of the rentier state in the future: for example, by requiring the removal of the monopoly of the state oil company (YPFB). Although tin itself remained an important export in the two decades of military rule that followed the coup of 1964, the capacity of the sector to provide the fiscal basis for a rentier state had been perhaps permanently crippled. After the Revolution, although there is some evidence that tin briefly provided a source of rent that underwrote spending in the rest of the economy, this source of public finance was also fleeting under Bolivian democracy after 1952.

6.2.3 Oil, Gas, and the Rise and Demise (and Rise) of the Rentier State

A final episode in the fiscal evolution of the Bolivian state, and one of particular interest for our argument, concerns the increasing importance of rents from oil and, later, natural gas as a source of government revenue over the second half of the twentieth century and the beginnings of the twenty-first—though this increase was uneven over time and was even reversed in some periods, with important implications for our argument. Though oil production had long existed in Bolivia—which in 1937 became the first Latin American country to nationalize its oil sector, a year before Mexico—its importance grew in the later period.

As in Venezuela, the growing role of oil and gas rents in Bolivia coincided with brief democratic reforms in the late 1970s and, especially, with the return to full democracy in the early 1980s. Bolivia redemocratized at a time of profound international economic difficulties for Latin American countries in the wake of the debt crisis of 1982, and in the context of a domestic economic policy package of austerity and liberalization for which international economic consultants had advocated (Stokes 2001: 113). Though this put pressure on democratic institutions in various ways, the growing importance of oil and gas rents helped to counteract this pressure and, as I will argue later in this section, helped to promote the relatively stable alternation of power through several elections. Democratization and democratic stability coincided with an increase in oil and gas rents.

Also as in Venezuela, however, a subsequent *decline* in oil and gas rents coincided with both the destabilization of democracy and the exacerbation of conflict that was defined in part along lines of relative economic privilege. The decrease in rents was due in part to a discrediting by some bureaucrats, conservative politicians, and international financial advisors of the role of resource rents in the political economy. In the mid-1980s, even as the newly installed democratic government of Jaime Paz Zamorra passed a law requiring a heightened fiscal contribution of the oil and gas sector to the central government, the state oil company came under increasing attack for inefficiency and corruption, a campaign that had increasing success over time. A quasi-privatization of the industry and a lowering of tax and royalty rates under the guise of a "capitalization" campaign, during the first administration of President Sanchez de Losada (1993–1997), were supposed eventually to increase total tax and royalties through their effects on investment incentives. At least in the short term, however, this set of policies contributed to *reducing* the role of oil and gas as a fiscal basis of the rentier state: between 1985 and 1995, oil and gas rents made up between 38 and 60 percent of state revenues, yet by 2002 rents constituted just 7 percent of the national budget (YPFB, various years).

The intertemporal relationship between oil and gas rents and democratic stability is thus largely *positive* in Bolivia, contra the claim that rents promote authoritarianism. The Bolivian case, however, also suggests theoretical extensions to the argument developed in this study. As suggested by my theoretical approach, the rise of oil and gas rents in Bolivia did plausibly have the effect of removing threats of redistribution to elites, particularly to elites in Bolivia's relatively wealthy lowland departments. However, the territorial distribution of oil and gas reserves, which were located primarily in the lowland departments that surround Bolivia's highland *altiplano* departments to the east, also very plausibly shaped incentives for regional autonomy and secession movements—a factor I have not considered in previous cases but one that may have general relevance for other resource-rich countries as well. Thus, as in the case of Bolivian tin in the pre-revolutionary period, the rise of oil and gas in Bolivia partially confirms key intuitions undergirding the theory developed here—but it also suggests new extensions and theoretical directions as well. I consider briefly the evidence in the following section.

Oil and Gas after the Revolution Oil played a growing role in Bolivia's economy after the Revolution. As noted above, some of the tin rent was itself transferred to the state-owned oil company, *Yacimientos Petroleros Fiscales de Bolivia* (YPFB), to pay for exploration and production costs. However, the major growth of the sector came with the opening of oil and gas to foreign investment. This was initiated under the MNR governments with the drafting of a new Petrol Code in 1955, under the guidance of the United States, and the removal of the monopoly of YPFB in 1956, as a condition of U.S. and IMF loans. In 1964, however, YPFB still controlled 95 percent of the production while its main competitor, Gulf Oil, had just 3 percent. This situation was dramatically transformed after the military coup of 1964; 3 years after removal of restrictions on foreign investment and profit repatriation under the Barrientos regime, Gulf Oil had 82 percent of production and YPFB's share was under 20 percent (Dunkerley 1980: 29). Rent collection by the state was relatively limited in this period but, in the classic pattern of heavy sunk-cost industries (Monaldi 2002a), also increased over time. Under the military presidency of Banzer, which was the period that saw the greatest flowering of the economic fortunes of Santa Cruz, oil revenues increased from US$24 million in 1971 to US$154 million in 1974 (Dunkerley 1980: 41). The Hydrocarbons Law of 1972 allowed YPFB to grant new concessions to foreign companies (Dunkerley 1980: 42). The fiscal coffers of the state benefited richly from the oil boom of the 1970s: in 1974, export earnings from oil were 230 percent higher than the previous year: "Almost overnight the budget and debt could be balanced and met with income from oil alone" (Dunkerley 1980: 44). By 1978, oil and natural gas constituted more than 30 percent of exports (Dunkerley 1980), and oil and non-oil mineral production together accounted for more than 70 percent of government revenue (Dunkerley and Morales 1985: 14). Although production actually began to decline toward the end of the 1970s, as a result of attempts early in the decade to maximize production, by the end of the 1970s Bolivia had clearly witnessed an oil boom that, if not on the same scale as Venezuela's or Ecuador's, nonetheless exerted a subtantial impact of the coffers of the Fisc.

The peak of the oil boom in the world market also coincided with important moves toward democratization in Bolivia. Long strikes in 1976 and 1977 led Banzer to decree elections to be held in 1978, which

> sparked off an upsurge of popular mobilization which focused on the demand for an amnesty for political prisoners and exiles.... Within a few days Banzer was faced with one of the most remarkable popular democratic campaigns of Bolivian history.... Within a fortnight over 1,200 people had joined the strike in a highly publicized fast until death in schools, universities and churches throughout the

country. The Church and its press gave especial support to this movement which emphasized the broad, non-partisan but solely anti-dictatorial character it had acquired. (Dunkerley 1980: 49–50)

Banzer declared an unrestricted amnesty and lifted restrictions on trade union activity, and parties re-emerged from their clandestine organization into the public arena:

As the poll of 9 July approached without major upset it seemed that Bolivia was set on the path to parliamentary democracy, something it had never experienced before... the immediate legacy of the Banzer years was not the revival of an anti-imperialist movement nor the rejection of the reformist political parties by the working class. Instead, the vast majority of workers and peasants identified with the electoral experiments and the moderation implicit in parliamentary government (Dunkerley 1980: 50).

As in the Ecuadorian case I will study in the next section, these moves toward democratization at the height of the world oil boom do not very squarely match the intuitions of the literature on the authoritarian resource curse. Also as in the Ecuadorian case, the crash in world oil markets subsequently appeared to contribute to imperiling democratic stability. In the Bolivian case, this was heightened by the fall of production in 1977–1978 duc to exhaustion of existing wells and a lack of new exploration. As Dunkerley and Morales (1985: 20–11) put it,

The economic model... could function more or less adequately in its own terms whilst the price and volume of mineral and oil exports remained buoyant... such conditions obtained during most of Banzer's regime.... The termination of the flexible terms of this fragile mortgage can be dated to 1977 with a major slump in the production of crude oil and the effective disappearance of foreign exchange earnings from this sector.... Earnings from all mineral exports over the same period dropped from $646 million to $348 million, which underpinned a drop in total legal exports from $1.07 billion to $788 million. Already alerted to the gravity of the position between 1978 and 1980, when growth dropped to 2% and inflation rose to 50%, the institutions of finance capital restricted the flow of credit and began to impose highly exigent terms for both its repayment and the disbursement of further funds.

Strikingly, in view of the apparent moderation of the 1977–1978 period, Bolivian politics in 1979 and particularly 1980 was characterized by increasing polarization. "The two-year period leading up to the July 1980 coup was one of the most confusing and turbulent in Bolivian history... [which involved] a notable worsening of the economic crisis and increasing polarization between the forces of left and right. The search for a viable centrism developed in practice into a choice between dictatorship and revolution"

(Dunkerley 1980: 51). Although a heir apparent to Banzer was initially elected in openly fraudulent elections in 1978, popular protests forced a new election in June 1979, which was won by Siles Zuaso, president under the MNR from 1956–1960 and now (having split from the MNR) a candidate for the leftist UDP party. However, Paz Estenssoro's MNR-Historico party controlled Congress, which under the Constitution gave Paz an effective veto over ratification of Siles Zuazo's victory. In the end a compromise was reached, with the president of the Senate becoming interim president and new elections scheduled for May 1980. However, the economic crisis worsened considerably in the interim, strikes intensified, and a process of increasing polarization between Left and Right ensued. Indeed, the imposition of a new austerity program, sparked in part by the economic crisis to which the fall of oil prices contributed, provoked popular mobilization that precipitated the coup of June 1980 and brought a return of the repressive authoritarian regime of General Luis Garcia Meza to power.

Oil and Democracy Notwithstanding these perturbations, oil became an increasingly important source of revenue for the government during the 1980s. By 1985, the state oil company YPFB had assets worth nearly \$2.6 billion and a net worth of \$1.2 billion (Luoma et al. 2007). The government of Jaime Paz Zamora passed a law requiring YPFB to transfer 65 percent of its annual revenues from domestic sales and 50 percent of revenues from exports to the central government; the amount represented 60 percent of the national treasury's revenues (Antelo 2000: 17). Between 1985 and 1995, YPFB contributed between 38 and 60 percent of the national government's total revenues—around \$3.5 billion in all (Luoma et al. 2007).

The 1990s marked a new phase in the evolution of the Bolivian oil and especially natural gas sector, one strongly associated with the presidency of Gonzalo Sánchez de Losada. Elected president in 1993 with 35.6 percent of the valid vote, on a mixed ticket including his MNR party and an indigenous party (*Movimiento Revolucionario Tupac Katari de Liberación, MRTKL*), Sánchez de Losada helped to implement a variety of reforms, including the creation of municipal governments and direct elections at that level of government, the extension of bilingual education, and the constitutional designation of Bolivia as a "plurinational, multicultural" republic. On the economic policy front, the Sánchez de Losada government's reforms included various austerity and structural adjustment measures, including the privatization or quasi-privatization of more than 100 state-owned enterprises (Luoma et al. 2007). Most notably, unlike the earlier wave of neoliberal economic reforms under the government of Victor Paz Estenssoro (1985–1989) when Sánchez de Losada was the planning minister, the economic reforms also focused squarely on the energy sector.

Dubbed a "capitalization" campaign by Sánchez de Losada, the idea of the reforms in the energy sector was to attract increased foreign direct investment in oil and particularly natural gas by converting the state-owned company YPFB into three public-private enterprises: two exploration and production companies, Chaco and Andina (which would be capitalized through partnerships with British Petroleum and the Spanish energy concern Repsol, respectively), and a pipeline and distribution company, Transredes (a consortium of Enron and Shell). With the stated goal of attracting the increased investment necessary for capitalization, Sánchez de Losada amended Bolivia's oil and gas laws, decreasing taxes and royalties from 50 percent to 18 percent. As with the Laffer curve for personal or corporate income tax, the idea was that increased investment would eventually raise the absolute level of government revenues, notwithstanding the sharply lowered rates.

The medium-term consequences of the capitalization program, however, included a sharply diminished role for resource rents on the revenue side of the government's fiscal balance. Taxes and royalties on oil and gas (which, as noted above, had constituted between 38 and 60 percent of state revenues from 1985 to 1995) comprised just 7 percent of total government revenues in 2002. The absolute amount of government revenue from oil and gas eventually did increase (after 2004) but only by 10 percent relative to the period preceding capitalization (Luoma et al. 2007). Instead of increasing government rents from oil and gas, capitalization was perceived by many Bolivians as simply increasing profits for foreign firms and, moreover, following an old model in which Bolivia exported cheap raw materials with little in the way of domestic value-added. Indeed, the government eliminated subsidies for oil and gas derivatives, passing on the costs of "capitalization" to consumers in the form of increased fuel prices and taxes on gas products.

In some sense, even as investment poured into a burgeoning natural gas sector, the capacity of the sector to provide rents to the central government remained fairly limited. Yet, in the few years before this book went to press, a major boom in natural gas exports driven by new natural gas discoveries during the late 1990s and early 2000s has taken place. In 1997, the largest natural gas deposits in Latin America outside of Venezuela were discovered in the lowland departments (the so-called *media luna* departments of the

East that surround the Andean highlands in a half-moon crescent shape). By 2000, the department of Santa Cruz, already a region that was growing much faster than the rest of the country during the 1970s and 1980s, produced 40 percent of national export revenue and 42 percent of tax revenue, though it holds less than a quarter of Bolivia's population (Eaton 2007: 8). As discussed earlier, growing resource rents provided an important new font of central government revenue.

There is substantial evidence that, consistent with this book's argument, oil rents have provided a font of public spending that has contributed to soothing tensions over the redistribution of non-resource income, even as conflict over the distribution of rents has also proven an important (and destabilizing) force as well. Interestingly, however, the Bolivian case also suggests new extensions of this book's argument. This is because, in contemporary Bolivia, both distributive and redistributive tensions play themselves out along regional lines. It turns out that the framework developed in Chapter Three is useful for analyzing the interaction of distributive and redistributive tensions at the interregional level, and the implications of these tensions for the regime type at the national level as well. Though I do not formally extend the analysis of Chapter Three to take account explicitly of interregional dynamics, leaving that for future work, I do close the discussion of the Bolivian case with an analysis of these dynamics.[46]

In Bolivia, the increasing economic power of Santa Cruz and in particular the existence of large actual and potential rents from natural gas have potentially contributed to political developments at the national level in at least two ways. On the one hand, an important regional movement focused on gaining greater economic and political autonomy for the lowland departments has gathered strength during the later part of the 1990s. Although, as discussed further below, this can be viewed as a backlash against the rise to power of indigenous-based parties in the highlands as well as administrative reforms that weakened the political power of the regional departments (Eaton 2007), the question of oil and gas revenues has clearly been at the center of autonomy demands and threats of secession from Santa Cruz elites. For example, the Santa Cruz groups that have pushed for greater political and adminstrative autonomy from the central government—in particular, the Pro-Santa Cruz Committee (*Comité*

[46] In Dunning (2006), I formally extend the analysis of Chapter Three to consider the effect of rents on incentives for territorial secession, placing emphasis on the effects of rents on patterns of interregional distribution and redistribution.

Pro-Santa Cruz, CPSC)—demand keeping two-thirds of revenues from major national taxes, including oil and natural gas taxes. The bountiful gas deposits that have recently been discovered would make gas a particularly copious source of revenue for the regional administration: in 2005, British Petroleum quadrupled its estimate of Bolivia's proven reserves to 29 trillion cubic feet and valued the reserves at around $250 billion (Powers 2006). In the last decade, companies including British Gas, Repsol of Spain, and Brazil's Petrobras have invested billions in exploration and extraction of natural gas.

On the other hand, gas has also been at the epicenter of popular mobilization in the highlands, both in the second administration of President Sánchez de Losada (2002–2003) and that of Carlos Mesa that followed Sánchez de Losada's forced resignation from office in October 2003. In the "gas war" of that month, Sanchez de Losada called in the military to repress protests of his proposal to build a pipeline for the export of natural gas through Chile, and nearly sixty people were killed (Eaton 2007). After Sánchez de Losada's resignation, the Santa Cruz civic committee, CPSC, announced that it "now doubted whether Santa Cruz would stay within Bolivia" (Eaton 2007). Popular groups, particularly in the highlands, have also made the nationalization of gas a major part of their political platforms in the late 1990s and early 2000s. In July 2004, voters approved a referendum according to which the government would take greater control of the gas industry, leading Congress to pass a new hydrocarbons law in 2005 that returned the royalty rates on new gas fields to their levels prior to liberalization in the hydrocarbons law of 1994.[47] Politicians from traditional parties, especially those with support bases in the highlands, reminded leaders in Santa Cruz that gas reserves constituted sovereign (national) property: as Julio Garrett Aillón, former vice-president to Paz Estenssoro, put it in an interview in November 2004, gas rents could "subsidize the economy of the country and the struggle against poverty, using a small fraction of the immense gas riches discovered in the national territory, that is the dominion of the State not because of the referendum's mandate, but because of the Constitution" (*La Prensa* 2004, translation mine). In June 2006, the country was paralyzed by blockades and protests, particularly in the highlands, by indigenous groups that pushed for complete nationalization of Bolivia's natural gas reserves (Powers 2006). Thus, even as the lowland departments

[47] The 1994 law had reduced royalty rates from 50% to 18%; the new legislation of 2005 restored them to their prior level.

have pushed for greater autonomy that would allow heightened regional control over the rents from oil and gas, popular movements in the highlands have pushed for greater central and national control. It is plausible that the recent discovery of large natural gas reserves in Santa Cruz and other lowland departments has contributed to the growing strength of the regional autonomy movements there as well as the mobilization in defense of national control in the highlands. Indeed, as one observer put it, it is plausible that "Bolivia's energy-rich eastern states are agitating for 'autonomy' in a thinly disguised effort to deprive the poor Indian west of oil and gas revenues" (Powers 2006). It is worth probing the evidence for this claim further, an objective to which I now turn.

Santa Cruz and other lowland departments were not always advocates of greater regional autonomy. In fact, as noted above, the lowland departments and particularly Santa Cruz tended to be disproportionate beneficiaries of public spending under the MNR governments that followed the Revolution, a tendency that only heightened after the return to authoritarian rule in 1964. Under the MNR, the *Corporación Boliviana de Fomento* (CBF) contributed significant development funds to Santa Cruz, completing the construction of a highway from Cochabamba to Santa Cruz and of railway connections to the Amazon and Rio de la Plata river systems. Elites from Santa Cruz had a major role in the military governments that ruled Bolivia for nearly two decades after the coup against the MNR government (1964–1982), and their support played a crucial role in the selection of Hugo Banzer, who was himself from Santa Cruz, as president of the military regime from 1971 to 1978. The bias of public spending toward the development of Santa Cruz was even more pronounced during the military rule than it had been before the Revolution and under the MNR. Agro-businesses in Santa Cruz received 66 percent of agricultural credits from Bolivia's Agricultural Bank under Banzer, nearly a quarter of new public-sector industries were created in Santa Cruz, and agricultural prices were set to guarantee the coverage of production costs (Eaton 2007, citing Conaghan and Malloy 1994). That Santa Cruz's economic success was in large part created by subsidies and transfers from the center is underscored by a refrain apparently often heard by national officials in La Paz: "Santa Cruz is the daughter of the national government" (Eaton 2007). During the post-revolutionary period, Santa Cruz elites exercised critical political power at the national level, often in support of military governments; under democratic politics, the leading rightist party, the *Falange Socialista Boliviana* (Bolivian Socialist Falange or FSB), had its largest support base in Santa Cruz. As Eaton (2007) puts it, "Throughout the political volatility of the 1960s, 70s, and 80s, support for a change of government in La Paz—rather than demands for autonomy from La Paz—was the consistent response by Santa Cruz elites to national governments they did not like."

However, the terms of exchange between the lowland departments and the national government in the highlands were substantially altered during the 1990s. Some of this change was clearly a result of political innovations that threatened to weaken the political power of the regional governments. For instance, a new Law of Administrative Decentralization, introduced by President Sánchez de Losada in 1995, strengthened the autonomy of municipalities at the expense of the regional departments; municipalities would enjoy direct transfers. The increasing political power of indigenous parties, including the national emergency of Evo Morales' *Movimiento al Socialismo* (MAS) after 2000 and Felipe Quispe's *Movimiento Indigena Pachakuti* (MIP), was aided by new mechanisms that created more propitious mechanisms for indigenous political participation, including the 1994 Law of Popular Participation and the shift in 1997 to a mixed-member electoral system, under which half of all legislators would be elected in single-member districts (Eaton 2007). Increasing mobilization in the highlands, including the so-called water war of 2000, in which the Bechtel corporation was forced to back out of contracts for privatized water delivery in Cochabamba, and coordinated blockades later in the same year by coca-growing farmers (*cocaleros*) seemed to promise an increased radicalization in the highlands that might eventually carry a redistributive cost to elites in the lowlands. In the 2002 elections, the traditional parties, including the rightist *Acción Democratica Nacionalista* (ADN) that traditionally had support from Santa Cruz elites, did poorly, and Morales' MAS party garnered 20 percent of the vote and significant representation in Congress (Eaton 2007).

Yet, the shifting terms of exchange between the center and the regions also very plausibly depended on changing economic conditions and, in particular, the discovery in 1997 of large gas deposits in the *media luna* departments. These enormous deposits promised a financial bounty to whoever controlled them. It is also possible that the existence of greater territorially based natural resource rents has, perhaps counterintuitively, increased the *success* of Santa Cruz elites in winning opportunities for regional autonomy. As Eaton (2007) notes, "In a relatively compressed period of time, the CPSC made substantial progress toward its twin goals of political and policy-making autonomy for Santa Cruz," notwithstanding the greatly weakened position of Santa Cruz elites in the national government. Shortly before

Mesa's resignation as president in June 2005, he agreed to hold a nationwide referendum on departmental autonomy, scheduled for July 2006. The remarkable success of Santa Cruz elites in forcing this concession, notwithstanding their political weakness, may plausibly reflect their vocal threats of total secession, made increasingly credible by the natural gas boom and consequent flow of rent that would accrue solely to Santa Cruz in the event of secession. Faced with this credible threat of secession, Mesa may well have seen a referendum on autonomy as the lesser of evils.[48]

In conclusion, how has the increased value of natural gas shaped the incentives of elites in Santa Cruz, in their quest for regional autonomy? On the one hand, it is quite plausible that elites realize that the redistributive cost of integration, in terms of taxes and other levies on non-resource income, may be substantially reduced by the accrual of gas rents to the central government. Garret Aillón (MNR), former vice-president under Paz Estenssoro and currently dean of the Universidad Andina Simón Bolívar, perhaps reminded elites of this when he said in an interview,

> To raise ourselves from underdevelopment and poverty... [we should] turn not to external aid but to the internal aid that gas can generate.... Subsidies [to the prices of consumer products] are not paid for with the fiscal resources of the State but with natural gas.... With the socialization of gas the concessionaires will have the opportunity to contribute, in their own interest, to the social governability of the country and the creation of a climate of peace, social cohesion and political stability.... The gas should be for the *campesinos*.... The Revolution yesterday gave them land, today it should give them water (*La Prensa* 2004).

On the other hand, as this discussion suggests, it is also quite plausible that the boom in resource rents in Santa Cruz and other lowland departments has created new incentives in favor of autonomy movements. In fact, as we will see further, it is quite possible that the effect of gas rents on the incentives for secession is analogous to the effect of rents on incentives of elites for coups against democracy. On the one hand, the indirect effect is to reduce redistributive threats to non-resource wealth and therefore decrease incentives for secession or autonomy, given the cost of autonomy or secession movements; on the other hand, the direct effect is to increase incentives for secession or autonomy, as this would allow direct control

[48] Organizational variables, including the way that Santa Cruz elites have been able to frame their demands for autonomy, undoubtedly play a role as well; see Eaton (2007) for a fuller discussion.

over the distribution of public rents from gas. These are hypotheses that future research on the Bolivian case should be geared toward evaluating further.

6.3 Ecuador: Oil Booms and Democratization

I now turn to the Ecuadorian case, where oil rents became an important source of government revenue in the early 1970s, after a military coup spurred in part by the possibility that a left-wing populist mayor of the country's largest city would ascend to the presidency. Though the literature on the authoritarian effects of petroleum would suggest that oil would then have provided the foundations for an authoritarian regime, Ecuador in fact redemocratized in 1979. I argue here that oil rents played an important role in this process of redemocratization. Intertemporal variation in political outcomes supports the idea of a democratic effect of resource rents—even as it is at odds with the predictions of the literature on oil rents and authoritarianism. Because the importance of the case lies, in part, in the evidence it provides that oil rents may play an active and important role in promoting democratization, I focus the analysis in this chapter on the temporal period just prior to and just after Ecuador's democratization.[49]

The rise of the Ecuadorian rentier state was sharp and rapid. Although the National Assembly had extended a concession for extraction of "bituminous substances . . . such as petroleum, tar, and kerosene" as early as 1878 (Martz 1987: 45), and petroleum extraction began in earnest in the first decades of the twentieth century, by 1970 Ecuador produced just 1.4 million barrels of crude oil a year, and revenues from oil constituted a negligible proportion of the government budget; Ecuador was in fact a net importer of crude (Martz 1987). Although oil production had remained geographically concentrated in coastal areas, particularly in Santa Elena Peninsula, this situation changed dramatically over the next 3 years, due almost entirely to the coming onstream of crude oil from large deposits in the eastern Amazonian province of Oriente. Only in 1967 had there been public acknowledgment of the possible discovery of large oil reserves in the eastern Oriente region; however, both the extent of later discoveries and their value were unpredictable at the beginning of the 1970s. By 1973, Ecuador was producing 76.2 million barrels of crude oil a year; buoyed by

[49] For another recent analysis that suggests Ecuador may have democratized not despite oil but *because* of oil, see Smith and Kraus (2005).

the price shock in world oil markets brought about by the Arab oil embargo of 1973, oil's share of exports rose from 18 percent in 1973 to 55 percent in 1976. The oil boom was a windfall for the fiscal coffers of the government: the national budget grew by 21 percent in 1974, 32 percent in 1975, and 32 percent in 1976.[50]

6.3.1 *The Coup of 1972 and Redemocratization in 1979*

The timing and rapidity of the rise of the Ecuadorian rentier state provide a valuable opportunity for studying the political consequences of oil rents in a highly unequal country, in which redistributive pressures have played an important role in shaping the emergence and persistence of democracy.[51] Ecuador experienced a military coup on February 15, 1972, just prior to the oil boom. Although the social bases of support for the coup were heterogeneous, and although the military regime that was installed in 1972 was a reformist one in some respects, it is also fairly clear that an important raison d'être for the coup was to put down the threat of redistribution from below. At the time of the coup, the victory of Assad Bucaram, a left-wing, populist mayor of the port city of Guayaquil, in the upcoming presidential elections of June 1972 seemed increasingly likely. As Martz (1987: 45) puts it, "The difficulty in somehow blocking a Bucaram presidency lay in the fact . . . that he had the support of only one group in Ecuador—the marginalized subproletariat, which was the largest and most oppressed cohort of voters." Although intellectuals on the Left also resented Bucaram's repression of the student movement while mayor of Guayaquil, the strongest opposition to a Bucaram presidency came from the traditional social bases of the Right. A likely Bucaram victory in 1972 "brought dismay . . . to the Guayaquil elite, who had already had a taste of Bucaram's populism during his term as mayor" (Fitch 1977: 178). Indeed,

> the Right could not forgive [Bucaram's] plebian-moralizing outbursts, which during the municipal administration had taken the form of verbal insults against the oligarchy . . . and rigorous tax collection from the bourgeoisie. . . . The army, which certainly did not mind his outbursts, feared that Bucaram might become a factor

[50] Oil production, revenue, and export data given in this paragraph come from Martz (1987: 51, Table 2-1; 159, Table 5-4; 404, Table A-3).

[51] In the data set used for the cross-national analysis in Chapter Four, Ecuador's average Gini coefficient between 1960 and 2001 was 53.1; its average labor share as a percentage of economic output was 30.4 (thus, its score on the labor share measure of inequality is $100 - 30.4 = 69.6$).

toward disorder, since his personality somehow represented the irruption of the masses in national political life (Cueva 1982: 54, cited in Martz 1987: 85).[52]

Quito's conservative newspaper *El Comercio* "soberly editorialized that the nation's problems virtually required intervention by the armed forces" (Martz 1987: 88). Thus, a credible interpretation privileges the role of class conflict and the threat of redistribution as a motivation for the coup of 1972 (see also Pérez Sáinz 1984: 50).

In possible contrast to the argument developed here, it is possible that the prospect of oil rents played a role in motivating the coup, and the realization of oil rents may have played a role in supporting authoritarian rule after 1972. Indeed, one finds some striking similarities in the literature on Ecuadorian politics during this period to case studies of the authoritarian, oil-rich regimes of the Middle East. Some analysts have suggested that the prospect of future government revenues from oil played a role in motivating the coup itself. According to Martz (1987: 84, 89–90), "The reality of newly-found petroleum wealth in Oriente was not the sole, but clearly among the important elements, which provoked [the] coup d'état.... Officers shared the national fervor over exaggerated dreams of the wealth of black gold.... Corporate benefits for the military institution could be anticipated, ranging from higher wages and greater fringe benefits to an improvement of training facilities and the purchase of modern weaponry." Isaacs (1993: 25–6) writes, "The petroleum boom would shift the locus of economic decision-making to the state. For the first time in Ecuadorian history, a relatively autonomous state, with significant resources at its disposal would find itself in a position to sponsor development and reform.... Institutional interests thus coincided with the national interest to push the military towards intervention." While the prospect of future oil rents seems somewhat debatable as an explanation for the coup itself—in part because the value of oil rents increased so greatly in 1973 after a world price shock that was ex-ante unpredictable—it is undeniable that oil did

[52] Not all scholars are in accord, however, that the apparent threat posed by the imminent election of Bucaram was the primary motivation of the officers who staged the coup d'état. Fitch (1977: 180, cited in Martz 1987: 89), e.g., argues that the "electoral veto of Bucaram was not the key element...it is not clear how many officers were acting to prevent a likely Bucaram victory or to what degree Bucaram really entered into military decisions to support or oppose the coup." Isaacs (1993: 22–7) also privileges corporatist explanations for the motives of officers involved in the coup, relegating class-based factors to a secondary role. Nonetheless, economic elites, whose support for the coup was also essential, were clearly anti-Bucaram: "to some, he was even seen... as a Marxist" (Martz 1987: 89).

provide an enormous increase in revenues to the Ecuadorian state in the *aftermath* of the coup. Expenditures for the armed forces "grew dramatically from $42 million in 1971 to $98 million in 1976. The regime also allocated 50 percent of its oil royalties to the military; this totaled an estimated $250,000 daily" (Martz 1987: 4). Non-oil taxes declined by the equivalent of two percentage points of GDP (World Bank, 1991), and "government elites ... engaged in ostentatious consumption" (Martz 1987: 4). According to this view, oil rents provided a source of direct benefits both to the ruling military and to elites under the authoritarian regime installed in 1972; they could therefore plausibly have increased the longevity of authoritarian rule.

Yet, Ecuador in fact *redemocratized* in 1978–1979—at the height of the second oil shock and at a moment at which the fiscal coffers of the state were swelling with oil revenues.[53] This appears to contradict the intuition provided by the existing literature on the authoritarian effects of resource wealth and raises an important question: given the apparent boon in the fortunes of elites and the military under oil-led authoritarianism, why would elites and the military allow a return to democratic rule?

Absent the effects of the oil boom, the return to democracy is puzzling because it implied a potential return to the kinds of social and political dynamics that had helped prompt the coup in the first place. Indeed, the inauguration of Bucaram's nephew and close advisor Jaime Roldós Aguilera, who took the plurality of the vote in the July 1978 elections, was followed by precisely the sorts of "populist" policies that Bucaram had advocated before the slated presidential elections of 1972. A day after his second-round victory in April 1978, Roldós announced his intention to "put an end to the contradiction betwen exploiters and exploited ... to lay down clear ideological lines to bring social justice to the majority and guarantee freedom to all Ecuadoreans" (Martz 1987: 247). Among the first acts of the new Parliament was the doubling of the minimum monthly wage, a reduction of the work week from 44 to 40 hours, and a price freeze on basic goods. The legislature also instituted a costly new adult education and literacy plan and increased subsidies to the domestic price of gasoline (Martz 1987: 34, 251, 292).

However, these new programs did not come at a redistributive cost to elites, in part because they were directly subsidized by oil rents. In the year

[53] Indeed, despite the increasing role of oil rents as a source of state finance after the coup, preparations for a redemocratization were underway as early as 1976, when a council of military officers avowedly sympathetic to redemocratization (the *Consejo Supremo de Gobierno*) took power from General Guillermo Rodríguez Lara, who had come to power after the coup of 1972.

after the inauguration of the new president, crude prices reached record levels; by January 1981, Ecuadorian crude was selling for $40 a barrel (Martz 1987: 379). Plans to use oil rents to subsidize the doubling of the minimum wage and the reduction of the work week, and the price freeze on basic goods were widely discussed in Congress (Corkill and Cubitt 1988). Simultaneously, a reduction in the tax burden on elites was extensive and linked directly to the rise of the oil economy. As a World Bank report put it in 1991, "The dependence of Government finances on oil revenues . . . has had the unfortunate consequence of . . . inducing a deterioration of the formal tax system" (World Bank 1991: xi–xii).[54]

At the same time, like the Venezuelan case, the Ecuadorian case, and particularly political developments in the wake of the plunge in oil prices in the 1980s, underscores the sometimes fragile nature of a democracy underwritten by oil rents. The collapse of oil prices in 1986 forced the government to enact emergency measures to address large fiscal deficits, including fuel price increases of up to 80 percent and 25 percent increases in bus fares (Corkill and Cubitt 1988). These measures to adjust to lower oil rents provoked widespread rioting, another general strike, assaults on members of Parliament, bombardment of government buildings with Molotov cocktails, and, in January 1987, the abduction of the president by air force paratroopers (Espinel et al. 1994). Febres Cordero was forced to reverse reforms and initiated enormous construction projects to benefit his coastal constituency. After his subsequent election, "President Borja inherited an inflation-riddled economy with a public sector deficit of 16 percent of GDP. His first package of economic reforms included moderate measures of fiscal austerity, but it too was met with a national strike, which was particularly damaging to oil exports. The powerful bus and truck drivers' union shut down transport across the country in June 1989" (Economist Intelligence Unit 1989), and the president's support quickly eroded as "continuing austerity measures reduced subsidies and restrained wages. As the Gulf conflict of 1990–91 escalated, the trade union federation, the military, and the business community descended on the state, demanding a share of increased oil revenues. Despite the expected temporary nature of high prices, Borja gave in and the entire oil windfall was used to finance increases in consumption" (World Bank 1991).

[54] Non-oil taxes were reduced by about 2 percent of GDP, relative to the pre-oil era. Ecuador's oil revenues, which were about 10 percent of GDP, played a growing role in financing total public expenditure, which was 6 percent of GDP higher in 1989 than in 1970 (World Bank 1991).

Even as oil revenue volatility has mapped onto patterns of mobilization from below, Ecuador has arguably continued to use periods of higher oil prices and thus higher oil rents to renew public spending in ways that ar-guably help to sustain Ecuador's "fragile democracy" (see Corkill a[illegible] 1988). As Eifert et al. (2003: 99–103) put it, "In eight years o[illegible] decade, fiscal impulses exacerbated the oil cycle"; in other words, booms have been followed by recourse to great public spending without recourse to taxation, while periods of contraction and adjustment have prompted increased mobilization from below that at various moments has posed an apparent threat to the stability of democracy. In combination with the evidence presented earlier on Chile and Bolivia, and later on Botswana, evidence from the Ecuadorian case thus helps to sustain the arguments advanced here. Most important from a theoretical perspective, the case suggests that oil rents may not only stabilize incumbent democracies but they may also promote democratization.

6.4 Botswana: An African Anomaly

Botswana is both a diamond-rich rentier state and, according to some observers, a nearly unique economic and political success story among the countries of post-colonial, sub-Saharan Africa (Acemoglu et al. 2003; Dunning 2005; Harvey and Lewis 1990; Samatar 1999). On the economic side, at the time of independence from the British in 1966, Botswana was the second-poorest country in the world (Edge 1998: 343). Between 1970 and 1997, however, Botswana achieved the highest average rate of economic growth in the *world* (Samatar 1999), which vaulted the country into the ranks of an "upper-middle income" developing country as classified by the World Bank. Botswana has also experienced substantial macroeconomic and fiscal stability, unusual among similar countries (Acemoglu et al. 2003). On the political side, the political opposition freely contests elections, and there is a significant degree of media freedom in this multi-party system. The fact that the Botswana Democratic Party (BDP) has won every election since independence has engendered some debate about how democratic the country should be considered (see Przeworski et al. 2000: 23; also Good 1992 and Picard 1987).[55] Yet, the identity of the highest office holder has changed three times since independence (that is, from President Seretse

[55] Interview, Professor Kenneth Good, Department of Political and Administrative Studies, University of Botswana; Gaborone, Botswana, August 7, 2003.

Khama to Ketumile Masire to Festus Mogae), and the existence of uninterrupted democratic participation and contestation throughout the post-independence period is nearly unique among sub-Saharan African countries (Bratton and van de Walle 1997: 79, table 3). Many analysts rate Botswana an unusually longstanding democracy in post-colonial Africa.

These striking economic and political developments have occurred even as diamond rents provided an increasingly dominant revenue source for the state, reaching an average of 51 percent of government revenue between 1983 and 1991 (Molutsi 1998: 364–5). The world diamond market itself produces substantial rents: the South African multi-national De Beers has substantial monopoly (as a significant "upstream" producer of diamonds) and monopsony (as the globe's principal "downstream" purchaser of rough diamonds) powers, allowing it substantial influence over the world diamond price; these elements of market structure have been married to the company's impressive marketing capacity to create a robust world market for gem diamonds.[56] Moreover, since independence Botswana's government has been well positioned to capture a high "state take" of diamond rents in proportional as well as absolute terms. Soon after the announcement in 1967 of the discovery of kimberlite diamond pipes at the Orapa mine, it was clear to De Beers that Botswana would become an important producer for the global diamond market.[57] This gave the country important leverage with respect to the company, which desired to maintain control over the production side of the world market.[58]

Thus, diamond rents have supplied the single most important supply for the fiscal coffers of the state in Botswana. When in 1974 De Beers asked for a lease to begin production at a second mine at Letlhakane, the government was able to increase its share of diamond mining profits from 50 percent to around 75 percent, and the Botswanan government also acquired a 50 percent equity interest in Debswana, a joint venture company half-owned by De Beers (Jefferis 1998: 304). Botswana's position as a dominant producer

[56] De Beers is thought to control around 80 percent of the world's supply of rough diamonds (Jefferis 1998: 306).

[57] Recall from Chapters One and Two that "kimberlite" diamonds—diamonds found in subterranean pipes that tend to be highly geographically specific and subject to large capital intensities in production—tend to provide a ready source of rents for the state. This contrasts with the case of "alluvial" diamonds, which have been scattered by waterways and tend to be easier for small private miners to exploit.

[58] Interview, Ribson Gabonowe, Director of Mines, Ministry of Minerals, Energy, and Water Affairs; Gaborone, Botswana, July 7, 2003.

in the world market and therefore its degree of bargaining power vis-a-vis De Beers were solidified by another discovery of diamond pipes, at Jwaneng in 1977: Botswana's share of total sales of De Beers' Central Selling Office grew from 3 percent in 1976 to 44 percent in 1987. Between 1976 and 1994, Botswana's diamond exports increased by an average of 30.2 percent annually (Dunning 2005: 462–3), supplying an ever-more important source of rents for the state. In other respects, Botswana conforms to the classic patterns of the rentier state: for instance, because of the geographic isolation of the mines, the capital intensity of kimberlite diamond mining, and the low numbers of people directly employed by the sector, diamond rents enter the domestic political economy largely through patterns of public revenue generation and spending, even though there have been some limited connections between diamonds and the private sector, for instance, in diamond cutting and polishing.[59]

The emergence of a diamond-based rentier state in Botswana therefore coincided with a period in which economic growth was pronounced and multi-party democracy was stabilized. Botswana appears to constitute an important exception to the idea of a political or economic "resource curse," particularly when contrasted with the many resource-rich sub-Saharan African countries that are poorer today than they were at independence and/or that have long histories of authoritarianism in the post-colonial period. Can the theory developed in this book help to illuminate this striking anomaly?

I argue here that key ingredients of the book's framework do help to elucidate the Botswanan case, in ways that have not been widely remarked by previous analysts. I begin by reviewing the aspects of Botswanan society and politics that are isomorphic with the basic assumptions of the theoretical model developed here: for instance, the existence of a more or less cohesive "elite" with well-defined economic interests, the political salience of inequality, and other factors. I also comment on aspects of the case that appear at odds with the basic presumptions of my framework, especially the apparent absence of significant challenges to elite rule "from below." Although one would obviously not expect isomorphism between the theory and the reality in all respects (like all theories in the social sciences,

[59] However, the Israeli concern Schachter & Namdar maintains an important diamond cutting and polishing plant outside Gaborone but employs less than 300 people, underscoring that even in the most labor-intensive part of the diamond production business, the numbers of employed may be low; diamonds are a capital-intensive sector. Interview, Willie Conradi, Production Manager, Schachter & Namdar; Gaborone, Botswana, July 7, 2003.

the one developed here is stylized and partial and may carry more explanatory power in some social and political settings than others), I suggest that the absence of challenges to elite rule can be viewed as an endogenous equilibrium outcome—endogenous, that is, to the existence of diamond rents that could be spent to mollify challenges to elite interests under democratic rule. This is one reason, I argue, why despite the dramatic inequality of assets and income, democratic rule has not posed a serious challenge to the private economic interests of the small Tswana elite. Although there are alternative explanations for why this might be so, I argue that diamond rents are part of the story. Exploring evidence on the mechanisms through which rents have helped to sustain the political regime in Botswana is the main goal of this section.

It is useful to begin by noting several widely discussed aspects of Botswanan politics and society. First, perhaps more than any other feature of society and politics in Botswana, observers have been struck by the power and cohesiveness of the traditional Tswana elite. Some scholars have attributed this elite cohesiveness to the historical legacy of "benign neglect" at the hands of British colonial authorities, who administered the Bechuanaland Protectorate from across the South African border at Mafeking, yet promoted strategies of indirect rule that were not as divisive of the elite as they were elsewhere in sub-Saharan Africa.[60] Robinson and Parsons (2006) instead emphasize the "defensive modernization" of traditional Tswana authorities, in the face of potential encroachments from the Boers, the British South Africa Company, and the Union of South Africa during Botswana's colonial period. Others analysts have emphasized the more recent period of transition to independence from Britain, when the country's first president, Seretse Khama, succeeded in uniting many of the traditional chiefs and leaders of the eight Tswana tribes behind his project of constructing a national, legal-rational state. Whatever the source of elite cohesiveness, it is clearly appropriate in the Botswanan context to say that there was an "elite" group that acted in a substantially corporate fashion.

Second, this cohesive elite also has substantial private economic interests, in particular, in cattle ranching. Cattle remains a profitable business in Botswana, one that generates substantial economic value for the Tswana elite.[61] Aside from diamonds, the cattle industry remains one of Botswana's dominant economic sectors, contributing nearly 80 percent of

60 Steenkamp (1991), however, challenges this standard account.

61 Interview, Richard White, Natural Resource Services; Gaborone, Botswana, July 10, 2003.

gross agricultural output in rural areas, where approximately 70 percent of Botswana's population live (Nengwekhulu 1998: 359). The key point here is not just about the continued economic importance of an alternate private sector in the wake of the diamond boom, which I discuss below; it is also that assets have been so unequally distributed in the cattle sector, with most of the wealth appropriated by a narrow elite. A National Migration study in the 1980s found that 45 percent of rural households did not own any cattle, with almost half of the national herd owned by the top 7 percent of owners (Nengwekhulu 1998: 359); in 1995, 49 percent of framing households had no cattle, while 10 percent had more than 100 cattle (Botswana NDP 8, 1997: 227). In other words, "incomes among cattle owners are themselves skewed.... Income from arable production is also unevenly distributed and in a pattern that is strongly influenced by the pattern of livestock ownership" (Nengwekhulu 1998: 359). The cattle-owning elite, or what Robinson and Parsons (2006: 120–21) call the "beefocracy," has reaped significant benefits from its economic dominance in this sector.

Thus, inequality of assets and income in non-resource sectors is a salient feature of the Botswanan regime; the socioeconomic reality involves the existence of poverty for a great majority of the population despite high average income levels. Some estimates have put 55 percent of residents below the poverty line, while other studies have estimated greater or lesser proportions.[62] As one government report put it, "The evidence surveyed... points unmistakeably to the conclusion that a majority of Batswana,[63] especially in the rural areas, are poor by any standards... income within Botswana is skewed, with most Batswana incomes [being] far below the average for all Botswana. There are few direct data concerning income distribution within Botswana, but there is considerable evidence of unequal distribution of the asset [sic] and opportunities upon which higher incomes depend" (Nengwekhulu 1998: 359). Nengwekhulu (1998: 359) adds, "It is not only that income is skewed but rather that it is skewed in favor of an extremely small minority."

With such a skewed distribution of income, one might think that democratic contestation and participation could prove injurious to the interests of the narrow elite. This has largely not been the case, and especially not

[62] Molutsi (1998: 373) gives the 55 percent figure; other estimates have reached as high as 70 percent, with 50 percent living in extreme poverty (all of which estimates depend on definitions of the poverty line, of course). Interview, Chris Sharp, mining and political consultant; Gaborone, Botswana, July 7, 2003.

[63] Batswana is the plural form of Motswana, i.e., a Tswana resident of the country of Botswana.

in cattle ranching, a sector in which the democratic Botswanan state has provided substantial protections for the relatively small cattle-owning elite. Not only has the private property of elites enjoyed de facto as well as de jure protection, but the land tenure regime has substantially favored large owners. As Nengwekhulu (1998: 352) puts it:

> The Tribal Grazing Land Policy (TGLP)... was introduced to facilitate the modernization and improvement of range and cattle management, but its application and implementation have had a negative impact on the land rights of the rural poor, especially hunters and gatherers. More specifically, it has had a negative effect on the land rights of the Basarwa[64] and non-stockholders.... Because the TGLP is essentially aimed at improving the lot of stockholders, large tracts of land have been zoned for them at the expense of the Basarwa and non-stockholders.

Of course, this cohesive Tswana elite has hardly faced a high degree of societal opposition "from below" in the post-independence period; in this sense (and here I turn to a third basic point about Botswanan politics and society), some observers might consider core elements of the theory developed in this book less analytically useful in the Botswanan context. Botswana remains a predominantly rural country, with a population of some 1.7 million people and a capital of just 170,000 residents; political opposition, however, has come largely from the towns where opposition parties have garnered some 65 percent of the popular vote (Molutsi 1998: 370). The prospect of high levels of redistribution under democracy has not seemed to pose a threat to elites' economic interests, despite the extreme inequality of assets and income found in both rural and urban areas. Scholars have remarked on a variety of reasons why this might be so. Some point to unique aspects of British colonial policy toward the Bechuanaland Protectorate, discussed above, which did not divide the elite to the same extent as in other sub-Saharan African cases. Others emphasize the role of the traditional authority of Tswana leaders in limiting challenges to elite rule; for instance, Seretse Khama, the first president after independence, was the hereditary chief of the Bangwato tribe, and Khama convinced other Tswana chiefs to follow him in the project of state-building at the national level, conceivably bolstering the unchallenged political eminence of this group (Parsons, Tlou, and Henderson 1995). The importance of this point for our purposes is that the relative lack of "mass" organization in this predominantly rural society of cattle herders, together with the traditional

64 The Basarwa (or San) people, sometimes called Bushmen, are hunters and gatherers who live largely in the Kalahari desert.

authority and Weberian charisma of elites, could imply that the potential redistributive costs to elites of holding elections may be relatively small.[65]

Yet, at least some of the explanation for this observed pattern—that is, the anemic challenge that democratic competition has posed to elite interests—may stem from patterns of spending diamond rents themselves. Botswana has invested heavily in education, health care, and infrastructure projects, and the country's high scores on social development indicators reflect these investments: "Botswana was able to direct between 32% and 44.5% of public expenditure towards social sector development during the years 1980–1991" (Edge 1998: 344). According to Molutsi (1998: 365), "the government was able to undertake a comprehensive social development programme which built schools, clinics, supplied water to villages, constructed rural roads and created limited job opportunities in rural areas . . . the economic prosperity resulting from mineral exploitation resulted in rapid job creation in the formal sector, with government as the leading employer." Primary and secondary schooling is free, and the government has embarked on "relief programmes which include feeding schemes. There have also been attempts to narrow income disparities, for example, by salary and wage increases" (Nengwekhulu 1998: 359–60).

There is also evidence that as electoral competition has stiffened, potentially posing a threat to the interests of the Tswana elite, the state has responded with increased welfare and transfer payments—all funded by diamond rents. In 1989, for instance, the BDP captured 64.7 percent of the popular vote and 91 percent of national assembly seats, matching its highest percentage since independence. Even in this election, however, the BDP captured only 12.8 percent of the vote in urban areas, an important challenge for the BDP because greatly increasing urbanization during the 1980s implied that fully one-quarter of the population now lived in cities; unemployment rates topped 30 percent in urban areas (Parson 1993: 68–71). In 1994, faced with a rising challenge from the opposition Botswana National Front (BNF) party, the BDP won only 54.5 percent of the popular vote, while the BNF captured 37.3 percent of the popular vote and 32.5 percent of seats in the national assembly (Molutsi 1998: 370–1, tables 23.2–3). The BNF took up "working-class issues," according to a number

[65] This view is bolstered by the claims of some critics of the BDP, who assert that "although elections since independence have been formally free and open, they function as a symbol of a style of political rule rather than as a mechanism for a change of government" (Picard 1987: 142, cited in Snyder 2001).

of analysts, engendering a serious threat to the BDP and forcing it to respond with increased transfers of diamond rents to popular groups (Parson 1993: 72).

As the BDP's electoral dominance began to wane, and especially in the wake of the elections of 1989 and 1994, the BDP responded to the increased competition by placing more emphasis on targeted subsidies for the poor, out of a development budget funded by mineral rents, and introduced pension benefits for the elderly.[66] The targeted transfers included direct payments of P170 a month (around US$30) to destitutes, who previously received monthly food rations of much lesser value; in 1995, pensions amounting to P117 (around US$20) a month were introduced.[67] According to the government's estimates, the proportion of poor and very poor households declined from 49 to 38 percent between 1986 and 1994 (Botswana NDP 8, 1997: 91).[68] One of the sadder commentaries on the demand for social spending includes a recent "hew and cry for the government to pay for funerals . . . which can bankrupt a family," in the wake of the recent sharp increase in deaths associated with HIV-AIDS.[69] The percentage of central government spending on housing also more than doubled from its 1980 level, to 13.5 percent in 1992–1993; by the mid-1990s, nearly 87 percent of all construction stemmed from the government and parastatals (Botswana NDP 8, 1997: 419). The public sector also continued to constitute a major employer, as the size of the civil service doubled between 1985/1986 and 1997/1998, while government spending contributed more than 17 percent to total GDP by 1995/1996 (Botswana NDP 8, 1997: 101, 452).[70] Finally, the government also spent one of the highest percentages of national income on health among African countries (N'Diaye 2001: 90); under-5 child mortality rates halved between 1981 and 1991 (Botswana NDP 8, 1997: 391). In total, Botswana directed between 32 and 45 percent of public expenditure toward social sector development up to the early 1990s (Edge 1998: 344).

[66] Interview, Chris Sharp, mining and political consultant; Gaborone, Botswana, July 7, 2003.

[67] The pension introduced in October 1996 was worth P100 per month paid in cash, and was raised to P110 per month in April 1998. Good (2002: 59), however, noting that pensions are larger in South Africa, characterizes the handout as "extremely mean in regional and national terms."

[68] The government's measurement of poverty is not uncontroversial, however; see Good (2002: 60), who suggests that reported declines in poverty are at least in part an artifact of new measurement criteria introduced in 1991.

[69] Interview, Chris Sharp, mining and political consultant; Gaborone, Botswana, July 7, 2003.

[70] By contrast, government spending as a proportion of GDP was less than 10 percent in 1966.

The theory developed in this book, in brief, does help to illuminate what is otherwise a striking puzzle: despite the presence of a cohesive elite with well-defined non-resource economic interests, and despite dramatic asset inequality and a highly skewed distribution of income, democratic participation and contestation have not posed an undue threat to the economic interests of this elite. Of course, there are a number of reasons this might be so that fall outside of our main analytic lens. For instance, there is a relative absence of mass organization "from below" in rural areas, where the BDP has historically had its strongest electoral base; in cities, opposition parties such as the BNF have greater electoral support. Yet, as political opposition and competition have increased (in part, perhaps, as a function of greater urbanization), the BDP leadership has responded by transferring diamond rents to the poor and other groups in the form of targeted subsidies. While there may be an economic opportunity cost to elites of doing so, the presence of diamond rents can also protect other elite interests under democracy: namely, continued predominance in the non-resource economy.

It is also important to note, however, that on some dimensions this book's theory would predict that Botswana would be more of an "intermediate" case than one in which the democratic effect of rents would be strongest (see Chapter One). For instance, despite the relative importance of the private sector, Botswana has been more resource-dependent than other democratic cases, particularly during its greatest boom period: between 1983 and 1991, the country's most resource-dependent period, mineral output constituted 58 percent of GDP on average (and 76 percent of exports; Molutsi 1998: 364). These proportions clearly do not put Botswana in the camp of a Saudi Arabia or Kuwait, but they do suggest a higher degree of economic dependence on resource wealth than the other democratic cases I have examined above.

This last consideration may be important for predicting Botswana's democratic future. Notwithstanding the media freedom, political space for opposition parties, and other elements that seem to qualify Botswana as a liberal multi-party democracy, some analysts wonder what would happen if the BDP actually lost an election: would the party relinquish power? As early as 1989 two local observers noted that "Botswana's ruling elite has yet to be tried. Those who won political power have not been challenged enough by those in opposition. When they do it remains to be seen whether they [sic] will step down" (Holm and Molutsi 1989). In the context of growing political opposition in the towns and the existence of a widespread "culture" of democracy (a set of expectations that the rule of law, elections, and so on will be respected), attempts to limit democratic participation and contestation would likely be resisted by important elements of Botswana's population.

Democratic reversals could thus be costly for elites, and the question of interest here is whether diamond rents make elites more or less likely to engage in these costly options. On the one hand, the opportunity cost of foregoing rents may make such costly actions to maintain power more likely, particularly as resource dependence grows: Botswana may not in the future be immune to the authoritarian effect of rents. On the other hand, living under democracy may not be so bad for elites, even after a fall from office on the part of the BDP, precisely because the presence of diamond rents could limit threats to other elite interests. This democratic effect of rents in Botswana has been and in all likelihood will continue to be an important way in which resource rents shape the Botswanan political regime.

7

Theoretical Extensions

Theoretical models, such as those developed in Chapter Three, might fruitfully be compared to Weberian ideal types.[1] They serve as useful devices for theoretical development; comparative statics analysis of models may suggest testable hypotheses that can be evaluated against the evidence. At the same time, of course, models simplify and abstract from "reality"; this is indeed what makes them models. Like Weberian ideal types, models often do not satisfactorily describe any given empirical case, yet they can be useful for organizing analysis of a set of empirical cases.

Nonetheless, points of disconnect between the models and the evidence should obviously be emphasized—not the least because these can provide new insights for theoretical development. As I have emphasized at various points, the case analysis of the previous two chapters, while confirming the importance of the political mechanisms I have emphasized, also suggests fruitful theoretical extensions. In this way (among others), the historical case-study analyses "talk back" to the theoretical models in various important ways. In this penultimate chapter, I develop several theoretical extensions suggested by the evidence presented in previous chapters.

In the first two sections, I begin by commenting briefly and informally on two important issues: the implications of the volatility of government revenues from natural resources for our argument, and the import for my thesis of the so-called Dutch Disease, that is, the often-noted tendency of resource booms to appreciate the real exchange rate and thereby cripple other non-resource tradeable sectors, such as agriculture. Both of these issues carry important implications for the thesis advanced in this book, and, although I have made reference to both topics at previous points in

[1] In conversation, Kathleen Thelen helpfully suggested the usefulness of this analogy to me.

the book, I have not engaged them systematically. I begin this chapter by discussing these two issues.

Then, I take up the topic of resource ownership, an issue upon which the evidence from several cases and particularly the historical evidence from Bolivia have focused our attention. In the basic framework of Chapter Three, resource rents are assumed to flow directly into the fiscal coffers of the state; this assumption was motivated by a long literature, reviewed in Chapters One and Two, that suggests that certain kinds of natural resources provide ready sources of government revenue, whether or not they are in fact owned by the government and whether or not the state is actually the entity extracting minerals from the ground. In this sense, as I discuss below, analyzing the form of ownership appears a second-order issue for understanding the effects of rents on the macro-outcomes of interest. Yet, in some cases, ownership forms certainly appear to matter for the political effects of rents. In the Bolivian case, for example, the fact that tin mines were controlled by a small private oligarchy in the pre-revolutionary period suggested quite different effects of rents on the political incentives of this elite from those suggested by my baseline model. While the first two sections of this chapter discuss revenue volatility and the Dutch Disease informally, in the third section I analyze the issue of resource ownership formally, extending the models of Chapter Three to analyze the impact of the form of ownership on political equilibria.[2]

7.1 *Revenue Volatility*

Revenue volatility is a key stylized fact of many rentier states. Because of the boom-and-bust cycles associated with many world commodity markets, the rent-producing sector can be a highly unreliable source of support for the government's fiscal coffers. The extent to which this is true, of course, varies from commodity to commodity and from historical period

[2] In Dunning (2006) I also developed a theoretical extension, inspired by the analysis of the Bolivian case, on the effects of resource rents on incentives for secession. The formal structure of the model developed in Chapter Three is useful for analyzing this question and suggests some perhaps surprising results: just as there may be competing effects of natural resource rents on the regime type, so there may be contrasting effects on incentives for territorial secession. Through some mechanisms, a resource boom can increase incentives for territorial secession in a resource-rich region; but through other mechanisms, the boom can also decrease these incentives. Though the formal model developed in Chapter Three is useful for analyzing this question, the topic itself is somewhat far from the main focus of this book and thus this theoretical extension was removed from this chapter.

to historical period. Some natural resources, such as Chilean nitrate, experience an initial boom, driven by a sharp increase in world demand, and thereafter provide a more-or-less constantly high level of revenues, until the appearance of substitutes (synthetics in the case of nitrate) or other factors obliterate altogether the ability of the resource sector to provide rents. (Peruvian guano in the nineteenth century provides another such case.) Markets for other natural resources, responding to longer-term cycles in the world economy as well as technological developments, may involve relatively long booms followed by sustained busts followed again by booms. For instance, though more stable in early decades of the twentieth century, petroleum markets have followed this pattern since the 1970s (Karl 1997).

How does this stylized fact relate to the theoretical framework developed in this book? In the formal models of Chapter Three, I proposed counterfactuals in which the level of resource rents R is more or less "permanently" altered; the comparative statics analysis then asks how the political equilibria vary as a function of changing levels of the resource rents. One justification for this approach is that a goal of the comparative statics analysis is to ask how being a relatively resource-rich country shapes the regime type, relative to the counterfactual of being resource-poor. Because this counterfactual may involve cross-sectional rather than intertemporal comparisons, and because even countries that experience volatility in revenues nonetheless remain "resource-rich" (witness Saudi Arabia in the second half of the twentieth century), the issue of within-country volatility of resource revenues is less important in this respect. Nonetheless, the model is also explicitly dynamic, in that the anticipation of future events shapes current political incentives; if actors anticipate that resource rents will be volatile, this clearly may affect these incentives. It might therefore seem that abstracting from the question of volatility imperils the validity of the theoretical approach.

Though an important concern, I argue that volatility is a second-order issue within the context of the framework developed here, which is why I treat it as a theoretical extension. In a specific way discussed later, however, volatility may well matter, especially empirically, and it is therefore important to discuss this issue.

On the one hand, even if revenues are volatile, we should still see the same kinds of tendencies as when revenue changes are relatively "permanent." It does not seem crucial to develop this claim formally; an intuitive argument should suffice. Following the model of coups in Chapter Three, let us imagine that in the wake of a resource boom, rich elites contemplate a coup against an existing democracy. Now, however, elites anticipate that with some probability resource rents will remain "high" in future periods, while with some probability resource rents will be "low" in future periods. The impact of a current boom on the political incentives of elites, however, will be qualitatively similar to the case where a resource boom is "permanent." Although they will take into account the probability that revenues will revert to a "low" state in future periods, the current boom will still have the dual effects of both increasing and reducing incentives to stage coups against democracy today. Thus, the predictions of the model developed here will carry through, even if the specific impact of a resource boom may depend on subjective evaluations of the probability of a future bust, as well, perhaps, as the degree of risk aversion and time preference of the actors involved. In this sense, although volatility is important, it may be a matter of "quantitative" size of the effects rather than the "qualitative" theoretical predictions.

Moreover, notwithstanding the empirical reality of revenue volatility, there may be compelling reasons to analyze the effects of resource booms "as if" these booms had an important degree of permanence. The apparent myopic behavior by government and private actors in the wake of resource booms, often noted by previous analysts (e.g., Karl 1997), might provide one such justification. If resource booms and busts are experienced as relatively permanent in the minds of the actors involved, and if we want to understand how resource rents shape the political incentives of those actors, then treating booms as more-or-less permanent seems like a useful approximation. While the models developed in Chapter Three do not countenance myopia or similar behavioral justifications, these considerations do provide another reason why abstracting from volatility may not undermine the central goals of our models: to analyze the qualitative impact of the presence or absence of resource rents on the political incentives of various actors.

On the other hand, understanding the "size" of effects as well as their direction is also important. For this reason, revenue volatility may well matter. For instance, anticipated revenue volatility may place limits on the ability of resource booms to enable "credible commitments" by a relatively poor democratic majority to restrict future redistribution away from the rich. Indeed, I briefly discussed just this issue in Chapter Five, in my discussion of contemporary Venezuela under Chávez. Thus, volatility may well limit the size of the "democratic" effect of rents, even as it decreases the opportunity cost of staying out of power, and thus also reduces the "authoritarian" effect of rents. (For instance, if rents are expected to decline with some probability in the future, then the threat of being cut out of the future distribution of rents may be less powerful in raising the incentives of elites to stage coups.) In sum, while volatility appears to be a somewhat second-order issue theoretically, in the context of the framework developed here, it may well be crucial for understanding empirically the degree to which resource booms or busts do in fact shape political incentives and thus the observed incidence of democracy and authoritarianism.

7.2 *The Dutch Disease*

Further considerations are raised by the often-remarked Dutch Disease, named in honor of the economic effects of a natural gas boom in Holland. By raising the real exchange rate (in a context in which resources are exported to be sold on world markets), resource booms make other exported products more expensive abroad and thus inhibit demand for those products. Through this mechanism, resource booms may inhibit other tradeable sectors such as agriculture or even industry; the specific sectors that are affected will of course depend on the structure of the economy in question. At the same time, resource booms can result in the growth of local non-tradeables such as many services (as well as inflationary pressures on these sectors) because of the cash that flows into the economy as a result of government spending.

The key concern for purposes of our argument is that according to this Dutch Disease mechanism, resource booms may endogenously structure the size of non-resource sectors of the economy (e.g., by inhibiting agriculture or industry). Yet, in our theoretical models, the size of resource rents is taken as independent of the size of the private, non-resource economy.[3] In the theoretical analysis, I ask questions about how the political effects of rents might vary as a function of (exogenously given) resource dependence, that is, as a function of the size of resource rents relative to the overall size of the economy.[4] Yet, I do not consider the possibility of feedback between resource rents and the absolute size of the non-resource economy.

Such feedback may well heighten the authoritarian effects of a resource boom, at least over the medium term. Imagine that a resource boom

[3] That is, in the models of Chapter Three, R is taken as independent of $\bar{y}$.
[4] That is, I investigate the import of the extent of resource dependence, or $\frac{R}{R+\bar{y}}$.

increases resource dependence through two channels, the direct positive effect of the boom itself on the size of rents and the indirect negative effect on the size of the private economy. Because I have argued that the authoritarian effects of resource booms may be particularly pronounced when resource dependence is high, the apparent tendency of resource booms to exaggerate resource dependence suggests another channel through which resource rents might promote authoritarianism. There might, however, be a countervailing effect: if resource booms lead to growth in sectors such as services that are comparatively difficult to tax, elites holding assets or income in these sectors might also not be as threatened by anticipated redistribution under democratic institutions. The importance of the specific character of the assets or income of elites recalls the argument of Boix (2003) about asset mobility and also suggests that the political effects of the Dutch Disease may well depend on the particular sectoral composition of the economy and the economic basis of elites.

On the other hand, the issue of feedback between the natural resource sector and the non-resource economy may also suggest effects that cut in other directions. For instance, suppose that under some conditions natural resources might themselves promote the development of non-resource sectors; the Indonesian case discussed in the concluding chapter provides one telling illustration of this dynamic. Then feedback between natural resources and other sectors could lead to a virtuous cycle as resource dependence is lessened and the democratic effects of resource wealth are enhanced.

These important considerations do not undercut the usefulness of the models developed in previous chapters but rather suggest additional directions for theoretical development. Indeed, the theoretical framework developed in this book helps to bring these issues into starker relief. For instance, a key contribution of the models developed here is to emphasize the importance of the relationship between the size of the resource sector and the size of the private sectors; the importance of the contrasting political effects of the distribution of resource rents and redistribution in the non-resource sectors of the economy brings to the fore the importance of resource dependence as a conditioning variable. Thus, by providing a vehicle through which issues such as resource dependence can be fruitfully analyzed, the models allow us a window onto an important channel through which the Dutch Disease may contribute to shaping political incentives and thereby the longer-term political effects of resource booms.

7.3 Resource Ownership

A third important theoretical extension relates to the issue of resource ownership. For reasons discussed at length in previous chapters and earlier in this chapter, I developed the theoretical framework assuming that resource rents accrue directly to the state. However, some of our empirical evidence, and particularly the case-study analysis of the political influence of tin barons in pre-revolutionary Bolivia, suggests the importance of considering this variable; I do so here. As we will see in this section, the form of resource ownership clearly does matter theoretically. I show this through a formal extension to the game-theoretic models developed previously.

Suppose that in the models of Chapter Three, resource rents do *not* flow into the fiscal coffers of the state like "manna from heaven"—that is, without requiring the state to appropriate resources from citizens. Instead, suppose that natural resource wealth is owned by the domestic elite. In this case, the country in question (as in the tin mining heyday of *la Rosca* in pre-revolutionary Bolivia) is not, in fact, a resource-rich rentier state, as that concept has been developed in this study. What are the political effects of resource rents, given the model of politics developed in Chapter Three?

To investigate this question formally, let us redefine elite income as follows:

$$\tilde{y}^r = y^r + R,$$

where, as before, y^r is the non-resource income (wealth) of elites and R is resource rent—which is now assumed to accrue directly to elites. As in Chapter Three, the income of the poor will be given by y^p, and a proportional income tax τ is levied in each period of the infinitely repeated game. Then government revenues are given by

$$\tau\left[\int_0^{\delta} \tilde{y}^r di + \int_{\delta}^{1} y^p di\right] = \tau\left[\delta\tilde{y}^r + (1-\delta)y^p\right] = \tau\tilde{y},$$

where $\tilde{y}$ is now total (and average) private income, which includes both resource and non-resource elements. (As before, denote $\bar{y}$ as total (and average) non-resource private income.) The government budget constraint is therefore

$$g = \tau\tilde{y}, \tag{7.1}$$

where I abstract from the non-linearity associated with the extraction of tax revenue (as in Chapter Three) because, in this economy, there is no resource rent flowing directly into the fiscal coffers of the state—and thus no need to model the difference between resource rent and rent that stems from taxation of private income.

With this reformulation, consider the ideal tax rates of rich and poor citizens. The optimization problem for the rich is to solve

$$\max_{\tau}(1-\tau)\tilde{y}^r + V(g) \tag{7.2}$$

subject to the government budget constraint in equation (7.1). The first-order condition for a maximum is

$$\frac{\tilde{y}^r}{\tilde{y}} = V'(\tau^r \tilde{y}). \tag{7.3}$$

Similarly, the optimization problem for the poor is

$$\max_{\tau}(1-\tau)y^p + V(g) \tag{7.4}$$

subject to equation (7.1). The first-order condition gives

$$\frac{y^p}{\tilde{y}} = V'(\tau^p \tilde{y}). \tag{7.5}$$

As in Chapter Three, because $\tilde{y}^r > y^p$, $\tau^r < \tau^p$.

Now consider the critical coup cost analyzed in Chapter Three. As we saw in equation (3.25), the exogenous coup cost φ^H at which the rich are indifferent between staging a coup and continuing to live under democracy (under the supposition that once society reverts to authoritarianism, it will remain authoritarian forever) is simply

$$\hat{\varphi}^{H*} = \eta[U^r(\tau^r(R), R) - U^r(\tau^p(R), R)],$$

where $\eta = \frac{\beta(1-p)}{(1-\beta(1-q))}$. This can also be expressed as

$$\hat{\varphi}^{H*} = \eta[(1-\tau^r)\tilde{y}^r + V(\tau^r\tilde{y}) - (1-\tau^p)\tilde{y}^r - V(\tau^p\tilde{y})]$$

or, substituting for $\tilde{y}^r$ and $\tilde{y}$,

$$\begin{aligned}\hat{\varphi}^{H*} = \eta[&(1-\tau^r)(y^r+R) + V(\tau^r(\bar{y}+R)) \\ &-(1-\tau^p)(y^r+R) - V(\tau^p(\bar{y}+R))].\end{aligned}$$

The key question is how an increase in resource rents affects this critical coup cost—that is, how do resource rents affect the incidence of coups against democracy? Taking derivatives with respect to R—and ignoring terms involving $\frac{\partial \tau^r}{\partial R}$ because $\frac{\partial U^r(\tau(R), R)}{\partial \tau^r} = 0$; recall that τ^r is the tax rate that maximizes $U^r(\tau(R), R)$—we have

$$\frac{\partial \hat{\varphi}^{H*}}{\partial R} = \eta[(\tau^p - \tau^r) + (V'(\tau^r \tilde{y})\tau^r - V'(\tau^p \tilde{y})\tau^p) + \frac{\partial \tau^p}{\partial R}(\tilde{y}^r - y^p)]. \quad (7.6)$$

Recall that the first-order condition for the preferred tax rate of the poor is

$$y^p = V'(\tau^p \tilde{y})\tilde{y}.$$

We can rearrange equation (7.5) and implicitly differentiate with respect to R to obtain an expression for $\frac{\partial \tau^p}{\partial R}$:

$$\frac{\partial \tau^p}{\partial R} = \frac{-V''(\tau^p \tilde{y})\tau^p \tilde{y} - V'(\tau^p \tilde{y})}{V''(\tau^p \tilde{y})\tilde{y}^2}.$$

Then, combining the last two terms on the right-hand side of equation (7.6) gives

$$\frac{\partial \hat{\varphi}^{H*}}{\partial R} = (V'(\tau^r \tilde{y})\tau^r - V'(\tau^p \tilde{y})\tau^p) + \frac{-V''(\tau^p \tilde{y})\tau^p \tilde{y} - V'(\tau^p \tilde{y})}{V''(\tau^p \tilde{y})\tilde{y}^2}(\tilde{y}^r - y^p)].$$

Rearranging, we can obtain

$$\frac{\partial \hat{\varphi}^{H*}}{\partial R} = \left. \frac{V''(\tau^p \tilde{y})\tilde{y}^2 V'(\tau^r \tilde{y})\tau^r - V''(\tau^p \tilde{y})[\tilde{y}^2 V'(\tau^p \tilde{y})\tau^p - \tau^p \tilde{y}(\tilde{y}^r - y^p)] - V'(\tau^p \tilde{y})(\tilde{y}^r - y^p)}{V''(\tau^p \tilde{y})\tilde{y}^2} \right]. \quad (7.7)$$

Because the denominator on the right-hand-side of equation (7.7) is negative, $\frac{\partial \hat{\varphi}^{H*}}{\partial R}$ is positive as long as the numerator is also negative. The first and the third terms in the numerator on the right-hand-side of the equation are clearly negative. Thus, the question is the sign of the term in brackets. As long as R is big enough, this expression is clearly negative, giving a sufficient condition for a positive sign of $\frac{\partial \hat{\varphi}^{H*}}{\partial R}$ to hold.[5] Even if this condition does not hold, under many parameter values the impact of R on the critical coup cost will be unambiguous:

$$\frac{\partial \hat{\varphi}^{H*}}{\partial R} > 0.$$

In this extension to the model, where resource rents are owned by the rich elite (rather than flowing into the coffers of the state as rent from, e.g., foreign-owned resource companies), the political effects of resource rents

[5] For example, such a sufficient condition is $y^p < \frac{1}{2}(y^r + R)]$.

can be quite different: namely, an increase in resource rents will unambiguously *increase* the incidence of coups against democracy. Because, as in Chapter Three, the expression for the critical repression cost is identical in key respects to the critical coup cost, resources will also increase the persistence of authoritarian forms of rule. This finding differs from recent work that suggests natural resources may promote democracy when they are privately owned (Jones Luong and Weinthal 2006; see also Jones Luong 2004 and Jones Luong and Weinthal 2001b). As discussed in Chapter Three, the result also underscores a key difference between the modeling approach in this study—where resource rents create the fiscal basis of a rentier state—and the approach in, for instance, Boix (2003), where immobile assets like oil are assumed to be owned by the elite. In the theoretical extension developed earlier, as in Boix's (2003) work, resource rents have an authoritarian effect. This extension may therefore help to illuminate the influence of tin mining on Bolivian politics during the rule of the tin oligarchy known as *la Rosca*.

8

Conclusion: Whither the Resource Curse?

Oil and other natural resources, many political scientists have argued, promote autocracy. In support of this claim, analysts have presented an impressive range of evidence, from case studies of resource-rich countries in the Persian Gulf and Africa to regression analyses of global time-series cross-section data. However, this valuable research has not elucidated a range of apparent anomalies to the authoritarian "resource curse." Botswana, Norway, and other resource-rich (though not necessarily resource-dependent) democracies such as Australia, Canada, the United Kingdom, or the United States appear to pose not just anomalies to the idea of an unconditional authoritarian resource curse, but also a fundamental challenge to the idea that resources must promote autocracy. Nor has the claim that resources promote autocracy been reconciled with the claim of many country experts that resource rents have promoted democracy in Venezuela. As I have shown in this study, the range of cases in which resources have very plausibly had a democratic effect is much broader than suggested by previous comparative studies: Bolivia, Chile, and Ecuador, for instance, may be added to the list.

I have argued here that the list of countries that have escaped the authoritarian resource curse is not merely idiosyncratic. Variation in the political effects of resource rents instead reflects structural factors that are systematic and, at least in part, explicable on the basis of theory. Contra Friedman's (2006) "law of petropolitics," according to which "the price of oil and the pace of freedom always move in opposite directions," there is a quite general mechanism through which resource rents may promote the emergence and persistence of *democracy*. Moreover, I have proposed and tested hypotheses about the conditions under which resource rents may promote democracy rather than authoritarianism and thus taken a step toward what should be an important goal for the literature on the political effects of resource wealth: how can we explain variation in political outcomes across resource-rich countries?

To be sure, this study will be far from the last word on the important question of how to explain political variation across resource-rich countries. One of its main contributions is simply to focus the attention of scholars on an under-studied mechanism through which rents may promote democracy, and also to show that there is substantially more variation to be explained than previous analyses have suggested. Yet, this study has also used a variety of theoretical approaches and a variety of kinds of empirical evidence to probe the validity of the main hypotheses advanced here. The formal model shows that there can be dual authoritarian and democratic effects of resource rents; moreover, analyzing these effects within a single model provides an opportunity to derive hypotheses about the conditions under which one or the other effect may be more important. The predictions of the formal model are in turn put to the test of both quantitative cross-section time-series data from a global set of countries and to the more fine-grained detail provided by the extensive case study of Venezuela and the somewhat briefer analyses of Chile, Bolivia, Ecuador, and Botswana. The case-study analyses both provide support for the democratic effect of resource rents and also suggest new directions for theoretical development.

8.1 *Crude Democracies and Crude Autocracies*

Nonetheless, there are many important resource-rich cases I have not examined in detail in previous chapters of this book. I have offered several justifications for this omission. For one, as noted in the discussion of case selection in Chapter Five, a large body of previous literature has extensively analyzed authoritarian resource-rich cases and explicitly explored the mechanisms through which resource wealth (or, more appropriately, resource dependence) may promote authoritarianism. More value therefore seems to be added by focusing my analysis on the relatively underexplored, relatively democratic cases. For another, and more importantly, I have focused on cases for which values of my key independent variables would predict a relatively democratic effect of resource rents. A major benefit of this strategy is that it helps us assess the extent to which case-study evidence supports the importance of the *mechanisms* through which I have argued that resource rents may have a democratic effect.

However, having explored several relatively democratic resource-rich cases in some detail in this book, it will be useful to compare several of these cases more explicitly to authoritarian resource-rich cases. Although it is obviously not possible to survey all cases of interest in this concluding chapter, for reasons both of lack of space and limited knowledge, I nonetheless attempt to pick several different types of cases for analysis here. I begin briefly with a set of cases in which my theory clearly predicts a robustly authoritarian effect of rents—and which, in fact, are robustly authoritarian. These cases include such diverse countries as Equatorial Guinea, São Tomé and Príncipe, and many of the Gulf monarchies. I then move to analysis of a more nuanced set of cases in which it may not be immediately obvious what predictions my theory yields: in particular, contemporary Iraq and Indonesia under Suharto. I nonetheless argue that the theory does help to illuminate outcomes in these cases. Finally, I turn to a set of cases that instead seem to pose important challenges to, or provide useful extensions of, the theory: these include post-Soviet Russia and Indonesia during and after Suharto. The course of future events in these countries, beyond the time period that history allows me to cover here, may help readers evaluate the predictive power of the model developed here.

Several questions will guide my inquiry in this section. First, beyond the broad statistical analysis of Chapter Four, can the theory developed here help to explain and predict variation at a more fine-grained level of detail? That is, can it help explain why the authoritarian resource-rich countries are authoritarian rather than democratic? Second, what predictions would the theory develop here for the course of politics in several resource-rich countries I have not considered? In this section, I attempt answers to such questions by turning to additional cases. Although I did not conduct original fieldwork in the cases I discuss in this section, and although my review of the secondary literature is necessarily somewhat cursory, I use the work of other scholars to compare the predictions of the theory developed in this book against the empirical reality other researchers have described.

I begin with a set of cases in which my theory rather unequivocally predicts an authoritarian effect of rents. Equatorial Guinea, in the wake of its massive oil boom in the late 1990s, would seem to be the poster child. A country of around 500,000 people, Equatorial Guinea has become Africa's third-biggest oil producer in absolute terms since large deposits of off-shore oil were discovered in the mid-1990s. The oil sector in Equatorial Guinea today comprises more than 90 percent of GDP (International Monetary Fund 2005; McSherry 2006); due solely to the influence of these discoveries, and given its small population size, Equatorial Guinea has become the country with the second-highest per capita income in the *world*. Measured private inequality prior to the boom was also very low: the non-resource industrial capital share was 39.5, according to UNIDO data, well below the regional average for sub-Saharan Africa (see Table 4.1 in Chapter Four).

The key point for our purposes is that oil in Equatorial Guinea today must clearly constitute the only economic "game in town." Conflict over the distribution of oil rents, and perforce the authoritarian effects of an oil boom, is likely to overwhelm the oil boom's potentially democratizing effects. Indeed, in the wake of the discovery of oil, the country was the site of a well-publicized coup attempt: in March 2004, a plane with 64 mercenaries alleged to be en route to stage a coup in Equatorial Guinea was detained in Zimbabwe, while coup plotters inside Equatorial Guinea were arrested as well.[1] To be sure, authoritarianism seems over-determined in post-independence Equatorial Guinea, where President Teodoro Obiang has ruled since he himself seized power from his uncle in a coup in 1979; the attempted coup in Equatorial Guinea obviously does not provide an example of a coup against democracy. The point here, however, is simply about the role that oil rents very plausibly played, in a country in which the distribution of rents is now overwhelmingly the key economic issue, in inciting the coup plotters. In this highly resource-dependent country, the theory predicts that conflict over the distribution of rents would be the main result of the resource boom.

On this logic, we would also expect a relatively authoritarian effect of rents in São Tomé and Príncipe, a small island state and former Portuguese colony off the coast of West Africa. Though one-party rule followed independence from Portugal in 1975, representative multi-party elections were held in 1991, and democracy has survived (uneasily) as of the time of this writing. This may well change in the wake of recent expectations of an imminent and substantial oil boom, however. Though no commercially viable discoveries have yet been announced, expectations based on the review of geological data in the past 5 years put recoverable reserves at up to 15 billion barrels of oil. After resolving a territorial dispute with Nigeria over ownership of off-shore oil (the countries agreed to a 60–40 split in favor of Nigeria), São Tomé and Príncipe sold its first exploration leases in 2004. Humphreys et al. (2006: 590–1) suggest that under one

[1] International forces also seemed to play a role in the coup; an executive of the security firm Executive Outcomes was alleged to be involved in the failed coup attempt, and Sir Mark Thatcher (son of the former UK prime minister) was arrested in South Africa and pleaded guilty to "negligence" in financing the aircraft detained in Zimbabwe.

scenario (crude oil prices at $50 a barrel and a 50 percent effective tax rate) annual per capita rents could reach nearly $1 million dollars, though the actual size of realized rents will likely be smaller. In a country in which per capita GDP in 2003 was around $1,200 and the population numbers less than 200,000, the size of prospective rents implies a level of resource dependence exceeding even Equatorial Guinea's. The prospect of these enormous oil rents flowing into the economy appears to have influenced domestic politics already. As Humphreys et al. (2006: 590–1) put it,

> In what seemed like a textbook example of the logic of resource curse, disclosure of the possible oil discoveries was soon followed by an attempted coup d'état. On July 16, 2003, while President Menezes was in Nigeria, a small group of former mercenaries, allied with the armed forces, arrested the prime minister and members of the cabinet. Although likely motivated largely by personal interests, the coup makers voiced grievances that centered on fears over impending mismanagement of the oil sector and the future oil economy.

Indeed, it is plausible that concerns over the capacity of the government to commit to distribution of future oil rents could have increased incentives for a coup, much as the theory developed here would predict—that is, in a highly resource-dependent country with little in the way of a non-resource economy (relative to the expected size of oil rents). Although democracy has thus far survived, the theory developed here (like other theories of the authoritarian resource curse) would suggest that the prospects of its continuation are poor. As oil rents come onstream in the future, of course, future work will be able to test this claim.

Other highly resource-dependent cases in which resources appear to have an authoritarian effect are not difficult to find; as many scholars have emphasized, many of the Gulf monarchies seem to fit this pattern. To be sure, my framework does not elucidate all the mechanisms through which resource rents might promote democracy, as I discussed in previous chapters. My theory is mostly about elite incentives to resist or accept democratization, while other theories have focused on capabilities as well: resources may be used to fuel the repressive capacity of the state, for instance.[2] However, the rich set of case studies on the authoritarian effects of resource wealth in the Middle East have tended to focus, in one

[2] Note, however, that the line between incentives and capacities may be blurred. Some analysts emphasize that resources may promote the *capacity* of autocrats to remain in power by allowing them to "buy out" the political opposition. In fact, however, this can also be seen as an argument about the impact of resources on the *incentives* of the political opposition.

way or another, on the influence of what I call the *distribution* of resource rents.[3]

Interestingly, however, among the Gulf states, Iraq may seem to fit less easily the profile of a state in which the authoritarian effect of rents would be comparatively strong—in part because it is historically less resource-dependent than several of the other resource-rich Gulf states, and in part because of the historical strength of elites in non-resource economic sectors (see Batatu 1978). It may be worthwhile to develop a more detailed analysis of the Iraqi case, particularly because, at the time of writing, perhaps no resource-rich country commands the world's attention as much as contemporary Iraq. I therefore turn to this case for the next several paragraphs.

As I noted in the opening chapter, while some analysts thought that Iraq's oil wealth might finance the construction of democracy after the U.S.-led invasion, others pointed out that the lessons of the authoritarian "resource curse" did not augur well for democracy's prospects in Iraq (see Wibbels 2004). At the time of this writing, history seems to have borne out these concerns. Far from funding a stable democracy, issues concerning the distribution of oil revenues instead have fueled interregional and interethnic conflict. As one reporter for the *New York Times* in Iraq put it, "The minority Sunni Arabs, who ruled Iraq for decades before the toppling of Saddam Hussein and are now leading the insurgency, have chafed at rule by the Shiites and Kurds partly because they fear that those two groups might hoard oil wealth for themselves" (Wong 2007). It is perhaps notable in this vein that leaders of the Iraqi cabinet reached agreement on a draft law regarding the regional distribution of oil revenues at the end of February 2007, only *after* an announcement that estimates of oil deposits in Sunni-controlled territory had been substantially revised upwards (Glanz 2007; Wong 2007).[4] As the same reporter notes, "The attitudes of Sunni Arabs

[3] See, e.g., Mahdavy (1970), Beblawi (1987), Skocpol (1982), and Shambayati (1994) on Iran; Batatu (1978) and Chaudhry (1994) on Iraq; Crystal (1990) on Kuwait; and Entelis (1976), Quandt (1981), or Chaudhry (1997) on Saudi Arabia.

[4] It was reported in the *New York Times* on February 19, 2007, that the Iraqi government had hired foreign consultants to reevaluate seismic data from areas to the north and east of Baghdad, which had not previously been analyzed with state-of-the-art technology. The re-examination resulted in a near-doubling of the estimate of recoverable reserves from fields in Anbar province, to nearly 15 billion barrels, and suggested that the fields might contain up to a trillion cubic feet of natural gas. Production from one of the fields (the Akkas field) could reach the energy equivalent of 100,000 barrels of oil a day (Glanz 2007). The draft law approved on February 26, 2007, which affords regions substantial control over signing contracts with foreign companies for exploration and development, would certainly be more advantageous to the Sunni regions should their territory prove richer in oil.

[towards the draft oil law] could . . . soften if more oil exploration is done on their land. Iraqi officials recently increased their estimates of the amount of oil and natural gas deposits in Sunni Arab territory" (Wong 2007).

Yet, even if approved by the Parliament in 2008, this draft law may prove a tenuous solution. In theory, it provides for an equitable distribution of rents, which will be collected by the central government and distributed to regional or provincial governments according to population. In practice, a central government controlled by Shiites or a Shiite–Kurdish coalition may have a difficult time credibly committing to uphold this practice over time; if the threat posed by the Sunni insurgency were to recede, there might be little to prevent the majority government from reneging on this agreement. How does this empirical reality in contemporary Iraq relate to the theory developed here?

Imagine the following counterfactual scenario. Suppose that after the fall of Saddam Hussein, an economically dominant and disproportionately wealthy Sunni minority had faced significant concerns about redistribution of its private assets. In part because of demographics, Iraqi democracy in the wake of the U.S.-led invasion threatened to be dominated at least to some extent by the Shiite majority or by a coalition of Shiites and Kurds. This relatively poor Shiite or Shiite–Kurdish majority might well have targeted Sunni wealth, redistributing private assets away from the Sunni minority. Under such conditions, the potential for redistribution could easily have been a salient concern for the Sunni elite. If this concern had been important enough, the theory developed in this study would have predicted a relatively democratic net effect of resources: that is, a resource-rich Iraq could have had a better chance for democracy than an Iraq in which the oil dried up, because resources could have helped to mitigate Sunni concerns about such redistribution of private wealth.

Yet, this scenario is, indeed, a counterfactual. Though there certainly were economic disparities between the Sunni minority and the Shiite–Kurdish majority at the time of the U.S.-led invasion, it is far from clear that they were important enough for redistribution of private assets to top a list of Sunni priorities or concerns. The invasion itself and the looting that followed destroyed many sources of private wealth in the country and particularly in Baghdad, making it less likely that democratic redistribution of Sunni-controlled assets would be politically salient in the wake of the invasion. Even notwithstanding the destruction of assets during the invasion, Iraq was already not just a resource-rich but also a highly resource-dependent country. The fact that Iraq is resource-dependent implies that the threat that the Shiites and Kurds might "hoard oil wealth for themselves" is relatively more salient than oil's impact on the mitigation of redistribution of private wealth. We should therefore not be surprised that oil does not appear to have promoted but rather has quite plausibly hindered the prospects for democracy in contemporary Iraq.

It may also be instructive to review briefly some historical evidence on oil and regime change in Iraq. Prior to 1958, the Iraqi monarchy that the British had returned to power in 1941 was closely associated with the landed elite, "in an alliance that did much to make the regime unpopular among educated urbanites and in the army" (Herb 1999: 214). This was also a period in which oil revenues provided a negligible source of government revenues; only by the 1950s had revenues come to constitute an important revenue source, rising sharply from just a few thousand Iraqi dinars in 1950 to more than 70,000 dinars just 5 years later (Herb 1999: 215, chart 8.1; based on Batatu 1978). In 1958, the Iraqi army overthrew the royal family to widespread acclaim in Baghdad. As Herb (1999: 215–16) notes, "Oil revenues . . . could have solved the problem of the regime's alliance with the landlord class . . . [an] alliance that made it difficult for the monarchy to try to adjust its policies in a direction more congenial to its nationalist opponents." However, other factors mitigated against a possible tendency for oil rents to ease the threat of redistribution or to counterbalance an arrangement of political forces that, following Barrington Moore (1966), "was barren ground for the growth of liberal politics" (Herb 1999: 214). For instance, "the close link between the monarchical leaders . . . and the British made [a strategy of liberalization] enormously difficult. . . . It would have been difficult indeed for [the monarchs] to have radically reoriented the regime away from its former allies, the British and the landed class, and toward urban nationalists" (Herb 1999: 216; see also Chaudhry 1994). It may therefore be these other factors that help explain why the growth of oil rents in the 1950s did not help encourage liberalization on the part of the political and economic elite.[5]

[5] The ascendency of the Baath party during the 1960s and the eventual consolidation of Saddam Hussein's power came in the context of an oil boom in which oil increasingly became the major economic "game in town." Saddam Hussein's tenure in power also coincided with an important economic liberalization in the 1980s (in the wake of the decline in oil revenues) that diminished the importance of the state in the economy and perhaps perforce increased the importance of the private elite. As Chaudhry (1994: 8) notes, "On the eve of the reforms [in 1987], the government directly owned approximately 50 percent of all agricultural lands; by January 1989, 88 percent of land was privately owned, 11 percent was rented from the state by private companies, and only 1 percent was state managed." On the other hand,

The claim being made here is not that this book's theoretical framework predicts all the effects of oil wealth on regime outcomes in Iraq. The point is that the theory, which argues that oil may bolster democracy and authoritarianism through different mechanisms, helps us to evaluate evidence from Iraq in a new and illuminating light. The authoritarian effect of oil, driven by conflict over the distribution of rents, has played an important role; yet relative to several other oil-dependent states in the region, the democratic effects of rents working through the mechanisms emphasized in this book also appear stronger.

In contrast, there are a number of cases that provide a greater challenge for the theory, and it is crucial to pay special attention to these cases. Post-Soviet Russia may provide one such case. The demise of the Soviet Union and the rapid liberalization and privatization that followed were accompanied by a dramatic increase in private inequality; the emergence of the so-called oligarchs, who benefited from the privatizations of state-owned firms, was perhaps the most widely noted aspect of this increasing inequality (Hoffman 2003). Many of these oligarchs enriched themselves in part through their connections to the democratically elected Yeltsin government. Standard theories, however, from Tocqueville (1835) to Acemoglu and Robinson (2006a), would suggest that this sharply increased economic inequality would pose significant threats to the stability of the incipient Russian democracy after the collapse of the Soviet Union. Yet, under circumstances of high private inequality, and lower economic dependence on natural resource wealth than in the countries of, say, the Persian Gulf, the theory developed in this study would predict that oil rents would have a relatively democratic effect.[6] Did they?

Many country experts have argued otherwise. Fish (2005: 114–38), for example, has recently argued compellingly that natural resource wealth has contributed to undermining democracy in contemporary Russia, though he argues that only some of the mechanisms suggested by standard accounts of the authoritarian "resource curse" are important. While other analysts have noted a more mixed relationship between natural resources and the political regime in post-Soviet Russia (see Rutland 2006), the predominant account

"dramatic as they appear, the reforms did not signal a fundamental change in the absolute balance between public and private shares in industry" (Chaudhry 1994: 9).

6 Although oil exports have constituted a preponderant share of *exports* at various points in post-Soviet Russia, they nonetheless have comprised a smaller share of GDP than in, e.g., the Gulf states.

among country experts is that oil rents have hindered the strengthening of democracy in Russia.

From the perspective of the theory developed here, however, there may be a number of salient points to make. The first is that in the context of the privatizations that followed the demise of the Soviet Union, resources were sold off to the members of the emerging "oligarchy"—and thus constituted assets of the rich. As such, the relevant analytic framework might be found in the theoretical extension of Chapter Seven, or in Boix's (2003) emphasis on how ownership of immobile assets (like oil) might make democracy less palatable to a private elite. Especially in the context of Russia's ever-widening income inequality gap in the 1990s, democracy could clearly threaten the interests of this nouveau elite; however, rather than mitigate the threat that democracy might pose to elite interests, a boom in the value of elite-owned resources could instead exacerbate it. It may be useful to recall that although private owners of resource wealth in post-Soviet Russia, such as Mikhael Khodorkovsky, have come to be seen in some circles as heros of liberal democracy—and opponents of Putin's apparent centralization of political power—they certainly did not begin post-Soviet life this way. In the 1990s, the beneficiaries of privatizations, the so-called oligarchs, were instead seen by many analysts as among the biggest threats to the consolidation of democracy in Russia.

Indeed, in the wake of privatizations of Russia's natural resource wealth, the country did not closely approximate the conditions of a rentier state. Yet, given the typical attractiveness of the oil and gas sector as a target for taxation, it was perhaps only a matter of time before Russia, like many countries before it, moved closer to this model. In the conflict between Putin and hydrocarbon oligarchs like Khodorkovsky, there were perhaps heightened political incentives to do so as well. Perhaps only in the wake of Putin's crackdown on Khodorkovsky, and the expropriation of many the assets of his firm (Yukos), did post-Soviet Russia become a rentier state.

This move against Khodorkovsky and the centralization of oil and gas revenues are generally interpreted by Russia experts as exhibit A in the creeping authoritarianism of the political regime. The framework developed here, however, would suggest that over the longer term the effects could be more mixed. It would predict that in a highly unequal country like Russia, appropriation of resource rents by the state could indeed blunt the detrimental impact of inequality on the long-run prospects for democracy.[7] This is, of course, a *ceteris paribus* claim. Yet, it provides a counter-intuitive claim against which future readers may evaluate the predictive power of the theoretical model proposed in this book.

A final case that may be useful to consider is Suharto's (as well as post-Suharto) Indonesia.[8] In some ways, Indonesia during the Suharto period might seem to exemplify the logic of the resource curse. In other ways, however, the case is anomalous from that perspective. For one, economic performance was much better over both boom and bust periods, relative to comparable resource-rich countries (see, e.g., Karl 1997): GDP per capita not only did not decline in the two decades following the oil boom of the 1997, as it did in many oil exporters outside the Middle East, but it instead grew at an annual rate of 5 percent from 1966 to 1997 (World Bank 2000).

Indonesia was anomalous in another way as well: though highly resource-dependent at the start of the Suharto regime, the economy diversified substantially during Suharto's tenure. When Suharto came to power, oil constituted the bulk of economic production and exports, along with a few agricultural products (rice, coffee, sugar, and palm oil). Yet, the structural composition of the economy subsequently underwent important changes. Manufactures, which were less than 10 percent of GDP in 1966, grew to 25 percent by 1996, while oil and liquified natural gas fell from more than 80 percent of exports as late as 1981 to less than 26 percent in 1989 (World Bank 1989, 2000). Some of this was obviously the result of the oil price bust, but the diversification went far beyond these effects: Suharto himself made major efforts to encourage the development of the private sector, developing symbiotic relations with networks of Chinese entrepreneurs (Dunning 2005: 468–9; Mackie and MacIntyre 1994; Robison 1986: 41–5; Rock 1999). The general picture is one of strong resource dependence when Suharto came to power in 1965–1967 and much lower resource dependence when he finally fell, in 1998.

Elsewhere I have analyzed the political economy factors that may have helped to engender a shift away from resource dependence in Indonesia (Dunning 2005: 468–71). The main point for my present purposes is to emphasize the extent to which over-time changes in the level of resource dependence might help explain changes to the political regime—and,

[7] This effect could be heightened by the fact that Russia is not extremely resource-dependent, at least on some metrics; while resources constitute a predominant share of exports, they do not comprise an overwhelming share of GDP.

[8] Some of the material in this section draws on Dunning (2005: 468–71).

indeed, the impact of oil rents on that regime. The middle-class business community, and even the influential business association, the Indonesian Chamber of Commerce and Industry (KADIN), played an important role over time in pressing for political change. Initially seen as a moribund association of native Indonesian (*pribumi*) businessmen who exercised neither economic nor political power, this association began to be used by economically powerful Chinese (*cucong*) industrialists to make independent claims on the state (MacIntyre 1990). Independent business interests also began to play an independent role through their support for the Indonesian Democratic Party (PDI) of Megawati Sukarnoputri (Eklof 2003).

What is perhaps striking from the point of view of the theory elaborated in this book is that the minority business class, economically empowered and politically protected (but also politically impotent) during the Suharto period, did not apparently anticipate undue threats from democracy. Perhaps some members of this community might have done well to do so, given the wave of, for example, anti-Chinese violence that coincided with democratization in Indonesia (see, e.g., Chua 2003). Yet, from the perspective of the theory developed here, the important role of elements of the elite private-sector business class in acquiescing to and even promoting democratization may be revealing. The move from a resource-dependent to a merely resource-abundant Indonesia thus witnessed political changes that appear to be broadly consistent with the theory developed in this book.

Clearly, in this brief concluding chapter, it is not possible to engage in a full analysis of many relevant cases, including both rentier autocracies and other rentier democracies (or near democracies) not discussed in this book. Yet, the cases discussed above, and the backdrop of the large previous literature on the authoritarian effect of natural resource rents, provide a useful comparative investigation of the mechanisms I have emphasized here. The review suggests, on the one hand, that reality is more complex than theory; but it also suggests that the parsimonious framework advanced in this book does have an important degree of predictive power. The evidence explored in this book suggests not only that there are democratic as well as authoritarian effects of rents but also that it is possible to explain variation in political outcomes across resource-rich states.

8.2 Resources and Democracy: A Normative Coda

This study has rather self-consciously stayed away from explicitly normative issues, focusing instead on the positive question of how resource rents may shape the emergence and persistence of Schumpeterian democracy. Yet, for a book that engages the literature on the authoritarian "resource curse"—a term with apparent normative connotations—it may be worth reflecting on some of the normative implications of the approach to resource rents and democracy developed in this study.

I have argued here that resource rents may promote democracy as well as authoritarianism. Yet, if resource rents might therefore seem not an unmitigated normative bad, neither is democracy necessarily an unqualified normative good. The approach to democracy in this study is not only Schumpetarian; it also privileges the role of economic class and particularly redistributive conflict between elites and masses. Like other recent approaches to the political economy of political regimes (e.g., Acemoglu and Robinson 2006a; Boix 2003; Rueschemeyer et al. 1992), my approach therefore emphasizes that democracy may persist when it is not "too" threatening to elites, either because inequality is not too great or, more particular to my argument, because resource rents help to mitigate the redistributive cost to elites.

Clearly, however, the ability of a regime that meets the procedural minimal requirements for democracy to persist, only because rents provide a form of public spending that does not threaten the economic interests of elites, may leave something normative to be desired, at least from the perspective of more "substantive" or "outcome-oriented" definitions of democracy. Rents may then be desirable because they can help democracy persist—but the political democracy they allow to persist also hardly represents the full economic or social democracy that some substantive political theorists may have in mind. I have not directly engaged the literature on the "quality" of democracy here, but this would seem an important issue to address briefly in closing.

Indeed, many of the resource-rich democracies I have studied in this book are democracies that may leave much to be desired, particularly from the point of view of liberal theories of democracy: contemporary Venezuela, Ecuador, Bolivia, Botswana, even Chile. This point merely underscores my basic argument: in the kinds of high-inequality settings I have studied in this book, the limited role for checks and balances and for protections of minority (elite) rights might ordinarily make democracy of this kind highly threatening to elites. That Schumpetarian democracy nonetheless persists, in one form or another, is remarkable from a positive point of view; but it is not necessarily to be recommended from a normative point of view. These are perhaps "crude" democracies in the multiple senses of that phrase.

This study is therefore not a normative corrective to past views about the corrosive influences of rentierism. It is instead a positive argument that seeks to further our understanding of a particular set of political consequences that may follow from the mode of public finance that lies at the basis of rentier states. I have attempted to explain and generalize the apparently anomalous democratic effect of rents in a few previously discussed cases and have developed a general theory that helps to explain variation in outcomes across resource-rich states. In doing so, I have not contradicted the assertion that resources may support authoritarian regimes, yet I have attempted to refine such arguments by pointing out the ways in which resource wealth may also bolster democracy. Oil and other forms of mineral wealth can promote both authoritarianism and democracy, I argue, but they do so through different mechanisms; an understanding of these different mechanisms can help us understand when either the authoritarian or democratic effects of resource wealth will be relatively strong. This is surely far from the last word on this question. Yet, in building a theory that seeks to explain political variation across resource-rich states, and that elucidates the democratic as well as the authoritarian effects of natural resources, this book suggests new avenues for exploring the construction not just of crude autocracies but also of crude democracies.

Appendix: Construction of the Simulations

The goal of this appendix is to sketch the procedures used to obtain the simulation results presented in Chapter Three.[1] I will illustrate these procedures using a simulation of the impact of resource rents on the critical coup cost depicted in Figure 3.1 in Chapter Three.

The idea of the simulation is to see how the impact of resource rents on the critical coup cost varies with the exogenous parameters of the model, for instance, inequality. In Chapter Three, the impact of rents on the critical coup cost is given by

$$\frac{\partial \hat{\varphi}^{H*}}{\partial R} = \eta \left[V'(H(\tau^r \bar{y}) + R) + \frac{\partial \tau^p}{\partial R} y^r \right], \tag{A.1}$$

where $\eta = \frac{\beta(1-p)}{(1-\beta(1-q))}$. (Because η is a constant that does not depend on R or inequality, it is ignored in conducting the simulation.)

To conduct the simulation, we must choose parameter values for R, $\bar{y}$, and δ (the size of resource rents, the size of average and total income, and the size of the rich group, respectively) and functional forms for $V(\cdot)$ and $H(\cdot)$ that are consistent with the assumptions of the model. For instance, in the simulation depicted in Figure 3.1 in Chapter Three, I chose $R = 1.25$, $\bar{y} = 3.75$, and $\delta = 0.1$. Because $\frac{R}{R+\bar{y}} = \frac{1.25}{1.25+3.75} = 0.25$, these assumptions imply that resource rents are 25 percent of "GDP" (i.e., the sum of resource rents and non-resource income). Also, because $\delta \in (0, \frac{1}{2})$ is the size of the rich group in a population of mass one, $\delta = 0.1$ implies that the rich comprise 10 percent of the population. Finally, we must assign functional forms to $V(\cdot)$ and $H(\cdot)$ so that both functions are concave and have positive third

[1] All simulations were done using Mathematica software, version 5.2 (student version). The code used to construct the simulations will be posted at the author's Web site at a later date.

derivatives on $\mathbb{R}_{++}$. In the simulation depicted in Figure 3.1 in Chapter Three, these functional form assumptions are $V(x) = U(x) = x^{\frac{1}{2}}$.

Given these parameter values and functional form assumptions, the algorithm for computing $\frac{\partial \hat{\varphi}^{H*}}{\partial R}$ as a function of inequality is as follows:

(1) Choose a level of inequality; that is, $\theta \in (\delta, 1]$.
(2) Calculate τ^r.
(3) Calculate τ^p and $\frac{\partial \tau^p}{\partial R}$.
(4) Use the results in **(2)** and **(3)** to calculate $\frac{\partial \varphi^{H*}}{\partial R}$ in equation (A.1).
(5) Repeat.

I will now illustrate this approach assuming $\delta = \theta = 0.1$ in step **(1)**, so that there is perfect equality of non-resource income between the rich and the poor. To calculate τ^r in step **(2)**, we use the first-order condition for utility maximization of the rich, which is

$$-y^r + V'(H(\tau^r \bar{y}) + R)H'(\tau^r \bar{y})\bar{y} = 0. \tag{A.2}$$

Because $y^r = \frac{\theta}{\delta}\bar{y} = 3.75$ (where the final equality comes from the assumption of $\delta = \theta$ in this example), we can substitute the assumed functional forms and parameter values into equation (A.2) to obtain

$$-3.75 + \frac{1}{2\sqrt{(\tau^r \cdot 3.75)^{\frac{1}{2}} + 1.25}}\left(\frac{1}{2\sqrt{\tau^r \cdot 3.75}}\right)(3.75) = 0, \tag{A.3}$$

which allows me to pin down $\tau^r \cong 0.011$. (The solution is approximate only due to rounding error.)

For step **(3)**, we need first to pin down τ^p by using the first-order condition for utility maximization of the poor and plugging in the appropriate parameter values and functional form assumptions, just as we did in step **(2)** to calculate τ^r. Using the first-order condition for utility maximization of the poor, we have

$$-y^p + V'(H(\tau^p \bar{y}) + R)H'(\tau^p \bar{y})\bar{y} = 0, \tag{A.4}$$

which gives

$$-3.75 + \frac{1}{2\sqrt{(\tau^p \cdot 3.75)^{\frac{1}{2}} + 1.25}}\left(\frac{1}{2\sqrt{\tau^p \cdot 3.75}}\right)(3.75) = 0. \tag{A.5}$$

Here, the incomes of the "rich" and the "poor" are identical because there is perfect equality of non-resource income. Thus, equation (A.5) is identical to equation (A.3) and therefore $\tau^p = \tau^r \cong 0.011$. In general, of course, this will not be the case, because in general, $y^r \neq y^p$. Now, having obtained a solution for τ^p, I use the expression for $\frac{\partial \tau^p}{\partial R}$ that is given in Chapter Three; that is

$$\frac{\partial \tau^p}{\partial R} = \frac{-V''(H(\tau^p \bar{y}) + R)H'(\tau^p \bar{y})\bar{y}}{[V''(H(\tau^p \bar{y}) + R)(H'(\tau^p \bar{y})\bar{y})^2 + V'(H(\tau^p \bar{y}) + R)H''(\tau^p \bar{y})(\bar{y})^2]}.$$

Plugging in the parameter values and functional form assumptions gives an approximate solution for $\frac{\partial \tau^p}{\partial R}$, which in this case is $\frac{\partial \tau^p}{\partial R} \cong -0.007$. (Note that we can verify here the negative sign on $\frac{\partial \tau^p}{\partial R}$.)

For step **(4)**, simply plug $\tau^r \cong 0.011$ and $\frac{\partial \tau^p}{\partial R} \cong -0.007$ into equation (A.1) and use the functional form assumptions on $V(\cdot)$ and $H(\cdot)$ as well as $\bar{y} = 3.75$, $R = 1.25$, and $y^r = 3.75$ to obtain $\frac{\partial \hat{\varphi}^{H*}}{\partial R} \cong 0.387$. Thus, with perfect equality of non-resource income, resource rents drive up the critical coup cost and thereby increase the incidence of coups against democracy in the model.

At step **(5)**, we simply iterate the algorithm, choosing different values of θ. In the simulation depicted in Figure 3.1 in Chapter Three, for example, I chose the following values $\theta = \{0.1, 0.2, 0.3, 0.4, 0.5, 0.6, 0.7, 0.8, \text{and } 0.9\}$. The approximate values of $\frac{\partial \hat{\varphi}^{H*}}{\partial R}$ obtained for each of these values of θ are as follows:

θ	$\frac{\partial \hat{\varphi}^{H*}}{\partial R}$
0.1	0.387
0.2	0.362
0.3	0.310
0.4	0.225
0.5	0.086
0.6	−0.153
0.7	−0.602
0.8	−1.600
0.9	−4.750

Figure 3.1 in Chapter Three then plots these values of $\frac{\partial \hat{\varphi}^{H*}}{\partial R}$ as a function of θ, using the ListPlot routine in Mathematica. The other simulations reported in Chapter Three are conducted similarly. In the simulation reported in Figure 3.4, for example, we proceed exactly as above, except now in the simulation depicted with the solid line in the figure, $R = 3.75$, $\bar{y} = 1.25$, and $\frac{R}{R+\bar{y}} = \frac{3.75}{3.75+1.25} = 0.75$, so resource rents are now 75 percent of "GDP" (i.e., I have increased the extent of resource dependence).

Bibliography

Acemoglu, Daron, María Angélica Bautista, Pablo Querubín, and James A. Robinson. 2007. "Economic and Political Inequality in Development: The Case of Cundinamarca, Colombia." Manuscript, Department of Government, Harvard University, and Department of Economics, MIT.

Acemoglu, Daron, Simon Johnson, and James Robinson. 2003. "An African Success: Botswana." In Dani Rodrik, ed., *In Search of Prosperity: Analytic Narratives on Economic Growth*. Princeton, NJ: Princeton University Press.

Acemoglu, Daron and James Robinson. 2000. "Political Losers as Barriers to Economic Development." *American Economic Review* 90: 126–30.

Acemoglu, Daron and James Robinson. 2001. "A Theory of Political Transitions." *American Economic Review* 91: 938–63.

Acemoglu, Daron and James Robinson. 2006a. *Economic Origins of Democracy and Dictatorship*. Cambridge: Cambridge University Press.

Acemoglu, Daron and James Robinson. 2006b. "De Facto Political Power and Institutional Persistence." *American Economic Review* 96 (2): 326–30.

Acemoglu, Daron, James A. Robinson, and Thierry Verdier. 2004. "Kleptocracy and Divide-and-Rule: A Model of Personal Rule." *Journal of the European Economic Association* 2 (2–3): 162–92 (Alfred Marshall Lecture).

Achen, Christopher H. 2002. "Toward a New Political Methodology: Microfoundations and ART." *Annual Review of Political Science* 5: 423–50.

Alesina, Alberto, Sule Ozler, Nouriel Roubini, and Phillip Swagel. 1996. "Political Instability and Economic Growth." *Journal of Economic Growth* 1: 189–211.

Alexander, Robert. 1982. *Bolivia: Past, Present and Future of Its Politics*. Stanford: Praeger and Hoover Institution Press.

Al-Ubaydli, Omar. 2005. "Diamonds Are a Dictator's Best Friend: Natural Resources and the Tradeoff between Development and Authoritarianism." Ph.D. dissertation, University of Chicago, Department of Economics.

Ameyima, Takeshi. 1985. *Advanced Econometrics*. Cambridge, MA: Harvard University Press.

Anderson, Lisa. 1991. "The State in the Middle East and North Africa." *Comparative Politics* 20 (1): 1–18.

Antelo, Eduardo. 2000. "Políticas de Estabilización y de Reformas Fiscales en Bolivia a Partir de 1985." Manuscript, Department of Economics, Universidad Católica Boliviana.

AP-IPSOS. 2006. "Venezuela Pre-Election Study." An Associated Press-IPSOS Poll released November 24, 2006.

Baena, Cesar. 1999. *The Policy Process in a Petro-State: An Analysis of PDVSA's (Petróleos de Venezuela SA's) Internationalisation Strategy*. Aldershot, UK: Ashgate.

Baptista, Asdrúbal. 1997. *Bases Cuantitativas de la Economía Venezolana 1830-1995*. Caracas: Fundación Polar, 2° edición.

Baptista, Asdrúbal. 2004. *El Relevo del Capitalismo Rentístico: Hacía un Nuevo Balance de Poder*. Caracas: Fundación Polar.

Baptista, Asdrúbal and Bernard Mommer. 1988. "Renta Petrolera y Distribución Factorial del Ingreso." Monograph, Instituto de Estudios Superiores de Administración (IESA): Caracas, Venezuela.

Baptista, Asdrúbal and Bernard Mommer. 1992. *El Petróleo en el Pensamiento Económico Venezolano*. Caracas: Ediciones IESA, Segunda edición, Segunda reimpresión.

Baptista Gumucio, Fernando. 1985. *La Crisis del estaño*. La Paz: Biblioteca Popular Boliviana.

Barro, Robert J. 1991. "Economic Growth in a Cross Section of Countries." *Quarterly Journal of Economics* 106: 407–44.

Barro, Robert J. 1999. "Determinants of Democracy." *Journal of Political Economy* 107 (6): 158–83.

Bartolini, Stefano and Peter Mair. 1990. *Identity, Competition, and Electoral Availability: The Stabilisation of European Electorates 1885–1985*. Cambridge: Cambridge University Press.

Batatu, Hanna. 1978. *The Old Social Classes and the Revolutionary Movements of Iraq*. Princeton, NJ: Princeton University Press.

Bates, Robert and Da-Hsieng Donald Lien. 1985. "A Note on Taxation, Development, and Representative Government." *Politics and Society* 14 (1): 53–70.

Bauer, Arnold J. 1975. *Chilean Rural Society from the Spanish Conquest to 1930*. Cambridge: Cambridge University Press.

Bauer, Arnold J. 1994. *La Sociedad Rural Chilena: Desde la conquista española a nuestros dias*. Santiago: Editorial Andres Bello.

Beard, Charles A. 1913. *An Economic Interpretation of the Constitution of the United States*. New York: The Free Press.

Beblawi, Hazem. 1987. "The Rentier State in the Arab World." In Hazem Beblawi and Giacomo Luciani, eds., *The Rentier State: Nation, State and the Integration of the Arab World*. London: Croom Helm, pp. 85–98.

Beck, Nathaniel L. and Jonathan N. Katz. 1995. "What to Do (and Not to Do) with Time-Series Cross-Section Data." *American Political Science Review* 89: 634–47.

Beck, Nathaniel L. and Jonathan N. Katz. 1996. "Nuisance vs. Substance: Specifying and Estimating Time-Series Cross-Section Models." *Political Analysis* VI: 1–36.

Belkin, Aaron and Evan Schofer. 2003. "Toward a Structural Understanding of Coup Risk." *Journal of Conflict Resolution* 47 (5): 594–620.

Bibliography

Bergquist, Charles. 1986. *Labor in Latin America: Comparative Essays on Chile, Argentina, Venezuela, and Colombia*. Stanford, CA: Stanford University Press.

Bernanke, Ben S. and Refet S. Gúrkaynak. 2001. "Is Growth Exogenous? Taking Mankiw, Romer, and Weil Seriously." NBER Working Paper 8365, Cambridge, MA.

Betancourt, Rómulo. 1979 [1956]. *Venezuela, Política y Petróleo*. Caracas: Monte Ávila Editores Latinoamericana.

Blakemore, Harold. 1974. *British Nitrates and Chilean Politics, 1886–1896: Balmaceda and North*. London: The Athlone Press, for the Institute of Latin American Studies, University of London.

Boix, Carles. 2003. *Democracy and Redistribution*. New York: Cambridge University Press.

Bollen, Kenneth and Robert Jackman. 1985. "Political Democracy and the Size Distribution of Income." *American Sociological Review* 50: 438–57.

Bolt, Katharine, Mampite Matete, and Michael Clemens. 2002. "Manual for Calculating Adjusted Net Savings." Mimeo, Environment Department, World Bank.

Bolton, Patrick and Gérard Roland. 1997. "The Breakup of Nations: A Political Economy Analysis." *Quarterly Journal of Economics* 112: 1057–90.

Botswana NDP 8. 1997. *National Development Plan 8: 1997/98–2002/03*. Government of Botswana, Ministry of Finance and Development Planning. Gaborone: Government Printer.

Boué, Juan Carlos. 1997. *The Political Control of State Oil Companies. A Case Study of the International Vertical Integration Programme of Petróleos de Venezuela (1982–95)*. Oxford: Oxford University Press.

Boué, Juan Carlos. 2003. "El programa de internacionalización en Pdvsa: ¿triunfo estratégico o desastre fiscal?" In Luis E. Lander, ed., *Poder y Petróleo en Venezuela*. Caracas: Faces-UCV, PDVSA, 133–84.

Brady, Henry E. 2002. "Models for Causal Inference: Going Beyond the Neyman-Rubin-Holland Theory." Paper presented at the Annual Meeting of the APSA Political Methodology Working Group, Seattle, Washington, July 16.

Bratton, Michael and Nicolas van de Walle. 1997. *Democratic Experiments in Africa: Regime Transitions in Comparative Perspective*. Cambridge: Cambridge University Press.

British Petroleum. 2005. "Statistical Review of World Energy 2005." Data available for download at: www.bp.com/genericsection.do?categoryID=92&contentid=7005893 as of March 2006.

Bueno de Mesquita, Bruce D., James D. Morrow, Randolph M. Siverson, and Alastair Smith. 2003. *The Logic of Political Survival*. Cambridge, MA: MIT Press.

Bulmer-Thomas, Victor. 1995. *The Economic History of Latin America since Independence*. Cambridge: Cambridge University Press.

Buxton, Julia. 2004. "Economic Policy and the Rise of Hugo Chávez." In Steve Ellner and Daniel Hellinger, eds., *Venezuelan Politics in the Chávez Era: Class, Polarization, and Conflict*. Boulder: Lynne Rienner Publishers, pp. 113–30.

Carter Center. 2004. "Report on an Analysis of the Representativeness of the Second Audit Sample, and the Correlation between Petition Signers and the Yes Vote in the Aug. 15, 2004 Presidential Recall Referendum in Venezuela." Atlanta, GA: Carter Center.

Caselli, Francesco. 2005. "Accounting for Cross-Country Income Differences." Manuscript, Department of Economics, London School of Economics. In Philippe Aghion and Steven Durlauf, eds., *Handbook of Economic Growth*, Elsevier, pp. 679–741.

CEPAL. 1999. *Estudio económico de América Latina y el Caribe, 1998–1999*. Santiago: Comisión Económica para America Latina y el Caribe.

Chaudhry, Kiren A. 1989. "The Price of Wealth: Business and State in Labor Remittance and Oil Economies." *International Organization* 43 (1): 104–45.

Chaudhry, Kiren A. 1994. "Economic Liberalization and the Lineages of the Rentier State." *Comparative Politics* 27 (9): 1–25.

Chaudhry, Kiren A. 1997. *The Price of Wealth: Economies and Institutions in the Middle East*. Ithaca and London: Cornell University Press.

Cheibub, José Antonio and Jennifer Gandhi. 2004. "Classifying Political Regimes: A Six-fold Measure of Democracies and Dictatorships." Presented at the American Political Science Association Annual Meeting, Chicago, September 2–5, 2004.

Chua, Amy. 2003. *World on Fire: How Exporting Free Market Democracy Breeds Ethnic Hatred and Global Instability*. New York: Anchor Books.

Cobbe, James. 1979. *Governments and Mining Companies in Developing Countries*. Boulder, CO: Westview.

Collier, David, Henry Brady, and Jason Seawright. 2004. "Sources of Leverage in Causal Inference: Toward an Alternative View of Methodology." Chapter 13 in David Collier and Henry Brady, eds., *Rethinking Social Inquiry: Diverse Tools, Shared Standards*. Lanham, MD: Rowman & Littlefield.

Collier, Paul and Anke Hoeffler. 1998a. "On Economic Causes of Civil War." *Oxford Economic Papers* 50: 563–73.

Collier, Paul and Anke Hoeffler. 1998b. *Greed and Grievance in Civil War*. World Bank Policy Research Working Paper 2355. Washington, DC: World Bank.

Collier, Ruth Berins. 1999. *Paths towards Democracy: The Working Class and Elites in Western Europe and South America*. New York: Cambridge University Press.

Collier, Ruth Berins and David Collier. 2001. *Shaping the Political Arena: Critical Junctures, the Labor Movement and Regime Dynamics in Latin America*, 2nd ed. Notre Dame: University of Notre Dame Press. (1st ed.: Princeton, NJ: Princeton University Press, 1991).

Conaghan, Catherine and James Malloy. 1994. *Unsettling Statecraft: Democracy and Neoliberalism in the Central Andes*. Pittsburgh: University of Pittsburgh Press.

Contreras, Manuel C. 1993. "The Bolivian tin mining industry in the first half of the 20th century." Research Paper 32, Institute of Latin American Studies, University of London.

Contreras, Carlos and Marcos Cueto. 1999. *Historia del Perú Contemporaneo*. Lima: IEP.

Coppedge, Michael. 1994. *Strong Parties and Lame Ducks: Presidential Partyarchy and Factionalism in Venezuela*. Stanford: Stanford University Press.

Corkill, David and David Cubitt. 1988. *Ecuador: Fragile Democracy*. London: Latin American Bureau.

Coronil, Fernando. 1997. *The Magical State: Nature, Money and Modernity in Venezuela*. Chicago: University of Chicago Press.
Corrales, Javier. 2002. *Presidents without Parties: Economic Reforms in Argentina and Venezuela*. University Park: Pennsylvania State University Press.
Corrales, Javier. 2006. "Hugo Boss." *Foreign Policy*, January/February issue.
Corrales, Javier and Michael Penfold. 2007. "Venezuela: Crowding out the Opposition." *Journal of Democracy* 18 (2): 99–113.
Crabtree, John, Gavan Duffy, and Jenny Pearce. 1987. *The Great Tin Crash: Bolivia and the World Tin Market*. London: Latin American Bureau, Monthly Review Foundation.
Crisp, Brian. 2000. *Democratic Institutional Design: The Powers and Incentives of Venezuelan Politicians and Interest Groups*. Palo Alto, CA: Stanford University Press.
Crystal, Jill. 1990. *Oil and Politics in the Gulf: Rulers and Merchants in Kuwait and Qatar*. New York: Cambridge University Press.
Crystal, Jill. 1995. *Oil and Politics in the Gulf: Rulers and Merchants in Kuwait and Qatar*. Cambridge: Cambridge University Press. (First published 1990).
Cueva, Agustín. 1982. *The Process of Political Domination in Ecuador*, trans. Danielle Salti. New Brunswick, NJ: Transaction.
DeShazo, Peter. 1983. *Urban Workers and Labor Unions in Chile: 1902–1927*. Madison: University of Wisconsin Press.
Deves, Eduardo. 2002. *Los que van a morir te saludan: Historia de una masacre, Escuela Santa María de Iquique, 1907*. Santiago: Ediciones LOM, Cuarta edición.
Dunkerley, James. 1980. *Bolivia: Coup d'Etat*. London: Latin America Bureau.
Dunkerley, James. 1984. *Rebellion in the Veins: Political Struggle in Bolivia, 1952–82*. London: Verso Editions.
Dunkerley, James and Rolando Morales. 1985. "The Crisis in Bolivia." Working Paper #54. Kellogg Institute for International Studies.
Dunning, Thad. 2004. "Conditioning the Effects of Aid: Cold War Politics, Donor Credibility, and Democracy in Africa." *International Organization* 58 (2): 409–23.
Dunning, Thad. 2005. "Resource Dependence, Economic Performance and Political Stability." *Journal of Conflict Resolution* 49 (4): 451–82.
Dunning, Thad. 2006. "Does Oil Promote Democracy? Regime Change in Rentier States." Ph.D. Dissertation, Department of Political Science, University of California, Berkeley.
Dunning, Thad. 2007. "Does Oil Promote Democracy? Regime Change in Rentier States." Working paper, Yale Program on Democracy, Yale University.
Dunning, Thad. 2008. "Model Specification in Instrumental-Variables Regression." *Political Analysis*. Advance Access published February 10, 2008.
Dunning, Thad and Leslie Wirpsa. 2004. "Oil and the Political Economy of Conflict in Colombia and Beyond: A Linkages Approach." *Geopolitics* 9 (1): 81–108.
Eaton, Kent. 2007. "Backlash in Bolivia: Regional Autonomy as a Reaction against Indigenous Mobilization." *Politics and Society* 35 (1): 1–32.
Economist Intelligence Unit. 1989. *Quarterly Economic Report, No. 3*. London, UK: The Economist.

Edge, Wayne. 1998. "Botswana: A Developmental State." In Wayne Edge and Mogopodi Lekorwe, eds., *Botswana: Politics and Society*. Pretoria, South Africa: J.L. van Schaik Publishers, pp. 331–48.

Eifert, Benn, Alan Gelb, and Nils Borje Tallroth. 2003. "The Political Economy of Fiscal Policy and Economic Management in Oil-Exporting Countries." In J. M. Davis, R. Ossowski, and A. Fedelino, eds., *Fiscal Policy Formulation and Implementation in Oil-Producing Countries*. Washington, DC: International Monetary Fund.

Eklof, Stefan. 2003. *Power and Political Culture in Suharto's Indonesia: The Indonesia Democratic Party (PDI) and Decline of the New Order (1986–98)*. London: Taylor & Francis.

Ellner, Steve. 2004. "Introduction: The Search for Explanations." In Steve Ellner and Daniel Hellinger, eds., *Venezuelan Politics in the Chávez Era: Class, Polarization, and Conflict*. Boulder: Lynne Rienner Publishers, pp. 7–26.

Engel, Eduardo, Alexander Galetovic, and Claudio Raddatz. 1999. "Taxes and Income Distribution in Chile: Some Unpleasant Redistributive Arithmetic." *Journal of Development Economics* 1 (59): 155–92.

Englebert, Pierre and James Ron. 2004. "Primary Commodities and War: Congo Brazzaville's Ambivalent Resource Curse." *Comparative Politics* 37 (1): 61–68.

Entelis, John P. 1976. "Oil Wealth and the Prospects for Democratization in the Arabian Peninsula: The Case of Saudi Arabia." In Naiem A. Sherbiny and Mark A. Tessler, eds., *Arab Oil: Impact on the Arab Countries and Global Implications*. New York: Praeger.

España, Luis Pedro. 1989. *Democracia y Renta Petrolera*. Caracas: Universidad Católica Andrés Bello.

Espinel, Ramón, Alison Graham, Alain de Janvry, Elisabeth Sadoulet, and Walter Spurrier. 1994. "Ecuador." In Alain de Janvry and Christian Morrisson, eds., *The Political Feasibility of Adjustment in Ecuador and Venezuela*. Paris: OECD Development Center.

Evans, Peter B. 1989. "Predatory, Developmental, and Other Apparatuses: A Comparative Political Economy Perspective on the Third World State." *Sociological Forum* 4: 561–87.

Evans, Peter B. 1995. *Embedded Autonomy: States and Industrial Transformation*. Princeton, NJ: Princeton University Press.

Evans, Peter B. and James Rauch. 1999. "Bureaucracy and Growth: A Cross-National Analysis of the Effects of 'Weberian' State Structure on Economic Growth." *American Sociological Review* 64 (5): 748–65.

Evans, Peter B. and James Rauch. 2000. "Bureaucratic Structure and Bureaucratic Performance in Less Developed Countries." *Journal of Public Economics* 75: 49–62.

Fearon, James D. 1991. "Counterfactuals and Hypothesis Testing in Political Science." *World Politics* 43 (January): 169–95.

Fearon, James. 2005. "Civil War since 1945: Some Fact and a Theory." Manuscript, Department of Political Science, Stanford University.

Fearon, James D. and David D. Laitin. 2003. "Ethnicity, Insurgency, and Civil War." *American Political Science Review* 97 (1): 75–90.

Feng, Yi and Paul Zak. 1999. "The Determinants of Democratic Transitions." *Journal of Conflict Resolution* 43 (2): 162–77.

First, Ruth. 1980. "Libya: Class and State in an Oil Economy." In Petter Nore and Terisa Turner, eds., *Oil and Class Struggle*. London: Zed Press.

Fish, M. Steven. 2005. *Democracy Derailed in Russia: The Failure of Open Politics*. New York: Cambridge University Press.

Fitch, John Samuel. 1977. *The Military Coup d'Etat as a Political Process: Ecuador, 1948–1966*. Baltimore: Johns Hopkins University Press.

Fourcade-Gourinchas, Marion and Sarah L. Babb. 2002. "The Rebirth of the Liberal Creed: Paths to Neoliberalism in Four Countries." *American Journal of Sociology* 108 (3): 533–79.

Freedman, David. 2005. *Statistical Models: Theory and Practice*. New York: Cambridge University Press.

Freedman, David and S. C. Peters. 1984. "Bootstrapping a Regression Equation: Some Empirical Results." *Journal of the American Statistical Association* 2: 150–58.

Friedman, Thomas. 2006. "The First Law of Petropolitics." *Foreign Policy*, May/June 2006.

Fudenberg, Drew and Jean Tirole. 1991. *Game Theory*. Cambridge, MA: MIT Press.

García, Gustavo, Rafael Rodríguez, and Silvia Salvato de Figueroa. 1998. "Dinámica de la tributación en Venezuela 1980–1994: Un período de turbulencia y contracción." *Debates IESA* 3 (3).

García Larralde, Humberto. 2000. "Limitaciones de la política económica actual: la ideología económica en el deterioro del bienestar del venezolano." *Revista Venezolana de Economía y Ciencias Sociales* 6 (Jan.–April): 83–143.

Geddes, Charles F. 1972. *Patiño, the Tin King*. London: R. Hale.

Gil Yepes, José Antonio. 1978. *El reto de las elites*. Madrid: Editorial Tecnos.

Glanz, James. 2007. "Iraqi Sunni Lands Show New Oil and Gas Promise." *New York Times*, February 19, 2007.

Gollin, Douglas. 2002. "Getting Income Shares Right." *Journal of Political Economy* 90: 458–74.

Good, Kenneth. 1992. "Interpreting the Exceptionality of Botswana." *Journal of Modern African Studies* 30: 69–95.

Good, Kenneth. 2002. *The Liberal Model and Africa: Elites against Democracy*. New York: Palgrave.

Goodwin, Jeff. 2001. *No Other Way Out: States and Revolutionary Movements, 1945–1991*. New York: Cambridge University Press.

GQR. 2006. "Venezuela General Population, Demographic Time Series, May 14, 2006." Public opinion data provided to the author by Greenberg Quinlan Rosner.

Grandmont, Jean-Michel. 1978. "Intermediate Preferences and the Majority Rule." *Econometrica* 46: 317–30.

Grossman, Gene and Elhanan Helpman. 2001. *Special Interest Politics*. Cambridge, MA: MIT Press.

Haber, Stephen and Victor Menaldo. 2007. "Do Natural Resources Fuel Authoritarianism?" Manuscript, Departments of Political Science and History, Stanford University.

Hamilton, Kirk and Michael A. Clemens. 1999. "Genuine Savings Rates in Developing Countries." *World Bank Economic Review* 13 (2): 333–56.

Harvey, Charles and Stephen R. Lewis. 1990. *Policy Choice and Development Performance in Botswana*. London: Macmillan.

Hausmann, Ricardo and Roberto Rigobón. 2003. "An Alternative Interpretation of the 'Resource Curse': Theory and Policy Implications." In Jeffrey M. Davis, Rolando Ossowski, and Annalisa Fedelino, eds., *Fiscal Policy Formulation and Implementation in Oil-Producing Countries*. Washington, DC: International Monetary Fund.

Hausmann, Ricardo and Roberto Rigobón. 2004. "In Search of the Black Swan: Analysis of the Statistical Evidence of Electoral Fraud in Venezuela." Manuscript, Harvard University and Massachusetts Institute of Technology.

Hellinger, Daniel. 1984. "Populism and Nationalism in Venezuela: New Perspectives on Acción Democrática." *Latin American Perspectives* 11 (4): 33–59.

Hellinger, Daniel C. 1991. *Venezuela: Tarnished Democracy*. Boulder, CO: Westview.

Hellinger, Daniel. 2004. "Political Overview: The Breakdown of *Puntofijismo* and the rise of *Chavismo*." In Steve Ellner and Daniel Hellinger, eds., *Venezuelan Politics in the Chávez Era: Class Polarization and Conflict*. Boulder: Lynne Rienner Publishers.

Herb, Michael. 1999. *All in the Family: Absolutism, Revolution, and Democracy in the Middle Eastern Monarchies*. Albany: State University of New York Press.

Herb, Michael. 2005."No Taxation without Representation? Rents, Development, and Democracy." *Comparative Politics* 37 (3): 297–317.

Hirschman, Albert O. 1963. "Inflation in Chile." In Albert O. Hirschman, ed., *Journeys toward Progress: Studies of Economic Policy-Making in Latin America*. New York: Norton, pp. 159–223.

Hirschman, Albert O. 1977. "A Generalized Linkage Approach to Development, with Special Reference to Staples." *Economic Development and Cultural Change* 25 (supplement): 67–98.

Hodges, Tony. 2001. *Angola from Afro-Stalinism to Petro-Diamond Capitalism*. Bloomington: Indiana University Press.

Hoffman, David Emanuel. 2003. *The Oligarchs: Wealth and Power in the New Russia*. Cambridge, MA: Perseus Books.

Holm, J. and P. Molutsi, eds. 1989. *Democracy in Botswana*. The proceedings of a symposium held by the Botswana Society in Gaborone, August 1–5, 1988. Gaborone: Macmillan Botswana.

Humphreys, Macartan. 2005. "Natural Resources, Conflict, and Conflict Resolution: Uncovering the Mechanisms." *Journal of Conflict Resolution* 49 (4): 508–37.

Humphreys, Macartan, William A. Masters, and Martin E. Sandbu. 2006. "The Role of Leaders in Democratic Deliberations: Results from a Field Experiment in São Tomé and Príncipe." *World Politics* 58 (4): 583–622.

Humud, Carlos. 1971. "Chilean Economic Policy during the Nineteenth Century." Thesis submitted for the degree of Bachelor of Philosophy. St. Antony's College, Oxford.

Huntington, Samuel P. 1991. *The Third Wave: Democratization in the Late Twentieth Century*. Norman: University of Oklahoma Press.

Hurtado Ruiz-Tagle, Carlos. 1988. *De Balmaceda a Pinochet: cien años de desarrollo y subdesarrollo en Chile, y una digresión sobre el futuro.* Santiago: Ediciones Logos.

IDB. 1998. "Facing Up to Inequality in Latin America." Report of the Inter-American Development Bank. Washington, DC.

Instituto Nacional de Tierras. 1998. Reforma Agraria: 1960–1998." Available at www.inti.gov.ve, accessed June 6, 2006.

International Monetary Fund. 2005. "IMF Executive Board Concludes Article IV Consultation with Equatorial Guinea." Public Information Notice (PIN) No. 05/61. Downloaded February 1, 2007, from http://www.imf.org/external/np/sec/pn/2005/pn0561.htm.

Isaacs, Anita. 1993. *Military Rule and Transition in Ecuador, 1972–92.* Pittsburgh: University of Pittsburgh Press.

Isham, J., M. Woolcock, L. Pritchett, and G. Busby. 2003. "The Variety of Resource Experience: How Natural Resource Export Structures Affect the Political Economy of Economic Growth." Middlebury College Economics Discussion Paper No. 03-08R.

Jefferis, K. 1998. "Botswana and Diamond-Dependent Development." In W. A. Edge and M. H. Lekorwe, eds., *Botswana: Politics and Society*, Pretoria: J. L. van Schaik.

Jensen, Nathan and Leonard Wantchekon. 2004. "Resource Wealth and Political Regimes in Africa." *Comparative Political Studies* 37: 816–41.

Jones Luong, Pauline. 2004. "Rethinking the Resource Curse: Ownership Structure and Institutional Capacity." Paper prepared for the Conference on Globalization and Self-Determination, Yale University, May 14–15, 2004.

Jones Luong, Pauline and Erika Weinthal. 2001a. "Energy Wealth and Tax Reform in Russia and Kazakhstan." *Resources Policy* 27: 215–23.

Jones Luong, Pauline and Erika Weinthal. 2001b. "Prelude to the Resource Curse: Explaining Energy Development Strategies in the Soviet Successor States and Beyond." *Comparative Political Studies* 34 (4): 367–99.

Jones Luong, Pauline and Erika Weinthal. 2006. "Rethinking the Resource Curse: Ownership Structure, Institutional Capacity, and Domestic Constraints." *Annual Review of Political Science* 9: 241–63.

Judis, John B. 2003. "Blood for Oil: Will Black Gold Stymie Democracy in Iraq?" *The New Republic*, March 31, 2003.

Karl, Terry Lynn. 1987. "Petroleum and Political Pacts: The Transition to Democracy in Venezuela." *Latin American Research Review* 22 (1): 63–94.

Karl, Terry Lynn. 1990. "Dilemmas of Democratization in Latin America." *Comparative Politics* 23 (1): 1–23.

Karl, Terry Lynn. 1997. *The Paradox of Plenty: Oil Booms and Petro-States.* Berkeley: University of California Press.

Kaufman, Robert R. 1972. *The Politics of Land Reform in Chile, 1950–1970.* Cambridge, MA: Harvard University Press.

Klein, Herbert S. 1969. *Parties and Political Change in Bolivia 1880–1952.* Cambridge, MA: Cambridge University Press.

Klein, Herbert S. 1982. *Bolivia: The Evolution of a Multi-Ethnic Society.* New York: Oxford University Press.

Kornblith, Miriam and Thais Maignon. 1985. *Estado y Gasto Público en Venezuela, 1936–1980*. Caracas: UCV, Ediciones de la Biblioteca.

La Prensa. 2004. "Julio Garrett Aillón: Una Entrevista." La Paz, Bolivia, November 28, 2004.

Lam, Ricky and Leonard Wantchekon. 2004. "Dictatorships as a Political Dutch Disease." Manuscript, Department of Politics, New York University.

Lander, Luis E. and Margarita López Maya. 2005. "Referendo revocatorio y elecciones regionales en Venezuela: geografía electoral de la polarización." *Revista Venezolana de Economía y Ciencias Sociales* 11 (1): enero-abril.

Lane, Philip and Aaron Tornell. 1999. "The Voracity Effect." *American Economic Review* 89: 22–46.

Le Billon, Philippe. 2001. "The Political Ecology of War: Natural Resources and Armed Conflict." *Political Geography* 20 (5): 561–84.

Le Billon, Philippe. 2005. *Fuelling War: Natural Resources and Armed Conflict*. New York: Routledge and the International Institute for Strategic Studies.

Levi, Margaret. 1988. *Of Rule and Revenue*. Berkeley: University of California Press.

Levine, Daniel H. 1978. "Venezuela since 1958: The Consolidation of Democratic Politics." In Juan J. Linz and Alfred Stepan, eds., *The Breakdown of Democratic Regimes: Latin America*. Baltimore: Johns Hopkins University Press.

Lindert, Peter. 1994. "The Rise of Social Spending, 1880–1930." *Explorations in Economic History* 33 (1): 1–34.

Lindert, Peter. 2004. *Growing Public: Social Spending and Economic Growth since the Eighteenth Century*. New York: Cambridge University Press, Volumes 1 and 2.

Londregan, John B. 2000. *Legislative Institutions and Ideology in Chile*. New York: Cambridge University Press.

López Maya, Margarita. 2004. "Exposición con motivo del reconocimiento en la Asamblea Nacional de la ratificación del presidente." Speech given to the National Assembly, August 27, 2004.

López-Maya, Margarita and Luis E. Lander. 2006. "Novedades y Continuidades de la Protesta Popular en Venezuela." *Revista Venezolana de Economía y Ciencias Sociales* 12 (1): 11–30.

Loveman, Brian. 1976. *Struggle in the Countryside: Politics and Rural Labor in Chile, 1919–1973*. Bloomington: Indiana University Press.

Luciani, Giacomo. 1987. "Allocation vs. Production States: A Theoretical Framework." In Hazem Beblawi and Giacomo Luciani, eds., *The Rentier State: Nation, State and the Integration of the Arab World*. London: Croom Helm.

Lujala, Paivi, Nils Petter Gleditsch, and Elisabeth Gilmore. 2005. "A Diamond Curse? Civil War and a Lootable Resource." *Journal of Conflict Resolution* 49 (4): 538–62.

Luoma, Aaron, Gretchen Gordon, and Jim Shultz. 2007. "Oil and Gas Policy in Bolivia." Mimeo, The Democracy Center, Cochabamba, Bolivia.

MacIntyre, Andrew. 1990. "State-Society Relations in New Order Indonesia: The Case of Business." In Arief Budiman, ed., *State and Civil Society in Indonesia*, Monash Papers on Southeast Asia No. 22, Monash University, Victoria, Australia.

Mackie, Jamie and Andrew MacIntyre. 1994. "Politics." In Hal Hill, ed., *Indonesia's New Order: The Dynamics of Socioeconomic Transformation*. Honolulu: University of Hawaii Press.

Magee, Stephen P., William A. Brock, and Leslie Young. 1989. *Black Hole Tariffs and Endogenous Policy Theory: Political Economy in General Equilibrium*. Cambridge: Cambridge University Press.

Mahdavy, Hussein. 1970. "The Patterns and Problems of Economic Development in Rentier States: The Case of Iran." In M. A. Cook, ed., *Studies in Economic History of the Middle East*. London: Oxford University Press.

Mahon, James. 2007. "Revenues and Regimes." Book Manuscript, Department of Political Science, Williams College.

Malloy, James. 1970. *Bolivia: The Uncompleted Revolution*. Pittsburgh: University of Pittsburgh Press.

Mamalakis, Markos. 1976. *The Growth and Structure of the Chilean Economy: From Independence to Allende*. New Haven: Yale University Press.

Mamalakis, Markos. 1989. *Historical Statistics of Chile*, vol. 6. (Government services and public sector and a theory of services). New York: Greenwood Press.

Marcano, Cristina and Alberto Barrera Tyszka. 2005. *Hugo Chávez Sin Uniforme: Una historia personal*. Caracas: Random House Mondadori.

Márquez, Gustavo, ed. 1993. *Gasto Público y Distribución del Ingreso en Venezuela*. Caracas: Ediciones IESA.

Márquez, Humberto. 2005. "British Corporation and Government Smoke Agrarian Peace Pipe." Inter Press Service News Agency (BBC), March 24, 2006.

Márquez, Patricia. 2004. "The Hugo Chávez Phenomenon: What Do 'the People' Think?" In Steve Ellner and Daniel Hellinger, eds., *Venezuelan Politics in the Chávez Era: Class, Polarization, and Conflict*. Boulder: Lynne Rienner Publishers, pp. 197–214.

Marshall, Monty G. and Keith Jaggers. 2002. "Polity IV Project: Political Regime Characteristics and Transitions, 1800–2000. Dataset Users Manual." Retrieved from http://www.cidcm.umd.edu/inscr/polity/.

Martz, John D. 1987. *Politics and Petroleum in Ecuador*. New Brunswick, NJ: Transaction.

McGowan, Patrick J. 2003. "African Military Coups d'État, 1956–2001: Frequency, Trends, and Distribution." *Journal of Modern African Studies* 41 (3): 339–70.

McSherry, Brendan. 2006. "The Political Economy of Oil in Equatorial Guinea." *African Studies Quarterly* 8 (3): 23–45.

Meltzer, Allan H. and Scott F. Richard. 1981. "A Rational Theory of the Size of Government." *Journal of Political Economy* 89: 914–27.

Ministry of Energy and Mines. Various years. *Petróleo y otros datos estadísticos*. Caracas: Republic of Venezuela.

Mitre, Antonio. 1993. "Bajo un cielo de estaño: fulgor y ocaso del metal en Bolivia." La Paz: Asociación Nacional de Mineros Medianos, ILDIS.

Molutsi, P. P. 1998. "Elections and Electoral Experience in Botswana." In W. A. Edge and M. H. Lekorwe, eds., *Botswana: Politics and Society*. Pretoria: J.L. van Schaik, pp. 363–77.

Mommer, Bernard. 2002. *Global Oil and the Nation State*. Oxford: Oxford University Press for the Oxford Institute for Energy Studies.

Mommer, Bernard. 2003. "Petróleo Subersivo." In Luis E. Lander, ed., *Poder y Petróleo en Venezuela*. Caracas: Faces-UCV, PDVSA, 19–40. Published in English as "Subversive Oil," in Steve Ellner and Daniel Hellinger, eds., *Venezuelan Politics in the Chávez Era: Class, Polarization, and Conflict*. Boulder: Lynne Rienner Publishers, 2004, pp. 131–48.

Monaldi, Francisco. 2002a. "Rent-Seeking, Institutions, and Commitment: The Political Economy of Foreign Investment in the Venezuelan Oil Industry." Ph.D. Dissertation, Department of Political Science, Stanford University.

Monaldi, Francisco. 2002b. "Government Commitment Using External Hostages: Attracting Foreign Investment to the Venezuelan Oil Industry." Paper prepared for delivery at the 2002 Meeting of the American Political Science Association.

Monaldi, Francisco, Rosa Amelia González, Richard Obuchi, and Michael Penfold. 2005. "Political Institutions, Policymaking Processes, and Policy Outcomes in Venezuela." *Working Paper R-507*. Washington, DC: Inter-American Development Bank.

Moore, Clement Henry. 1976. "Petroleum and Political Development in the Maghreb." In Naiem A. Sherbiny and Mark A. Tessler, eds., *Arab Oil: Impact on the Arab Countries and Global Implications*. New York: Praeger.

Moore, Barrington. 1966. *Social Origins of Dictatorship and Democracy: Lord and Peasant in the Making of the Modern World*. Boston: Beacon Press.

Moore, Mick. 2004. "Revenues, State Formation, and the Quality of Governance in Developing Countries." *International Political Science Review* 25: 297–319.

Moran, Theodore. 1974. *Copper in Chile: Multinational Corporations and the Politics of Dependence*. Princeton, NJ: Princeton University Press.

Morrison, Kevin M. 2007. "Natural Resources, Aid, and Democratization: A Best-Case Scenario." *Public Choice* 131: 365–38.

MPD-SISOV. 2005."Sistema Integrado de Indicadores Sociales de Venezuela." Ministerio del Poder Popular para la Manificación y Desarrollo. Available at www.sivov.mpd.gov.ve, accessed April 18, 2008.

Muñoz, Jorge. 2000. "Rural Poverty and Development." In John Crabtree and Laurence Whitehead, eds., *Towards Democratic Viability: The Bolivian Experience*. London: Palgrave Macmillan.

Myers, David. 1986. "The Venezuelan Party System: Regime Maintenance under Stress." In John D. Marts and David Myers, eds., *Venezuela: The Democratic Experience*. New York: Praeger.

Myers, David. 1998. "Venezuela's Political Party System: Defining Events, Reactions, and the Diluting of Structural Cleavages." *Party Politics* 4 (4): 495–521.

Naím, Moises and Ramón Piñango. 1984. *El caso Venezuela: Una ilusión de armonía*. Caracas: Ediciones IESA.

Nash, June C. 1979. *We Eat the Mines and the Mines Eat Us: Dependency and Exploitation in Bolivian Tin Mines*. New York: Columbia University Press.

N'Diaye, Boubacar. 2001. *The Challenge of Institutionalizing Civilian Control: Botswana, Ivory Coast, and Kenya in Comparative Perspective*. Lanham, MD: Lexington Books.

Nengwekhulu, R. 1998. "Human Rights, Development and the Rule of Law in Post-Colonial Botswana." In W. A. Edge and M. H. Lekorwe, eds., *Botswana: Politics and Society*, Pretoria: J.L. van Schaik, pp. 351–62.

Neuhouser, Kevin. 1992. "Democratic Stability in Venezuela: Elite Consensus or Class Compromise?" *American Sociological Review* 57 (1): 117–35.

Norden, Deborah L. 2004. "Democracy in Uniform: Chávez and the Venezuelan Armed Forces." In Steve Ellner and Daniel Hellinger, eds., *Venezuelan Politics in the Chávez Era: Class, Polarization, and Conflict.* Boulder: Lynne Rienner Publishers, pp. 93–112.

North, Douglass and Barry Weingast. 1989. "Constitutions and Commitment: The Evolution of Institutions Governing Public Choice in Seventeenth Century England." *Journal of Economic History* 49: 803–32.

O'Donnell, Guillermo. 1973. *Modernization and Bureaucratic Authoritarianism: Studies in South American Politics.* Berkeley: Institute of International Studies, University of California.

O'Donnell, Guillermo and Philippe Schmitter. 1986. *Transitions from Authoritarian Rule: Tentative Conclusions about Uncertain Democracies*. Baltimore: Johns Hopkins University Press.

Ortega, Daniel and Francisco Rodríguez. 2006. "Are Capital Shares Higher in Poor Countries? Evidence from Industrial Surveys." Manuscript, Corporacin Andina de Fomento (CAF) and IESA, and Department of Economics, Wesleyan University.

Ortega, Daniel, Francisco Rodríguez, and Edward Miguel. 2006. "Freed from Illiteracy? A Closer Look at Venezuela's *Robinson* Literacy Campaign." Manuscript, IESA and the Departments of Economics, Wesleyan University and the University of California, Berkeley.

Paige, Jeffrey. 1997. *Coffee and Power: Revolution and the Rise of Democracy in Central America*. Cambridge, MA: Harvard University Press.

Palma, Pedro. 1993. "La Economía Venezolana en el perodo 1974–1988: Ultimos Años de una Economía Rentista?" En *Venezuela Contemporáneo 1974–1989.* Caracas: Grijalbo.

Parra Luzardo, Gastón. 2005. "La Nueva Distribución del Ingreso Petrolero: Un Cambio de Estructura." Discurso del Presidente del BCV, Gastón Parra Luzardo, en el acto de juramentación de la directiva de FONDEN. Caracas: Banco Central de Venezuela.

Parson, Jack. 1993. "Liberal Democracy, the Liberal State, and the 1989 General Elections in Botswana." In Stephen John Stedman, ed., *Botswana: The Political Economy of Democratic Development*. Boulder, CO: Lynne Rienner Publishers.

Parsons, Q. Neil, T. Tlou, and W. Henderson. 1995. *Seretse Khama, 1971–1980.* Bloemfontein: Macmillan.

Pérez Alfonso, Juan Pablo. 2003 [1967]. *The Petroleum Pentagon*. Vienna: Organization of the Petroleum Exporting Countries. (Translation of *El Pentágono Petróleo*, Caracas 1967).

Pérez Sáinz, Juan Pablo. 1984. *Clase Obrera y Democracia en el Ecuador*. Quito: El Conejo.

Persson, Torsten and Guido Tabellini. 1994. "Does Centralization Increase the Size of Government?" *European Economic Review* 38: 765–73.

Persson, Torsten and Guido Tabellini. 2000. *Political Economics: Explaining Economic Policy*. Cambridge, MA: MIT Press.

Picard, Louis. 1987. *The Politics of Development in Botswana: A Model for Success?* Boulder, CO: Lynne Rienner Publishers.

Pinto Santa Cruz, Aníbal. 1962. *Chile, un caso de desarrollo frustrado*, 2nd ed. Santiago.

Powell, John Duncan. 1971. *Political Mobilization of the Venezuelan Peasant*. Cambridge, MA: Harvard University Press.

Powell, Robert. 2004. "The Inefficient Use of Power: Costly Conflict with Complete Information." *American Political Science Review* 98 (2): 231–41.

Powers, William. 2006. "Poor Little Rich Country." *New York Times*, June 11, 2005.

Przeworski, Adam. 1988. "Democracy as a Contingent Outcome of Conflicts." In Jon Elster and Rune Slagstad, eds., *Constitutionalism and Democracy*. Cambridge: Cambridge University Press.

Przeworski, Adam. 1991. *Democracy and the Market: Political and Economic Reforms in Eastern Europe and Latin America*. Cambridge: Cambridge University Press.

Przeworski, Adam, Michael Alvarez, José Antonio Cheibub, and Fernando Limongi. 2000. *Democracy and Development: Political Institutions and Well-Being in the World, 1950–1990*. New York: Cambridge University Press.

Przeworski, Joanne Fox. 1980. *The Decline of the Copper Industry in Chile and the Entrance of North American Capital, 1870–1914*. New York: Arno Press.

Quandt, William B. 1981. *Saudi Arabia in the 1980's: Foreign Policy, Security, and Oil*. Washington, DC: Brookings Institution.

Quandt, William B. 1998. *Between Ballots and Bullets: Algeria's Transition from Authoritarianism*. Washington, DC: Brookings Institution Press.

Ramsey, Kris. 2006. "Natural Disasters, the Price of Oil, and Democracy." Manuscript, Department of Politics, Princeton University.

Republica de Venezuela. 1995. "Venezuela ante la cumbre mundial sobre desarrollo social." Caracas.

Rey, Juan Carlos. 1989. *El futuro de la democracia*. Caracas: Serie Estudios Colección Idea.

Reynolds, Clark Winton. 1965. "Development Problems of an Export Economy: The Case of Chile and Copper." In Markos Mamalakis and Clark Winton Reynolds, eds., *Essays on the Chilean Economy*. Homewood, IL: Richard D. Irwin, pp. 201–398.

Rivera Letelier, Hernán. 2002. *Santa María de las flores negras*. Santiago: Grupo Editorial Planeta, segunda edición.

Roberts, Kenneth. 2004. "Social Polarization and the Populist Resurgence in Venezuela." In Steve Ellner and Daniel Hellinger, eds., *Venezuelan Politics in the Chávez Era: Class, Polarization, and Conflict*. Boulder: Lynne Rienner Publishers, pp. 55–72.

Roberts, Kevin W. S. 1977. "Voting over Income Tax Schedules." *Journal of Public Economics* 8: 329–40.

Robinson, James. 1997. "When Is a State Predatory?" Manuscript, Department of Government, Harvard University.

Robinson, James A. and Q. Neil Parsons. 2006. "State Formation and Governance in Botswana." *Journal of African Economies* 15 (AERC Supplement 1): 100–40.

Robinson, James A., Ragnar Torvik, and Thierry Verdier. 2006. "Political Foundations of the Resource Curse." *Journal of Development Economics* 79: 447–68.

Robison, Richard. 1986. *Indonesia and the Rise of Capital*. Sydney, Australia: Allen & Unwin.

Rock, Michael. 1999. "Reassessing the Effectiveness of Industrial Policy in Indonesia: Can the Neoliberals be Wrong?" *World Development* 27(4): 691–704.

Rodríguez Balsa, Rafael Antonio. 1993. "La economía política de la reforma tributaria en Venezuela." Trabajo presentado para la obtención del grado de Master en Administración. Caracas: IESA.

Rodrik, Dani. 1999. "Democracies Pay Higher Wages." *Quarterly Journal of Economics* CXIV: 707–38.

Roemer, John. 1998. "Why the Poor Do Not Expropriate the Rich: An Old Argument in New Garb." *Journal of Public Economics* 70 (3): 399–424.

Roemer, John. 2006. "Prospects for Achieving Equality in Market Economies." Manuscript, Department of Political Science, Yale University.

Rogowski, Ronald. 1989. *Commerce and Coalitions: How Trade Affects Domestic Political Alignments*. Princeton, NJ: Princeton University Press.

Romer, David. 2001. *Advanced Macroeconomics*, 2nd ed. New York: McGraw-Hill.

Romer, Thomas. 1975. "Individual Welfare, Majority Voting, and the Properties of a Linear Income Tax." *Journal of Public Economics* 7: 163–8.

Romero, Aníbal. 2005. "Nostalgia Socialista." *El Nacional*, May 18, 2005. Available at http://luisdelion.free.fr/ar200518051621.html. Downloaded September 2005.

Romero, Simon. 2006a. "Venezuelans Square Off over Race, Oil and a Populist Political Slogan." *New York Times*, November 12, 2006.

Romero, Simon. 2006b. "Chávez Wins Easily in Venezuela." *New York Times*, December 4, 2006.

Ross, Michael L. 1999. "Political Economy of the Resource Curse." *World Politics* 51: 297–322.

Ross, Michael L. 2001. "Does Oil Hinder Democracy?" *World Politics* 53 (3): 325–61.

Ross, Michael. 2006. "A Closer Look at Oil, Diamonds, and Civil War." Manuscript, Department of Political Science, University of California at Los Angeles.

Rueschemeyer, Dietrich, Evelyn Huber Stephens, and John D. Stephens. 1992. *Capitalist Development and Democracy*. Chicago: University of Chicago Press.

Rutland, Peter. 2006. "Oil and Politics in Russia." Paper presented at the annual meeting of the American Political Science Association, Philadelphia, PA, August 31, 2006.

Sachs, Jeffrey and Andrew Warner. 1995. "Natural Resource Abundance and Economic Growth." National Bureau for Economic Research (NBER) Working Paper 5398. Cambridge, MA.

Samatar, Abdi Ismail. 1999. *An African Miracle: State and Class Leadership and Colonial Legacy in Botswana Development*. Portsmouth, NH: Heinemann.

Schrank, Andrew. 2004. "Reconsidering the Resource Curse: Selection Bias, Measurement Error, and Omitted Variables." Manuscript, Department of Sociology, Yale University.

Schumpeter, Joseph. 1976. *Capitalism, Socialism, and Democracy*. New York: Allen & Unwin.

Seawright, Jason. 2006. *Crisis of Representation: Voters, Party Organizations, and Party-System Collapse in South America*. Ph.D. dissertation, Department of Political Science, University of California at Berkeley.

Segall, Maurice. 1953. *Desarrollo de capitalismo en Chile*. Santiago (privately published).

Shafer, Michael D. 1983. "Capturing the Mining Multinationals: Advantage or Disadvantage?" *International Organization* 37 (1): 93–119.

Shambayati, Hootan. 1994. "The Rentier State, Interest Groups, and the Paradox of Autonomy: State and Business in Turkey and Iran." *Comparative Politics* 26 (3): 307–31.

Shapiro, Ian. 2003. *The State of Democratic Theory*. Princeton, NJ: Princeton University Press.

Skocpol, Theda. 1979. *States and Social Revolutions: A Comparative Analysis of France, Russia, & China*. New York: Cambridge University Press.

Skocpol, Theda. 1982. "Rentier State and Shi'a Islam in the Iranian Revolution." *Theory and Society* 11.

Smith, Benjamin. 2004. "Oil Wealth and Regime Survival in the Developing World, 1960–1999." *American Journal of Political Science* 48 (2): 232–46.

Smith, Benjamin and Joseph Kraus. 2005. "Democracy despite Oil: Transition and Consolidation in Latin America and Africa." Manuscript, Department of Political Science, University of Florida.

Snyder, Richard. 2001. "Does Lootable Wealth Breed Disorder? States, Regimes, and the Political Economy of Extraction." Paper presented at the annual meeting of the American Political Science Association, San Francisco.

Snyder, Richard and Ravi Bhavnani. 2005. "Diamonds, Blood, and Taxes: A Revenue-Centered Framework for Explaining Political Order." *Journal of Conflict Resolution* 49 (4): 563–97.

Soifer, Hillel. 2006. "Authority over Distance: Explaining Variation in State Infrastructural Power in Latin America." Ph.D. thesis, Department of Government, Harvard University.

Stallings, Barbara. 1978. *Class Conflict and Economic Development in Chile, 1958–1973*. Stanford: Stanford University Press.

Steenkamp, Philip. 1991. "Cinderella of the Empire? Development Policy in Bechuanaland in the 1930s." *Journal of Southern African Studies* 17 (2): 292–308.

Stepan, Alfred. 1985. "State Power and the Strength of Civil Society in the Southern Cone of Latin America." In Peter B. Evans, Dietrich Rueschemeyer, and Theda Skocpol, eds., *Bringing the State Back In*. New York: Cambridge University Press.

Stephens, Evelyn Huber. 1987. "Minerals Strategies and Development: International Political Economy, State, Class and the Role of the Bauxite/Aluminum and Copper Industries in Jamaica and Peru." *Studies in Comparative International Development* 22 (3): 60–102.

Stokes, Susan C. 2001. *Mandates and Democracy: Neoliberalism by Surprise in Latin America*. Cambridge: Cambridge University Press.

Stolper, Wolfgang and Paul A. Samuelson. 1941. "Protection and Real Wages." *Review of Economic Studies* 9: 58–73.

Taylor, Charles L. and Michael Hudson. 1972. *World Handbook of Political and Social Indicators*, 2nd ed. New Haven, CT: Yale University Press.

Tilly, Charles. 1985. "War Making and State Making as Organized Crime." In Peter Evans, Dietrich Rueschemeyer, and Theda Skocpol, eds., *Bringing the State Back In*. Cambridge: Cambridge University Press.

Tilly, Charlcs. 1990. *Coercion, Capital, and European States, AD 990– 1990.* Oxford: Blackwell.

Tilly, Charles. 1995. "Democracy Is a Lake." In George Reid Andrews and Herrick Chapman, eds., *The Social Construction of Democracy, 1870–1990* (pp. 365–87). London: Macmillan.

Tilly, Charles. 2004. *Contention and Democracy in Europe, 1650–2000.* Cambridge: Cambridge University Press.

Tocqueville, Alexis de. 1835 [1966]. *Democracy in America*. New York: Harper & Row.

Treier, Shawn and Simon Jackman. 2005. "Democracy as a Latent Variable." Manuscript, Department of Political Science, Stanford University. At http://jackman.stanford.edu/papers/download.php?i=1, downloaded March 14, 2006.

Tugwell, Francis. 1975. *The Politics of Oil in Venezuela*. Stanford: Stanford University Press.

UNU-WIDER. 2005. "World Income Inequality Database." United Nations University and the World Institute for Development Economics Research. v 2.0a, June 2005.

Urbaneja, Diego Bautista. 1992. *Pueblo y petróleo en la política venezolana del siglo XX.* Caracas: Centro de Formación y Adiestramiento de Petróleos de Venezuela y sus Filiales.

US-EIA. 2008. "World Crude Oil Prices." United States Energy Information Administration. Downloaded February 1, 2008; http://tonto.eia.doe.gov/dnav/pet/pet*priwcokw.htm.*

Valenzuela, Arturo. 1976. "Political Constraints to the Establishment of Socialism in Chile." In Arturo Valenzuela and J. Samuel Valenzuela, eds., *Chile: Politics and Society*. New Brunswick, NJ: Transaction.

Valenzuela, Arturo. 1978. *The Breakdown of Democratic Regimes: Chile.* Baltimore: Johns Hopkins University Press.

Valenzuela, Arturo. 1985. "Origins and Characteristics of the Chilean Party System: A Proposal for a Parliamentary Form of Government." Working Paper, Latin American Program, Wilson Center, Washington, DC.

Vandewalle, Dirk. 1998. *Libya since Independence: Oil and State-Building*. Ithaca, NY: Cornell University Press.

Vernon, Raymond. 1967. "Long-Run Trends in Concession Contracts." Proceedings of the American Society for International Law, pp. 81–90. April 1967.

Villasmil Bond, Ricardo. 2005. *Lecciones Aprendidas de Política Económica en Venezuela: 1936–2004*. Caracas: Instituto Latinoamericano de Investigaciones Sociales (Ildis).

Villasmil, Ricardo, Francisco Monaldi, G. Rios, and M. Gonzalez. 2004. "Understanding Reform: The Case of Venezuela." Manuscript, Global Development Network. Washington, DC.

Wade, Terry. 2006. "Venezuelan Democracy Looks Alive, Despite Doubts." Reuters, August 16, 2006.

Wantchekon, Leonard. 1999a. "Strategic Voting in Conditions of Political Instability: The 1994 Elections in El Salvador." *Comparative Political Studies* 32 (7): 810–34.

Wantchekon, Leonard. 1999b. "Why Do Resource Abundant Countries Have Authoritarian Governments?" Yale University Leitner Center Working Paper 99-12. New Haven, CT: Yale University.

Wantchekon, Leonard. 2002. "Why Do Resource Dependent Countries Have Authoritarian Governments?" *African Finance and Economic Development* 5 (2): 57–77.

Weinthal, Erika and Pauline Jones Luong. 2002. "Energy Wealth and Tax Reform in Russia and Kazakhstan." *Resources Policy* 27: 215–23.

Wells, Louis T. 1971. "The Evolution of Concession Agreements in Developing Countries." Harvard Development Advisory Service, March 19, 1971.

Weyland, Kurt. 2003. "Economic Voting Reconsidered: Crisis and Charisma in the Election of Hugo Chávez." *Comparative Political Studies* 36 (7): 822–48.

White, Halbert. 1980. "A Heteroscedasticity-Consistent Covariance Matrix Estimator and a Direct Test for Heteroscedasticity." *Econometrica* 48: 817–38.

Wibbels, Erik. 2004. "Democracy in Iraq?" *Seattle Times*, August 2, 2004.

Wibbels, Erik and Ellis Goldberg. 2007. "Natural Resources, Development, and Democracy: The Quest for Mechanisms." Manuscript, Departments of Political Science, Duke University and the University of Washington.

Wittman, Donald. 1995. *The Myth of Democratic Failure: Why Political Institutions are Efficient*. Chicago: University of Chicago Press.

Wong, Edward. 2007. "Iraqis Reach an Accord on Oil Revenues." *New York Times*, February 27, 2007.

World Bank. 1989. "Indonesia: Strategy for Growth and Structural Change." Country Department V, Report No. 77758-IND, World Bank, Washington DC.

World Bank. 1991. "Ecuador: Public Sector Reforms for Growth in the Era of Declining Oil Output." Washington, DC: International Bank for Reconstruction and Development (World Bank).

World Bank. 2000. *World Development Indicators* 2000, CD-ROM Washington, DC: International Bank for Reconstruction and Development.

Wright, Gavin. 2001. "Resource-Based Growth Then and Now." Manuscript, Department of Economics, Stanford University, Palo Alto, California.

Yergin, Daniel. 1991. *The Prize: The Epic Quest for Oil, Money, and Power*. New York: Simon & Schuster.

Young, Crawford. 1983. "Zaire: The Politics of Penury." *SAIS Review* 3: 115–30.

YPFB. "Annual Report." Yacimientos Petroliferos Fiscales Bolivianos, various years. Available online at www.ypfb.gov.bo, consulted April 18, 2008.
Zambrano Sequín, Luis and Luis Pedro España N. 1991. *Buenos o Malos gobiernos? : estadísticas seleccionadas de ocho gobiernos venezolanos*, 1951–1990. Caracas: Universidad Católica Andrés Bello.
Zeitlin, Maurice. 1984. *The Civil Wars in Chile (or the Bourgeois Revolutions That Never Were)*. Princeton, NJ: Princeton University Press.

Index

Acción Democrática (AD), 158, 166, 168
Acemoglu, Daron, 9, 10, 13, 14, 21, 34, 54–56, 62–64, 69, 81, 82, 91, 101, 110, 116, 117, 149, 290
Alessandri, Arturo, 220, 221
Allende, Salvador, 227
Anaconda, 226
  Chuquicamata copper mine of, 223

Banzer, Hugo, 250
Barro, Robert J., 27
Bauer, Arnold, 219, 222, 224
Beard, Charles, 10
Bechuanaland Protectorate, *see* Botswana, 263
Bergquist, Charles, 158
Betancourt, Rómulo, 158
Bhavnani, Ravi, 6, 18, 19, 41, 42
Boix, Carles, 10, 14, 81, 82, 110, 290
Bolivia, 4, 210, 211
  Comité Pro-Santa Cruz, 249
  la Rosca tin oligarchy, 32, 211, 233, 234, 236
  COB, 238
  Comibol, 238
  Comité Pro-Santa Cruz, 249, 251
  coup of 1964, 33
  FSTMB, 235, 238
  inequality in, 236
  MNR and, 235, 238
    relations with the FSTMB of, 235
  Patiño, Simón, 211
  pre-revolutionary period in, 33, 233
  regional autonomy movements in, 249–253
  Revolution of 1952 in, 33, 236
  role of resource ownership in, 212, 232, 234, 235, 237
  tin
    as source of rents, 238
    decline of, 239, 240
Bolivian Socialist Falange (FSB), 250
Botswana, 34, 210
  and cattle ranching, 261
  and diamonds, 259, 260
  and inequality, 262
  and resource dependence, 266
  as a democracy, 259, 264, 266, 267
  as a rentier state, 260
  as an anomaly to the resource curse, 2, 35, 213, 258, 260
  BDP and electoral competition in, 258, 264, 267
  British colonial legacy in, 261, 263
  Debswana, 259
  democratic effects of diamonds in, 213
  social indicators in, 265
  spending of diamond rents and, 264, 265
  the Tswana elite and, 261, 263
  Tribal Grazing Land Policy, 263
Bueno de Mesquita, Bruce, 14

Caldera, Rafael, 178
Calderón, Alvaro Silva, 183
capital shares
  as measure of inequality, 116–119
case selection
  discussion of, 149–151, 211
causal-process observations, 148, 151
  examples of, 211

Chaudhry, Kiren, 23, 237
Chávez, Hugo, 184, 194, 201
 allegations of electoral fraud and, 201
 approval of, 196
 attempted coup against, 68, 154, 175
 attempted coup of, 176
 constitutional reforms and, 174, 198, 199
 election of, 154, 168, 173, 174, 176
 oil rents and, 154, 192, 198, 202
 private-sector elites and, 194, 195, 205
 public spending, 196
 redistribution and, 30, 155, 174–176, 188, 192
 relations with PDVSA of, 175
 socialism of, 183
 support for, 174, 195–197
Chile, 4, 210
 agrarian reform in, 228
 and copper, 211, 213
 and CORFO, role of copper rents, 225
 and nitrate, 211, 213, 216, 217, 219
 and the price of copper, 229
 and the social question, 224
 as a rentier state, 211, 213, 216
 as a stable democracy, 211, 214
 counterfactual reasoning and, 215
 coup of 1973 in, 211, 214, 230
 democratic effect of rents in, 215, 230
 entrance of North American copper companies, 223
 Gran Minería, 223
 nationalization of copper, 228, 230
 patterns of spending in, 217
 Popular Front, 224, 225
 redistributive conflict and, 32, 215, 220, 229–231
 resource dependence and, 20, 211
 taxation in, 217
 War of the Pacific, 216, 218
Chileanization of copper industry, 227, 228, 230
Christian Democrats
 in Chile, 227
Collier, David, 29, 106, 148, 151, 153, 158, 166, 167, 218–220, 222, 224, 226
Collier, Ruth Berins, 29, 55, 56, 63, 128, 153, 158, 166, 167, 219, 220, 222, 224, 226
comparative statics, 76
 on the role of inequality, 81–86
 on the role of resource dependence, 87, 88
COPEI, 166, 168
Coppedge, Michael, 166
copper
 and market power, 230
 as a source of rents, 6
copper companies
 taxes paid by, 224
Coronil, Fernando, 5
coups
 against democracy, 8
 and commitment problems, 9
 and natural resources, 7
 costs of, 7
 payoffs to, 8
crude democracy
 concept of, 1, 14
 normative implications of, 290

De Beers, 259
 Central Selling Office, 260
democracy
 and redistribution, 10, 12
 economic sources of, 5
 measurement of, 119, 120
 Schumpetarian definition of, 12, 290
democratic effect of rents, *see* natural resources, democratic effect of, 129
 in Latin America, 129–131
democratization
 and natural resource wealth, 12
 formal model of, 89–92, 94–96, 98–100
diamonds
 alluvial *v.* kimberlite, 6, 41
 as a source of rents, 6, 259
distribution
 v. redistribution, 11
 of resource rents, 8
Dutch Disease, 23, 272
 definition of, 268
 political effects of, 272, 273

Ecuador, 4, 34, 210, 212
 as a rentier state, 253, 254
 authoritarian effects of oil in, 212, 256

Index

Bucaram, Assad, 254, 255
class conflict in, 255
democratic effects of oil in, 212, 253, 256–258
inequality in, 254
military coup in, 254
redemocratization of, 256–258
resource dependence in, 20, 211
envelope theorem
application of, 79
Equatorial Guinea
authoritarian effects of oil in, 280, 281
effects of oil in, 280, 281
inequality in, 281
oil dependence in, 280
resource dependence and, 20
Evans, Peter, 57

Fearon, James, 215
Fish, M. Steven, 286
foreign aid
as a source of rents, 33
Frei, Eduardo, 227
Friedman, Thomas, 1

Gabonowe, Ribson, 259
Goldberg, Ellis, 144
Gómez, General Juan, 158
Good, Kenneth, 258
Gran Minería, *see* Chile, 223
Grove, Marmaduque, 224
guano
boom in Peru, 270

Haber, Stephen, 4, 143
Herb, Michael, 4, 145
Hirschman, Albert O., 6, 23, 226
Humud, Carlos, 221, 222

Ibáñez del Campo, Carlos, 224
Indonesia
effects of oil in, 288, 289
oil dependence in, 288
industrial capital shares
as a measure of inequality, 22, 116, 117
inequality
as shaped by resource rents, 23
concept of, 17, 114
measurement of, 114–119
capital shares, 22, 116, 117
Gini coefficients, 115, 116
Iraq
effects of oil in, 283–285
oil and ethnic conflict in, 283, 284
resource dependence in, 283
role of elites in, 283, 285
sharing of oil revenues in, 284

Jamaica
bauxite and, 229
policies toward resource TNCs in, 229
Jensen, Nathan, 2, 14, 27

Karl, Terry Lynn, xv, 3
Kennecott, 226
El Teniente copper mine of, 223
Khama, Seretse, 261

Latin America
coups against democracy in, 166
Le Billon, Philippe, 6, 19
Levine, Daniel H., 153, 166, 167
Londregan, John, 63
López Contreras, José Eleazar, 158
Loveman, Brian, 225

Mahon, James, 145
Mamalakis, Markos, 218, 221, 222
Markov-perfect equilibrium
definition of, 70
Martz, John, 256
Medina Angarita, Isaías, 158
Menaldo, Victor, 143
Mesa, Carlos, 249
Missions
role in Venezuela of, 188
Misión Habitat, 188
Misión Ribas, 188
Misión Robinson, 188
Mommer, Bernard, 6, 40, 173
Monaldi, Francisco, 224
Moore, Barrington, 5
Moran, Theodore, 6, 224, 227

natural resources
v. non-resource economic sectors, 16
authoritarian and democratic effects of, compared, 11, 12, 14–24, 81
authoritarian effect of, 2, 10, 13, 79

natural resources (*cont.*)
democratic effect of, 2, 3, 5, 11, 80
diffuse *v.* point-source, 41
form of ownership of, 6, 44, 45
liberal tax and royalty treatments of, 43
linkages to other sectors of, 6, 23, 114
lootable *v.* non-lootable, 41, 42
Neuhouser, Kevin, 165
non-resource sectors
and taxation, 9
as private sectors, 9
Norway
as an anomaly to the resource curse, 2

O'Donnell, Guillermo, 5
Orapa mine
discovery of, 259
Organization of Petroleum Exporting Countries (OPEC), 42
Ortega, Daniel, 22

Pact of Punto Fijo, *see* Venezuela, 166
Patiño, Simón, 233, 234
Pauline Jones Luong, 24, 44, 277
Paz Estenssoro, Víctor, 236, 238
Pequeña Minería, 223
Persian Gulf
resource dependence in, 211
Persian Gulf countries
effects of oil in, 282
Popular Front, *see* Chile, 224
Przeworski, Adam, 5

rentier states
foundations of, 18, 24, 40–44
resource curse
anomalies to, 2
normative implications of, 290
resource dependence
v. resource abundance, 19–21, 111
concept of, 16
measurement of, 113
resource ownership
role of, 33, 38, 42, 44, 45, 274–277
resource rents
and public spending, 7
and taxation, 7, 45
definition of, 2, 6, 39, 40, 114
measurement of, 111–113
sources of, 6, 40–42
revenue volatility
role of, 269
revolutionary threats, 26
Reynolds, Clark, 223, 224
Robinson, James, 9, 10, 13, 14, 21, 54–56, 62–64, 69, 81, 82, 91, 101, 110, 116, 117, 120, 121, 125, 128, 261, 262, 286, 290
Rodríguez, Francisco, 22
Rodríguez Lara, General Guillermo, 256
Rodrik, Dani, 22
Ross, Michael, 2, 13, 27, 41, 146
Rueschemeyer, Dietrich, 5, 10, 290
Russia
and the oligarchs, 287
effects of oil in, 286–288
inequality in, 286
oil dependence in, 286

Sachs, Jeffrey, xv
Sánchez de Losada, Gonzalo, 247, 249
São Tomé and Príncipe
effects of oil in, 281, 282
expected oil dependence in, 282
Saudi Arabia
and resource dependence, 20
Schmitter, Philippe, 5
Shapiro, Ian, 5
Silez Zuazo, Hernán, 236
simulations
description of, 293–295
Smith, Benjamin, 4
Snyder, Richard, 6, 18, 19, 41, 42
Stephens, Evelyn H., 5, 10
Stephens, John D., 5, 10
sub-Saharan Africa
resource dependence in, 211

Tarre Briceño, Gustavo, 168, 171, 172
Thelen, Kathleen, 268
Tilly, Charles, 5
Tocqueville, Alexis de, 5, 21
Torres Uribe, Alfredo, 158
Tremont, Arturo, 185

Urriolagoitia, Mamerto, 236

Valenzuela, Arturo, 225, 230
Velasquez, Ramón J., 158

Index

Venezuela, 4
  as a democracy, 184, 200, 201
  as an anomaly to the resource curse, 3
  authoritarian effect of oil in, 202
  Causa Radical party, 30
  class conflict and, 29, 30, 168, 189, 193
  decline of oil rents and, 30
  democratic effect of oil in, 3, 184, 202
  land reform in, 189–192
  Pact of Punto Fijo in, 30, 166
  price of oil and, 183
  redistribution and, 188, 189, 192
  renewal of rents and, 31
  resource dependence and, 20
  role of *Misiones* in, 186–188
  social spending in, 185, 186

Wantchekon, Leonard, 2, 14, 27, 63
War of the Pacific, *see* Chile, 218
Weinthal, Erika, 24, 44, 277
Wells, Theodore T., 6
Wibbels, Erik, 144

Other Books in the Series (*continued from page iii*)

Catherine Boone, *Political Topographies of the African State: Territorial Authority and Institutional Change*
Michael Bratton and Nicolas van de Walle, *Democratic Experiments in Africa: Regime Transitions in Comparative Perspective*
Michael Bratton, Robert Mattes, and E. Gyimah-Boadi, *Public Opinion, Democracy, and Market Reform in Africa*
Valerie Bunce, *Leaving Socialism and Leaving the State: The End of Yugoslavia, the Soviet Union, and Czechoslovakia*
Daniele Caramani, *The Nationalization of Politics: The Formation of National Electorates and Party Systems in Europe*
Kanchan Chandra, *Why Ethnic Parties Succeed: Patronage and Ethnic Headcounts in India*
José Antonio Cheibub, *Presidentialism, Parliamentarism, and Democracy*
Ruth Berins Collier, *Paths toward Democracy: The Working Class and Elites in Western Europe and South America*
Christian Davenport, *State Repression and the Domestic Democratic Peace*
Donatella della Porta, *Social Movements, Political Violence, and the State*
Alberto Diaz-Cayeros, *Federalism, Fiscal Authority, and Centralization in Latin America*
Gerald Easter, *Reconstructing the State: Personal Networks and Elite Identity*
M. Steven Fish, *Democracy Derailed in Russia: The Failure of Open Politics*
Robert F. Franzese, *Macroeconomic Policies of Developed Democracies*
Roberto Franzosi, *The Puzzle of Strikes: Class and State Strategies in Postwar Italy*
Geoffrey Garrett, *Partisan Politics in the Global Economy*
Miriam Golden, *Heroic Defeats: The Politics of Job Loss*
Jeff Goodwin, *No Other Way Out: States and Revolutionary Movements*
Merilee Serrill Grindle, *Changing the State*
Anna Grzymala-Busse, *Rebuilding Leviathan: Party Competition and State Exploitation in Post-Communist Democracies*
Anna Grzymala-Busse, *Redeeming the Communist Past: The Regeneration of Communist Parties in East Central Europe*
Frances Hagopian, *Traditional Politics and Regime Change in Brazil*
Henry E. Hale, *The Foundations of Ethnic Politics: Separatism of States and Nations in Eurasia and the World*
Gretchen Helmke, *Courts under Constraints: Judges, Generals, and Presidents in Argentina*

Yoshiko Herrera, *Imagined Economies: The Sources of Russian Regionalism*

J. Rogers Hollingsworth and Robert Boyer, eds., *Contemporary Capitalism: The Embeddedness of Institutions*

John D. Huber and Charles R. Shipan, *Deliberate Discretion? The Institutional Foundations of Bureaucratic Autonomy*

Ellen Immergut, *Health Politics: Interests and Institutions in Western Europe*

Torben Iversen, *Capitalism, Democracy, and Welfare*

Torben Iversen, *Contested Economic Institutions*

Torben Iversen, Jonas Pontussen, and David Soskice, eds., *Union, Employers, and Central Banks: Macroeconomic Coordination and Institutional Change in Social Market Economics*

Thomas Janoski and Alexander M. Hicks, eds., *The Comparative Political Economy of the Welfare State*

Joseph Jupille, *Procedural Politics: Issues, Influence, and Institutional Choice in the European Union*

Stathis Kalyvas, *The Logic of Violence in Civil War*

David C. Kang, *Crony Capitalism: Corruption and Capitalism in South Korea and the Philippines*

Junko Kato, *Regressive Taxation and the Welfare State*

Robert O. Keohane and Helen B. Milner, eds., *Internationalization and Domestic Politics*

Herbert Kitschelt, *The Transformation of European Social Democracy*

Herbert Kitschelt, Peter Lange, Gary Marks, and John D. Stephens, eds., *Continuity and Change in Contemporary Capitalism*

Herbert Kitschelt, Zdenka Mansfeldova, Radek Markowski, and Gabor Toka, *Post-Communist Party Systems*

David Knoke, Franz Urban Pappi, Jeffrey Broadbent, and Yutaka Tsujinaka, eds., *Comparing Policy Networks*

Allan Kornberg and Harold D. Clarke, *Citizens and Community: Political Support in a Representative Democracy*

Amie Kreppel, *The European Parliament and the Supranational Party System*

David D. Laitin, *Language Repertoires and State Construction in Africa*

Fabrice E. Lehoucq and Ivan Molina, *Stuffing the Ballot Box: Fraud, Electoral Reform, and Democratization in Costa Rica*

Mark Irving Lichbach and Alan S. Zuckerman, eds., *Comparative Politics: Rationality, Culture, and Structure*

Evan Lieberman, *Race and Regionalism in the Politics of Taxation in Brazil and South Africa*

Julia Lynch, *Age in the Welfare State: The Origins of Social Spending on Pensioners, Workers, and Children*
Pauline Jones Luong, *Institutional Change and Political Continuity in Post-Soviet Central Asia*
Doug McAdam, John McCarthy, and Mayer Zald, eds., *Comparative Perspectives on Social Movements*
Beatriz Magaloni, *Voting for Autocracy: Hegemonic Party Survival and its Demise in Mexico*
James Mahoney and Dietrich Rueschemeyer, eds., *Historical Analysis and the Social Sciences*
Scott Mainwaring and Matthew Soberg Shugart, eds., *Presidentialism and Democracy in Latin America*
Isabela Mares, *The Politics of Social Risk: Business and Welfare State Development*
Isabela Mares, *Taxation, Wage Bargaining, and Unemployment*
Anthony W. Marx, *Making Race, Making Nations: A Comparison of South Africa, the United States, and Brazil*
Bonnie Meguid, *Competition between Unequals: The Role of Mainstream Parties in Late-Century Africa*
Joel S. Migdal, *State in Society: Studying How States and Societies Constitute One Another*
Joel S. Migdal, Atul Kohli, and Vivienne Shue, eds., *State Power and Social Forces: Domination and Transformation in the Third World*
Scott Morgenstern and Benito Nacif, eds., *Legislative Politics in Latin America*
Layna Mosley, *Global Capital and National Governments*
Wolfgang C. Müller and Kaare Strøm, *Policy, Office, or Votes?*
Maria Victoria Murillo, *Labor Unions, Partisan Coalitions, and Market Reforms in Latin America*
Ton Notermans, *Money, Markets, and the State: Social Democratic Economic Policies since 1918*
Aníbal Pérez-Liñán, *Presidential Impeachment and the New Political Instability in Latin America*
Roger Petersen, *Understanding Ethnic Violence: Fear, Hatred, and Resentment in Twentieth-Century Eastern Europe*
Simona Piattoni, ed., *Clientelism, Interests, and Democratic Representation*
Paul Pierson, *Dismantling the Welfare State?: Reagan, Thatcher, and the Politics of Retrenchment*

Marino Regini, *Uncertain Boundaries: The Social and Political Construction of European Economies*

Marc Howard Ross, *Cultural Contestation in Ethnic Conflict*

Lyle Scruggs, *Sustaining Abundance: Environmental Performance in Industrial Democracies*

Jefferey M. Sellers, *Governing from Below: Urban Regions and the Global Economy*

Yossi Shain and Juan Linz, eds., *Interim Governments and Democratic Transitions*

Beverly Silver, *Forces of Labor: Workers' Movements and Globalization since 1870*

Theda Skocpol, *Social Revolutions in the Modern World*

Regina Smyth, *Candidate Strategies and Electoral Competition in the Russian Federation: Democracy Without Foundation*

Richard Snyder, *Politics after Neoliberalism: Reregulation in Mexico*

David Stark and László Bruszt, *Postsocialist Pathways: Transforming Politics and Property in East Central Europe*

Sven Steinmo, Kathleen Thelen, and Frank Longstreth, eds., *Structuring Politics: Historical Institutionalism in Comparative Analysis*

Susan C. Stokes, *Mandates and Democracy: Neoliberalism by Surprise in Latin America*

Susan C. Stokes, ed., *Public Support for Market Reforms in New Democracies*

Duane Swank, *Global Capital, Political Institutions, and Policy Change in Developed Welfare States*

Sidney Tarrow, *Power in Movement: Social Movements and Contentious Politics*

Kathleen Thelen, *How Institutions Evolve: The Political Economy of Skills in Germany, Britain, the United States, and Japan*

Charles Tilly, *Trust and Rule*

Daniel Treisman, *The Architecture of Government: Rethinking Political Decentralization*

Lily Lee Tsai, *Accountability without Democracy: How Solidary Groups Provide Public Goods in Rural China*

Joshua Tucker, *Regional Economic Voting: Russia, Poland, Hungary, Slovakia and the Czech Republic, 1990–1999*

Ashutosh Varshney, *Democracy, Development, and the Countryside*

Jeremy M. Weinstein, *Inside Rebellion: The Politics of Insurgent Violence*

Stephen I. Wilkinson, *Votes and Violence: Electoral Competition and Ethnic Riots in India*
Jason Wittenberg, *Crucibles of Political Loyalty: Church Institutions and Electoral Continuity in Hungary*
Elisabeth J. Wood, *Forging Democracy from Below: Insurgent Transitions in South Africa and El Salvador*
Elisabeth J. Wood, *Insurgent Collective Action and Civil War in El Salvador*